MW01089964

A GUIDE TO CIVIL PROCEDURE

A Guide to Civil Procedure

Integrating Critical Legal Perspectives

Edited by
Brooke Coleman, Suzette Malveaux,
Portia Pedro, *and* Elizabeth Porter

NEW YORK UNIVERSITY PRESS
New York

NEW YORK UNIVERSITY PRESS
New York
www.nyupress.org

References to Internet websites (URLs) were accurate at the time of writing. Neither the author nor New York University Press is responsible for URLs that may have expired or changed since the manuscript was prepared.

Library of Congress Cataloging-in-Publication Data
Names: Coleman, Brooke D., editor. | Malveaux, Suzette, editor. | Pedro, Portia, editor. | Porter, Elizabeth (Law teacher), editor.
Title: A guide to civil procedure : integrating critical legal perspectives / edited by Brooke Coleman, Suzette Malveaux, Portia Pedro, and Elizabeth Porter.
Description: New York : New York University, [2022] | Includes bibliographical references and index.
Identifiers: LCCN 2021039779 | ISBN 9781479805938 (hardback) | ISBN 9781479805976 (ebook) | ISBN 9781479805945 (ebook other)
Subjects: LCSH: Civil procedure—Social aspects—United States. | Critical legal studies—United States.
Classification: LCC KF8840.A2 G85 2022 | DDC 347.73/5—dc23
LC record available at https://lccn.loc.gov/2021039779

New York University Press books are printed on acid-free paper, and their binding materials are chosen for strength and durability. We strive to use environmentally responsible suppliers and materials to the greatest extent possible in publishing our books.

Manufactured in the United States of America

10 9 8 7 6 5 4 3 2 1

Also available as an ebook

To my kids, Cole, Ardon, and Ezzy, who inspire me to work hard, laugh a lot, and snuggle more.—BDC

To my parents, Floyd and Myrna Malveaux, whose memory, love, and example inspire me every day.—SMM

To the memory of Jack Greenberg, who taught me the power and peril of civil procedure.—EGP

To my clients, my students, and the communities who have inspired this work.—PDP

CONTENTS

WHY PROCEDURE IS CRITICAL, CONSTITUTIVE, AND VULNERABLE

A Reconstruction Foreword

JUDITH RESNIK

In 1935, the US Supreme Court moved to a building of its own. Carved in stone atop the entry are the words "Equal Justice Under Law." Three years later, in 1938, the Court promulgated the first set of Federal Rules of Civil Procedure. One of the drafters toasted that event by echoing the phrase etched into the Supreme Court's façade: "Drink to our Rules—they know of no flaw: 'Equal Justice Under the Law!'"[1]

References to "equal justice" in the 1930s did not mean what those words denote today, and the original Rules did have flaws. Racial segregation was commonplace, as were barriers based on color, gender, and much else that precluded ready access to economic, professional, and political opportunities. The justices on the Supreme Court and the lawyers appearing before them were almost all white men. The law they shaped helped to sustain multiple forms of subordination and discrimination.

Fast-forward to the contemporary era. As a result of political and social movements, courts are now obliged to welcome all persons as litigants, witnesses, jurors, staff, lawyers, and judges. The Court's inscription has become its motto, as if it always memorialized an understanding of equality that has become central to the identity and the legitimacy of courts themselves.[2] In the 1960s, the Federal Rules were revised to reflect and enable these changing understandings of courts' obligations, as rule drafters expanded the 1938 premise of ready access to enable a more diverse group of users, including those proceeding through class actions, to make their way into the federal courts.

This volume is a testament to these new metrics of legitimacy for judiciaries. Yet as the chapters unfold, the authors document the incompleteness and the fragility of commitments to an inclusive court system, as they describe the many revisions required to end subordination. Before I sketch the distance between the "actual" as compared to the "aspirational"[3] function of courts and the distinctions between symmetrical opportunities to participate in lawsuits and substantive equality,[4] I need to underscore the distance traveled that has resulted in rereading the 1935 invocation of "equal justice under law" to apply to all people.[5]

One way to see the change is by looking at the large mural (reproduced in Figure F.1) that was installed in a courthouse in 1938, the same year that the Federal Rules of Civil Procedure were rolled out. In the wake of the Great Depression, the federal government funded construction and art; one commission went to a Northeast artist whose mural, a depiction of "Justice as Protector and Avenger," was placed behind a judge's bench in Aiken, South Carolina's new federal courthouse and post office.[6]

The central female figure is a reference to the Renaissance Virtue Justice—familiar because that personification can be found in courthouses around the world. The artist explained that, rather than adorn his "figure of Justice" with the conventional attributes of scales and sword, the only "allegory" he had permitted himself was "to use the red, white and blue [of the United States flag] for her garments."

What did others see? A local newspaper objected to this "barefooted mulatto woman wearing bright-hued clothing." The federal judge assigned to the courtroom called it a "monstrosity"—a "profanation of the otherwise perfection" of the courthouse. The artist asserted that impartial observers would not think "that the figure's face . . . appears to have negroid traits," but that he was nevertheless eager "to obliterate this 'blemish'" and proposed to "lighten Justice's skin color." As the events made national news, the National Association for the Advancement of Colored People and other groups weighed in to oppose the removal or repainting. The denouement was that, for decades, tan curtains (seen at the edges of the photograph) covered the mural.

We should not lose sight of this image. It marks courthouses as one of many venues making and enforcing racial, gender, and class hierarchies. Just as a perceived "mulatto" woman could not serve uncontested in 1938 as a representation of the Virtue Justice, people labeled "mulattos" or otherwise denoted as people of color were often excluded from many occupations and accorded fewer rights than people perceived to be white.

Figure F.1. "Justice as Protector and Avenger," Stefan Hirsch, 1938, Charles E. Simons, Jr. Federal Courthouse, Aiken, South Carolina. Image provided courtesy of the Fine Arts Collection, United States General Services Administration.

Given the role that courts had played in sustaining discrimination, today's impression that courts *ought* to welcome everyone is a major achievement.[7] Yet, as the authors of the chapters that follow make plain, that welcome is far from complete.[8] This volume represents the success of political and social movements reshaping the expectations, practices, culture, and laws of courts and, in addition, details how that project is haunted by a justice gap; the differences between what courts purport to provide and what they deliver are substantial. Of course, concerns about courts' adequacy are long-standing. In the 1980s and 1990s, state and federal judiciaries launched "task forces" on gender, race, and sexual orientation to examine courts' practices and laws; the results included dozens of reports on what some termed "bias" and others "fairness,"[9] and in 2021, Washington State's Gender and Justice Commission issued its report of its three-year study, 2021: How Gender and Race Affect Us Now.[10]

This book underscores the continuing need to renew as well as to deepen such inquiries. The volume's editors have chosen the word "critical" in their title, and in the 2020s, the phrase "critical studies" has become freighted. Some commentators think of critical studies as a critique from the left, engaged in elaborating liberal and progressive agendas and sometimes presumed to be focused on deconstructing extant institutions. "Legal estrangement"—a sense that law will either do harm or is not helpful—is an experience that many people share, and such alienation could prompt a turn away from courts and other government institutions.[11] Yet even as the chapters in this volume explain many of the sources for such estrangement, they brim with *legal engagement*. The authors aim to be reconstructive—to instantiate substantive equality in courts—first by unearthing procedures and decisions that limit participatory parity and that undercut public accountings of alleged illegalities, and second by proposing remedies.

In contrast, conservatives (with a few exceptions[12]), aligned with what is sometimes styled "the right" and identified with fiscal and social conservativism, are at the forefront of an effort to circumscribe the authority of courts, to limit their remedial role, and to curb government regulation on many fronts. Thus, atop the failures *within* courts, efforts are underway to undermine reforms by closing off access *to* courts, diffusing disputes, and privatizing whatever processes for resolution remain.[13]

What commentators from left to right share, however, is a view that procedure is critical and constitutive. Across these differing perspectives, commentators illuminate the importance as well as the vulnerability of recently crafted procedural norms that value equality of access and of participation. Underscoring the centrality of procedure, Marc Galanter explained in the 1970s that the "haves" always play for the "rules" and often come out "ahead."[14] Readers of this volume should appreciate that this "critical guide" is a collective cri de coeur that aims to interrupt that trajectory in an optimistic effort to generate participatory parity through new understandings of what "equal justice under law" entails.

* * *

The template for judging in democratic polities reflects Enlightenment political thought. Before then, judges were required to be loyal to the governments that appointed them; members of the audience were passive spectators watching rituals of power; and a limited set of persons were eligible to participate as disputants, witnesses, or decision makers. In contrast, today judges are supposed to function as independent actors in complex and critical relationships with the governments that employ them and with the public.[15] At a formal level, the public has a right of access to observe court proceedings.[16] What the second half of the twentieth century added is that, at a formal level, everyone is entitled to be in all of the seats in the courtroom. Today's questions are the extent to which courtrooms will remain open (physically or online) to disputants (proceeding individually or in the aggregate) and to third parties who seek to observe interactions.

Many of the chapters in this book take up the challenges that people with limited economic resources face when they seek to use courts. Elsewhere in this volume, I join others in discussing the pervasive lack of participatory parity.[17] As several authors document, the inequalities in courts are problems that not all want to solve. Instead, in many decisions, the US Supreme Court has restrictively interpreted the federal class action rule,[18] constricted standing,[19] rejected arguments to imply statutory and constitutional causes of action,[20] cut back on the jurisdictional reach of states,[21] often limited the authority of tribal courts,[22] marginalized undocumented claimants,[23] and expanded the use of summary judgment.[24]

Of course, the courts are never solo actors. Other branches of the federal government, as well as those of many states, have also limited access to courts as well as to subsidies for those needing the resources to participate. Congress has sent disputants to administrative tribunals, and the Supreme Court has been at the forefront of outsourcing adjudication to private providers. Because of the Court's reinterpretation of the 1925 Federal Arbitration Act, millions of consumers and employees have been closed out of courts and left to proceed, if at all, single-file into closed arbitrations run by entities selected by the companies whose actions they contest.[25] The Court's new arbitration doctrine cuts off remedies in state as well as in federal courts and, in addition, limits collective action in arbitration itself.[26]

These barriers to court, coupled with the expenses and challenges of using courts, have had an impact. Filings are flattening or declining in both federal and state courts. For decades, federal filings (civil and criminal) have remained relatively constant at about 325,000 cases per year. The bulk of litigation is brought in the state systems. Not too long ago, at the end of the 2010s, some 100 million cases of all kinds were filed; as of 2020, about 80 million were filed. After filing, a tiny fraction end with a trial. In the federal courts, a trial starts in fewer than one in one hundred civil cases. Information on state court litigation comes from the National Center for State Courts; one of its studies on the "landscape of civil litigation" looked at almost a million cases in ten major counties and concluded that most dispositions involve management, not adjudication; about 4 percent of the civil docket ended with a trial, arbitration, or dispositive motion.[27]

* * *

This volume's "critical guide" is premised on the ideas that courts ought to be accessible and accountable and that procedures should mitigate against biases predicated on class, race, gender, and other facets of identity. The capacity to level such criticism stems from the public nature of courts. Historically, judges were obliged to make much of what they do public. But with the rise of alternative dispute resolution (ADR) in courts,[28] of technologies enabling online dispute resolution (ODR), and of the outsourcing to private providers, third-party access has declined.[29] Indeed, in arbitration, under current legal rules the public has no right to attend.[30] Absent statutes that impose disclosure requirements or by virtue of targeted research, the public has no way to learn about the few arbitrations that take place.[31] When the public has nothing to see, whatever critiques or praise that might flow become silenced.

Through the privatization of processes inside courts and the outsourcing to private actors, the public loses its opportunities to engage. Gone are what Jeremy Bentham in the nineteenth century called "auditors"[32] and the potential for his imagined "Tribunal of Public Opinion" to function.[33] Today, Bentham's optimism about what he termed "publicity," which assumed a unity of perspective grounded in rational assessments of self-interest, has been undercut by experiences with misinformation, false facts, and deep divides among the many "publics" often in conflict with each other. Yet without third-party access to the processes for responding to disputes, no one can evaluate the abilities of decision makers and the views of the disputants. Lost are opportunities to assess whether procedures and decision makers are fair, how resources affect outcomes, whether similarly situated litigants are treated comparably, and why one would want to get into (or avoid) court.

Instead, a private transaction has been substituted and, unlike in public adjudication, control over the meaning of the claims made and the judgments rendered rests with the corporate provider of the service.[34] Just as Michel Foucault mapped how governing powers, eager to maintain control, moved punishment practices from public streets into closed institutions, adjudication itself is at risk of being removed from public purview—rendering the exercise and consequences of public and private power hard to ascertain. Foucault famously focused on criminal punishment. As Robert Cover explained in the mid-1980s, when courts issue rulings in civil or in criminal cases they alter people's lives through affecting their liberty, households, and property; thus, a form of violence is intrinsic to adjudication.[35] When such decision-making processes occur in public, accountings permit assessments that in turn generate debates about their legitimacy. Yet, the privatization of procedure closes off such interactions. All the more chilling is that in many instances, public and private sector decision makers do not acknowledge that their exercise of power and the violence it entails *require* explanation.

To be clear, the devolution of adjudication to tribunals and administrative agencies and the reliance on private providers should not be equated with inevitably ending public access and oversight. For example, enforcement of clauses in consumer and employee documents that mandate the use of private providers for dispute resolution could be unenforceable (as some federal legislators have proposed) or could be accompanied by requirements of third-party access, an accounting of the diversity of decision makers, and other disclosure obligations.[36] Regulation of the many forms of dispute resolution that exist could be imbued with the norms discussed in this volume—if the political will to do so existed.

* * *

Given the demand for adjudication, the high-profile lawsuits and jurists sparking press coverage of some court-based activities, the influx of some persons of diverse backgrounds as litigants, lawyers, and on the bench, and many impressive courthouse buildings (including the 1935 Supreme Court's temple-like structure), the diminution in the aegis of

Figure F.2. Decorative cloth with repeated pattern of the High Court's figure Lady Justice, made for the Zambia Association of Women Judges, circa 2004. Cloth provided by Elizabeth Brundige and courtesy of the Zambia Association of Women Judges. Facsimile by Yale University Press.

adjudication could be overlooked. Yet even as many new courthouses with cutting-edge technologies have been constructed, they are at risk of being anachronistic. While monumental in ambition and often in physical girth, the durability of courts as active sites of public exchange, where litigants could participate on an equal footing and debate facts and legal norms before independent judges, should not be taken for granted.

I opened this foreword with the image of a "Justice" whom lawmakers rejected because she was perceived to have dark skin. I close with another version: the logo from the Zambia Association of Women

Judges,[37] shown in Figure F.2. This organization of women judges reclaimed this artifact of colonialism and put a Justice on a pattern of brightly colored kente cloth. This volume likewise aims to reengage with practices that have a long pedigree and, through excavating the limits of their impact, to remake judiciaries and their procedures to render them vital resources for the array of individuals and groups who aspire to interact with and in courts.

NOTES

1 George Wharton Pepper, *A Tast to the Federal Rules (Circa 1938)*, 137 U. Pa. L. Rev. 1877 (1989), appended to Stephen N. Subrin, *Preface—The 50th Anniversary of the Federal Rules of Civil Procedure, 1938–1988*, 137 U. Pa. L. Rev. 1877 (1989).

2 *See* Judith Resnik, *Representing What? Gender, Race, Class, and the Struggle for the Identity and the Legitimacy of Courts*, 15 J. Ethics and Human Rights 1 (2021).

3 *See, e.g.*, Norman W. Spaulding, Barbara Allen Babcock, and Toni Massaro, *The Ideal and the Actual in Procedural Due Process* [this volume].

4 *See e.g.*, Matthew L. M. Fletcher and Neoshia R. Roemer, *Procedure and Indian Children* [this volume].

5 Annette Kolodny, *A Map for Rereading: On Gender and the Interpretation of Literary Texts* (1980).

6 Mural by Stefan Hirsch, "Justice as Protector and Avenger" (1938) at US Courthouse and Post Office, Aiken, SC. The Aiken building was subsequently named the Charles E. Simons Jr. Federal Courthouse in honor of that court's Chief Judge who served from 1980 to 1986. *See also* Marlene Park & Gerald E. Markowitz, *Democratic Vistas: Post Offices and Public Art in the New Deal* 61, 90 n.30 (1984); Karel Ann Marling, *Wall-to-Wall America: A Cultural History of Post Office Murals in the Great Depression* 64–65 (1982). For more discussion and for the sources for the quoted references in the text, see Judith Resnik & Dennis Curtis, *Representing Justice: Invention, Controversy, and Rights in City-States and Democratic Courtrooms* 110–13 (2011), and *Mural: "Justice as Protector & Avenger," by Stefan Hirsch*, Libr. of Cong., (Nov. 16, 2016), https://www.loc.gov.

7 Judith Resnik, *Constitutional Entitlements to and in Courts: Remedial Rights in an Age of Egalitarianism: The Childress Lecture*, 56 St. Louis U. L.J. 916 (2012).

8 The title of Brooke Coleman's chapter in this volume (chapter 19)—"*#SoWhite Male*"—makes that point.

9 *See, e.g.*, *The Effects of Gender in Courts: The Ninth Circuit Gender Bias Task Force*, 67 S. Cal. L. Rev. 731 (1994); *see generally* Judith Resnik, *Asking About Gender in Courts*, 21 Signs 952 (1996).

10 Washington State Supreme Court Gender and Justice Commission, *2021 Gender Justice Study* (2021), www.courts.wa.gov.

11 Monica Bell, *Police Reform and the Dismantling of Legal Estrangement*, 126 Yale L.J. 2054 (2017).

12 *See, e.g.*, Brian Fitzpatrick, *The Conservative Case for Class Actions* (2019).
13 I analyze many of the efforts to do so in Judith Resnik, *Diffusing Disputes: The Public in the Private of Arbitration, the Private in Courts, and the Erasure of Rights*, 124 Yale L.J. 2804 (2015).
14 Marc Galanter, *Why the "Haves" Come Out Ahead: Speculations on the Limits of Legal Change*, 9 Law & Soc'y Rev. 95 (1974).
15 How they are supposed to do so is the subject of several essays in this volume. *See, e.g.*, Brian Soucek, *Can a Gay Judge Judge a Gay Rights Case?* (chapter 15 in this volume); Elizabeth Thornburg, *(Un)conscious Judging* (chapter 16 in this volume).
16 *See* Judith Resnik, *The Functions of Publicity and of Privatization in Courts and Their Replacements (from Jeremy Bentham to #MeToo and Google Spain)*, in *The Role of Courts in a Democratic Society* 177 (Burkhard Hess & Ana Koprivica eds., 2019).
17 *See, e.g.*, Judith Resnik, *Class in Courts* (chapter in this volume); Miriam Gilles, *When Law Forsakes the Poor* (chapter 14 in this volume); Andrew Hammond, *The Master of the Complaint? Pleadings in our Inegalitarian Age* (chapter 27 in this volume).
18 *See, e.g.*, Suzette Malveaux, *The Benefits of Class Actions and the Increasing Threats to Their Viability* (chapter 7 in this volume); Brooke Coleman & Elizabeth Porter, *Reinvigorating Commonality: Gender and Class Actions* (chapter 36 in this volume). Judith Resnik, Comment, *Fairness in Numbers: A Comment on* AT&T v. Concepcion, Wal-Mart v. Dukes, *and* Turner v. Rogers, 125 Harv. L. Rev. 78 (2011).
19 *See* Thole v. U.S. Bank N.A., 140 S. Ct. 1615, 1619 (2020). An exception—whose implications are not clear—is the 2021 decision of *Uzuegbunam v. Preczewski*, 141 S. Ct. 792 (2021).
20 *See, e.g.*, Hernandez v. Mesa, 140 S. Ct. 735 (2020) (Thomas, J., concurring).
21 Charlton Copeland, *Building a Litigation Coalition, Business Interests and the Transformation of Personal Jurisdiction* (chapter 20 in this this volume).
22 Angelique EagleWoman, *Jurisprudence and Recommendations for Tribal Court Authority Due to Imposition of U.S. Limits* (chapter 23 in this volume). The 2020 decision of *McGirt v. Oklahoma*, 140 U.S. 2412 (2020), is an exception, and its implications are being debated as I write.
23 Stephen Lee, *Undocumented Civil Procedure* (chapter 28 in this volume).
24 *See* Nancy Gertner, *Losers' Rules* (chapter 12 in this volume); Jasmine Gonzales Rose, *Civil Rights Summarily Denied: Race, Evidence, and Summary Judgment in Police Brutality Cases* (chapter 30 in this volume); Suja A. Thomas, *Summary Judgment, Factfinding, and Juries* (chapter 32in this volume); Elizabeth M. Schneider, *Gender and Summary Judgment* (chapter 31 in this volume).
25 Judith Resnik, Stephanie Garlock & Annie J. Wang, *Collective Preclusion and Inaccessible Arbitration: Data, Non-disclosure, and Public Knowledge*, 24 Lewis & Clark L. Rev. 611 (2020).
26 Epic Sys. Corp. v. Lewis, 138 S. Ct. 1612 (2018); Stephanie Bornstein, *When Forum Determines Rights: Forced Arbitration of Discrimination Claims* (chapter 39 in this volume).

27 Civ. Just. Initiative, *The Landscape of Civil Litigation in State Courts*, Nat'l Ctr. for State Cts., 31–32 (2015), https://www.ncsc.org.

28 *See, e.g.*, Deborah R. Hensler, *Our Courts, Ourselves: How the Alternative Dispute Resolution Movement Is Re-shaping Our Legal System*, 108 Pa. State. L. Rev. 165 (2003); Carrie Menkel-Meadow, *Mothers and Fathers of Invention: The Intellectual Founders of ADR*, 16 Ohio St. J. Disp. Resol. 1 (2000); Carrie Menkel-Meadow, *Whose Dispute Is It Anyway? A Philosophical and Democratic Defense of Settlement (in Some Cases)*, 83 Geo. L.J. 2663 (1995); Judith Resnik, *Many Doors? Closing Doors? Alternative Dispute Resolution and Adjudication*, 10 Ohio St. J. Disp. Resol. 211 (1995).

29 Judith Resnik, *The Contingency of Openness in Courts: Changing the Experiences and Logics of Publics' Role in Court-Based ADR*, 15 Nev. L.J. 1631 (2015).

30 The Supreme Court's arbitration case law is a part of this construction. *See* Resnik, *Diffusing Disputes*, supra note 13; Eric K. Yamamoto, *Critical Procedure: Alternative Dispute Resolution and the Justices' "Second Wave" Constriction of Court Access and Claims Development* (chapter 37 in this volume).

31 Michael Z. Green, *Reconsidering Prejudice in Alternative Dispute Resolution for Black Work Matters* (chapter 38 in this volume).

32 Jeremy Bentham, *Rationale of Judicial Evidence: "Of Publicity and Privacy, as Applied to Judicature in General, and to the Evidence in Particular," in* 6 *The Works of Jeremy Bentham* 356 (J. Bowring ed., 1843).

33 Frederick Rosen, *Jeremy Bentham and Representative Democracy: A Study of Constitutional Code* 26–27 (1983).

34 Judith Resnik, *The Privatization of Process: Requiem for and Celebration of the Federal Rules of Civil Procedure at 75*, 162 U. Pa. L. Rev. 1793 (2014). This shift is not limited to the United States. *See generally The Multi-Tasking Judge: Comparative Judicial Dispute Resolution* (Archie Zariski & Tania Sourdin eds., 2013).

35 Robert M. Cover, *Violence and the Word*, 95 Yale L.J. 1601 (1986). *See* Shirin Simmar, *Civil Procedure in the Shadow of Violence* (chapter in this volume).

36 For example, in response to a European decision requiring that search platforms such as Google must, under certain circumstances, delist individuals (a "right to be forgotten") and in light of European regulations, Google publishes what it styles as a "Transparency Report" providing its own account of how it weighs public access and personal privacy. *See Google Transparency Report*, Google (Apr. 9, 2021), https://transparencyreport.google.com. The key EU decision was Case C-131/12, Google Spain SL v. Agencia Española de Protección de Datos, 2014 E.C.R. 317. *See* Judith Resnik, *The Functions of Publicity and of Privatization in Courts and Their Replacements (from Jeremy Bentham to #MeToo) and* Google Spain, in *The Role of Courts in a Democratic Society* 177 (Burkhard Hess & Ana Koprivica eds., 2019); Resnik, Garlock & Wang, *supra* note 25, at 611.

37 This picture is a facsimile, made by Yale University Press, of a piece of cloth that was given to me and that has a repeat pattern of the Justice image.

Introduction

BROOKE COLEMAN, SUZETTE MALVEAUX, PORTIA PEDRO, AND ELIZABETH PORTER

The United States civil court system is held up as a symbol of justice and constitutional due process—a place where everyone can get their "day in court." But reality falls short of this ideal. Particularly for certain groups—such as Indigenous people and tribes; people of color; immigrants; prisoners; women; people with disabilities; and LGBTQ+ people—courts and judicial decisions may function as tools of exclusion rather than instruments of justice. And civil procedure—the rules of the game—plays a central role in this reality.

Yet despite procedure's impact on marginalized people, discussions of systemic inequality are frequently viewed as beyond the scope of civil procedure courses—a detour from supposedly neutral black-letter law. But it is not possible to fully understand or fairly apply procedural rules without awareness of the potential impacts of those rules on vulnerable members of our communities. Considerations of equity and justice belong at the center of the study and application of civil procedure—and at the center of the promulgation and interpretation of procedure by judges, scholars, and rule makers. Indeed, the very perception of these issues as marginal to civil procedure perpetuates exclusion.

This book represents our efforts, and the efforts of our contributors, to center questions of inequality in the teaching, learning, and practice of civil procedure. The chapters represent voices of a diverse group of scholars, including longtime leaders in the field, as well as new voices. The chapters draw on a range of literatures—from critical theory to social science, from doctrinal examination to empirical analysis. The critical perspectives expressed are as diverse as our authors and subjects. But they share an overarching goal: to shine a light on the ways in which civil procedure may privilege—or silence—voices in our courts. Each chapter shows how the seemingly dry and technocratic tone of the civil rules and process may conceal—or perpetuate—apathy, injustice, brutality, poverty, abuse of power, or discrimination. For many, the civil litigation system may connote images of contract lawsuits or intellectual property disputes. But the rules of civil procedure also govern litigation over police killings, deportation of immigrants fleeing atrocities, climate change, prisoners subject to abhorrent conditions of confinement, defrauded consumers, and people seeking racial or gender justice in the workplace.

We have designed this book to maximize ease of use for instructors, students, scholars, and judges. It can be used as a stand-alone resource or as a supplement to a traditional casebook. Each chapter is concise, lightly footnoted, and readable. Part I includes chapters addressing theoretical frameworks for analyzing procedure, as well as critiques of the judicial and rulemaking processes. The remaining chapters are organized into Parts II–V, corresponding roughly with the order in which topics are covered in civil procedure textbooks—beginning with personal and subject matter jurisdiction; moving to pleading, discovery, and summary judgment; and concluding with aggregate litigation and arbitration. While the majority of the chapters in this volume are original works, we have also included excerpts from classic articles that have helped change our understanding of procedure.

We hope that this collection will provide a road map toward a fairer, more equitable approach to civil procedure—an approach that listens to diverse voices and recognizes its own limitations.

PART I

Theoretical Concepts in Civil Procedure

The chapters in this section add to our understanding of the theoretical underpinnings of critical perspectives in the area of civil procedure. The authors push us to question the foundational norms underpinning the Federal Rules of Civil Procedure. Despite its name and theoretical separation from criminal litigation and the individual merits of each case, civil procedure can, in fact, be substantive and a site of state or private violence. In these chapters, scholars situate the work of various social theorists and empiricists within civil procedure. In chapter 1, Roy Brooks revisits his groundbreaking work, *Critical Procedure*, by using a classic personal jurisdiction case, *Kulko v. Superior Court*, to propose a critical theory of procedural judicial decision-making. In chapter 2, Portia Pedro calls for proceduralists to build a more comprehensive theoretical analysis of procedure and suggests that prior failed attempts to exclude people of color and other marginalized groups from courts have been revived and framed as neutral procedural clarifications. Shirin Sinnar, in chapter 3, demonstrates how procedure and violence have been inextricably linked because the procedures we study often provide the mechanism or justification for state violence. And, in chapter 4, Rachel Kahn Best, Lauren Edelman, Linda Hamilton Krieger, and Scott Eliason bring to the fore an empirical lens through which to see how intersectional identities negatively impact a plaintiff's likelihood of success in employment discrimination claims. This study of theory ends with Danya Reda and her exploration in chapter 5 of how US courts construct an "other" to exclude certain foreign parties from litigation and how courts extend this exclusion to US litigants through civil procedure arbitration doctrine.

Next, other contributions offer insight into some of the foundational concepts of procedure—how we think about how the rules should function. We are often taught that the rules are trans-substantive—that the rules apply across the board to all claims regardless of the substantive rights or litigants before the court. Katherine Macfarlane shatters this myth in the context of prisoner procedure in chapter 6. She uncovers how various statutes, rules, and customs disadvantage prisoners at every turn, undermining prisoners' efforts to curtail constitutional violations in the carceral state. We may also presume that trans-substantivity is inherently fair. The trans-substantivity ideal, however, is also suspect. Suzette Malveaux, in chapter 7, reveals how this formal equality model masks an unfairness for civil rights claims and litigants. She contends that the Supreme Court's interpretation of the modern class action rule takes a heavier toll on the more vulnerable, whose reliance on this procedural tool has been and remains key to civil rights enforcement. Jasmine Harris, in chapter 8, drills down on this point, describing how judicial skepticism about the commonality of harm has detrimentally impacted employment discrimination cases under the Americans with Disabilities Act in particular and identifying helpful arguments that certain disability class actions can provide to civil rights employment antidiscrimination class actions and vice versa. Finally, in chapter 9, Matthew Fletcher and Neoshia Roemer highlight a statute, the Indian Child Welfare Act, that explicitly moves away from the trans-substantive model and instead provides greater procedural protections to Indian children and their families going through the child welfare system. This rebuke of trans-substantivity is made in favor of procedural justice. Together, these chapters challenge the reader to critique our traditional understanding of trans-substantivity and its normative value.

1

A Critical Perspective on Personal Jurisdiction

Kulko v. Superior Court

ROY L. BROOKS

In 1998, I opened *Critical Procedure*, my book about outsider perspectives on federal civil procedure, with this passage:

> "The life of the law has not been logic; it has been experience." That is one of the great aphorisms of Anglo-American law, written over one hundred years ago by Justice Oliver Wendell Holmes. From that legal truism it is natural to ask whether the experiences, or *values*, of racial minorities, women, and other "outsiders" inform the growth and direction of the law. . . . [W]ould the Federal Rules of Civil Procedure look different if the experiences of outsiders were consciously taken into account? Would civil procedure be the same today if nontraditionalists held seats on the original Rules Advisory Committee in 1934?[1]

In response to that question, I attempted to illustrate how civil procedure might operate when viewed from the perspective of outsiders. Framing procedural analysis in this fashion necessarily rejects the notion that fair and reasonable answers to complex questions of jurisdiction, pleading, joinder, res judicata, and the like are to be found in nothing more than a dictionary or literal reading of words, as textualists are wont to assert. My framework also teaches that the choice between "judicial action" and "judicial restraint" presents a false binary. In most so-called hard cases (cases that present polycentric, socially significant issues), judges are called upon to balance competing interests, which is often a personal calculation even though informed by external considerations. As it is said, every judge has a "puke test."[2] The judicial duty is to draw difficult lines in arriving at just outcomes.

In this chapter, I present a revised conceptual scheme. But rather than endeavoring to analyze the whole of civil procedure as I did in *Critical Procedure*, my ambition here is more modest. It is simply to apply the updated framework to an important case: *Kulko v. Superior Court* (1978).[3] The opinion was written by Justice Thurgood Marshall, one of the most progressive justices to sit on the United States Supreme Court. Although an old case, it addresses a modern problem and is still good law. My discussion will, for the most part, take place within the time frame of the case, 1978. That will enable us to see what options were available to the Court at the time of its decision. I begin with the revised framework.

The Framework

Broached in *Critical Procedure* and refreshed here, my conceptual scheme is informed by critical theory, an amalgamation of outsider criticisms of the received tradition in law. These criticisms come from Critical Race Theory, Critical Feminist Theory, LatCrit Theory, Asian Crit, QueerCrit Theory, and other outsider perspectives.[4] My goal has been to transform critical theory from a theory of legal criticism to a theory of judicial decision-making, something judges can use in deciding procedural issues of keen importance to outsiders. The challenge has been to create a judicial theory or process—one with cognitive, constructive, and critical dimensions—that is faithful to the mission (social transformation) and the diversity of thought in critical theory.

The process I offer begins with the "subordination question," a two-part inquiry of deconstruction and reconstruction. Deconstruction serves the cognitive function of judicial process and reconstruction serves the constructive function. To implement the critical function of judicial theory, the process ends with the "internal critique." The basic framework is:

> Subordination Question (Deconstruction/Reconstruction) and Internal Critique.

Deconstruction, the first part of the subordination question, begins the process. It asks, does a sociolegal arrangement (e.g., a specific case or legal doctrine) subordinate outsiders or a particular outsider group? This inquiry represents the cognitive feature of judicial theory. It enables one to see things that one would not otherwise see through the lens of traditional civil procedure. "Deconstruction . . . can be seen as the breaking down of the walls of a building in order to see why it leans in [a particular] . . . direction."[5] Thus, deconstruction makes visible what is otherwise invisible.

Reconstruction, the second part of the subordination question, redresses the defect unearthed through deconstruction. It serves the constructive dimension of judicial theory. "Reconstruction . . . rebuilds the defective edifice into a palace of justice."[6] Thus, reconstruction is more than an ordinary legal remedy. It aims to be socially transformative, to make society better and more just for outsiders.

Criticalists have different ways of framing the subordination question depending on their vision of equality. Some criticalists believe in equality-as-sameness. These "symmetricalists" assert that outsiders are better served in the long run by equal treatment. Outsider-specific laws are more detrimental than beneficial to outsiders because they undermine the equality claim (i.e., the claim that outsiders and insiders are equal). Such laws paint outsiders as hapless victims in need of special treatment. Symmetricalists believe that outsiders and insiders should be symmetrically situated in a society that is inclined to treat them differently. In procedure, symmetricalists deconstruct by asking a question: Whether the procedural matter under consideration involves an explicit outsider/insider classification or is applied in that manner. If the answer is yes, symmetricalists prescribe a facially neutral reconstructive procedural rule or standard.

Other crits believe in equality-as-difference. They see outsiders and insiders as asymmetrically situated. Yet, unlike symmetricalists, asymmetricalists believe outsiders and insiders *should* be asymmetrically situated. Social transformation is otherwise impossible. Asymmetricalists deconstruct by asking whether the procedural matter under consideration adversely affects outsiders or an outsider group in such a way as to suggest "insiderism." *Insiderism* is manifested as implicit bias, the protection or perpetuation of insider privilege, discounting important outsider values, and the creation of gender-status or other status harms.[7] Such inequality is reconstructed by prescribing outsider-conscious rules. Special rights and empowerment are essential strategies for overcoming society's built-in slant in favor of insiders.

Implicit in the foregoing analysis is a more nuanced equality model that I only hinted at in *Critical Procedure.* Some criticalists imbibe elements of both symmetrical equality and asymmetrical equality. Collectively, they agree with the asymmetrical deconstruction model, but favor a symmetrical-like reconstructive model (i.e., rules that are explicitly designed to aid outsiders but are equally accessible to insiders). Culturally coded rules, such as rules that grant family leave, are examples. Men have access to a company's family leave policy, yet the policy came into existence, ostensibly, to meet the needs of women. But for those needs, the policy would not exist. Proportional rules also follow this general path. These rules apportion benefits based on one's group affiliation. They are facially non-neutral rules designed to aid outsiders, but are equally accessible to insiders who also receive benefits. Criticalists who proceed in this *hybrid* fashion are more solicitous of the interest of insiders than asymmetricalists, but less so than symmetricalists.

Thus, we have three distinct approaches. Symmetricalists deconstruct by asking whether the procedural matter under consideration involves an explicit outsider/insider classification. If the answer is yes, they prescribe a facially neutral reconstructive procedural rule or standard. Asymmetricalists deconstruct by asking whether the procedural matter under consideration adversely affects outsiders or an outsider group in such a way as to suggest insiderism. If the answer is yes, they reconstruct by prescribing outsider-conscious rules. Finally, hybrid crits join the asymmetricalists in the deconstruction mode, but favor culturally coded or insider/outsider–conscious rules designed to empower outsiders while remaining equally accessible to insiders. If deconstruction does not unearth any subordination, the operative value underpinning the governing, nonsubordinating rule must be contextualized within the relevant outsider group. In this way, the court validates an outsider value, which is important for social transformation.

The internal critique, the last step in the process, applies to reconstruction (after a yes answer to the deconstruction question). It implements the critical function of judicial theory. That is, it enables us to determine whether crits, with all their diversity, are likely to be satisfied with the proposed reconstructive measure—the holding of the case.

This exercise takes a deep dive into critical theory. Whether proceeding pursuant to the symmetrical, asymmetrical, or hybrid model, each reconstructive rule is scrutinized under critical epistemologies, which ask in succession: Does the rule make sense because it: is logical or empirical (*rational/empirical*);[8] narrowly tailored to validate the experiences of the "representative" outsider, the outsider most represented in the factual pattern (*standpoint*);[9] validates relevant intersectional experiences or identities of relevant outsiders (*postmodernism*);[10] or promotes a hypertruth (*positionality*)?[11]

If the reconstruction rule passes scrutiny under each or most of these epistemologies, it wins critical acceptance and, therefore, can be presented as a progressive solution to the procedural problem. Still, there will be different critical resolutions to the procedural problem. I leave it to the reader to determine, in juxtaposition with the majority rule, which is the "best" way to resolve the procedural problem. I shall use personal jurisdiction, a central doctrine in civil procedure, to illustrate the process.

Application to *Kulko v. Superior Court*

"Minimum contacts" in personal jurisdiction jurisprudence is the touchstone of determining the proper place for trying a civil lawsuit.[12] When the parties live in different states, the judge must often decide whether the lawsuit should be litigated in the state wherein the plaintiff or the defendant resides. Who should travel? Plaintiff or defendant? That is what the court is ultimately deciding, using minimum contacts as its lodestar.

Kulko v. Superior Court is a seminal personal jurisdiction case. How would a criticalist approach this case? How would that analysis differ from the type of analysis traditionally taught in law schools?

Facts

The primary facts of the case are as follows.

Ms. Kulko lived with her husband, Mr. Kulko, and their two children in New York. After the couple separated, Ms. Kulko moved to California. While in California, she and Mr. Kulko entered into a separation agreement, executed in New York, which provided that the children would remain with their father during the school year and spend vacations with their mother. Under the agreement, Mr. Kulko paid child support when the children were in Ms. Kulko's custody. The agreement was later incorporated into a Haitian divorce decree. A year later, the couple's daughter wanted to live with her mother in California. The father bought her a one-way plane ticket to facilitate the move. Two years later, the couple's son took up residence with his mother in California after Ms. Kulko, without notifying Mr. Kulko, sent the son a plane ticket at his request. Ms. Kulko then sued Mr. Kulko in a California court to modify the divorce decree to, among other things, obtain full legal custody of their children and to increase child support.

Mr. Kulko appeared specially and moved to quash service of the summons on the ground that he was not a California resident and lacked sufficient minimum contacts with the state to warrant personal jurisdiction. Affirming the lower courts, the Supreme Court of California held that the state's exercise of personal jurisdiction was reasonable, because Mr. Kulko had purposely availed himself of the benefits and protections of the laws of California by sending his daughter to live with her mother in California.

The United States Supreme Court reversed by a 6–3 vote. In an opinion written by Justice Marshall, the Court held that California's exercise of in personam jurisdiction over the father violated the Due Process Clause of the Fourteenth Amendment, notwithstanding the fact that Mr. Kulko had acquiesced to his daughter's desire to live with her mother in California. The Court reasoned, in large part, that Mr. Kulko had not purposefully availed himself of the benefits and protection of California's laws and that California's assertion of jurisdiction was unreasonable because "[t]he cause of action herein asserted arises, not from the defendant's commercial transactions in interstate commerce, but rather from his personal, domestic relations."[13] As Mr. Kulko had been in the state only on two brief occasions in the distant past and had no business ties to the state, there was no sufficient connection or relationship between him and the state. Thus, basic considerations of fairness pointed decisively in favor of New York, the father's state of domicile, for adjudication of the claim since he had remained there while the mother had moved.

A Critical Lens

Let us consider how the case might be decided under the three equality models—symmetrical, asymmetrical, and hybrid. Each model begins by engaging the subordination question. If there is no finding of subordination, in this case gender subordination, the analysis proceeds to a confirmation that the operative value underlying the governing law (minimum contacts rule) is congruent with the values or experiences of the relevant outsider group (women). If there is no finding of subordination, there is no need to fashion a reconstructive rule. And if there is no reconstruction, there is no need for an internal critique. However, a finding of subordination would necessitate the creation of a reconstructive rule; and the latter would require application of the internal critique to contextualize the new rule within the outsider community.

It is important to underscore that the models offer different and sometimes contraposed perspectives on the question of gender subordination. Some perspectives will resonate with some readers while other perspectives will not. This is particularly true because women are not a monolithic group. In addition, our modern understanding of gender as a nonbinary construct certainly challenges the conventional meaning of terms such as "mother," "father," "daughter," "son," and "family." There may be disagreement concerning the extent to which, if any, a nonbinary perspective changes the construction or application of the models. Disagreement is a necessary, if uncomfortable, condition for learning and improving the social condition.

Symmetrical Equality Model

Like the asymmetrical and hybrid equality models, the symmetrical equality model begins with deconstruction. Unlike the former, however, the symmetrical equality model deconstructs by asking whether the minimum contacts rule involves an explicit outsider/insider classification or otherwise fails to validate or enforce the value of neutrality (i.e., gender neutrality) that may be an inherent norm in women's lives. In other words, is the minimum contacts rule gender-neutral? Does it embrace the belief in equality as sameness?

Reading the minimum contacts rule and the majority opinion in *Kulko*, symmetricalists would argue that the rule is gender-neutral on its face and in the Court's application. They would point out that no gender classification is explicit in the statement of the minimum contacts rule or in Justice Marshall's application of the rule. Thus, symmetricalists would not find gender subordination.

Given this finding, the next step is to determine whether the relevant value (gender neutrality) is an important norm within the relevant outsider community (women). If it is, then we can say that law embraces an important outsider norm. Validation is all-important in the quest for social transformation.

In making this determination, one need not discern what constitutes a culture among women,[14] a multifaceted subject.[15] One need only demonstrate that the gender-neutrality norm is among the questions and concerns that have preoccupied the lives of US women writ large. Gender neutrality, symmetricalists would argue, is one of many important values in the lives of some women. Though perhaps not an overarching or universally shared value, symmetricalists might say that gender neutrality is a value for which many women have fought long and hard to assert and defend through protest, politics, and litigation.

As one example, some women used litigation to defend a gender-neutral norm. Significantly, the ACLU Women's Rights Project initiated litigation in the 1970s to overturn state and federal laws that discriminated on the basis of sex. The Project's efforts resulted in significant victories for gender equality for both women and men. In *Frontiero v. Richardson*,[16] for example, the late Justice Ruth Bader Ginsburg (then a law professor) successfully argued that a law barring women serving in the military from receiving a housing allowance violated the United States Constitution. Two years later, in *Weinberger v. Wiesenfeld*,[17] Ginsburg represented a man denied the "mother's benefit" (social security payments to a surviving spouse) after the passing of his wife during childbirth. The Court unanimously held that the discriminatory rule was unconstitutional and, in its reasoning, acknowledged the impact that gender discrimination has on both sexes. Ginsburg continued to defend the gender-equality norm case by case and did so representing both women and men. Although the Women's Rights Project litigated on behalf of men—indeed most of the major constitutional sex discrimination cases filed during the 1970s were brought on behalf of male plaintiffs—women were viewed as the ultimate beneficiaries of these victories.

Similarly, symmetricalists would maintain that, as a general position, the gender-neutrality norm inures to the benefit of women in the long run. That is because special treatment undercuts the claim women are making—that they are equal to men—because special treatment portrays women as hapless victims. Thus, symmetricalists would argue that neither the minimum contacts rule nor its application in *Kulko* subordinates women; neither is gender-conscious. Both validate the gender-neutrality value historically embraced by many women. Due to the absence of a finding of gender subordination, symmetricalists would support the governing law as determined by *Kulko*. There is no need for reconstruction, and, consequently, there is no need for the internal critique.

Asymmetrical Equality Model

One proceeding under the asymmetrical equality model would deconstruct *Kulko* by asking whether the Supreme Court's application of the minimum contacts doctrine in that case adversely impacts women in such a way as to suggest insiderism. Asymmetricalists would likely answer that question in the affirmative. *Kulko* adversely affects women in child custody or support cases by making it difficult for them to litigate these cases involving a nonresident father. In addition, asymmetricalists would argue that *Kulko* reeks of insiderism in that it suppresses and, thereby, invalidates an important value ostensibly claimed by many women—care and connection—by privileging commercial ties over personal relations.

At the time *Kulko* was decided, women received custody of children in 90 percent of divorce cases involving minor children, and more than 50 percent of all divorced fathers did not meet their child support or spousal maintenance obligations.[18] Matters are pretty much the same today.[19] By placing the burden of travel on women in child custody or support cases, the doctrine of minimum contacts hurts women because it makes it more difficult for women to sue to protect their rights. This, then, makes it easier for divorced men to evade their responsibilities to divorced women, as well as to their children.

Turning to insiderism, the threshold question concerns whether *Kulko* ignores or discounts any value identified with women. Care and connection are arguably values identified with women. It is posited that men—more than women—tend to value independence and view the world and relationships in terms of status; and women—more than men—tend to value care and connection and express vulnerability to male violence.[20] Carrie Menkel-Meadow famously discussed psychological studies that arguably demonstrate "women experience themselves through connections and relationships to others while men see themselves as separately identified individuals."[21] As it encompasses "connections and relationships to others,"[22] the value of care and connection that allegedly animates much of the lived experiences of many women necessarily extends beyond caregiving for children. Women's experiences are not limited to caregiving for children. The value of care and connection is, in fact, present in other endeavors women pursue, including business.[23]

Of course, any theory that imputes distinct qualities, attitudes, or duties to outsiders and insiders is bound to invite sharp criticism as stereotypical and wrong. Arguments have been made on both sides of the issue. For purposes of this analysis, however, let us make the assumption for the asymmetricalists that the value of care and connection is identified more with women than with men.

The next question, then, is whether *Kulko*'s construction and application of the minimum contacts rule ignores or discounts this value. It could be argued that it does. The Court explicitly rules that minimum contacts recognize "commercial" ties, but not "personal" ones, as valid forum contacts.[24] This reasoning subordinates the value of care and connection by elevating commercial interests above the parental relationship.

Having found subordination, criticalists are free to fashion their own response—a reconstructive rule—to the jurisdictional issue. An asymmetrical reconstructive rule will typically provide special treatment for outsiders. Asymmetricalists might, therefore, prescribe the following rule: the state in which a female litigant resides is the proper place for trial in child custody and support cases. Thus, if a female litigant (plaintiff or defendant) resides in California and a male litigant (plaintiff or defendant) resides in New York, the case will be litigated in California.

Moving to the internal critique, the question is whether the female plaintiff residency jurisdictional rule passes scrutiny under the rational/empirical, standpoint, postmodern, and positionality epistemologies. Wearing the rational/empirical epistemological hat, one could reason that the rule makes sense based on the following logic: (1) the relative lack of flexibility and wealth make travel to litigate lawsuits difficult; (2) as discussed, even today women get child custody in the majority of divorce cases; (3) ergo, women are less able to travel to litigate child custody and support matters, at least in the majority of such cases, and, therefore, should not have to do so.

Arguing in the opposite direction on rational/empirical grounds, a symmetricalist would press the point that the rule, by portraying women as hapless victims in need of special treatment, reinforces gender stereotypes and, thus, undercuts the gender-equality principle. The rule might also spark a backlash, especially if men see rich women benefiting from the rule. A logical response to the gender stereotyping argument could be that if judges reject the female plaintiff residency rule, all doubt will be removed: women litigants will *in fact* be hapless victims in child custody and support cases.

Responding to that argument in this ongoing internal discussion, a symmetricalist might offer the following slippery-slope, line-drawing argument: If an exception is carved out for mothers in these cases, what's to stop courts from making exceptions for other groups in other cases? This type of argument might also resonate with insiders. If so, it is not by design, for the primary purpose of the internal critique is to advance arguments (opposing and supporting) that are meaningful to outsiders.

In rebuttal, it could be argued that we draw the line at outsider status: outsiders get the exception, insiders do not. A rejoinder to that argument might be that we risk balkanizing the rules governing civil litigation if exceptions are made for outsiders. However, litigation rules are riddled with exceptions; there is, in fact, little uniformity. This internal, Socratic discourse could continue for perhaps several more rounds.

Whether rational/empirical considerations suggest that the female plaintiff residency rule, on balance, passes muster under the rational/empirical epistemology is a conclusion readers will have to draw on their own. One should try as much as possible to view the matter from the woman's perspective—privilege that perspective—however difficult it might be to make that determination given the fact that women are not monolithic. This takes us to the other epistemologies.

It could be argued that the female litigant residency jurisdictional rule passes muster under both standpoint and postmodern epistemologies. *Standpoint* validates exclusively the values or experiences of the "representative" woman in child custody or support cases; or, if the validation is not exclusive, it at least is not detrimental to the representative outsider. In contrast, *postmodernism* validates the values and experiences of all female identities in these cases. In *Kulko*, the representative outsider is a woman with legal custody, because women in child custody or support cases typically get custody of their children. A woman without legal custody in these cases is atypical; in other words, she is the nonrepresentative outsider. The female litigant residency jurisdictional rule is not narrowly tailored to validate the values or experience of the representative woman in this case, because the nonrepresentative can use the rule to get a favorable jurisdictional ruling. Yet, that possibility is not detrimental to the representative outsider. It does not in any way prejudice the representative who otherwise has full, untrammeled access to the rule. Based on this reasoning, the asymmetrical jurisdictional rule passes scrutiny under standpoint epistemology. And because both the representative and nonrepresentative are validated, the rule also survives scrutiny under postmodern epistemology. But, again, readers must make this call on their own.

Positionality,[25] it could be argued, is something of a mixed bag. On the one hand, providing a preference to female litigants in child custody or support cases vindicates the gender-equality hypertruth.[26] It gives women a measure of social and economic equality in such cases. (If we assume women already have the children, they are less able to travel than fathers.) On the other hand, the gender-equality hypertruth can collide with the economic fairness hypertruth. Some fathers are less able to travel than some mothers. This can happen in cases involving custodial fathers and noncustodial mothers or mothers who are wealthier than fathers. One hypertruth (economic fairness) rubs against another hypertruth (gender equality). Asymmetricalists would resolve the conflict in favor of women litigants, the outsiders.

On balance, a jurisdictional rule granting a preference to women litigants in child custody or support cases is likely to pass scrutiny under the internal critique. Applied to the facts of this case, then, this rule would give the California courts personal jurisdiction since the female litigant, Ms. Kulko, resides in that state. But, again, readers have to decide the matter.

Hybrid Equality Model

Deconstruction under the hybrid equality model is the same as it is under the asymmetrical equality model. Because the latter finds gender subordination, so, too, does the former. The difference between these equality models is in their respective reconstructive modes.

Unlike an asymmetrical reconstructive—or equity—rule, a hybrid reconstructive rule is not explicitly skewed in favor of outsiders. It is subtle because it is driven by the criticalist belief in "[e]quality as acceptance"—in other words, a vision of equality in which "distinctly outsider and insider choices and roles [are] equally valued and equally accessible *to both* groups."[27] Thus, a hybrid reconstructive rule, like an asymmetrical rule, benefits outsiders, but unlike the latter it is equally accessible to insiders. Such a rule could be culturally coded in favor of outsiders (e.g., family leave policies) or overtly proportional (e.g., half outsiders, half insiders). Our civil rights laws are basically hybrid rules of conduct. The prohibition against discrimination on the basis of "race" or "sex,"[28] for example, is designed to benefit people of color and women, but is also accessible to white males (i.e., insiders).

Under the hybrid equality model, one might favor the following reconstructive rule in the present case: the state with which the *child* has the closest or most significant personal connections shall be the proper place for litigation in child custody and support cases. Three features about this jurisdiction rule should be noted at the outset. First, while it is unclear whether children ought to be deemed as an outsider group, it could be argued that the word "child" is culturally coded to benefit mothers. Children are closely associated with mothers in US culture; for example, mothers still get custody in the great majority of divorce cases.[29] Second, the hybrid rule does not assume that female identity is necessarily tethered to motherhood. The present case involves mothers, a specific type or subset of women. Third, a male litigant can certainly benefit from a child-centered jurisdictional rule if he lives in a state with which the child has the closest personal ties—physical as well as psychological.

Thus understood, the hybrid rule would seem to pass muster under the rational/empirical epistemology. A child-centered jurisdictional rule neutralizes the difference between mothers and fathers. Rationally, a child could be viewed as the "golden mean" between parents.[30] Also, the parent most responsible for the child's care and support should not bear the additional cost of litigating in a faraway place to establish or enforce child custody rights.

That being said, it could also be argued that the hybrid holding mediates differences between mothers and fathers only in form, not in substance. If mothers get custody of minor children in most divorce cases, then a child-centered jurisdictional rule effectively favors mothers in most cases. Thus, to the extent that rules seeking the golden mean appeal to a woman's rational sense of fairness,[31] the hybrid equality rule flunks that test. It does not, as an empirical matter, take a middle position as between mothers and fathers even though it purports to do so. But on balance the rule seems to make rational/empirical sense given the fact that the custodial parent should not assume additional child-rearing expenses created as a plaintiff or defendant in child custody or support cases.

In discussing the asymmetrical jurisdictional rule, the representative woman in child custody or support cases was defined as the woman with legal custody of her children, and the nonrepresentative woman in these cases was defined as the woman without such custody. Based on these definitions, it could be argued that the hybrid jurisdictional rule passes muster under neither standpoint nor postmodern epistemology. A child-centered jurisdictional rule takes the jurisdictional decision out of the hands of women—whether representative or nonrepresentative—and places it into children's hands. Women with legal custody of their children will not get a favorable jurisdictional ruling if the child has closer personal ties to the father's forum state. If both parents share custody, as in the present case, or if a child spends half her time with both parents, or if the significant occasions during the year (such as birthdays, holidays, and vacations) are spent with the father, then there is nothing in a child-centered jurisdictional rule that prevents a judge from concluding that the child's closest personal connections are with the father's state. Clearly, then, the rule is not narrowly tailored to validate the experiences or expectations of the representative, let alone nonrepresentative, female litigant in these cases. It is centered on children and not on women.

While the hybrid jurisdictional rule is unlikely to pass scrutiny under standpoint and postmodern epistemologies, it does survive scrutiny under positionality—in a big way. The rule, at bottom, is about children—specifically, the love and responsibility parents have (or should have) for their children. The love of one's child is a hypertruth. That view would arguably trump any deficiencies in the hybrid jurisdictional rule brought to light under standpoint and postmodern scrutiny. Any rule of law that validates children makes perfect sense under positionality.

Applied to the facts of this case, the hybrid jurisdictional rule gives the California courts personal jurisdiction. That is the forum state with which the litigants' children have the closest or most significant personal connections at the time the lawsuit was filed. They are living full time with their mother in California, and they have expressed a desire to be there. Their ties to the state relative to New York are quite substantial.

Conclusion

Underlying the framework presented in this chapter is an awareness that the sociolegal order is not objective as to outsiders and insiders. It is, instead, anti-objective. It leans in the direction of insiders. For that reason, the application of my framework in this case makes women's voices the touchstone for analyzing jurisdictional issues in child custody or support cases. Her perspective must be privileged. Room must be made for her voice.

I do not, however, decide which deconstruction or reconstruction best promotes social transformation. There is great pedagogical value in leaving that task to the reader. Through such reflection, one is also able to understand that the traditional way of understanding civil procedure—in which the focus is on extant rules—is a necessary starting point but hardly sufficient in doing justice to outsiders. Leaving the question open allows one to think outside of the box and begin to conceive of a forward-looking approach to civil procedure rooted in justice for all.

NOTES

1 Roy L. Brooks, *Critical Procedure* xxiii (1998).

2 Justice Oliver Wendell Holmes famously wrote that in certain cases he would consider "all the elements enumerated" and "accept the judgement unless it makes us puke." Oliver Wendell Holmes, *Washington, D.C., October 23, 1926*, in *Holmes-Laski Letters* 888 (Mark De Wolfe Howe ed., 1953).

3 436 U.S. 84 (1978).

4 For a discussion of some of the formative works in critical theory, *see* Brooks, *supra* note 1, at 3–36. *See also* Khiara M. Bridges, *Critical Race Theory: A Primer* (2018); Richard Delgado & Jean Stefancic, *Critical Race Theory: An Introduction* (3d ed. 2017); Nancy Levit & Robert R. M. Verchick, *Feminist Legal Theory: A Primer* (2d ed. 2016); Charles F. Abel & Arthur J. Sementelli, *Evolutionary Critical Theory and Its Role in Public Affairs* (2016); Adrien K. Wing, *Is There a Future for Critical Race Theory?*, 66 J. Legal Educ. 44 (2016); Mario L. Barnes, *Empirical Methods and Critical Race Theory: A Discourse on Possibilities for a Hybrid Methodology*, 2016 Wis. L. Rev. 443 (2016).

5 *See* Brooks, *supra* note 1, at 32.

6 *Id.* at 32.

7 Classic scholarship on this point includes: Ian Haney Lopez, *White by Law: The Legal Construction of Race* (1996); Charles R. Lawrence II, *The Id, the Ego, and Equal Protection: Reckoning with Unconscious Racism*, 39 Stan. L. Rev. 317 (1987).

8 "Rational/empirical epistemology" refers to the criticalist approach to legal problem-solving that mirrors the traditional mode of legal reasoning taught in American law schools, but assumes the law is *not* objective. Brooks, *supra* note 1, at 23–24.

9 "Standpoint epistemology" proceeds from the victim's or outsider's perspective, such as women or black people, and seeks judicial validation of the values or experiences of the most representative of the outsider group within the context of the case. Such essentialism is in conflict with postmodernism. *See id.* at 28. Groundbreaking criticalists such as Derrick Bell and Mari Matsuda have often referred to the "authentic" and "inauthentic" outsider, those who are "essentially connected" and those who are not. This distinction harkens back to the difference between "field Negroes" and "house slaves." *See id.* at 24–28.

10 "Postmodern epistemology" views outsider perspectives as fluctuating within "a complex set of social contexts" and as a "matter of social, historical, and cultural construction." *Id.* at 28 (quoting Katharine T. Bartlett, *Feminist Legal Methods*, 103 Harv. L. Rev. 829, 877 (1990)). This subjective approach helps to deal with the fragmentation of group identity. However, postmodernism is undermined by the absence of objectivity. Criticalists influenced by postmodernism struggle to maintain that oppression exists when their capacity to document it is limited by their denial of common truths. The rejection of universal truths also presents the challenge of determining which outsider perspective, all claimed to be of equal status, deserves advocacy. *Id.* at 29–30.

11 "Positionality epistemology" acknowledges the existence of "hypertruths." These truths are values that enjoy near-universal acceptance in the culture, e.g., children should be loved, killing another person not in self-defense is wrong, etc. *See id.* at 30–31.

12 Int'l Shoe Co. v. Washington, 326 U.S. 310, 316 (1945).

13 Kulko v. Superior Ct., 436 U.S. 84, 94, 96–97 (1978).

14 "Culture" is a complex and controversial concept, even among anthropologists. Fundamentally, it means the behaviors, values, and attitudes—the questions and concerns—that preoccupy the lives of a group. *See, e.g.*, Roy L. Brooks, *The Racial Glass Ceiling: Subordination in American Law and Culture* 70–71 (2017) (discussing race and culture). There are, of course, many characteristics (e.g., race and class) intersecting with sex that determine what is important in the lives of women. Some are personal while others are socially constructed. For a more detailed discussion, *see generally* Bell Hooks, *Ain't I a Woman: Black Women and Feminism* (2d ed. 2014). *See also* Mikki Kendall, *Hood Feminism: Notes from the Women That a Movement Forgot* (2020); Charlene Carruthers, *Unapologetic: A Black, Queer, and Feminist Mandate for Radical Movements* (2018).

15 *See* sources cited *supra* note 14 regarding the intersectionality of "women's culture."

16 411 U.S. 677 (1973).

17 420 U.S. 636 (1975).

18 *See, e.g.*, Deborah L. Rhode, *Justice and Gender: Sex Discrimination and the Law* 151 (1989).

19 *See Why Do Women Get Child Custody in 90 Percent of All Cases? Isn't It Gender Discrimination?*, Emy A. Cordano, Att'y L. Blog (June 28, 2018), www.cor-law.com.

20 It is most instructive that Justice Breyer devotes six pages of his dissenting opinion in *United States v. Morrison* discussing various government studies that came out around the time of *Kulko* and that demonstrated the extent to which women are victims of male violence. 529 U.S. 598, 629–635 (2000). For example, a Department of Justice report that Justice Breyer cites found: "Three out of four American women will be victims of violent crimes sometime during their life." *Id.* at 631

(citing U.S. Dep't. of Just., Report on the Nation on Crime and Justice 29 (2d ed. 1988)).

21 Carrie Menkel-Meadow, *Portia in a Different Voice: Speculations on a Women's Lawyering Process*, 1 Berkeley Women's L. J. 39, 43 (1985).

22 *Id.*

23 In the corporate world, for example, several studies have identified a "cooperative" as opposed to an "adversative" leadership style among female corporate executives. Some male executives have incorporated the care-and-connection value in their leadership style, perhaps because these studies have also shown that the presence of women in upper management positions in the Fortune 500 companies correlates with increased profits. *See, e.g.*, Yoni Blumberg, *Companies With More Female Executives Make More Money—Here's Why*, CNBC (March 2, 2018), www.cnbc.com (women leaders facilitate diverse approaches to problem-solving, reduce turnover, and enhance the quality of employees by reducing gender discrimination in recruitment, promotions, and retention); Valerie Ross, *Is There a Female Leadership Style?*, KelloggInsight: Kellogg Sch. Mgmt. Nw. Univ. (September 4, 2012), https://insight.kellogg.northwestern.edu (companies led by women make significantly fewer layoffs than male-led companies).

24 Kulko v. Superior Ct., 436 U.S. 84, 97 (1978).

25 *See* definition *supra* note 11.

26 *See id.*

27 Brooks, *supra* note 1, at 19–20 (*see* sources cited therein).

28 *See, e.g.*, Title VII of the Civil Rights Act of 1964, 42 U.S.C. § 2000e-2(a).

29 *See supra* notes 18–19.

30 The "golden mean" is Aristotle's idea of the middle position between two sides. *See* Aristotle, *Nicomachean Ethics* (W. D. Ross trans., 2016).

31 Again, this statement admittedly embeds a certain degree of essentialism not intended.

2

Forging Fortuity Against Procedural Retrenchment

Developing a Critical Race Theoretical Account of Civil Procedure

PORTIA PEDRO

There is no neutral. Race and racial subordination matter within civil procedure. But race, racism, white supremacy, and other aspects of identity-based marginalization course through the veins of civil procedural standards much more than scholarship has revealed. In this chapter, I emphasize the importance of, and begin to lay the theoretical groundwork for, a critical racial analysis of civil procedure.

The Import of a Critical Race Theoretical Account of Civil Procedure

Critical Race Theory reveals the ways in which racial subordination is embedded in social structures and bureaucracies. What other system could be more central to law than the procedure that decides who can access courts to request justice for harms? Naming and describing the racist effects of seemingly technocratic or neutral efforts are significant parts of the project of stopping the further retrenchment of racial equality.

There have been significant scholarly contributions of critical perspectives on civil procedure,[1] the racial implications of various aspects of civil procedure,[2] and critical race perspectives on numerous procedural doctrines and precedents.[3] But there is less civil procedural scholarship with a critical perspective on race than exists in some other areas such as constitutional and antidiscrimination law,[4] contracts,[5] corporations,[6] criminal procedure,[7] evidence,[8] property,[9] tax,[10] and voting rights and election law.[11] There is still not a comprehensive theoretical account of the interactions between racial subordination and procedure across various procedural mechanisms, doctrines, precedents, and principles. The literature to which I hope to add includes scholarship that provides models for how different criticalists might critique and rework areas of civil procedure,[12] integrate racial justice into teaching civil procedure,[13] and engage "critical race empiricism"[14] in civil procedure.[15]

Procedural justice scholars posit that individuals feel better about their litigation experiences and the law if they think that judges treat them fairly.[16] There are three key principles of procedural justice: (1) having an opportunity to tell your story; (2) thinking that decision makers are neutral and trustworthy; and (3) feeling that you are treated with respect.[17] Given that stated civil procedural ideals and rules are similar to these principles, it takes work to uncover the ways in which procedure might have been, currently is, or might in the future be mobilized to the disadvantage of marginalized groups, all while upholding a façade of procedural justice.

Bringing these insights together with Professor Derrick Bell's theory of racial fortuity,[18] we should expect attempts to retrench civil rights and the rights of marginalized groups to have a procedural focus—that is, procedural retrenchment. Racial fortuity is a cyclical process between interest convergence and involuntary sacrifice (of those same victories secured during interest convergence). Under interest convergence, "the interest of blacks in achieving racial equality is accommodated only when that interest converges with the interests of whites."[19] The less-discussed component of racial fortuity is involuntary sacrifice:

> To settle potentially costly differences between two opposing groups of whites, a compromise is effected that depends on the involuntary sacrifice of black rights or interests. Even less recognized, these compromises (actually silent covenants) not only harm blacks but also disadvantage large groups of whites, including those who support the arrangements. Examples of this involuntary racial-sacrifice phenomenon abound and continue. A few of the more important are: the slavery understandings, the Constitution, universal white male suffrage, the *Dred Scott v. Sandford* case, the Hayes-Tilden compromise, and the southern disenfranchisement compromise.[20]

Bell posits that "the rights of blacks are always vulnerable, subject to be sacrificed, or used as catalysts enabling whites to settle serious policy differences."[21] The involuntary sacrifice comes at a time when white[22] people are divided and need to be reunited across class or other lines, so they reunite by taking something away from Black people or other marginalized groups. Given current high levels of polarization,[23] it seems that we are currently in such a time.

Structural marginalization of people of color is one of the primary goals, and results, of procedural retrenchment. Procedural retrenchment of civil rights occurs when seemingly neutral and technocratic changes to the landscape of civil procedure or remedies doctrine effectively roll back constitutional and statutory civil rights in a way that cuts off marginalized groups from access to courts and the remedies needed to redress the wrongs that we suffer. We should expect substantial litigation attacks on people of color and other marginalized communities to be framed as technical and neutral by using procedure as a Trojan horse for substantive attacks.

If we bring a critical racial theoretical focus to areas such as pleading, discovery, and class actions, we may see a sort of procedural equilibration[24]—courts and defendants chipping away at substantive rights of communities of color and other marginalized groups through imposing procedural hurdles either instead of or in addition to primarily substantive attacks. This supposed objective framing leaves civil rights, constitutional rights, and impact litigation vulnerable to retrenchment and may gain more traction than attempts to cut back the underlying substantive rights directly.

To avoid involuntary sacrifice, "it is usually necessary to push the dynamics of fortuity hard."[25] Those who support the end of marginalized groups' subordination should "forge fortuity."[26] Forging fortuity requires unmasking the ways that procedural rules and doctrine work to subjugate marginalized communities:

> We can both think and plan within a context of what is, rather than idealism. We know, for example, that a great many whites will not maintain discriminatory policies, or even beliefs, if the cost is too high or if the benefits of easing discriminatory policies are sufficiently obvious.

Designing strategies based on this knowledge will lift the sights, providing a bird's eye view of discriminatory situations and how best to address them.[27]

The Need for an Intersectional Theoretical Approach

Although the focus of this chapter is on Critical Race Theory, and many of the theory's foundational concepts of focus on race (more specifically, how US structures reinforce white supremacy to subjugate Black people), we also need a broader development of Critical Race Theory in civil procedure. I am not the first to explore what applying Black/white paradigm critical race theorist concepts might mean for other racial groups or other marginalized groups such as women, immigrants, LGBTQ+ communities, Indigenous peoples, people with disabilities, and others.[28] A goal of my project is to help develop a theory that informs how we might deploy civil procedure to prevent the further structural oppression of all of these groups and how we can begin to undo prior attacks and even make gains.

As Professor Russell Robinson points out for substantive constitutional law, doctrinal intersectionality—"juxtaposing doctrinal domains that are often thought of as distinct"—"plac[es] cases from different silos in conversation with each other[, which] may make visible broader projects."[29] Because courts generally apply civil procedural mechanisms trans-substantively, theorizing in a doctrinally intersectional way in civil procedure is essential to consider implications across different types of claims and groups.

It is crucial to have an understanding of Critical Race Theory's procedural implications that goes beyond people of color. Attempts to retrench rights are likely to either start, or be most successful soonest, with groups perceived as more vulnerable, smallest, or "fringe"[30] (e.g., the transgender community) or more recently recognized rights[31] (such as marriage equality) instead of marginalized groups perceived as stronger, larger, or more traditional (such as Black people or women) or much longer recognized civil rights (such as the rights to free speech or voting).[32] After procedural protections have been denied to (or clawed back from) some vulnerable communities or for some vulnerable rights, that retrenchment is likely to spread to what we assume are more classic civil rights groups and core civil rights. For example, the US Supreme Court arguably imposed a heightened pleading standard on a Pakistani Muslim plaintiff in litigation alleging racial and religious discrimination in September 11, 2001 investigation–related detentions[33] and, because of the Court's opinion in *Ashcroft v. Iqbal*,[34] the heightened pleading standard from *Bell v. Twombly*[35] and *Iqbal* apply generally to civil pleadings.

These socially created categories[36] are not monolithic, so any procedural retrenchment for transgender people will also be a retrenchment for women, people of color, and people with disabilities who are also transgender. Additionally, because different claims, rights, and groups generally are not separated into different procedural silos, procedural retrenchment from one marginalized group likely will lead to procedural retrenchment for other marginalized groups and for litigants overall. The justifications for reduced procedural protections for one group or type of claim will serve as precedential and theoretical bases for extending the same treatment to others.

* * *

A comprehensive critical race theoretical analysis of procedural mechanisms and doctrines should reveal prior and current attempts to curtail procedural protections for people of color and other marginalized groups. Further, such analysis should identify the types of previously unsuccessful attacks that may be revived in cases with plaintiffs whom, or claims which, the judiciary might understand the least—plaintiffs from marginalized groups seen as smaller, more vulnerable, more suspect (or claims for more recently recognized rights) in a way that might limit procedural protections for these plaintiffs and all litigants. This is not a conclusion. Hopefully, this can, instead, serve as part of beginning a renewed conversation.

NOTES

1 *See, e.g.*, Brooke D. Coleman, *One Percent Procedure*, 91 Wash. L. Rev. 1005 (2016); Suzette Malveaux, *A Diamond in the Rough: Trans-Substantivity of the Federal Rules of Civil Procedure and Its Detrimental Impact on Civil Rights*, 92 Wash. U.L. Rev. 455 (2014); Roy Brooks, Critical Procedure (1998); Katherine A. Macfarlane, *Shadow Judges: Staff Attorney Adjudication of Prisoner Claims*, 95 Or. L. Rev. 97, 105 (2016); Andrew Hammond, *Pleading Poverty in Federal Court*, 128 Yale L.J. 1478, 1526 (2019); Eric K. Yamamoto, *Critical Procedure: ADR and the Justices'*

"Second Wave" Constriction of Court Access and Claim Development, 70 SMU L. Rev. 765 (2017).

2 *See, e.g.*, Victor D. Quintanilla, *Beyond Common Sense: A Social Psychological Study of* Iqbal*'s Effect on Claims of Race Discrimination*, 17 Mich. J. Race & L. 1 (2011); Suzette M. Malveaux, *Front Loading and Heavy Lifting: How Pre-Dismissal Discovery Can Address the Detrimental Effect of* Iqbal *on Civil Rights Cases*, 14 Lewis & Clark L. Rev. 65 (2010).

3 Victor D. Quintanilla, *Critical Race Empiricism: A New Means to Measure Civil Procedure*, 3 U.C. Irvine L. Rev. 187 (2013); Roy L. Brooks, Conley *and* Twombly*: A Critical Race Theory Perspective*, 52 How. L.J. 31 (2008); Roy L. Brooks, *Critical Race Theory: A Proposed Structure and Application to Federal Pleading*, 11 Harv. BlackLetter L.J. 85 (1994).

4 *See, e.g.*, T. Alexander Aleinikoff, *The Constitution in Context: The Continuing Significance of Racism*, 63 U. Colo. L. Rev. 325 (1992); Kimberlé Williams Crenshaw, *Race, Reform, and Retrenchment: Transformation and Legitimation in Antidiscrimination Law*, 101 Harv. L. Rev. 1331 (1988); Eric Schnapper, *Perpetuation of Past Discrimination*, 96 Harv. L. Rev. 828 (1983); Alan David Freeman, *Legitimizing Racial Discrimination Through Antidiscrimination Law: A Critical Review of Supreme Court Doctrine*, 62 Minn. L. Rev. 1049 (1978).

5 *See, e.g.*, Marjorie Florestal, *Is a Burrito a Sandwich? Exploring Race, Class, and Culture in Contracts*, 14 Mich. J. Race & L. 1 (2008); Michele Goodwin, *The Body Market: Race Politics & Private Ordering*, 49 Ariz. L. Rev. 599 (2007); Emily M.S. Houh, *Sketches of a Redemptive Theory of Contract Law*, 66 Hastings L.J. 951 (2015); Blake D. Morant, *The Relevance of Race and Disparity in Discussions of Contract Law*, 31 New Eng. L. Rev. 889 (1997); Patricia J. Williams, The Alchemy of Race and Rights: Diary of a Law Professor (1991).

6 *See, e.g.*, Richard R.W. Brooks, *Incorporating Race*, 106 Colum. L. Rev. 2023 (2006).

7 *See, e.g.*, Devon W. Carbado, *(E)Racing the Fourth Amendment*, 100 Mich. L. Rev. 946 (2002); Tracey Maclin, *Race and the Fourth Amendment*, 51 Vand. L. Rev. 333 (1998); Russell M. Gold, *Procedure's Racism* (unpublished manuscript) (on file with author).

8 *See, e.g.*, Jasmine B. Gonzales Rose, *Toward a Critical Race Theory of Evidence*, 101 Minn. L. Rev. 2243 (2017).

9 *See, e.g.*, Cheryl I. Harris, *Whiteness as Property*, 106 Harv. L. Rev. 1707 (1993).

10 *See, e.g.*, Andre L. Smith, Tax Law and Racial Economic Justice: Black Tax (2015); Critical Tax Theory: An Introduction (Anthony C. Infanti & Bridget J. Crawford eds., 2009); David A. Brennen, *Race and Equality Across the Law School Curriculum: The Law of Tax Exemption*, 54 J. Legal Educ. 336 (2004); Beverly I. Moran & William Whitford, *A Black Critique of the Internal Revenue Code*, 1996 Wis. L. Rev. 751 (1996); Dorothy A. Brown, *Race, Class, and Gender Essentialism in Tax Literature: The Joint Return*, 54 Wash. & Lee L. Rev. 1469 (1997).

11 *See, e.g.*, Lani Guinier, *Groups, Representation, and Race-Conscious Districting: A Case of the Emperor's Clothes*, 71 Tex. L. Rev. 1589 (1993); Heather K. Gerken, *Understanding the Right to an Undiluted Vote*, 114 Harv. L. Rev. 1663 (2001). For examples specific to teaching in various doctrinal areas, see Dorothy A. Brown, Critical Race Theory: Cases, Materials, and Problems (3rd ed. 2013); Kevin R. Johnson, *Integrating Racial Justice into the Civil Procedure Survey Course*, 54 J. Legal Educ. 242 (2004); Taunya Lovell Banks, *Teaching Laws with Flaws: Adopting a Pluralistic Approach to Torts*, 57 Mo. L. Rev. 443, 446–47 (1992).

12 Brooks, *supra* note 1.

13 Johnson, *supra* note 11.

14 Devon W. Carbado, *Blue-on-Black Violence: A Provisional Model of Some of the Causes*, 104 Geo. L.J. 1638 (2016).

15 *See, e.g.*, Quintanilla, *supra* note 3 (discussing social psychology and pleading).

16 Tom R. Tyler, *Procedural Justice and the Courts*, 44 Court Rev. J. Am. Judges Ass'n 26, 28 (2007); *see also* E. Allan Lind & Tom R. Tyler, The Social Psychology of Procedural Justice (1988); Tom R. Tyler, Social Justice: Outcome and Procedure, 35 Int'l J. Psych. 117 (2000).

17 Tyler, *Procedural Justice and the Courts*, *supra* note 16, at 30–31.

18 Derrick Bell, *Brown v. Board of Education: Reliving and Learning From Our Racial History*, 66 U. Pitt. L. Rev. 21, 26 (2004).

19 *Id.* at 22.; *see also* Derrick Bell, Race, Racism, and American Law 18, 40 (5th ed. 2004).

20 Derrick Bell, Silent Covenants: *Brown v. Board of Education* and the Unfulfilled Hopes for Racial Reform 51 (2005).

21 Bell, *supra* note 18, at 22.

22 I capitalize "Black," do not capitalize "white," and do not capitalize "people of color" because "Blacks, like Asians, Latinos, and other 'minorities,' constitute a specific cultural group and, as such, require denotation as a proper noun." Crenshaw, *supra* note 4, at 1332 n.2; *see also* Kimberlé Crenshaw, *Mapping the Margins: Intersectionality, Identity Politics, and Violence Against Women of Color*, 43 Stan. L. Rev. 1241, 1244 n.6 ("I do not capitalize 'white' which is not a proper noun, since whites do not constitute a specific cultural group"). "Although 'white' and 'Black' have been defined oppositionally, they are not functional opposites." Harris, *supra* note 9, at 1710 n.3.

23 *See, e.g.*, Katherine Schaeffer, *Far More Americans See "Very Strong" Partisan Conflicts Now Than in the Last Two Presidential Election Years*, Pew Rsch. Ctr., (Mar. 4, 2020), www.pewresearch.org (noting that the percentage of people in the United States who report perceiving strong or very strong "conflicts between Democrats and Republicans" in 2020 is significantly higher than it was in 2016 or 2012); Anne E. Wilson, Victoria A. Parker & Matthew Feinberg, *Polarization in the Contemporary Political and Media Landscape*, 34 Current Op. Behav. Sci. 223, 223 (2020) (noting that "[b]y 2010, opposition to cross-party unions had shot up

to 49% of Republicans and 33% of Democrats" compared to a small minority of people in the United States who opposed cross-party unions in 1960); Guy-Uriel E. Charles, *Motivated Reasoning, Post-Truth, and Election Law*, 64 St. Louis U. L.J. 595, 595–96 (2020) (arguing that polarization "has infected American electoral institutions, particularly Congress" and "the Supreme Court").

24 *See* Daryl J. Levinson, *Rights Essentialism and Remedial Equilibration*, 99 Colum. L. Rev. 857 (1999) (introducing remedial equilibration—there is no meaningful constitutional right unless there is also a concomitant remedy that redresses the full scope of the harm to the right).

25 Bell, *supra* note 18, at 31.

26 *Id.*

27 *Id.* at 32.

28 *See, e.g.*, Jeremiah A. Ho, *Queer Sacrifice in Masterpiece Cakeshop*, 31 Yale J.L. & Feminism, 249, 287–89 (2020); Amit Patel, *The Orthodoxy Opening Predicament: The Crumbling Wall of Separation Between Church and State*, 83 U. Det. Mercy L. Rev. 195, 209–11 (2006).

29 Russell K. Robinson, *Justice Kennedy's White Nationalism*, U.C. Davis L. Rev. 1027, 1030, 1030 n.7 (2019) ("By assigning cases to different silos . . . scholars and teachers might miss how these cases converge or clash.").

30 *See* Cynthia Lee, *The Trans Panic Defense Revisited*, 57 Am. Crim. L. Rev. 1411, 1447–53 (2020); Ho, *supra* note 28, at 287–89 (proposing that litigants "'more queer' than 'gay'" were less sympathetic litigants because their identities destabilized heterosexual hegemony and challenged mainstream normalcy):

> In contrast to the . . . identities that the *Obergefell* couples projected . . . , the same-sex couple in *Masterpiece* did not appear as readily assimilated nor as aligned with mainstream respectability. . . . They played with androgyny and avoided wearing conventional clothing. . . . [T]hey affirmatively challenged the assimilated image of normalcy the *Obergefell* plaintiffs had embodied and curtailed any sameness arguments to be made for successfully increasing the level[] of . . . interest convergence. . . . Unlike "gay and lesbian," the terminology "queer" does not merely describe sexual practices . . . ; instead, whatever features that embody "queerness" defy such identity-oriented classifications and exist as a means for "a destabilization of heterosexual hegemony." Applying queerness to Craig and Mullins's public personas, this observation could affirm and explain how their sexualities appeared more destabilizing to members of the Supreme Court than the *Obergefell* plaintiffs did previously. *Id.*

31 *See, e.g.*, Lisa Keen, *Strength and Longevity of Legal Gains May Change in 2016 Politics and Lawsuits*, Keen News Serv. (Jan. 5, 2016), www.keennewsservice.com; Caitlin Patler, Erin Hamilton & Robin Savinar, *The Limits of Gaining Rights While Remaining Marginalized: The Deferred Action for Childhood Arrivals (DACA) Program and the Psychological Wellbeing of Latina/o Undocumented Youth*, Soc. Forces 1, 19–21 (2020).

32 Eduardo Bonilla-Silva, *The Linguistics of Color Blind Racism: How to Talk Nasty About Blacks Without Sounding "Racist,"* 28 Critical Socio. 41 (2002); Philip J. Mazzocco, The Psychology of Racial Colorblindness: A Critical Review 35–37, 149 (2017); Katrina Rebecca Bloch, Tiffany Taylor & Karen Martinez, *Playing the Race Card: White Injury, White Victimhood and the Paradox of Colour-Blind Ideology in Anti-Immigrant Discourse*, 43 Ethnic & Racial Stud. 1130, 1130–33, 1140 (2020).

33 Ashcroft v. Iqbal, 556 U.S. 662 (2009).

34 *Id.*

35 Bell Atl. Corp. v. Twombly, 550 U.S. 544 (2007).

36 *See generally* Judith Butler, *Gender Trouble: Feminism and the Subversion of Identity* (1990).

3

Civil Procedure in the Shadow of Violence

SHIRIN SINNAR

In *Violence and the Word*, legal scholar Robert Cover proclaimed that "[l]egal interpretation takes place in a field of pain and death."[1] Cover wrote that legal interpretation inflicts violence while justifying doing so. The threat of violence shapes even routine legal acts, such as criminal sentencing: "[M]ost prisoners walk into prison because they know they will be dragged or beaten into prison if they do not walk."[2]

Outside criminal law, however, the relationship between interpretation and violence is often obscure. In civil procedure, the focus on the *civil* invokes a system for peaceful dispute settlement—a *civilized* realm far from inflicting pain and death. The focus on *procedure* suggests attention to the mechanics of rights enforcement rather than the content of rights—masking the extent to which procedural rules can systematically disadvantage certain groups.

Yet civil procedure, too, regulates the boundaries of legitimate violence. First, procedural regimes respond to private violence. Courts justified the creation of housing summary eviction proceedings, for example, on the ground that they would dissuade landlords from forcibly expelling tenants and tenants from forcibly resisting those expulsions. Second, civil adjudication operates in the shadow of potential state violence. Evictions rely on the threat of force, now in the form of an armed sheriff arriving with a court order to vacate. Third, procedural regimes offer special protection for state violence. As interpreted by courts, federal procedural rules shield law enforcement officers from having to answer for many allegations of excessive force.

Civil procedure need not invariably protect the powerful or the state. For instance, the civil rights movement spurred the development of the modern class action, liberal intervention, and other procedural mechanisms to facilitate the private enforcement of new substantive rights. But any procedural reform project requires dispensing with the pretense that procedure offers a neutral set of rules. This chapter illuminates the relationship between procedure and violence with respect to two pressing social issues: the massive scale of evictions and the infliction of police violence on communities of color.

Eviction Summary Procedures

Far more people in the US receive an eviction notice than a federal court summons. Landlords filed 2.3 million evictions in 2016,[3] while plaintiffs filed only 292,076 new cases in federal court in a comparable period.[4] Thus, eight times as many people encountered civil procedure through a potential state court eviction than in any federal court proceeding. For Black women, sociologist Matthew Desmond observed, the eviction crisis has reached proportions paralleling that of mass incarceration for Black men: "Poor black men were locked up. Poor black women were locked out."[5] In addition to displacement, evictions caused lost jobs, interrupted schooling, exacerbated depression and trauma, and disrupted communities.[6] When the COVID-19 pandemic catalyzed massive unemployment, only temporary moratoria on evictions kept many families from losing their homes.[7]

Eviction procedure is far from textbook federal or state civil procedure. Every state maintains summary eviction procedures designed to oust tenants expeditiously when they fall behind on rent. In most states, a landlord seeking to reclaim a home serves the tenant a notice and, after the notice period expires, an eviction action.[8] If the tenant does not respond, as is common, the landlord may obtain a default judgment. If the tenant responds, a trial may take place. A winning landlord then obtains a writ of possession and files it with the sheriff, who conducts the eviction.

The speed of this process makes it virtually impossible for tenants to mount a viable defense. In California, a landlord may obtain an eviction judgment as soon as the sixth day after filing.[9] Even where legal aid is available, few tenants can find lawyers in the time provided. Courts hearing eviction cases are full of lawyers representing landlords, while tenants are unrepresented or absent.[10] In New York City Housing Court, judges spent an average of five to fifteen minutes on cases, while landlords' lawyers pressured unrepresented clients—mostly poor women of color—to accept settlements in the courthouse hallways.[11]

All this raises the question: Why do states maintain summary eviction procedures when the stakes for tenants are so high? The US Supreme Court's historical answer is that such procedures protected landlords and tenants from violence. In *Lindsey v. Normet*, the Court upheld the constitutionality of an Oregon statute that required the holding of a trial a mere six days after service of a complaint, unless the tenant paid security for the accruing rent, and barred tenants from raising the poor condition of the premises as a defense.[12] The Court acknowledged that the speed and limitation on defenses diverged from standard civil procedure, but upheld the procedures because they "obviate[d] resort to self-help and violence."[13] Under the common law, landlords could reclaim property either through a cumbersome civil action for ejectment or through "self-help," which had often led to "'violence and quarrels and bloodshed.'"[14] The Court asserted that the Oregon statute would "protect tenants as well as landlords" with a "speedy, judicially supervised proceeding."[15]

The summary eviction process established in Oregon was not unusual. All fifty states enacted laws to settle housing possession disputes speedily.[16] As in *Normet*, courts described the overriding goal of these expedited procedures as preventing violence. Over time, most states abolished self-help and required landlords to evict only through legal proceedings. In the 1970s, tenants in most jurisdictions won the right, at least in theory, to defend against eviction where the premises were in such poor condition as to be uninhabitable.[17]

Yet the expedited adjudication of eviction cases persists across jurisdictions, and few tenants can resist expulsion even when landlords have failed to provide them a safe place to live.[18] When enacted, summary eviction statutes may have protected some tenants, given that the prevailing legal regime and social customs authorized forcible expulsion. But the persistence of these procedures—and the justification in nineteenth-century notions of protection from violence—seems anomalous at a time when our intuitive response to the threat of violence is to restrain the perpetrators and protect the victims, rather than stack the legal deck in favor of one side.

In fact, the replacement of private self-help with public legal process benefits the targets of self-help only if the new procedures actually provide greater protections than the system they replace. Sometimes, legal procedures merely codify and legitimize deep social inequalities by harnessing state power to unleash the violence that private parties otherwise would have inflicted. For example, Michael Klarman describes how southern states responded to criticism over lynchings by adopting summary procedures to convict and execute Black defendants in rape cases.[19] The replacement of private mob violence with official state violence—with only a veneer of process—did not reduce its horror or injustice.

The evictions context shows that expediting state procedure in the name of forestalling private violence is not restricted to criminal law. Eviction procedures still operate in the shadow of violence, although it is now the state that is solely authorized to inflict it. As Desmond observes, a tenant knows she must vacate because, if she does not, "the landlord would summon the sheriff, who would arrive with a gun, a team of boot-footed movers, and a folded judge's order saying that the house was no longer hers."[20] And, in contrast to the past, when the threat of an eviction might lead crowds to amass in protest, sheriffs armed with a gun and eviction order rarely elicit public response. The background knowledge of the violence at the disposal of the state—legitimized by legal interpretation—leads most tenants to move on long before the sheriff arrives.

Civil procedural regimes are designed not just to achieve internal "process values" in dispute resolution—such as the accuracy, efficiency, or participatory nature of decision-making—but also to structure the rights and relative advantage of different groups, enforced by the threat of force.

Procedure Immunizing Police Violence

Civil procedure has played a special role in protecting state violence. In 2020, the fatal police killings of Breonna Taylor and George Floyd catalyzed the largest protests in US history.[21] These killings and others also inflicted trauma upon Black communities facing the repeated killings of unarmed men, women, and children and the legal system's failure to hold accountable those responsible. But numerous aspects of both "civil and criminal process translate police violence into justifiable force."[22]

Over decades, the Supreme Court has largely immunized police officers from civil liability. Its Fourth Amendment test accords significant deference to officer perceptions of the reasonableness of the use of force.[23] Moreover, the Court's qualified immunity jurisprudence exempts officers from liability for federal civil rights violations except where officers violate "clearly established" rights.[24] In practice, the Court's decisions protect officers from excessive force claims in all but the most egregious circumstances.[25]

The Court has further protected the police with procedural decisions. Several procedural interventions fortify qualified immunity. First, the Court has allowed judges to grant qualified immunity even where there are factual disputes that would ordinarily go to a jury. In *Scott v. Harris*,[26] the Court approved qualified immunity for a police officer who rammed the car of a fleeing motorist, rendering the plaintiff a quadriplegic. The Court acknowledged that, on a defendant's summary judgment motion, a court should ordinarily view the facts, and draw reasonable inferences, in a manner favorable to the plaintiff. Yet, because, in the Court's view, a police videotape appeared to show the plaintiff driving dangerously, the Court concluded that the plaintiff's version of the facts was "blatantly contradicted by the record."[27] The *Scott* decision has given lower courts greater latitude to immunize police officers rather than allow juries to decide whether an officer's use of force was reasonable.

Second, the Court has widened interlocutory jurisdiction over trial courts' denials of qualified immunity—giving law enforcement agents an unusual second or even third shot at convincing a court to preempt trial. Ordinarily, parties cannot appeal until there is a final judgment.[28] The Court created a partial exception for qualified immunity in *Mitchell v. Forsyth*.[29] But, even after *Mitchell*, the Court prohibited immediate appeals of qualified immunity denials when the parties disagreed over the sufficiency of the evidence.[30] That prohibition now appears to be changing. In *Scott* and a later case involving a fatal police shooting, the Court found that appellate jurisdiction existed despite contested factual disputes, creating an additional opportunity to immunize police.[31]

Third, as William Baude has shown, the Supreme Court has deviated from its traditional criteria for reviewing cases in order to rebuke lower courts for allowing suits against police to proceed. While the Court mostly hears cases presenting an important legal question or a circuit split, it takes an unusual number of qualified immunity cases only to discipline lower courts for a perceived misapplication of existing law.[32] As Justice Sotomayor has observed, the Court's interest in qualified immunity cases is asymmetric: it almost always grants certiorari to protect police officers, not the victims of police violence.[33] And it decides many such cases through rare summary reversals, without the filing of merits briefs or oral argument.[34]

In addition to shielding law enforcement officers through procedural rules strengthening qualified immunity, courts have interpreted the Federal Rules of Civil Procedure (FRCP) to shield police violence. In a pair of decisions, the Court jettisoned a fifty-year-old liberal pleading standard in favor of a new plausibility standard.[35] In *Ashcroft v. Iqbal*, the Court rejected a post-9/11 immigrant detainee's claims against government officials while asserting that requiring government officials to answer to civil rights litigation would divert them from their duties—the same specter invoked in qualified immunity cases.[36] The Court also instructed judges to assess the plausibility of claims using their "judicial experience and common sense"[37]—an invitation to dismiss cases, such as police misconduct suits, where judges' life experiences differ sharply from those of the litigants before them.

Structural reform litigation against police departments also suffers from the Court's reinterpretation of FRCP Rule 23, the federal class action rule. Class actions offer a means for civil rights plaintiffs to highlight the "extent of state-imposed harm on Black and Brown communities" and seek an injunction reforming police practices.[38] But *Wal-Mart Stores v. Dukes* required a greater showing of "commonality" across the claims of a plaintiff class, pushing courts toward an earlier merits determination more likely to end the legal challenge.[39]

Finally, courts interpret still more arcane rules within the FRCP to protect police violence. For example, appellate courts have largely held that, when a statute of limitations runs after the filing of a complaint, the plaintiff cannot add defendants whose names were unknown to them when they first filed—even if they specifically described the intended "John Doe" defendants in the original complaint. On that basis, appellate courts have ruled that a man could not sue the officers who broke his hand;[40] a pro se (self-representing) prisoner could not sue officers for excessive force;[41] and another man could not sue the officers who punched, tased, and chemical-sprayed him.[42]

Victims of police violence often do not know the names of the officers who beat or shot them, and police departments often refuse to release officers' names.[43] Thus, plaintiffs often name John Doe defendants in a complaint filed before the statute of limitations expires and then seek discovery to learn defendants' names.[44] Naming individual defendants is crucial because plaintiffs generally cannot recover directly against local government entities.[45]

Relying on the text of FRCP Rule 15,[46] most courts have ruled that an amendment that adds the defendants' real names doesn't "relate back" to the filing of the original, timely complaint, because the initial naming of John Doe defendants stemmed from a lack of knowledge rather than "mistake."[47] Some courts acknowledge that civil rights plaintiffs suffer acutely from this interpretation.[48] But the Civil Rules Advisory Committee has rejected any change to the rule. It expressed, in part, an unwillingness to further expose federal officials to lawsuits and questioned whether the problem facing plaintiffs in police cases was significant enough to justify the political difficulties of revising the rule.[49] Police violence presents one of the most profound social issues of our time, but developments in procedural law seriously restrict the potential for civil accountability.

Conclusion

As in other areas of law, the application of civil procedure "takes place in a field of pain and death."[50] Procedural regimes respond to and regulate private violence, rely on the threat of state violence for enforcement, and often immunize state violence. The recognition of procedure's relationship to violence makes abundantly clear that procedural choices protect or reform particular relationships of power rather than simply reconciling internal process values in a neutral fashion.

NOTES

1 Robert M. Cover, *Violence and the Word*, 95 Yale L.J. 1601, 1601 (1986).
2 *Id.* at 1607.
3 *National Estimates: Eviction in America*, Eviction Lab (May 11, 2018), https://evictionlab.org (nearly 40 percent resulted in eviction).
4 Admin. Office of the U.S. Courts, *Table C—U.S. District Courts–Civil Federal Judicial Caseload Statistics (March 31, 2017)*, www.uscourts.gov.
5 Matthew Desmond, Evicted: Poverty and Profit in the American City 98 (2016).
6 *Why Eviction Matters*, Eviction Lab, https://evictionlab.org.
7 Peter Hepburn & Renee Louis, *Preliminary Analysis: Eviction Filings During and After Local Eviction Moratoria*, Eviction Lab (Nov. 15, 2020), https://evictionlab.org.
8 Randy G. Gerchick, *No Easy Way Out: Making the Summary Eviction Process a Fairer and More Efficient Alternative to Landlord Self-Help*, 41 UCLA L. Rev. 759, 792 (1993).
9 Cal. Civ. Proc. Code §§ 1161(2), 1167, 1167.3 (West 2020).
10 Jessica K. Steinberg, *Demand Side Reform in the Poor People's Court*, 47 Conn. L. Rev. 741, 750 (2015).
11 Russell Engler, *Out of Sight and Out of Line: The Need for Regulation of Lawyers' Negotiations with Unrepresented Poor Persons*, 85 Calif. L. Rev. 79, 106–09 (1997).
12 Lindsey v. Normet, 405 U.S. 56 (1972).
13 *Id.* at 71.
14 *Id.* at 71 (quoting Entelman v. Hagood, 22 S.E. 545, 545 (Ga. 1895)).
15 *Id.* at 71–72.
16 Gerchick, *supra* note 8, at 777.
17 Paula A. Franzese, Abbott Gorin & David J. Guzik, *The Implied Warranty of Habitability Lives: Making Real the Promise of Landlord-Tenant Reform*, 69 Rutgers U.L. Rev. 1, 3 (2016) (showing that few tenants assert the defense of breach of an implied warranty of habitability despite its recognition in most states' laws).
18 Jessica K. Steinberg, *Informal, Inquisitorial, and Accurate: An Empirical Look at a Problem-Solving Housing Court*, 42 Law & Soc. Inquiry 1058, 1064–65 (2017).
19 Michael J. Klarman, *The Racial Origins of Modern Criminal Procedure*, 99 Mich. L. Rev. 48, 56–57 (2000).
20 Desmond, *supra* note 5, at 2.
21 Larry Buchanan, Quoctrung Bui & Jugal K. Patel, *Black Lives Matter Puts Another Stamp on History*, N.Y. Times, July 8, 2020, at A15.
22 Devon W. Carbado, *Blue-on-Black Violence: A Provisional Model of Some of the Causes*, 104 Geo. L.J. 1479, 1528 (2016).
23 *See, e.g.*, Graham v. Connor, 490 U.S. 386, 396 (1989).
24 Harlow v. Fitzgerald, 457 U.S. 800, 818 (1982).
25 William Baude, *Is Qualified Immunity Unlawful?* 106 Calif. L. Rev. 45, 82 (2018).
26 Scott v. Harris, 550 U.S. 372 (2007).
27 *Id.* at 380.

28 28 U.S.C. § 1291.
29 472 U.S. 511, 526 (1985).
30 Johnson v. Jones, 515 U.S. 304, 307 (1995).
31 Scott, 550 U.S. at 376; Plumhoff v. Rickard, 572 U.S. 765, 773 (2014).
32 Baude, *supra* note 25, at 85.
33 Kisela v. Hughes, 138 S. Ct. 1148, 1162 (2018) (Sotomayor, J., dissenting).
34 Baude, *supra* note 25, at 85.
35 Bell Atl. Corp. v. Twombly, 550 U.S. 544 (2007); Ashcroft v. Iqbal, 556 U.S. 662 (2009).
36 Iqbal, 556 U.S. at 685.
37 *Id.* at 679.
38 Sunita Patel, *Jumping Hurdles to Sue the Police*, 104 Minn. L. Rev. 2257, 2281 (2020).
39 Wal-Mart Stores v. Dukes, 564 U.S. 338 (2011).
40 Worthington v. Wilson, 8 F.3d 1253 (7th Cir. 1993).
41 Barrow v. Wethersfield Police Dep't, 66 F.3d 466 (2d Cir. 1995), modified, 74 F.3d 1366 (2d Cir. 1996).
42 Smith v. City of Akron, 476 Fed. Appx. 67 (6th Cir. 2012).
43 John Sullivan, Derek Hawkins, Kate McCormick, Ashley Balcerzak & Wesley Lowery, *In Fatal Shootings by Police, 1 in 5 Officers' Names Go Undisclosed*, Wash. Post (Apr. 1, 2016), www.washingtonpost.com.
44 *See, e.g.*, Smith, 476 Fed. Appx. at 67; Worthington, 8 F. 3d at 1253.
45 Howard M. Wasserman, *Civil Rights Plaintiffs and John Doe Defendants: A Study in § 1983 Procedure*, 25 Cardozo L. Rev. 793, 823–25 (2003).
46 Fed. R. Civ. P. 15(c)(1)(C)(i) and (ii).
47 Note, Meg Tomlinson, Krupski *and Relation Back for Claims Against John Doe Defendants*, 86 Fordham L. Rev. 2071, 2084–85, 2092 (2018).
48 Singletary v. Penn. Dep't of Corrections, 266 F.3d 186, 190–91, 201–02 n.5 (3d Cir. 2001).
49 Minutes of the Civil R. Adv. Comm., May 22–23, 2006, at lines 1130–1139, 1140–41. www.uscourts.gov.
50 Cover, *supra* note 1, at 1601.

4

Multiple Disadvantages

An Empirical Test of Intersectionality Theory in Equal Employment Opportunity Litigation

RACHEL KAHN BEST, LAUREN B. EDELMAN, LINDA HAMILTON KRIEGER, AND SCOTT R. ELIASON

In a 1989 law review article, Kimberlé Crenshaw introduced the idea that civil rights laws are ill equipped to address the types of inequality and discrimination faced by people who suffer multiple, or "intersect[ing]," axes of discrimination.[1] Her work has inspired decades of research on intersectionality in many fields, including Critical Race Theory, stratification, social psychology, and women's studies. Yet despite the richness of the theoretical scholarship on the legal disadvantages confronted by women of color, there has been little empirical research that addresses the effects of intersectionality on litigation outcomes.

This chapter addresses that lacuna by examining the effects of intersectional demographic characteristics and intersectional legal claims on plaintiffs' likelihood of success in discrimination lawsuits. Using a representative sample of judicial opinions over thirty-five years of federal employment discrimination litigation, we show that nonwhite women are less likely to win their cases than any other demographic group. Additionally, plaintiffs who make intersectional claims—alleging that they were discriminated against based on more than one ascriptive characteristic—are only half as likely to win their cases as are other plaintiffs. Our results suggest that antidiscrimination lawsuits provide the least protection for those who already suffer multiple social disadvantages, thus limiting the capacity of civil rights law to produce social change.

Methods

Our study draws upon a representative sample of judicial opinions in equal employment opportunity (EEO) cases, allowing us to provide generalizable findings on patterns in EEO decisions. We first retrieved all federal employment opinions decided by the US district and circuit (appellate) courts between 1965 and 1999 and available in the Westlaw database, which yielded a sampling frame of more than 50,000 opinions. We then selected a 2 percent random sample, yielding 328 circuit court opinions and 686 district court opinions. We coded each opinion for court (which circuit or which district), judges, plaintiff characteristics, defendant characteristics, statutory claims involved in the case, challenged actions, legal theories on which the claims were based, which party prevailed (and the extent to which they prevailed), and a variety of other variables. In our coding, we identified two types of intersectionality that might affect case outcome.

Demographic Intersectionality

Demographic intersectionality disadvantages occur when discrimination and/or stereotyping targets plaintiffs who occupy the intersection of two or more demographic categories. For these plaintiffs, overlapping axes of disadvantage may add up to more than the sum of their parts.

Indeed, recent empirical research on hiring and discrimination provides evidence that employers hold discrete stereotypes for various intersectional categories. Employers may stereotype inner-city blacks (but not necessarily other blacks or white inner-city residents) as lazy and dangerous. Employers also hold different stereotypes about black men and black women. They sometimes stereotype black women negatively as desperate single mothers or positively as responsible "matriarchs."[2] Black men, by contrast, are stereotyped as "unmanageable workers [who are] more likely to resist authority."[3]

Judges, juries, and lawyers are subject to the same institutionalized stereotypes as are employers. If they introduce these stereotypes into legal decision-making, the types of stereotypes discussed in the literature on labor-market discrimination may also affect court outcomes, with courts replicating the discriminatory practices that operate in the labor market.

Claim Intersectionality

Claim intersectionality is present when plaintiffs allege discrimination on the basis of two or more ascriptive characteristics. Critical race theorists have argued that since antidiscrimination law organizes demographic traits into formal, one-dimensional categories—race, sex, national origin, and so forth—legal doctrine often fails to capture the types of discrimination suffered by intersectional subjects. So, for example, sex discrimination is conceptualized in antidiscrimination case law as a problem affecting all women equally and in the same ways (with white women as the prototypical case), while race discrimination is understood as affecting all blacks (prototypically male) in the same ways. Intersectionality theorists argue that this one-dimensional, categorical approach to understanding discrimination prevents civil rights law from adequately protecting members of groups that experience more than one axis of prejudice.

For example, an employer might be willing to hire black men and white women as retail salespeople but unwilling to hire black women because he thinks that customers will stereotype them in disparaging ways that will harm his business. Or, as another example, an employer might fire a black female employee because the employer is discomfited by her Afrocentric feminine attire or hairstyle. Their employees might make what we call "intersectional" claims: allegations that they were discriminated against due to more than one ascriptive characteristic. But since these types of discrimination would not affect minority men or white women, under some interpretations of EEO law the employer could parry a claim of race discrimination by pointing to the hiring of men belonging to the plaintiff's racial group and deflect a claim of sex discrimination by pointing to his hiring of white women.

Thus, plaintiffs who make intersectional discrimination claims may be less likely to win their cases not only because they are members of particularly derogated subgroups but also because, given the categorical nature of discrimination law, intersectional claims are particularly hard to establish. While demographic intersectionality can produce unequal outcomes in all arenas of social life, claim intersectionality is a mechanism of disadvantage that is particular to civil rights litigation.

While there is an extensive research literature exploring intersectional experiences and identities, researchers have rarely sought to document the effects of intersectionality on inequality. Attributing this neglect to methodological preferences, McCall argues that suspicion of statistics has "restrict[ed] the scope of knowledge that can be produced on intersectionality."[4] This neglect is so extreme that the hypothesis that Crenshaw introduces in her foundational article on intersectionality—that intersectional plaintiffs fare worse in discrimination lawsuits—has not been systematically tested. Our study is designed to test this hypothesis.

Results

Both "demographic intersectionality" and "claim intersectionality" disadvantage plaintiffs (see table 4.1). Bivariate relationships between both claim and demographic intersectionality and case outcomes yield strong support for intersectionality theory. First, plaintiffs making intersectional claims are less than half as likely to win their cases as are other plaintiffs (15 percent compared to 31 percent). Second, race and sex disadvantages do not operate independently. White male plaintiffs were more likely to lose their cases than white women were (61 percent as compared to 55 percent). This female advantage, however, does not apply to black women, who are slightly more likely than black men to lose their cases (71 percent as compared to 69 percent).

The bivariate relationships between both types of intersectionality and employee victory provide suggestive evidence of an intersectionality penalty. Next, we conducted generalized ordered logistic regressions to control for other features of cases that might account for the relationships (see table 4.2). In each model we present, the first column of coefficients denotes each variable's effects on the odds that the plaintiff will achieve at least a partial victory (a mixed outcome or a complete victory), and the second column of coefficients focuses on the odds of a complete victory.

Model 1 (table 4.2) shows the effects of claim intersectionality on the likelihood of employee victory. Even when controlling for multiple aspects of the case, compared to plaintiffs who allege a single basis of discrimination, plaintiffs making intersectional claims have only about half the odds of attaining at least a partial victory and approximately one-third the odds of a complete victory. All else equal, we predict that plaintiffs alleging only one basis of discrimination will win their cases 28 percent of

TABLE 4.1. Case outcome by claim and demographic intersectionality

	Victor		
	Employer	Mixed	Employee
Claim intersectionality			
Intersectional bases of discrimination (N = 178)	69%	16%	15%
Nonintersectional bases of discrimination (N = 836)	56%	14%	30%
Demographic intersectionality			
White male plaintiff (N = 36)	61%	3%	36%
White female plaintiff (N = 20)	55%	10%	35%
Nonwhite male plaintiff (N = 196)	69%	14%	17%
Nonwhite female plaintiff (N = 109)	71%	17%	13%
Plaintiff's race or sex is missing (N = 653)	53%	15%	32%

the time, whereas plaintiffs bringing otherwise identical cases that allege intersectional bases of discrimination will win only 13 percent of the time. This finding provides strong evidence for the hypothesis that EEO law disadvantages plaintiffs who allege intersectional discrimination.

One interpretation of this finding might be that cases alleging multiple types of discrimination were intrinsically weaker, with desperate plaintiffs adding bases of discrimination and hoping that one would be successful. At least one federal judge adopts this view, suggesting that plaintiffs who allege multiple bases of discrimination are "throwing spaghetti at the wall to see what sticks."[5]

We test for this possibility in three ways. First, we control for multiple challenged actions because desperate plaintiffs might be just as likely to challenge multiple employer actions (e.g., compensation and promotion) as to allege multiple bases of discrimination. We do find a significant negative effect of the number of challenged actions on complete plaintiff victory, but the effect's magnitude is much smaller than is the claim intersectionality effect. Second, if desperate plaintiffs were likely to add both challenged actions *and* bases of discrimination to their cases, then controlling for the number of challenged actions would decrease the size of the coefficient for intersectional claims. In fact, including the number of challenged actions in the model has no such effect. Third, if

TABLE 4.2. Generalized ordered logistic regressions of employee victory on demographic and claim intersectionality

	Model 1		Model 2		Model 3		Model 4	
	Claim intersectionality		Traditional demographics		Demographic intersectionality		Claim and demographic intersectionality	
Independent Variables	At least partial victory	Complete victory	At least partial victory	Complete victory	At least partial victory	Complete victory	At least partial victory	Complete victory
Claims								
Intersectional claim	−0.63** (0.20)	−1.00*** (0.24)					−0.51* (0.21)	−0.90*** (0.25)
Multiple non-intersectional claims	0.0062 (0.17)	−0.33^{t} (0.19)					0.070 (0.17)	−0.22 (0.19)
Single claim (omitted)								
Demographics								
Nonwhite plaintiff			−0.37 (0.30)	−1.17*** (0.31)	−0.14 (0.31)	−0.94** (0.33)	−0.17 (0.32)	−0.91** (0.33)
Missing race			0.019 (0.28)	−0.55^{t} (0.29)	−0.019 (0.28)	−0.59* (0.29)	−0.090 (0.29)	−0.67* (0.30)
White (omitted)								
Female plaintiff			0.28^{t} (0.14)	0.13 (0.16)	0.48** (0.17)	0.33^{t} (0.18)	0.47** (0.17)	0.38* (0.18)
Missing sex			1.25*** (0.25)	1.11*** (0.24)	1.24*** (0.24)	1.10*** (0.24)	1.26*** (0.25)	1.12*** (0.24)
Male (omitted)								
Nonwhite female plaintiff					−0.68* (0.30)	−0.73* (0.36)	−0.55^{t} (0.31)	−0.64^{t} (0.37)

Standard errors in parentheses.
All models control for the number of challenged actions, circuit vs. district court, legal publication, length in pages, and post-1986.
***$p < 0.001$, **$p < 0.01$, *$p < 0.05$, $^{t}p < 0.1$.

alleging multiple bases of discrimination were an indicator of intrinsically weak cases, it should not matter whether or not the additional alleged bases of discrimination are based on ascriptive characteristics.

Our results show that whether or not the bases of discrimination are ascriptive matters: we find a large significant negative effect for intersectional claims (those alleging discrimination based on multiple ascriptive characteristics) but only a small, marginally significant effect for cases alleging multiple nonintersectional bases of discrimination (i.e., cases in which only one or none of the alleged bases of discrimination is an ascriptive characteristic). These findings suggest that intersectional claims are not the result of plaintiffs' frivolously adding additional claims.

Model 2 (table 4.2) shows the effects of plaintiffs' demographics on the likelihood of employee victory without considering demographic intersectionality. Besides the control variables, Model 2 includes only the main effects for race and sex, which are measured by dummy variables for nonwhite plaintiffs and plaintiffs with missing race data (white plaintiffs are the omitted category) and variables for female plaintiffs and plaintiffs with missing sex data (male plaintiffs are the omitted category). Model 2 shows that, all else equal, nonwhite plaintiffs have less than one-third of white plaintiffs' odds of achieving complete victories. Female plaintiffs are slightly more likely than male plaintiffs to achieve at least partial victories, but this coefficient is significant only at the .1 level. If we stopped at Model 2 (thus ignoring demographic intersectionality), as do previous studies, we would likely conclude that there are no important differences between men's and women's outcomes in EEO litigation.

Model 3 (table 4.2) improves on Model 2 (and on previous research) because it accounts for demographic intersectionality by including a variable set to one if the plaintiff is a nonwhite woman. The interaction effect has a negative and statistically significant effect on plaintiffs' odds of at least partial victory and on plaintiffs' odds of complete victory. When we include it in the model, the main effect for sex becomes a significant predictor of at least partial plaintiff victory.

Based on Model 3, and holding all control variables constant at their means or modes, white women have the highest predicted probability of a full victory (38 percent), followed by white men (31 percent), nonwhite men (15 percent), and nonwhite women (11 percent). This intersectional relationship between race and sex can be understood in two ways. First, there are larger race effects for women than for men: nonwhite women fall further behind white women than nonwhite men fall behind white men. Second, there are different gender effects for whites and nonwhites: white women get ahead of white men, while nonwhite women fare similarly to nonwhite men. Our findings, then, suggest that studies that fail to account for demographic intersectionality miss the fact that sex and race disadvantages do not operate independently in the courts.

Whereas Models 1 and 3 in table 4.2 consider demographic and claim intersectionality separately, Model 4 includes both, thus allowing us to test whether either intersectionality effect is an artifact of omitted variable bias. Given that plaintiffs making intersectional claims are disproportionately likely to be nonwhite women, the effect of claim intersectionality observed in Model 1 might actually reflect nonwhite women's disadvantage. Alternatively, the negative coefficient for nonwhite women in Model 3 might be explained by the fact that nonwhite women are disproportionately likely to make intersectional claims. Model 5 shows, however, that each type of intersectionality has an independent effect on plaintiffs' likelihood of winning. The claim intersectionality coefficient remains statistically significant and decreases only slightly. Regarding demographic intersectionality, the interaction effect between plaintiffs' race and sex is significant only at the $p < 0.1$ level in Model 5, but its magnitude is virtually unchanged. The fact that the coefficients for both measures of intersectionality remain large and at least marginally statistically significant when included in the same model suggests that demographic and claim intersectionality represent two distinct pathways of disadvantage for plaintiffs. Demographic and claim intersectionality are each associated with dramatically reduced odds of plaintiff victory.

Discussion

Our analysis provides the first systematic empirical test of intersectionality theory by examining the effects of demographic intersectionality and claim intersectionality on plaintiff win rates in employment discrimination cases. We find strong support for the ideas that race and sex disadvantages do not operate independently in the courts (*demographic intersectionality*) and that antidiscrimination law provides less protection in cases that involve intersecting bases of discrimination (*claim intersectionality*).

Our results suggest, moreover, that these two types of intersectionality represent two distinct processes of disadvantage. Although nonwhite women are more likely to bring intersectional claims, this does not explain all of the disadvantage they face in court. Likewise, claim intersectionality harms plaintiffs' chances of winning, regardless of their demographic characteristics. EEO law itself seems to disadvantage intersectional plaintiffs, above and beyond any discrimination they may face in the courtroom on the basis of their race or sex.

Our findings have important implications for several theoretical debates in the intersectionality literature. One point of disagreement among scholars is whether intersectionality applies only to members of traditionally disadvantaged groups or whether all identities are intersectional. Some researchers subscribe to a "multiple jeopardy" approach that assumes that women of color are more disadvantaged than other groups in all contexts.[6] However, other critiques of the intersectionality literature from within argue that, when limited to the case of black women, intersectionality is insufficiently developed as a general theory and view intersectionality as a broader theory that can apply "to any grouping of people, advantaged as well as disadvantaged."[7] A related debate focuses on whether intersectional disadvantages are "ubiquitous or contingent."[8] Some scholars argue that intersectionality affects outcomes and experiences in every social setting, while others suggest that its effects are contingent, with single categories sometimes dominating.[9]

Our findings demonstrate that intersectionality is context-dependent. Whereas intersectionality theory generally presumes that white men tend to fare the best and nonwhite women are the most disadvantaged, our findings suggest a somewhat different pattern. In our sample, white female plaintiffs had the highest chances of winning their cases, a pattern that is likely specific to the context of EEO litigation.

Our findings regarding demographic intersectionality demonstrate that intersecting demographic characteristics shape outcomes in the courts as well as in the labor market. Moreover, our findings regarding claim intersectionality establish that EEO law provides little protection for plaintiffs facing intersectional discrimination in the labor market.

Plaintiffs who suffer multiple disadvantages in society fare worse than do singly disadvantaged plaintiffs when they seek to assert their civil rights in court. This disadvantage operates through demographic intersectionality, where the intersection of race and sex puts black women at a disadvantage, and through claim intersectionality, where those who assert two or more types of discrimination fare worse than do those whose cases are simpler. By assuming that disadvantages based on race, sex, and other ascriptive characteristics operate independently, civil rights law perpetuates intersectional disadvantages.

NOTES

Acknowledgment: This chapter is updated and adapted from the article Rachel Kahn Best, Lauren B. Edelman, Linda Hamilton Krieger, and Scott R. Eliason, *Multiple Disadvantages: An Empirical Test of Intersectionality Theory in EEO Litigation*, 45 Law & Soc'y Rev. 991 (2011).

1 Kimberlé Crenshaw, *Demarginalizing the Intersection of Race and Sex: A Black Feminist Critique of Antidiscrimination Doctrine, Feminist Theory and Antiracist Politics*, 1989 U. Chi. Legal F. 139, 140.

2 Johanna Shih, *". . . Yeah, I Could Hire This One, but I Know It's Gonna Be a Problem": How Race, Nativity and Gender Affect Employers' Perceptions of the Manageability of Job Seekers*, 25 Ethnic & Racial Stud. 99, 111 (2002).

3 *Id.* at 102.

4 Leslie McCall, *The Complexity of Intersectionality*, 30 Signs 1771, 1772 (2005).

5 Minna J. Kotkin, *Diversity and Discrimination: A Look at Complex Bias*, 50 Wm. & Mary L. Rev. 1439, 1442 (2009) (quoting District Judge Ruben Castillo).

6 *E.g.*, Deborah K. King, *Multiple Jeopardy, Multiple Consciousness: The Context of a Black Feminist Ideology*, 14 Signs 42, 47 (1988).

7 Nira Yuval-Davis, *Intersectionality and Feminist Politics*, 13 Eur. J. Women's Stud. 193, (2006).

8 Irene Browne & Joya Misra, *The Intersection of Gender and Race in the Labor Market*, 29 Annual Rev. Sociology 487, 492 (2003).

9 *Id.* at 492–93.

5

Orientalizing Procedure

Insiders and Outsiders in the Doctrine of Arbitration

DANYA SHOCAIR REDA

When courts in the US decide cases, particularly those involving international elements, they are simultaneously constructing an "Other" jurisdiction. This jurisdiction is a repository for the features of law and courts that US courts reject. Thus, in creating this Other, the US courts construct themselves. Conceptions of the foreign have been pivotal to helping craft a vision, and a doctrine, of our courts—who they serve and how. In procedural doctrine, the foreign has played a foil, helping to draw and redraw the procedural lines and to remake procedural values. In this chapter, I draw on Edward Said's concept of Orientalism[1] to capture this process of self-understanding and self-justification through one's definition against an imagined Other.

In the opening paragraphs of Said's *Orientalism*, we are presented with words of British politician Lord Balfour, defending Britain's continued colonization of Egypt.[2] In the face of a growing nationalist movement and calls for self-determination, Balfour explains that it is right and good—necessary, even—for Britain to rule the Egyptians through "absolute government," because the history of Egypt shows us that they have never had self-government and, by implication, are not capable of it. In contrast, Balfour says, Western nations "as soon as they emerge into history show the beginnings of those capacities for self-government."[3] It is this special quality of the West—its inhabitants' supposed inherent capacity for self-government—that justifies the West's domination of Egypt (and, presumably, all colonies). Balfour does not seem to notice the paradox: That the very quality that defines Europe—self-government—should be the basis for a relationship built entirely upon the negation of Egyptian self-government; that Britain should govern Egypt undemocratically and autocratically *because it has the special capacity of democratic self-government.*

This kind of contradiction is at the heart of the concept of Orientalism that Said described in his landmark study. Through their descriptions of the Orient and the Other, European scholars, writers, government officials, and colonial courts simultaneously defined Europe. Yet time and again, the characteristics that Europeans believed defined the Other were apt descriptions of Europe's own conduct in its colonies and, indeed, at times, of Europe's citizens. What drew Said's attention to these discourses is that they cannot be understood merely as rationalizations for European control, as they were when wielded by Balfour in 1910. In fact, what seemed so peculiar to Said, and suggested the *power* of Orientalism, is that the discourse developed *prior to* the advent of colonial control. Instead of post hoc rationalizations of imperial control, Orientalism serves an expansive terrain for conceptualizing the Other and, concomitantly, the self. Thus, ideas about the Orient have not always been pejorative, but they frequently include romanticized conceptions of an alternative geography and culture.

Teemu Ruskola builds on Said's work to develop the concept of "legal Orientalism"—"the ways in which 'the Orient,' as well as the Euro-American 'West,' have been produced through discourses of law."[4] As Ruskola describes it, legal Orientalism is a discourse that produces a conception of rule of law through a description of the legal Other that lacks law.[5] The legal Orientalism discourse is "a set of usually unarticulated cultural assumptions about that which is not law, and about those who do not have it."[6] "[I]deas of Chinese lawlessness" are central to constructing the United States' own self-regard as The Lawful, as a paragon of the "rule of law."[7] Drawing on Ruskola's concept, I focus in this chapter on the US Supreme Court's conception of the foreign as legal Other, through which the Court defines the parameters of US courts and procedure, as well as the procedural values that the courts will seek to vindicate.

The Orientalizing of procedure in the United States is a tale of outsiders and of foreignness and how those tales help to construct, and reconstruct, the United States' conceptions of its own law. Law's Other helps to construct law's self.[8] The realm of law is governed by universality, certainty, order, predictability, and democratic accountability, in contrast to the nonlegal Other characterized by particularity, uncertainty, disorder, unpredictability, and Oriental despotism.[9] The presence of the Other in US litigation has significant consequences for how the Supreme Court understands the appropriateness of the use of US courts and who ought to be in them.

More specifically, in this chapter, I focus on one dimension of the phenomenon of legal Orientalism: the ways that ideas of the lawlessness of Others "had important consequences also for the development of *domestic* U.S. law in several areas."[10] I suggest that the Orientalizing of US law is ongoing and continues to remake what we call US "domestic" law. I extend this application to US procedural law and, specifically, to the jurisprudence of arbitration (although similar analyses might be made in the fields of general jurisdiction, specific jurisdiction, and summary judgment, among others).

Since the early 1970s, the US Supreme Court has reinterpreted the existing statute governing arbitration, the Federal Arbitration Act[11] (FAA), to gradually expand arbitration.[12] Today, this expansion has reached something of a crisis point. Scholars and commentators widely proclaim, with good reason, that large swaths of US law are being siphoned off into arbitration[13]—barred entirely from entering a court—or, even worse, placed beyond the bounds of enforcement, as many cases that would have been brought to court are prevented from entering the courthouse, yet cannot be arbitrated due to arbitration's procedural constraints.[14] That is, arbitration, something of a nonlegal forum, has been expanded by the highest US court to swallow up the traditional legal forum of the courts, to displace legal for nonlegal in numerous types of cases and for numerous types of litigants.

This designation of some cases and litigants as not requiring a legal forum but rather being better suited to a nonlegal forum begins with the presence of Others, but then it migrates into the core of the law, applying to Others and US residents (which we might call "proper" legal subjects), alike. That is, the conception of the Other—the Foreign—enables jurists to construct a US nonlegal regime of arbitration doctrine that converts large sections of legal regulation into a nonlaw, nonlegal area.

Viewing foreign-related cases as somehow bracketed or "Other," or not implicating the same concerns as the cases that procedure is concerned with in the domestic context, ends up Orientalizing US procedural rights. That is, it transforms US procedural rights into the very unrelated Orient that modern procedure is constructed in opposition to, with all of its associated attributes regarding lawlessness, lack of accountability, and an undemocratic or autocratic character. Thus, this tale is one of the remaking of the FAA into a federally imposed requirement of a nonlegal forum, often imposed without functional consent on unsuspecting litigants, and even in litigation contexts when those claims will not be able to be brought in arbitration at all.

The first step in that legal transformation is the 1974 Supreme Court opinion in *Scherk v. Alberto-Culver Co.*,[15] determining that the FAA requires enforcement of an arbitration clause even if the lawsuit concerns the validity of the contract itself. Previously, it was understood that, if a lawsuit challenged the validity of the contract itself, the arbitration clause that was part of that contract would not be enforceable. That is, if it is unclear that the contract is valid, one cannot use an arbitration provision in the contract to force the question of validity into arbitration. The *Sherck* reasoning expanded the reach of the FAA considerably, a significant early development in the Supreme Court's evolving and expansive arbitration jurisprudence. At the time, the significance of the decision was uncertain. Indeed, the Supreme Court's reasoning turned a considerable degree on the fact that the case concerned an international contract. The *Sherck* Court distinguished precedent by claiming that any attempt to rely on the prior case law "ignores the significant and, we find, crucial differences between the agreement involved in [the precedent] and the one signed by the parties here. [The contract here] was a truly international agreement."[16] It was this "truly international" quality of the agreement that led to the reasonableness of banishing the case to the nonlegal forum.[17] What made it international? One party was a US resident and the other party was German. Negotiations took place in several countries; the signing and closing were overseas. The subject matter of the contract was itself the sale of business enterprises organized under foreign laws.[18] For the Court, the foreign-related character of the dispute suggested a different balance of procedural values and protections.[19] In this "international" contract case, there was the prospect of an international choice-of-laws question that was absent in an ordinary contract case.[20] Accordingly, in the international case there would be considerable uncertainty about which law applies.[21] But, nonetheless, by banishing the case to the nonlegal forum, the Court avoided having to worry about whether the legal application of a choice-of-law rule adheres to the legal standard.

The Court was clear that the problem that justified the utility of enforcing arbitration clauses in international contracts would exist "almost inevitably . . . with respect to any contract touching two or more countries, each with its own substantive laws and conflict-of-laws rules."[22] The Court seemed to think that the abyss of uncertainty into which international agreements are thrust must be illuminated and plugged and, further, that privately negotiated choice of law and forum provisions are the only way to do so. Privately negotiated choice-of-law and forum provisions are, in the words of the Court, "an almost indispensable precondition to achievement of orderliness and predictability essential to any international business transaction."[23]

So, according to the Court, out of the chaos of the international, the nonlaw forum forges the orderliness and predictability—the "lawfulness," if you will. Moreover, the threat of a forum "hostile to the interests of one of the parties"[24] or ignorant, not versed in one of the areas of law addressed, is also held at bay by forcing the parties into the nonlegal forum. The nonlegal forum saves the litigants from the threat of nonlegal ignorance and hostility and restores the legal prospect of unbiased expertise. If the threat of placing the international contract into a legal forum of the courts were allowed to stand, the very existence of international commerce would be threatened. The legal operation of international commerce requires the cabining of dispute into a nonlegal private forum.

In addition, while in earlier jurisprudence courts sought to protect a US litigant's choice of forum and ability to plead to the US court of its choice, the *Scherk* Court determined that this benefit/right doesn't really exist for the US litigant in international litigation. Because the other party can simply rush to the door of a foreign court and block the litigants from the US court and because it is possible a foreign law might be invoked, there remains no reason to seek to protect a US forum as well.[25] Rather than allow the development of a "legal no-man's-land" through the prospect of competing claims to jurisdiction between US courts and an Other jurisdiction, *Scherck* determined that it is better to simply place the jurisdiction in a predetermined nonlegal land (of arbitration).

Oddly, this case appeals in particular to a cosmopolitan conception of US engagement with the world and denounces any effort to maintain a legal court forum for international disputes as a "'parochial concept that all disputes must be resolved under our laws and in our courts. . . . We cannot have trade and commerce in world markets and international waters exclusively on our terms, governed by our laws, and resolved in our courts.'"[26] As I have recounted, the bulk of the reasoning centered on international-ness, Otherness, and some sense that, to maintain engagement with international trade requires a relinquishing of the public, legal court forum. Yet the holding and its balance of protections migrated across the border from foreign to wholly domestic alike.

The *Scherck* opinion is but one example of Orientalizing procedure. Viewing foreign-related cases as somehow bracketed or "Other"—not really implicating the same concerns as the cases with which procedure is concerned in the domestic context—has ended up Orientalizing US procedural rights. That is, it transforms US procedural rights into the very unrelated Orient that modern procedure is constructed in opposition to, with all of its associated attributes regarding lawlessness, lack of accountability, and undemocratic or autocratic character.

The Orientalizing of procedure is a phenomenon worth recognizing in itself, but it also serves as a cautionary tale suggesting that the domestic/international divide is one that must be more intently theorized by procedural scholarship. To what extent should foreignness determine a case's procedural fate—in what contexts and for what reasons? These are questions that demand attention so that procedure is not unwittingly Orientalized. Moreover, scholarly attention to Orientalizing effects on procedure promises to be valuable as it can provide structure to consider vital questions about procedural values and the function of courts.

NOTES

1 Edward W. Said, Orientalism (1978).

2 *Id.* at 31. Balfour had previously been prime minister of Britain and heavily involved in affairs throughout the British Empire.

3 Great Britain, Parliamentary Debates (Commons), 5th ser., 17, 1140–46 (1910) *quoted in* Said, *supra* note 1, at 32.

4 Teemu Ruskola, Legal Orientalism: China, The United States, and Modern Law 5 (2013).

5 *Id.* at 4.

6 *Id.* at 10.
7 *Id.* at 141.
8 "There is no discourse of rule-of-law that is not at the same time a discourse of legal Orientalism . . . there is no world of legal modernity without an unlegal, despotic Orient to summon it into existence." *Id.* at 10.
9 *Id.* at 8–16.
10 *Id.* at 141.
11 United States Arbitration Act, ch. 213, 43 Stat. 883 (1925) (current version at 9 U.S.C. §§ 1–16 (2018)).
12 *See, e.g.*, Adam M. Samaha, *On Law's Tiebreakers*, 77 U. Chi. L. Rev. 1661, 1719, 1720 n.166 (2010); Aaron-Andrew P. Bruhl, *The Unconscionability Game: Strategic Judging and the Evolution of Federal Arbitration Law*, 83 N.Y.U. L. Rev. 1420, 1424 (2008); Jean R. Sternlight, *Creeping Mandatory Arbitration: Is It Just?*, 57 Stan. L. Rev. 1631, 1638 (2005); Mastrobuono v. Shearson Lehman Hutton, Inc., 514 U.S. 52, 57 (1995).
13 *E.g.* Myriam Gilles, *The Day Doctrine Died: Private Arbitration and the End of Law*, 2016 U. Ill. L. Rev. 371 (2016); Myriam Gilles, *The Demise of Deterrence: Mandatory Arbitration and the "Litigation Reform" Movement, in* Forced Arbitration and the Fate of the 7th Amendment: The Core of America's Legal System at Stake? 7 (Pound Civil Justice Institute, 2014).
14 *See, e.g.*, Judith Resnik, *Diffusing Disputes: The Public in the Private of Arbitration, the Private in Courts, and the Erasure of Rights*, 124 Yale L.J. 2804, 2809 (2015); Jessica Silver-Greenberg & Robert Gebeloff, *Arbitration Everywhere, Stacking the Deck of Justice*, N.Y. Times: Dealbook (Oct. 31, 2015) (first of three-part series on such arbitration clauses), www.nytimes.com.
15 417 U.S. 506 (1974).
16 *Id.* at 515.
17 *Id.*
18 *Id.*
19 It should be made clear that there *were* reasons to think procedural values and protections were in issue. The defendant in the case, who was attempting enforcement of the arbitration provision, appeared to have engaged in unethical if not fraudulent conduct, the plaintiff and US party appeared to have suffered inequities, and the selected arbitral forum might require interpretation and application of US securities laws by foreign nonlawyers.
20 *Id.* at 516.
21 *Id.*
22 *Id.*
23 *Id.*
24 *Id.*
25 *Id.* at 517.
26 *Id.* at 519 (citing The Bremen v. Zapata Off-Shore Co., 407 U.S. 1 (1972)).

6

Prisoner Procedure

KATHERINE MACFARLANE

Prisoner litigation matters. Civil prisoner litigation is a vital tool for remedying the worst excesses of a racist carceral state. Prisoner suits have resulted in the release of inmates from overcrowded California prisons, where uncared-for inmates regularly died;[1] they have successfully challenged the denial of medical care to transgender inmates;[2] and they have also set constitutional standards of decency on death row in Louisiana's Angola prison.[3] Writs of habeas corpus, though rarely granted, can save the lives of inmates unconstitutionally sentenced to death and can set other inmates free. As recently as 2018, prisoner litigation represented nearly 20 percent of the federal docket.[4]

Yet, despite its central importance to civil rights, most prisoner civil litigation is pro se *(i.e., by an individual not represented by a lawyer).*[5] For the last thirty years, pro se prisoner litigants have been forced to run the gauntlet of prisoner procedure—a body of civil procedure that applies only, and onerously, to prisoners. Prisoner procedure is based on a presumption—either tacit or explicit—that prisoners file frivolous claims. In an oft-cited statement in *Jones v. Bock*,[6] Chief Justice Roberts proclaimed that prisoner cases "'account for an outsized share of filings' in federal district courts," and most "have no merit."[7] In fact, the volume of prisoner litigation has increased only in proportion to the massive growth of prison populations.[8] But in the world of prisoner procedure, the goal is to keep these cases out of federal court.

Federal procedure generally is trans-substantive: it does not vary based on the kind of claim being brought or the identity of the party bringing the claim. Yet the differential treatment of prisoners and their cases is embedded in federal statutes, the Federal Rules of Civil Procedure, and federal district courts' local rules and customs.

Unrepresented, isolated, and vulnerable prisoner litigants are forced to contend with rules that target their claims, giving procedural advantages to the entities and individuals they sue.

Prisoner Pleading Rules

Judicial intervention at the pleadings stage is the norm in prisoner litigation, upending the common law litigation model, which is adversarial.[9] Typically, plaintiffs file complaints and defendants respond by answering or moving to dismiss. Defendants must identify and raise their own defenses. Most defenses are waived when they are not raised at the pleadings stage.

In prisoner civil rights cases, by contrast, district courts review prisoners' complaints before service of process occurs.[10] The Prison Litigation Reform Act—designed to filter prisoner suits out of the federal judicial system—requires a district court to "identify cognizable claims or dismiss the complaint, or any portion of the complaint, if the complaint—(1) is frivolous, malicious, or fails to state a claim upon which relief may be granted; or (2) seeks monetary relief from a defendant who is immune from such relief."[11] Unlike defendants in all other federal civil cases, defendants in prisoner litigation need only respond to a complaint when ordered to do so by the court.[12]

Rule 4 of the Rules Governing Section 2254 Cases provides for similar screening of habeas petitions.[13] Even when habeas respondents waive affirmative defenses such as the statute of limitations, courts may raise defenses sua sponte, well past the pleadings stage.

Prisoner Discovery Rules

Prisoner procedure also departs from the otherwise trans-substantive Federal Rules with respect to the issuance of a summons, special masters, default judgments, and discovery.[14] Here again, the presumption is that prisoner cases are nuisance suits. For example, Rule 26(a)'s initial disclosure requirement, added in 1993, was intended to speed up the exchange of basic yet valuable information,[15] including the name of "each individual likely to have discoverable information—along with the subjects of that information—that the disclosing party may use to support its claims or defenses." Initial disclosures help "under-equipped litigants" more than others.[16]

However, Rule 26(a) exempts prisoner cases—including habeas petitions and pro se civil suits—from the initial disclosure requirement.[17] In 2000, the Rules Advisory Committee explained that the exemptions apply to cases "in which there is likely to be little or no discovery, or in which initial disclosure appears unlikely to contribute to the effective development of the case."[18]

The opposite is true in prisoner cases, where defendants have access to the very information that, if shared with a prisoner plaintiff through initial disclosures, could make the plaintiff's case. Most prisoners proceed pro se and may struggle to propound discovery without receiving initial disclosures to guide them. In fact, they may be unable to propound any discovery at all. Coupled with the difficulties associated with accessing a prison law library and other logistical obstacles related to incarceration, prisoner plaintiffs who do not receive initial disclosures stand to lose more than the average plaintiff.

Take, for example, a prisoner civil rights action alleging that prison guards failed to protect a transgender inmate from assault and that the prison subsequently refused to provide adequate medical care to the inmate. Both claims would require extensive discovery. Initial disclosures should include the prison's policies regarding transgender inmates and identify the guards on duty—both vital forms of information for seeking depositions and making claims.

In fact, prisoners—unlike other plaintiffs—are at the mercy of the prisons in which they are incarcerated with respect to gaining access to their own medical records. Unlike other defendants, wardens and prison employees both create and store documents relevant to prisoners' civil rights claims. Initial disclosures are crucial in litigation with such a power imbalance.

Habeas rules impose additional discovery barriers. In federal habeas litigation involving prisoners in state custody, petitioners must obtain leave of court to propound discovery. Discovery may be granted only upon a showing of good cause,[19] and the request for discovery must include the proposed discovery itself.[20] The Advisory Committee has noted that "the requirement of prior court approval of all discovery is necessary to prevent abuse,"[21] though discovery abuse by the incarcerated is difficult to imagine. Discovery in habeas petitions challenging federal confinement is similarly curtailed.[22] As a result, not only is a petition's likelihood of success limited by a lack of initial disclosures; it is further limited due to discovery rules that permit it only with court approval.

At least one court has pushed back. In 2000, the Advisory Committee clarified that even when a case is categorically excluded from the initial disclosure requirement, "the court can order exchange of similar information in managing the action under Rule 16."[23] Judge Anthony W. Ishii of the Eastern District of California requires defendants in prisoner civil rights actions to provide plaintiffs with initial disclosures, despite vehement resistance from defendants.[24]

Prisoner Local Rules

Federal Rule of Civil Procedure 83 gives federal district courts the power to adopt and amend local rules applicable within their districts, so long as the rules govern practice.[25] Additionally, local rules may not contradict or duplicate federal rules and federal statutes.[26] Local rules are both drafted and approved by district judges. As of 2012, there were more than 6,000 local rules.[27]

Despite federal procedure's trans-substantive tradition, two common categories of local rules have emerged: those specific to particular claims, and those specific to particular parties. In the first category, a growing number of district courts have adopted local rules specific to patent claims. The patent rules are often the result of input from patent practitioners, bar associations, and district judges. Local patent rules are intended to render patent litigation predictable, at least procedurally. They appear to function as intended.[28]

In the second category, many district courts have also adopted local rules applicable to cases brought by prisoners. Unlike local patent rules, local rules targeting prisoner cases are not the result of compromise involving all stakeholders. These rules curtail prisoners' ability to litigate their cases. For example, some local rules establish different tracks for cases depending on their complexity. Those deemed complex receive more judicial attention and access. Local rules frequently label habeas and prisoner civil rights actions as the least complex, with correspondingly less access to judges. Other local rules limit the length of prisoners' complaints, sometimes permitting only four pages in which to allege a civil rights claim. A four-page prisoner complaint is much more vulnerable to pleadings-stage dismissal.

Local rules generally require that parties expressly consent to magistrate judge jurisdiction. But local rules governing prisoner litigation may automatically assign litigation to a magistrate judge when a prisoner fails to opt out of such jurisdiction. This is a consequential assignment for politically unpopular prisoners suing their state custodians. Unlike Article III judges, who are appointed for life, magistrates are appointed under Article I for an eight-year term by a majority of a district's district court judges. To assist them in obtaining reappointment, magistrate judges may be more likely to follow the preferences, political or otherwise, of the judge to whom they submit a report and recommendation.[29] Consequently, magistrate judges may be more likely to rule against disfavored parties, such as prisoners.

Local rules also limit prisoners' access to discovery. In suits alleging use of force, one district court limits prisoner plaintiffs' discovery to interrogatories and requests for production of documents.[30] Other forms of discovery are available only with the court's permission upon a showing of good cause. As a result, prisoners must engage in motion practice to obtain discovery to which all other parties are automatically entitled.

Limiting prisoners' access to depositions, especially in use of force cases, is particularly punitive. Depositions test a witness's credibility and are often useful settlement tools—a party's or witness's performance at a deposition predicts their performance at trial. A good cause standard means that depositions must be earned, even though parties in all other cases may automatically take ten depositions each. Local rules also limit prisoners' access to alternative dispute resolution, despite its acknowledged benefits. Finally, as discussed below, local rules delegate important aspects of prisoner case management, and perhaps even decision-making, to law clerks commonly known as staff attorneys.

The Federal Rules of Civil Procedure invite district courts to use local rules to treat prisoner cases differently. The Advisory Committee's note to Rule 16(b) encourages the promulgation of local rules exempting certain cases, including those involving habeas petitions, from the mandatory scheduling order. The scheduling order requirement was adopted in 1983 as part of a "package of reforms" aimed at curbing "abusive practices and tactical behavior" in discovery.[31] The scheduling order's time limits "stimulate litigants to narrow the areas of inquiry and advocacy to those they believe are truly relevant and material," forcing parties "to establish discovery priorities and thus to do the most important work first."[32]

Scheduling orders are efficiency tools. Nevertheless, the Rules encourage creation of local exemptions, and the Advisory Committee identified several types of cases as "[l]ogical candidates" for this treatment—including habeas corpus petitions.[33] Thus, despite the scheduling order's documented advantages, local rules could ensure that prisoners will never enjoy them.

Staff Attorneys and Prisoner Procedure

Since 1975, when a federal pilot program established "pro se law clerk" positions, district courts have hired attorneys assigned exclusively to pro se prisoner cases.[34] Today, such positions exist in most district courts. The attorneys are commonly known as staff attorneys. Unlike elbow clerks, whose offices are located inside judges' chambers and who serve limited, one- or two-year terms, staff attorneys labor in their own designated space within a federal courthouse—the "Pro Se Office"—and hold permanent positions. Staff attorneys do not work on behalf of pro se prisoners, but, rather, work on prisoner cases on behalf of district courts. Because pro se prisoner cases represent nearly 20 percent of civil cases filed in the district courts, staff attorneys control a significant aspect of the federal civil docket.

This delegation arguably contravenes Congress's intent that judges decide certain aspects of prisoner cases.[35] In 2016, with this concern in mind, I reviewed pro se prisoner staff attorney practices in each district court in the Ninth Circuit.[36] My research suggested that judicial decision-making, in addition to case management, was being delegated to staff attorneys. Information regarding the delegation of judicial tasks to staff attorneys was not easy to find. Only one district court—the District of Arizona—used its local rules to assign administration of habeas and prisoner civil rights actions to staff attorneys. More often, information about staff attorneys could be found only in less obvious places, such as job postings, externship information, local rules committee rosters, and state of the court reports. From those sources, I determined that the Districts of Alaska; the Central, Eastern, and Southern Districts of California; and the Western District of Washington also assign prisoner litigation to staff attorneys.

Local rules cannot exceed the authority delegated to the district courts through Rule 83, which prohibits local procedure that conflicts with federal law. Federal law provides that judges must engage in the initial screening of prisoner habeas petitions and prisoner civil rights actions. Therefore, the formal and informal procedure governing staff attorneys oversteps the federal courts' rulemaking authority. Federal courts have the power to make procedural rules as a result of a limited delegation from Congress and cannot take action that exceeds that delegation.

Delegating decision-making authority to staff attorneys also may transfer judicial power to non–Article III actors. Life tenure ensures that Article III judges are free to make politically unpopular decisions without fear of retribution. This kind of independence is particularly preferable when judicial decisions may grant relief to disfavored litigants such as prisoners. Yet when decision-making authority is transferred to non–Article III actors, their continued employment may depend upon decisions that align with majoritarian values.

Of course, because staff attorneys' work frees up judicial time, there are practical reasons to maintain the status quo, and valid concerns about dismantling it. Still, prisoners bring claims of constitutional and social significance, claims that speak to the consequences of mass incarceration and the racial injustice perpetuated by it. Perhaps cases brought by prisoners are the worst candidates for delegation to nonjudicial actors.

Conclusion

Prisoners' civil litigation sheds light on the constitutional injustices suffered by some of the more vulnerable and isolated members of society. The litigation should be carefully shepherded through the federal courts. Instead, prisoner litigation and prisoners themselves are vilified. This animosity informs and justifies the punitive procedure that prisoner litigation is subject to.

Prisoner procedure is easy to miss. It hides out in advisory committee notes and district courts' local customs. And it is rarely part of the law school curriculum, even though it applies to cases that represent nearly 20 percent of the federal courts' civil dockets. Given prisoner procedure's impact, it could be studied alongside the otherwise transsubstantive Federal Rules of Civil Procedure—or in a class of its own. For now, that kind of pedagogical and cultural shift is unlikely. The continued existence of prisoner procedure suggests that Congress and judges still disdain prisoner litigants. Those are powerful norms to overcome. Until incarceration is itself suspicious, the incarcerated will catch no breaks, both with respect to the rights that protect them and the procedure through which those rights are enforced.

NOTES

1 Brown v. Plata, 563 U.S. 493 (2011) (upholding three-judge panel's decision to order a "population reduction" where prisoners were deprived of adequate medical care).

2 Edmo v. Corizon, Inc., 935 F.3d 757 (9th Cir. 2019) (upholding district court's order that a state prison provide gender affirmation surgery to the incarcerated plaintiff).

3 Ball v. LeBlanc, 881 F.3d 346 (5th Cir. 2018) (upholding district court's order to control the temperature in a prison for death-row inmates with preexisting medical conditions that rendered them vulnerable to heat-related injuries).

4 *See* U.S. Courts, Table C-2, U.S. District Courts–Civil Statistical Tables For The Federal Judiciary, U.S. District Courts—Civil Cases Commenced, by Basis of Jurisdiction and Nature of Suit (Dec. 30, 2018) (Table C-2), www.uscourts.gov.

5 *See* U.S. Courts, Table C-13, U.S. District Courts–Civil Judicial Business, U.S. District Courts—Civil Pro Se and Non-Pro Se Filings (Sept. 30, 2018) (Table C-13), www.uscourts.gov (in 2018, more than 91 percent of prisoner litigation was brought pro se, compared with 11 percent of nonprisoner litigation).

6 549 U.S. 199 (2007).

7 *Id.* at 203; *see* Katherine A. Macfarlane, *Shadow Judges: Staff Attorney Adjudication of Prisoner Claims*, 95 Or. L. Rev. 97, 137 n.70 (2016).

8 Patricia W. Hatamyar Moore, *The Civil Caseload of the Federal District Courts*, 2015 U. Ill. L. Rev. 1177, 1216 (2015).

9 Francesco Parisi, *Rent-Seeking Through Litigation: Adversarial and Inquisitorial Systems Compared*, 22 Int'l Rev. L. & Econ. 193, 195 (2002).

10 28 U.S.C. § 1915A; Joseph T. Lukens, *The Prison Litigation Reform Act: Three Strikes and You're Out of Court—It May Be Effective, But Is It Constitutional?*, 70 Temp. L. Rev. 471, 514 (1997).

11 28 U.S.C. § 1915A(b).

12 *Jones*, 549 U.S. at 213–14.

13 Kiser v. Johnson, 163 F.3d 326, 328 (5th Cir. 1999) (quoting 28 U.S.C. foll. § 2254 Rule 4).
14 Margo Schlanger, *Inmate Litigation*, 116 Harv. L. Rev. 1555, 1561 (2003).
15 Fed. R. Civ. P. 26(a) advisory committee notes (1993).
16 William B. Rubenstein, *The Concept of Equality in Civil Procedure*, 23 Cardozo L. Rev. 1865, 1880 (2002).
17 Fed. R. Civ. P. 26(a)(1)(B).
18 Fed. R. Civ. P. 26(a) advisory committee notes (2000).
19 28 U.S.C. foll. § 2254 Rule 6(a).
20 28 U.S.C. foll. § 2254 Rule 6(b).
21 Advisory Committee Notes, 28 U.S.C. foll. § 2254 Rule 6.
22 28 U.S.C. foll. § 2255 Rule 6.
23 Fed. R. Civ. P. 26(a) advisory committee notes (2000).
24 Quiroga v. Green, No. 1:11CV00989 AWI DLB, 2013 WL 6086668, at *1 (E.D. Cal. Nov. 19, 2013).
25 Fed. R. Civ. P. 83(a)(1).
26 *Id.*
27 Katherine A. Macfarlane, *A New Approach to Local Rules*, 11 Stan. J. C.R. & C.L. 121, 121 (2015).
28 Macfarlane, *Shadow Judges*, *supra* note 7, at 142.
29 *Id.* at 146.
30 *See* S.&E. D.N.Y. U.S. Dist. Ct. Civ. Rule 33.2.
31 Macfarlane, *Shadow Judges*, *supra* note 7, at 146.
32 *Id.*
33 *Id.*
34 *Id.* at 105.
35 Federal law clerks draft orders and opinions, which are reviewed and approved by Article III judges. However, unlike term clerks, staff attorneys do not enjoy easy access to federal judges, rendering close supervision less likely. Also, staff attorneys often focus on a single type of case and may develop assumptions regarding those cases and parties. This specialization creates the risk of confirmation bias regarding prisoners' likelihood of success.
36 Macfarlane, *Shadow Judges*, *supra* note 7. My article received significant negative feedback from judges and court administrators, who argued that staff attorneys are highly valued court employees who perform essential work. My decision to study staff attorneys was the subject of inquiry during my tenure review. No one questioned the accuracy of my arguments. Instead, it was my decision to study the topic that came under fire.

7

The Benefits of Class Actions and the Increasing Threats to Their Viability

SUZETTE MALVEAUX

Plaintiffs challenging discrimination in the workplace and elsewhere are finding it more difficult to act collectively by aggregating their claims in a class action because the United States Supreme Court has interpreted Rule 23's class certification requirements in such a way that putative class actions have a higher bar to clear to get certified.[1] Although applicable to all cases, heightened certification is a major issue for claims alleging systemic discrimination.

The modern class action rule, Rule 23, is critical to curtailing workplace discrimination and civil rights violations. Far from simply an intricate joinder device, this aggregation method was designed to empower everyday people to promote and enforce public policy.[2] As indicated by the drafters,[3] the Rule was revised extensively in 1966 "so that it would provide a useful procedural vehicle, particularly for civil rights cases."[4] Through class actions and statutory delegation of private attorney general status to ordinary citizens, private individuals and their counsel supplemented, subsidized, and even substituted official government regulation.[5] Against this backdrop, federal courts applied a liberal approach to class certification, especially in the civil rights context.[6]

Recently, that liberal approach has ended. Aggregate ligation—while relatively rare—has been criticized, largely by those in the business community[7] who argue that the tremendous financial exposure caused by class actions makes class certification akin to blackmail and the pressure to settle irresistible.[8] Critics also argue that class actions are motivated primarily by self-interested plaintiffs' lawyers who use group litigation to enrich themselves to the public's detriment.[9] Although there are certainly dramatic examples of class action abuse, this concern is largely overblown and unsupported empirically.[10]

The class certification inquiry is appropriately "rigorous," but this rigor must be tempered by recognition that aggregation serves at least three important objectives: access, enforcement, and efficiency. As of now, class action law has become increasingly obstructionist. Claimants seeking to challenge discriminatory practices in the workplace and elsewhere have been hit particularly hard by increasingly restrictive applications and interpretations of Rule 23—applications that have curtailed access and weakened the law enforcement objective of collective litigation, functionally shutting civil rights plaintiffs out of court.

Access

The civil justice system works only if ordinary people can use it. For many employees and others, a class action is their only meaningful access to the court system. Those with small claims and limited resources are often disinclined, or unable, to challenge powerful corporations on their own,[11] and litigation costs and attorney's fees may exceed the value of the recovery,[12] resulting in employees foregoing legal action altogether. Additionally, in the absence of aggregate litigation, an employee may be too fearful of losing her job or of other retaliation to challenge her employer—especially a multinational mega-corporation.[13] For example, a plaintiff who sues her employer directly may suddenly be scheduled for too few hours to qualify for benefits, or she may be passed over for promotion, or receive a poor employment evaluation. Passive participation in a class action is much less likely to invoke such retaliatory measures. In this regard, the class action helps level the playing field between those with differential power and resources.

Enforcement

Aggregate litigation also promotes law enforcement. Even if employees are able to seek redress for individual harms, in the absence of collective action, they often cannot challenge widespread misconduct as successfully. A class-wide challenge enables plaintiffs to more easily obtain evidence[14] that can unearth trends and show systemic wrongdoing. In turn, this enables plaintiffs to craft remedies and injunctive relief far greater in scope than what could be done in an individual capacity.

The class action also casts a sufficiently broad net to put others on notice of discriminatory practices and subsequent remedies of which they may not have been aware.[15] Class actions led by private attorneys fill the gap left by government agencies that are often burdened by budgetary and political constraints.[16] In fact, as recognized by the Supreme Court and Congress, class actions are a central part of the Title VII enforcement scheme.[17]

Efficiency

In addition, enabling plaintiffs—especially those with small-value claims and limited resources—to jointly challenge widespread conduct in a single stroke fosters efficiency. Together, employees can share the risks and burdens of litigation and pool their resources, making it economically feasible to challenge misconduct through the court system.[18] Aggregate litigation saves judges and parties substantial time and money by resolving similar claims in one case. Not insignificantly, employers also benefit from the efficacy and closure a class settlement can offer.

New Limits on Class Actions

Not only does the class action device play a critical role in the US civil justice system generally through the benefits of access, enforcement, and efficiency, the device plays a special role in the civil rights context. Historically, class actions have been central to the civil rights movement—as the procedural vehicle for structural reform in cases from school desegregation to prisoners' rights to employment discrimination. For example, one of the most preeminent Supreme Court cases of the twentieth century—*Brown v. Board of Education*[19]—was a class action.[20]

In 2011, in one of the largest private-employer civil rights class actions in US history, *Wal-Mart Stores, Inc. v. Dukes*,[21] the Supreme Court imposed new obstacles to class certification by imposing a heightened Rule 23(a)(2) commonality requirement. This 5–4 ruling by the conservative majority raised the bar for one of the easiest class action thresholds, thereby jeopardizing Title VII and related claims going forward.

Dukes involved former and current female employees who brought a class action against Wal-Mart Stores, Inc., on behalf of approximately

1.5 million women, alleging nationwide gender discrimination, in violation of Title VII.[22] Plaintiffs alleged that Wal-Mart gave its local managers unfettered discretion when making pay and promotions decisions, resulting in women being disproportionately underpaid and denied advancement.[23] To demonstrate that class members had enough in common with each other to justify collective action—as required by Rule 23(a)(2)[24]—plaintiffs proffered statistics showing gender disparities in pay and promotions; 120 employee affidavits reporting discrimination; and testimony from a sociologist, concluding that Wal-Mart's corporate culture and personnel practices made it susceptible to gender discrimination.[25]

Conceding that even a single common question would suffice under Rule 23(a)(2), the Court concluded that the women failed to make even this minimal showing.[26] The Court required plaintiffs to demonstrate commonality with "'[s]ignificant proof' that Wal-Mart 'operated under a general policy of discrimination.'"[27] Applying this new elevated commonality standard, the Court concluded that the statistical disparities, anecdotal accounts, and "social framework" evidence[28] proffered fell short of demonstrating that there was sufficient glue to hold the class together.[29]

The Court's application of heightened commonality[30] to the evidence in *Dukes* portends a difficult future for workers attempting to collectively challenge alleged discrimination. As Professor Catherine Fisk and Dean Erwin Chemerinsky recognize:

> [I]n *Wal-Mart* . . . the Supreme Court abandoned any pretense of equilibration and handed large companies huge victories. The significance, of course, is not simply that Wal-Mart's employees who suffered sex discrimination are unlikely ever to recover damages. . . . The larger concern is that big companies know that it will be much harder to sue them in class actions, and the unscrupulous ones will more often make the choice to enrich themselves at the expense of . . . employees.[31]

At the very least, *Dukes* hands defendants another tool for dismantling group action. Unquestionably, classes the size and scope of the one proposed in *Dukes* will become even rarer.[32] But even classes of less magnitude and scope are suffering a fate similar to *Dukes* because of their underlying theory of liability. As in *Dukes*, many employment discrimination class actions are premised on excessive subjectivity as a discriminatory policy, which grounds Rule 23(a)(2) commonality. Thus, claimants arguing that a policy of unfettered discretionary decision-making is a vehicle for systemic workplace discrimination and disparities face a more formidable battle post-*Dukes*.[33] *Dukes*'s impact has gone even beyond Title VII and employment discrimination claims: cases brought under the Equal Credit Opportunity Act,[34] the Fair Housing Act,[35] and § 1981[36] challenging lenders' discretionary pricing policies as discriminatory have also suffered this fate.[37]

Plaintiffs are adjusting to the harsher certification climate to minimize the potentially damaging impact of *Dukes*. Plaintiffs' counsel is bringing smaller cases that are more geographically limited to create a tighter nexus between decision makers and alleged discriminatory conduct. Other strategies include seeking issue certification under Rule 23(c)(4), creating subclasses, defining the class more narrowly, distinguishing *Dukes*, filing class actions in state court, and relying on statutes other than Title VII to challenge certain employment practices. These strategies come with costs, some at their peril.[38]

In sum, the Court's heightened commonality standard potentially undermines court access and denies formal resolution on the merits. Withholding class certification—especially in cases involving small value claims and poor claimants—may deny relief altogether for such litigants[39] and compromise enforcement of antidiscrimination statutes more generally.[40]

However, it bears acknowledging that plaintiffs permitted to seek class certification at all are the fortunate ones.[41] Arbitration agreements that compel employees to forgo class actions—along with other procedural protections—are increasingly found in employment contracts[42] and enforced by the courts. The Supreme Court's endorsement of arbitration over several decades has encouraged employers to increasingly condition employment on an individual's willingness to forego court access.[43] Consequently, to the extent that those with small claims and resources are unlikely to challenge powerful corporate employers on their own, class action bans will function as exculpatory clauses, shielding an employer from accounting for widespread discrimination.

NOTES

Acknowledgment: This chapter is updated and adapted from the article Suzette Malveaux, *A Diamond in the Rough: Trans-Substantivity of the Federal Rules of Civil Procedure and its Detrimental Impact on Civil Rights*, 92 Wash. U. L. Rev. 455 (2014).

1 *See* Mary Kay Kane, *The Supreme Court's Recent Class Action Jurisprudence: Gazing Into a Crystal Ball*, 16 Lewis & Clark L. Rev. 1015, 1036–41 (2012).

2 *See* David Marcus, *The History of the Modern Class Action, Part I*: Sturm Und Drang, *1953–1980*, 90 Wash. U. L. Rev. 587, 594 (2013).

3 *See* Fed. R. Civ. P. 23 advisory committee's note.

4 *See* Arthur R. Miller, *Some Very Personal Reflections on the Rules, Rulemaking, and Reporters*, 46 U. Mich. J.L. Reform 651, 652–53 (2013).

5 Arthur R. Miller, *Simplified Pleading, Meaningful Days in Court, and Trials on the Merits: Reflections on the Deformation of Civil Procedure*, 88 N.Y.U. L. Rev. 286, 316 (2013).

6 *See* Robert H. Klonoff, Edward K.M. Bilich & Suzette M. Malveaux, *Class Actions and Other Multi-Party Litigation: Cases and Materials* 788 (West, 3d ed. 2012).

7 *See, e.g.*, Press Release, *U.S. Chamber Commends Supreme Court for Limiting Class Action Abuses*, U.S. Chamber of Commerce (Mar. 18, 2013, 8:00 PM), www.uschamber.com.

8 *See, e.g.*, In re Rhone-Poulenc Rorer, Inc., 51 F.3d 1293, 1298 (7th Cir. 1995) ("blackmail settlements"); Waste Mgmt. Holdings, Inc. v. Mowbray, 208 F.3d 288, 293 (1st Cir. 2000) ("irresistible pressure to settle"); Ross v. A.H. Robins Co., 607 F.2d 545, 557 (2d Cir. 1979) ("*in terrorem*" settlements).

9 Daniel Fisher, *Plaintiff? Is That Really Necessary in a Class Action?* Forbes (Feb. 4, 2014, 10:04 AM), http://www.forbes.com.

10 *See* Thomas E. Willging, Laura L. Hooper & Robert J. Niemic, *An Empirical Analysis of Rule 23 to Address the Rulemaking Challenges*, 71 N.Y.U. L. Rev. 74, 177–78 (1996).

11 *See* Carnegie v. Household Int'l, Inc., 376 F.3d 656, 661 (7th Cir. 2004) (Posner, J.) ("The *realistic* alternative to a class action is not 17 million individual suits, but zero individual suits, as only a lunatic or a fanatic sues for $30.").

12 This is known as a "negative value suit." *See* Jay Tidmarsh, 1 Class Actions: Five Principles to Promote Fairness and Efficiency § 1.03 at 2 (2013).

13 Catherine Fisk & Erwin Chemerinsky, *The Failing Faith in Class Actions*: Wal-Mart v. Dukes *and* AT&T Mobility v. Concepcion, 7 Duke J. Const. L. & Pub. Pol'y 73, 76 (2011).

14 For example, class representatives can justify getting access to statements from management, corporate documents, and companywide statistics.

15 *See* Fisk & Chemerinsky, *supra* note 13, at 76 (employees unlikely to sue because they are unaware of illegality).

16 *Id.* at 75.

17 *See* Griggs v. Duke Power Co., 401 U.S. 424, 426 (1971).

18 *See* Fisk & Chemerinsky, *supra* note 13, at 76.
19 347 U.S. 483, 495 (1954).
20 The case was, in fact, a consolidation of four separate class actions originating in Delaware, Kansas, South Carolina, and Virginia. *Id.* at 486. There was also a companion case that originated in the District of Columbia. *See* Bolling v. Sharpe, 347 U.S. 497 (1954).
21 131 S. Ct. 2541 (2011).
22 *Id.* at 2547.
23 *Id.* at 2548.
24 Fed. R. Civ. P. 23(a)(2). "Commonality" is satisfied when "there are questions of law or fact common to the class."
25 *Dukes*, 131 S. Ct. at 2549.
26 *Id.* at 2556–57.
27 *Id.* at 2553 (quoting Telephone Co. of the Southwest v. Flacon, 457 U.S. 147, 159 n.15 (1982)).
27 *Id.* at 2549.
29 *Id.* at 2556–57.
30 The Court elevated the commonality standard in a number of ways. *See* Suzette M. Malveaux, *How Goliath Won: The Future Implications of* Dukes v. Wal-Mart, 106 Nw. U. L. Rev. Colloquy 34, 39, 42–43 (2011) (describing "same injury," "common mode" necessary for commonality); A. Benjamin Spencer, *Class Actions, Heightened Commonality, and Declining Access to Justice*, 93 B. U. L. Rev. 441, 463–75 (2013) (describing new same injury, centrality, and efficiency requirements of commonality).
31 Fisk & Chemerinsky, *supra* note 13, at 77.
32 This is not surprising. Cases the magnitude and scope of *Dukes* are rare. Even among those sympathetic to the plaintiffs in *Dukes* concede that the class scope was ambitious. *See, e.g.*, Deborah M. Weiss, *A Grudging Defense of* Wal-Mart v. Dukes, 24 Yale J.L. & Feminism 119, 163–64 (2012).
33 *See* Joseph M. Sellers, *Class Actions After* Wal-Mart v. Dukes, *Am. Law Inst.* 113, 114 (2013).
34 15 U.S.C. § 1691 (2006).
35 42 U.S.C. §§ 3601–3619 (2006).
36 42 U.S.C. § 1981 (2006).
37 *See, e.g.*, Barrett v. Option One Mortg. Corp., No. 08-10157-RWZ, 2012 U.S. Dist. LEXIS 132775, at *9–13 (D. Ma. Sept. 18, 2012); Rodriguez v. Nat'l City Bank, 277 F.R.D. 148, 155 (E.D. Pa. 2011), *aff'd*, 726 F.3d 372 (3d Cir. 2013); In re Wells Fargo Residential Mortg. Lending Discrimination Litig., No. 08-MD-01930, 2011 WL 3903117, at *1–5 (N.D. Cal. Sept. 6, 2011).
38 Malveaux, *A Diamond in the Rough*, *supra* first unnumbered note, at 498–99 nn.263–70 (citing cases).
39 Miller, *supra* note 5, at 318 ("Realistically, the choice for class members is between collective access to the judicial system or no access at all.").

40 *See* George Rutherglen, *Wal-Mart, AT&T Mobility, and the Decline of the Deterrent Class Action*, 98 Va. L. Rev. In Brief 24, 29 (2012) ("In sum, the holding on commonality in *Wal-Mart* diminishes the prospect of certification and in doing so, diminishes the likelihood that a class action will be brought. The net effect is to reduce the defendant's exposure to class-wide liability and the deterrent effect of class actions generally.").

41 *See* Judith Resnik, Comment, *Fairness in Numbers: A Comment on* AT&T v. Concepcion, Wal-Mart v. Dukes, *and* Turner v. Rodgers, 125 Harv. L. Rev. 78, 118–22 (2011); David S. Schwartz, *Claim-Suppressing Arbitration: The New Rules*, 87 Ind. L.J. 239, 267 (2012) (*AT&T v. Concepcion* essentially "destroys . . . employment class actions").

42 Predispute compulsory arbitration agreements in the employment arena have been on the rise. *See* Suzette M. Malveaux, *Is It the "Real Thing"?: How Coke's One-Way Binding Arbitration May Bridge the Divide between Litigation and Arbitration*, 2009 J. Disp. Resol. 77, 80 nn.11–12 (citing Theodore Eisenberg & Geoffrey P. Miller's empirical analysis of 2,858 corporate contracts, which "revealed that employment contracts are more likely to have arbitration clauses than other types of contracts"). A troubling feature of those agreements—the class action ban—is consequently on the rise. *See* Suzette M. Malveaux, *Clearing Civil Procedural Hurdles in the Quest for Justice*, Ohio N.U. L. Rev. 621, 639 (2011).

43 *Id.* at 83.

8

Disability Employment Class Actions

JASMINE HARRIS

A basic premise underwriting federal procedural rules is their presumed trans-substantivity. That is, the Rules Enabling Act of 1934 gave the United States Supreme Court the authority to issue procedural and evidentiary rules for federal courts to the extent that they do not "abridge, enlarge, or modify any substantive right."[1] Many chapters in this anthology, however, challenge assumptions of trans-substantivity by applying various critical lenses to demonstrate the ways in which the rules have a disparate impact on the substantive rights of marginalized communities. This chapter focuses on the ways in which Rule 23 of the Federal Rules of Civil Procedure—a critical tool for public interest litigation and the framework for key antidiscrimination civil rights victories in education and public accommodations along racial and gender axes—interacts with the Americans with Disabilities Act's (ADA)[2] prohibitions on employment discrimination.

Thirty-plus years after the 1990 passage of the ADA—the most comprehensive civil rights legislation for people with disabilities in the United States—courts continue to restrict the broad scope of congressional intent to remedy employment discrimination experienced by people with disabilities by means of aggregate litigation. One way to narrow substantive civil rights is to attack procedural rules. The strategy of narrowing civil rights by restricting the use of procedural mechanisms for aggregate litigation, and thus structural reform, has a long history in the context of civil rights.[3]

Yet the need for structural reform in the employment context for people with disabilities[4] is pronounced. Employment rates for people with disabilities are 19.1 percent compared with 65.9 percent of nondisabled people.[5] When people with disabilities are present in the workforce, they disproportionately work in the less formal economy and/or are more self-employed relative to nondisabled workers,[6] meaning there are fewer structural employment protections and benefits in place.

Title I of the ADA provides a remedy for employment discrimination experienced by "qualified" individuals with disabilities.[7] I argue that judges have improperly narrowed the use of aggregate litigation tools to the detriment of broader structural reforms in employment for people with disabilities. A critical tension exists between the structural goals of the ADA to end discrimination against people with disabilities in employment and the reluctance of judges to certify disability rights class actions to achieve those goals. Several courts have reasoned that Congress did not intend for individual claims of reasonable accommodations to proceed as a class action because they are highly fact-specific and as such defeat the requirements of FRCP 23(a) such as commonality or typicality and, when seeking damages, FRCP 23(b)(3)'s predominance requirement. However, the current doctrine fundamentally misunderstands the ways in which Title I claims are well-suited to class certification and adjudication.

In this chapter, I argue that courts reviewing motions for class certification of ADA Title I employment cases should revisit Congress's broad remedial directives that demand greater recognition of the structural roots of disability employment discrimination. Title I, although billed as the same remedial model as Title VII of the Civil Rights Act of 1964,[8] offered a broader vision for disability antidiscrimination in employment than its predecessor. Yet, unlike Title VII, since the inception of Title I, motions for certification of disability employment class actions have faced the type of judicial skepticism about common aggregate harm that ultimately characterized the Supreme Court's landmark decision in *Wal-Mart v. Dukes*.[9] I join other disability scholars in prescribing the adoption of broader theories of disability discrimination as a means to certify employment classes (e.g., "pandisability," akin to "panethnicity"),[10] while also suggesting narrower definitions of putative classes to facilitate the certification process, develop a foundational jurisprudence over time, and address the concerns proffered by some courts regarding individualization and potential conflicts of interest among members of the class.

The Role of Class Actions in Structural Reform

The class action is a procedural device rooted in efficiency and designed to aggregate individuals who have similar legal claims against a common defendant. In order to proceed as a class action, the putative class must meet the requirements of FRCP 23(a), which include demonstrating commonality, typicality, and representativeness or adequacy. In addition to these prerequisites, plaintiffs seeking class certification must show that (a) separate adjudications will create a risk of decisions that are inconsistent with or dispositive of other class members' claims,[11] (b) injunctive or declaratory relief is appropriate based on the actions of the defendant with respect to the class more generally,[12] *or* (c) common questions predominate *and* a class action is superior to individual actions.[13]

Decisions about class certification often require courts to resolve a threshold question of how to frame the nature of discrimination experienced by a putative class. Renowned proceduralist Robert Cover opined that, despite the rule drafters' intent that the FRCP be trans-substantive, courts should interpret rules contextually, with attention to the particular area of law to which the rule is applied.[14] In other words, Cover explained that FRCP 23 required courts to contextualize its application.

Before the promulgation of the ADA, courts initially adopted a broad interpretative view when certifying Title VII class actions. Courts identified a shared, common experience of racial discrimination among class members, particularly relative to the dominant white male norm for employees. Judges differentiated between employment-based discrimination claims with respect to the employers' motives: "disparate treatment" (where an employer's motivation is intentional) and "disparate impact" (where the employer lacks the intent to discriminate but nevertheless advances seemingly "neutral" policies or practices that cause certain groups of people to be disproportionately negatively impacted).[15] Courts in disparate impact cases focused on the consequences of employment actions and not solely on the motivation.[16] At times, court interpretations were so broad that they even allowed one racial and ethnic minority group to stand in for another racial minority group.[17] "This flexible approach to class certification countenanced a judicial recognition of the need and desirability of group-driven litigation challenging policies and practices that favored the traditional labor force of white male employees."[18]

Yet, this flexible approach did not hold for long in Title VII cases. First, the nature of employment discrimination (and discrimination writ large) shifted from clear evidence of animus-based employment decisions in the early years of Title VII to contemporary forms of implicit biases that may be more subtle and difficult to smoke out because they are baked into long-standing organizational structures and designs.[19] Simultaneously, the substantive doctrine in Title VII cases began to narrow over time to reflect a normative position hostile to employment discrimination claims by racial and ethnic minorities and women. This normative shift was accomplished, in part, by narrower interpretations of FRCP 23 certification standards such that courts certified fewer employment discrimination class actions.[20] Judicial interpretation generally has shifted from a focus on an intergroup shared experience of workplace subordination to emphasizing intragroup distinctions, particularly regarding the facts surrounding the employer's alleged adverse employment action and differences in the specific remedies sought by putative plaintiff classes.[21]

A Flawed Application of Rule 23 to Disability Rights Law

To understand the difficulties with successfully litigating ADA Title I class actions, it is important to understand the success of class actions under Titles II and III of the ADA. Title II prohibits discrimination in public programs and services and Title III prohibits discrimination based on disability by private entities operating places of public accommodations. While there is room for more progress, class actions under both titles have had greater success relative to Title I cases.[22]

Title I of the ADA gives people with disabilities employment protection by extending to private employers the Civil Rights Act Title VII protections. Specifically, Title I provides a remedy for employment discrimination experienced by "qualified" individuals with disabilities.[23] "Qualified" employees who can meet the federal definition of disability are protected from forms of "disability discrimination" in employment, including failure to make reasonable accommodations and imposition of discriminatory qualification standards or examinations.[24]

In contrast to the relative success of Title II and III class actions in generating institutional changes in education, housing, public accommodations, and transportation, Title I class actions have not radically transformed access to employment for people with disabilities.[25] These employment discrimination class action cases emerged in disability rights litigation over time, with courts consistently expressing their doctrinal discomfort with these types of class actions. Two analytical moves stand out.

First, courts have denied certification for ADA Title I class actions by distinguishing disability as a "different" immutable characteristic than race or gender. For example, the court in *Lintemuth v. Saturn Corp.*[26] denied certification of a Title I disability class, explaining that "the shared characteristic is being disabled, which unlike race or gender, involves varying degrees."[27] These arguments assume that race, gender, and disability are all immutable characteristics—that they are biologically determined and not socially constructed. The association of disability with medical impairment rather than sociopolitical identity leads courts to assume that the root of disability employment discrimination lies in the individual and not society. Thus, courts may reduce failure to accommodate claims to individual bad actors who harm individuals with impairments seeking specific statutory entitlements rather than ableist institutions that have chosen to design employment spaces, job requirements, and methods of accomplishing the organization's goals without regard for physically different and neurodiverse employees based on assumptions about their value as employees.

Second, courts have opined that, while Title I should be enforced, the class action is not a good vehicle for that enforcement because Congress prescribed individualization—best embodied in Congress's requirement that employers provide reasonable accommodations—as a remedy for some disability employment discrimination claims. In *Davoll v. Webb*, a putative class of police officers with work-related disabilities sued their department under Title I for failure to provide reasonable accommodations.[28] The district court denied plaintiffs' certification motion, reasoning that "necessarily individualized inquiries are best suited to a case-by-case determination."[29] Because the requests for accommodation varied according to disability, functional limitations, and job performed, the court viewed the class action as an inefficient procedural device because the court would have to engage in a highly fact-intensive inquiry for each putative plaintiff.

Lessons for Disability and Employment Law

By examining the disability class action in this broader context, we can identify arguments from Title VII cases to employ in ADA Title I cases and reciprocal arguments from the disability context to apply in Title VII employment discrimination cases in areas of race discrimination.[30] The class action is not a dead tool for disability rights in employment. Instead, disability discrimination demands more creative use of existing procedural rules to advance structural reform. This section offers initial ideas on procedural reforms that could assist advocates reimagining the disability class action. By studying class actions through a critical disability lens, we can also better understand how we could restructure classes and advance legal theories to focus courts on what unites, rather than what distinguishes, putative class members.

First, in response to concerns regarding how certain employment actions differently impact individuals with different disabilities, lawyers can focus on antisubordination harm theories. Lawyers should demonstrate how employers systematically fail employees with disabilities—failure to accommodate, hostile work environment, improper discharge, or failure to hire. While this may require disaggregation along different axes such as nature of the accommodation or specific disabilities, a single antisubordination theory unites the subclasses around a discriminatory pattern or practice of a defendant employer.

For example, in *McDonald*, the court addressed the propriety of a class of "[a]ll individuals employed by Corrections Corporation of America ('CCA') at any time since July 1, 2007, who have been or may be subjected to termination, discipline, or reprimand, resulting from CCA's failure to comply with the ADA."[31] The district court held this definition overly broad and "unascertainable" because of the definition's unlimited geographic scope.[32] Furthermore, the court held that the plaintiffs failed to meet the typicality requirement because plaintiffs' individual claims varied as did defendants' potential defenses. Upon closer examination, factors unrelated to disability or disability law (such as overly broad geographic definition or prospective discrimination of unnamed future putative class members) appear to drive judicial decisions to deny class certification.

Second, instead of private enforcement, agency-led "class" actions may offer an additional opportunity to remedy employment discrimination harms. The Equal Employment Opportunity Commission (EEOC) is exempt from FRCP 23 when it brings an enforcement action "in its own name."[33] The Supreme Court held that, although the "pattern or practice" method of proof is often deployed in class actions, strict application of the FRCP's certification requirements would hamper the EEOC's ability to proceed in one enforcement action.[34] Furthermore, even when the EEOC acts on behalf of specific individuals, "it acts also to vindicate the public interest in preventing employment discrimination."[35]

Third, the fragmented approach to employment discrimination—one that sees only race or gender or disability—is ill-equipped to address the realities of individuals' lived experiences and multiple forms of oppression. An intersectional approach to employment discrimination litigation would help courts to better understand how discrimination occurs and, as a result, how to remedy intersectional harms.[36] This could be similar to the "race plus" approach in Title VII employment discrimination cases that have begun to acknowledge intersectional discrimination even if the current legal framework is insufficient to remedy intersectional harms.[37]

Consider the following example. Anya, a Black woman who is now bald due to alopecia,[38] works as a hotel and casino bartender. She used to straighten her hair but has donned a wig with the texture of her natural, curly hair since she became bald. Her employer's grooming policy states that women must straighten their hair or wear it neatly pulled back in a bun or ponytail tightly secured to their heads. Anya's supervisor denies her request for an accommodation to appear bald at work even though restyling the wig to comply irritates Anya's scalp and exacerbates her alopecia. Her supervisor suspends Anya from work for noncompliance and docks a week's pay. Then, the hotel-casino fires Anya.

Anya experiences discrimination as a Black woman with a disability: the policy required her to perform a white, abled identity by wearing her hair in a style typical of white women, and her disability meant that she could not comply with the policy. All three of these identities are important to remedying the harm. Yet, if Anya tries to organize a class of Black women with disabilities to sue her employer, she—and every person who joins her with these identity components—would have a more onerous burden of proof than if the class reflected only one of those identities.[39] Thus, the current antidiscrimination framework fails to capture and remedy the harm precisely because it requires individuals to structure litigation around a single identity trait—disability, race, or gender—which simply reinforces the fallacy that discrimination can (or should) be neatly compartmentalized or strained into its component parts.

* * *

As employment law scholars, courts, and practitioners contemplate the future of employment class actions, disability must be a key part of those discussions. On one hand, the ADA lacks a robust doctrine with respect to class certification of actions alleging structural discrimination because some courts have taken Congress's emphasis on individualization as a directive to structure the lawsuits individually. On the other hand, the doctrinal trajectory of deploying class actions as a strategic device in employment discrimination under Title VII has moved from greater acceptance of legal theories based on group subordination to skepticism and denials of certification that have effectively limited the availability of disability employment class actions. Returning to the history of the class action and congressional intent of the ADA, therefore, can help us better understand some of the contemporary backlash against broader certification.

NOTES

1 Rules Enabling Act of 1934, 28 U.S.C. § 2072.
2 42 U.S.C. § 12101 et seq.
3 *See, e.g.*, A. Benjamin Spencer, *Substance, Procedure, and the Rules Enabling Act*, 66 UCLA L. Rev. 654 (2019).
4 I refer to "people with disabilities" or "disabled people" interchangeably and include those with more apparent, less apparent, and invisible disabilities. I employ "people first" ("people with disabilities") and "identity first" ("disabled people") language to reflect an ongoing self-identification debate. *See* Lydia X.Z. Brown, *Identity-First Language*, Autistic Self Advocacy Network, https://autisticadvocacy.org. To center disability, I use "nondisabled people" and "people without disabilities" interchangeably.

5 News Release, U.S. Bureau of Labor Statistics, Persons with Disability: Labor Force Characteristics—2020 (Feb. 24, 2021), www.bls.gov.

6 *Id.*

7 42 U.S.C. § 12111(8) ("The term 'qualified individual' means an individual who, with or without reasonable accommodation, can perform the essential functions of the employment position that such individual holds or desires.") *and* § 12102(1) ("The term 'disability' means, with respect to an individual—(A) a physical or mental impairment that substantially limits one or more major life activities of such individual; (B) a record of such an impairment; or (C) being regarded as having such an impairment.").

8 *See, e.g.*, Tory L. Lucas, *Disabling Complexity: The Americans with Disabilities Act of 1990 and Its Interaction with Other Federal Laws*, 38 Creighton L. Rev. 871, 917 (2005).

9 564 U.S. 338 (2011).

10 *See* Michael Ashley Stein and Michael E. Waterstone, *Disability, Disparate Impact, and Class Actions*, 56 Duke L.J. 861, 863–66 (2006).

11 Fed. R. Civ. P. 23(b)(1).

12 Fed. R. Civ. P. 23(b)(2).

13 Fed. R. Civ. P. 23(b)(3).

14 Robert M. Cover, *For James Wm. Moore: Some Reflections on a Reading of the Rules*, 84 Yale L.J. 718, 738–39 (1975).

15 *Compare* International Brotherhood of Teamsters v. United States, 431 U.S. 324 (1977) *with* Griggs v. Duke Power, Co., 401 U.S. 424 (1971).

16 Griggs, 401 U.S. at 432.

17 *See, e.g.*, Sanchez v. Standard Brands, Inc., 431 F.2d 455 (5th Cir. 1970).

18 Stein & Waterstone, *supra* note 10, at 873.

19 Susan Sturm, *Second Generation Employment Discrimination: A Structural Approach*, 101 Colum. L. Rev. 458, 465–78 (2001).

20 *But see* Michael Selmi and Sylvia Tsakos, *Employment Discrimination Class Actions After Wal-Mart v. Dukes*, 48 Akron L. Rev. 803, 804 (2015) (arguing that *Wal-Mart* has had less of an impact on Title VII employment class action certification than feared).

21 In *Wal-Mart v. Dukes*, 564 U.S. 338 (2011), the Supreme Court held that class certification was inappropriate to remedy workplace gender bias because of what the Court perceived to be disparate facts, policies, and practices applicable to the named plaintiffs and putative class such that it failed to meet the commonality prerequisite.

22 Titles II and III class actions, arguably, have produced the most significant disability rights reforms. *See, e.g.*, Olmstead v. L.C. ex rel. Zimring, 527 U.S. 581 (1999).

23 See sources cited *supra* note 7.

24 Statutory law, not federal constitutional law, dominates the remedial landscape for the advancement of the civil rights of people with disabilities. *See, e.g.*, City of Cleburne v. Cleburne Living Cent., Inc., 473 U.S. 432 (1985).

25 Some empirical evidence suggests that Title I may have created additional barriers to employment. *See, e.g.*, Christine Jolls, *Accommodations Mandates*, 53 Stan. L. Rev. 225, 229, 272–78 (2000).

26 No. 1:93–0211, 1994 WL 760811 at *1 (M.D. Tenn. Aug. 29, 1994).

27 *Id.* at *5.

28 Davoll v. Webb, 160 F.R.D. 142, 144 (D. Colo. 1995), aff'd 194 F.3d 1116 (10th Cir. 1999).

29 *Id.* at 146.

30 *See, e.g.*, D. Wendy Greene, *Title VII: What's Hair (and Other Race-Based Characteristics) Got to Do With It?*, 79 U. Colo. L. Rev. 1355 (2008).

31 McDonald v. Corr. Corp. of Am., No. CV-09-00781-PHX-JAT, 2010 WL 4572758 at *1, *7 (D. Ariz., Nov. 4, 2010).

32 *Id.* at *3.

33 Equal Emp't Opportunity Comm'n v. Bass Pro Outdoor World, 826 F.3d 791, 797–98 (5th Cir. 2016).

34 Gen Tel. Co. of Northwest v. Equal Emp't Opportunity Comm'n, 446 U.S. 318, 330 (1980).

35 *Id.* at 326.

36 *See* Jasmine E. Harris, *Reckoning with Race and Disability*, 130 Yale L.J. Forum 916 (2021).

37 Alice Abrokwa, *"When They Enter, We All Enter": Opening the Door to Intersectional Discrimination Claims Based on Race and Disability*, 24 Mich. J. Race & L. 15, 58 (2018).

38 *What You Need to Know About Alopecia Areata*, Nat'l Alopecia Areata Ass'n, www.naaf.org; *see also* Merrit Kennedy, *"Freed From The Secret": Rep. Ayanna Pressley Opens Up About Living With Alopecia*, Nat'l Public Radio (Jan. 17, 2020), https://www.npr.org.

39 *See, e.g.*, Jeffers v. Thompson, 264 F. Supp. 2d 314, 327 (D. Md. 2003) ("[T]he more specific the composite class in which the plaintiff claims membership, the more onerous that ultimate burden [of proof] becomes."). *See also* Kathryn Abrams, *Title VII and the Complex Female Subject*, 92 Mich. L. Rev. 2479 (1994).

9

Procedure and Indian Children

MATTHEW L. M. FLETCHER AND NEOSHIA R. ROEMER

The Federal Rules of Civil Procedure were meant to infuse *equality* into civil proceedings. For decades, scholars have discussed the trans-substantive nature of the federal rules. That is, the federal rules apply equally to substantive legal matters across the board without distinction among the specific causes of action or parties involved.[1] But treating every litigant the same despite power differentials among some parties raises the question of how equality exists in modern US legal procedure.[2]

Today's legal system requires procedural justice, not just procedural symmetry.[3] Procedural justice is the idea that cases that are *truly* alike will be treated the same under the rules.[4] However, procedural justice must also be equitable—"[j]ust, fair, and right, in consideration of the facts and circumstances of the individual case."[5]

This chapter offers an example of procedural justice in the child welfare system: the procedural rules developed in response to the Indian Child Welfare Act of 1978[6] (ICWA). Perhaps no area of civil litigation requires procedural justice more than child welfare. Each year, child welfare systems across the United States handle thousands of cases involving children who need care for a variety of reasons, including foster care placements, guardianships, adoption, and more. However, procedural rules are sometimes applied to child welfare cases in ways that do not holistically account for historical and contemporary traumas that families and children face. The application of trans-substantive rules in child welfare cases most severely disadvantages minority children, who are already involved in the system at disproportionate rates.[7] Procedural mechanisms, generally guided by funding requirements, make the modern child welfare system work.

In contrast, the ICWA contains both substantive and procedural requirements that take into account the cultural devastation that state and federal child welfare practices wrought on tribal communities. At its core, the ICWA ensures that Indian children are not removed from their homes and communities without requiring state agencies to take appropriate remedial measures first. The ICWA's substantive mechanisms mandate placement preferences and expert witness testimony in some cases, among other requirements. But procedure plays a major role: the ICWA dictates how a court must serve notice, the type of findings the court must make in the record, standards of review, jurisdiction, and counsel for parents. For these reasons, the ICWA is considered the "gold standard" of child welfare practices.[8] In fact, as this chapter demonstrates, the ICWA has positively influenced the development of state child welfare law, thereby spreading the concept of procedural justice. Some states, such as Michigan and Minnesota, have enacted their own version of the ICWA.[9] Today, Minnesota has strengthened its child welfare code to require placement preferences for all children, including first placement preference considerations to the child's family members.[10] Minnesota is also considering legislation similar to the ICWA that would apply to Black children in the state's child welfare system.[11]

The ICWA's procedural protections—a step toward procedural justice in child welfare—continue to be the bellwether of a revolution in state court procedure and procedural justice, one that unfortunately remains incomplete and under attack.

The Indian Child Welfare Act of 1978 and Procedural Justice

Typically, Congress cannot outright craft child welfare policy and force states to follow the law.[12] However, American Indian children have a special relationship with the federal government. For centuries, the United States Supreme Court has recognized Indian tribes as "domestic dependent nations" to which the federal government owes a trust relationship.[13] Indian tribes, at least those that are federally recognized, are sovereign bodies.[14] As sovereigns, tribes have the ability to make membership determinations. Thus, to be American Indian is not merely a racial classification; it is a political classification.

Prior to 1978, federal and state programs often called for the removal of American Indian children in deadly assimilationist projects aimed to solve the "Indian problem."[15] Oftentimes, government entities allowed and encouraged the removal of children to religious orphanages or boarding schools, where leaders brutalized them in attempts to remove their indigeneity.[16] Because government officials often removed Indian children from their homes during their formative years, Indian children in boarding schools often did not receive education in their culture and native languages, leading to a gap in cultural knowledge and near cultural genocide for many tribes in the United States.[17] Moreover, the boarding school atmosphere—lacking in the attention and affection young children require—also lent itself to harsh physical and sexual abuse.[18] The ICWA was a partial remedy for the genocidal effect of decades of federally sanctioned programs that removed Indian children from their families and communities.[19]

To remedy the violent cultural devastation the removal of Indian children from their homes caused, the ICWA allowed tribes to exercise power over child placement outcomes.[20] In its findings prior to enacting the ICWA, the Senate found that the separation of Indian children from their families created a "socially and culturally" undesirable situation in which Indian children faced the loss of identity.[21] The Senate recognized that the special trust relationship that the US government held with Indian tribes required a remedy for this problem.[22] Therefore, Congress implemented the ICWA, intending to create fairer procedures for Indian children and families that acknowledged their specific cultural needs.

Today, the ICWA governs cases involving both the voluntary placement away from, and the involuntary removal of Indian children from, their families and oftentimes their tribal communities. The ICWA applies to child custody matters in four scenarios: (1) foster care placement; (2) termination of parental rights; (3) pre-adoptive placement; and (4) adoptive placement.[23] The ICWA applies where a child is enrolled in an Indian tribe *or* the child's parent is an enrolled member and the child is eligible for enrollment.[24] The ICWA sets forth procedural requirements that states must, at a minimum, follow in voluntary and involuntary child custody proceedings.[25]

The ICWA is a very narrow, special exception to legal doctrines that place states at the helm of child welfare law and procedure. Because the federal government owes Indian tribes a trust responsibility, Congress has the authority to create laws protecting Indian children and the rights of Indian tribes to maintain their membership.[26]

Because many Native Americans live outside the boundaries of Indian Country, state courts are often involved in child placement decisions from the start, prompting an evaluation of whether the ICWA requires tribal involvement and/or transfer to tribal court. In voluntary and involuntary proceedings, state courts are required to submit notice to a child's presumed tribe when they have reason to know the child is Indian.[27]

The ICWA vests tribes with exclusive jurisdiction in matters where children are domiciled on the reservation.[28] Where a child does not live within reservation boundaries, the ICWA provides for concurrent state and tribal jurisdiction.[29] However, there is a presumption that tribal jurisdiction is the appropriate jurisdiction.[30] In addition to state law and local court rules, where the ICWA applies, the ICWA procedural rules supersede the Federal Rules of Civil Procedure where applicable.

The ICWA also authorizes a transfer of jurisdiction mechanism under which child welfare cases can be transferred to tribal court. Absent good cause to the contrary, absent a parental objection, and upon the tribal court's acceptance, state courts may transfer jurisdiction to tribal courts.[31] That is, the ICWA generally vests original jurisdiction in tribal courts in child welfare matters where Indian children are involved.[32]

Under the ICWA, tribes maintain the right to intervene in dependency proceedings[33] and may intervene at any stage.[34] In addition, Indian tribes and parents of Indian children have the right to collaterally attack a decision where a state court has not complied with the ICWA.[35] As a matter of policy, these provisions exist as a stopgap of sorts because the general lack of ICWA education within many state courts leads to the improper compliance or the rejection of it altogether.

The ICWA also outlines a process, including evidentiary standards that courts must follow in the placement of Indian children. For example, prior to terminating a parent's rights, the state agency must provide preventative, remedial services to parents.[36] Additionally, a court may not terminate a parent's right without first hearing testimony from a qualified expert witness and making a finding *beyond a reasonable doubt* that the parent's continued custody of the child will result in "serious emotional or physical damage to the child."[37] Similarly, where a child is to be placed into foster care, a state court must make similar findings, including testimony from a qualified expert witness, on the record supported by *clear and convincing evidence*.[38] Where a higher evidentiary standard is applicable under federal or state law, the ICWA requires that the court use the higher evidentiary standard to provide the greatest protections of parental rights.[39] Procedurally, the ICWA's evidentiary standards are important because they tend to provide greater protections to parents of Indian children compared to traditional state legal standards.[40]

The ICWA is a remedial measure that requires states to implement substantive and procedural mechanisms that heighten the state's burden when contemplating the removal of Indian children from their families in child welfare proceedings. While the ICWA requires states to use greater caution when removing American Indian children from their families, the ICWA's procedural rules are equitable because the ICWA requires states to conduct a holistic review of the proceedings that considers the child's community. Not only is the ICWA at the crux of tribal development and maintenance and federal Indian policy, it also provides a gold standard for best practices for child welfare.[41]

Lessons in Procedural Justice and Child Welfare in Minnesota

In many ways, Minnesota has long led states in child welfare reform. Minnesota created its first juvenile courts in 1905[42] and was one of the first states to enact a child welfare law.[43] Although Minnesota was progressive in its child welfare initiatives, the state was also a leader in child welfare disparities, as much of its early child welfare policy was rooted in racism and eugenics.[44]

As of 2010, American Indians constitute approximately 1.1 percent of Minnesota's total population.[45] And as of 2017, African American and American Indian children are more likely than white children to experience placement in out-of-home foster care in Minnesota.[46] American Indian children are 18.5 times more likely to be placed in out-of-home care foster care than white children.[47] Similarly, African American children are three times more likely to be placed in out-of-home foster care than white children.[48] However, many of the Minnesota American Indian children who came into care in 2017 were placed under the care of tribal social services.[49] While Minnesota has significant racial disparities in the children its child welfare system serves, Minnesota has once again shown progressive leadership in crafting progressive child welfare policies.

The Minnesota state legislature enacted the Minnesota Indian Family Preservation Act (MIFPA) in 1985.[50] The MIFPA increases the procedural protections that the ICWA provides to Indian children, families, and tribal communities.[51] For example, the ICWA is silent on who constitutes a parent and the procedural mechanism to determine that fact.[52] However, the MIFPA expands the ICWA's notice requirements and outlines a procedural requirement to identify birth fathers of Indian children for the purposes of these proceedings.[53] The MIFPA also expands the situations in which state courts should transfer cases to tribal court absent good cause to the contrary.[54]

The MIFPA complements the ICWA and helps guide state agencies and courts in child welfare cases involving American Indian children.[55] The MIFPA furthers the ICWA's shift toward procedural justice. By filling in some of the gaps that the ICWA leaves open, the MIFPA further ensures fair and equitable process in child welfare proceedings where American Indian children are involved. For example, by expanding notice requirements in cases where a father is unknown, the MIFPA creates a procedural mechanism that speaks directly to a problem area in litigation that involves communities with different concepts of family and marriage than non–American Indian households.

The Minnesota state legislature has also begun to contemplate a law similar to the MIFPA for African American children. In 2019, state senators introduced the Minnesota African American Family Preservation Act (MAAFPA).[56] The goal of this bill is to promote the best interests of African American children and the stability of African American families.[57] The MAAFPA borrows language from the MIFPA and the ICWA.[58] The need for state agencies and courts to refrain from removing a child from their family and working toward family (re)unification where possible is at the crux of the MAAFPA.[59]

As an example of procedural justice, the MAAFPA outlines procedures that reinforce equity, not just symmetricality. Through the MAAFPA, the Minnesota legislature is attempting to solve the problem of the disproportionate number of African American children within its child welfare system through procedural rules that require a holistic application based on the facts of the case at hand. Procedural rules treating all children and families "equally" landed Minnesota in its current child welfare conundrum.

Conclusion

Through its progressive attempts at child welfare law, Minnesota demonstrates why procedural justice, not procedural symmetry, is necessary and how it can exist even in child welfare in contexts outside of Native American tribes. Though the MAAFPA attempts to address child welfare concerns in a manner similar to the MIFPA and the ICWA, the MAAFPA will also go beyond these two other laws to include procedural mechanisms that are wholly distinct from the procedures specific to Indian children. Because the MIFPA and the ICWA rely upon the political status of American Indian children and the trust relationship that the federal government has with Indian tribes, the MAAFPA attempts to apply child welfare procedure equitably to Black children and families. For Native American children and Black children, procedural trans-substantivity and equity are not one and the same. Instead of being a one-of-a-kind set of procedural protections due to the special status of Indian tribes and instead of being a ceiling on the types of procedural protections possible, the MAAFPA shows that the ICWA is just the beginning of looking beyond trans-substantivity toward procedural justice though equitable procedures.

NOTES

Acknowledgment: This chapter is updated and adapted from the article Neoshia Roemer, *Finding Harmony or Swimming in the Void: The Unavoidable Conflict Between the Interstate Compact on the Placement of Children and the Indian Child Welfare Act*, 9 N.D. L. Rev. 149 (2019).

1 Paul Stancil, *Substantive Equality and Procedural Justice*, 102 Iowa L. Rev. 1633, 1653 (2017).

2 *See* Suzette Malveaux, *A Diamond in the Rough: Trans-Substantivity of the Federal Rules of Civil Procedure and Its Detrimental Impact on Civil Rights*, 92 Wash. U. L. Rev. 455, 465 (2014).

3 *See* Stancil, *supra* note 1, at 1660 (discussing how civil actions have changed substantially since 1938).

4 *Id.* at 1684.

5 Black's Law Dictionary, 2d ed., https://thelawdictionary.org (2d edition online).

6 25 U.S.C. §§ 1901–63.

7 *See* Malveaux, *supra* note 2.

8 *See, e.g.*, Memorandum from Casey Family Programs on Notice of Proposed Rulemaking and Regulations for State Courts and Agencies in Indian Custody Proceedings to Elizabeth Appel, Office of Regulatory Affairs & Collaborative Action, Indian Affairs, U.S. Department of the Interior, at 1 (May 19, 2015) (available at www.regulations.gov) ("We believe that ICWA embodies the gold standard for child welfare policies and practices in the United States.").

9 Michigan Indian Family Preservation Act, Mich. Comp. Laws Ann. §§ 712B.1–41 (West 2013); Minnesota Indian Family Preservation Act, Minn. Stat. Ann. §§ 260.751–835 (West 2019).

10 *See* Minn. Stat. Ann. § 260C.181(2) (2001).

11 Minnesota African American Family Preservation Act, S.F. 730, 91st Leg. (Minn. 2019).

12 U.S. Const. amend. X. While child welfare is typically reserved to the states, Congress does stipulate child welfare procedures it wants states to follow through the exercise of its Spending Power and Title IV funds.

13 Cherokee Nation v. Georgia, 30 U.S. 1, 17 (1831).

14 *Id.*

15 Margaret Jacobs, A Generation Removed: The Fostering and Adoption of Indigenous Children in the Postwar World 5 (2014).

16 *Id.* at 13; *see also* Corp. of the Pres. of the Church of Jesus Christ of Latter-Day Saints v. RJ, 221 F.Supp. 3d 1317, 1328 (D. Utah 2016) (declining to declare the Navajo Nation lacked jurisdiction to hear a case filed by former child participant in the Mormon Indian Placement Program, citing physical and sexual abuse in the program where Indian children were placed in Mormon homes).

17 Jacobs, *supra* note 15, at 13.

18 *Id.*

19 25 U.S.C. § 1902.

20 *See id.*

21 Indian Child Welfare Act of 1977, Cmte. on Indian Affairs, S. Rpt. 95–597, at 1–2 (1977) (available at https://narf.org).

22 *Id.*; *see also* Comm. On Interior & Insular Affs., Establishing Standards for the Placement of Indian Children in Foster or Adoptive Homes, to Prevent the Breakup of Indian Families, H.R. Rep. No. 95–1386, at 2 (1978) (available at https://narf.org).

23 25 U.S.C. § 1903(1).

24 *Id.* § 1903(4).

25 *See id.* §§ 1912–13.

26 25 U.S.C. §§ 1901–63.

27 *Id.* at § 1912(a); 25 C.F.R. § 23.112.

28 25 U.S.C. § 1911(b).

29 *Id.*
30 Miss. Band of Choctaw Indians v. Holyfield, 490 U.S. 30, 36 (1989).
31 *Id.*
32 *Id.*; *see also* Watso v. Lourey, 929 F.3d 1024, 1025–26 (8th Cir. 2019).
33 25 U.S.C. § 1911(c).
34 *Id.*
35 *Id.* § 1914.
36 *Id.* § 1912(f).
37 *Id.*
38 *Id.* § 1912(e).
39 *Id.* § 1921.
40 *See* Interest of K.S.D., 904 N.W.2d 479, 486 (N.D. 2017).
41 *See* Memorandum from Casey Family Programs, *supra* note 8.
42 Edward F. Waite, *New Laws for Minnesota Children*, 1 Minn. L. Rev. 48, 48 (1917).
43 Edward N. Clopper, *The Development of the Children's Code*, 98 Annals Am. Acad. Pol. & Soc. Sci. 154, 158 (1921).
44 *See, e.g.*, Waite, *supra* note 42, at 53–54.
45 *See* Minn. Dept. of Human Servs., Populations of Color and American Indians, www.health.state.mn.us (citing 2010 U.S. Census Bureau data).
46 *See* Minn. Dept. of Human Servs. Children and Family Servs., Minnesota's Out-of-Home Care and Permanency Plan Report 9 (2018), https://www.leg.state.mn.us/docs/2018/mandated/181111.pdf.
47 *Id.* at 6.
48 *Id.*
49 *See id.* at 22 (42.8 percent of all American Indian children entering out-of-home placement in 2017 were placed under supervision of tribal social services, while 61.3 percent of all American Indian children continuing in out-of-home placement were under the supervision of tribal social services).
50 Minn. Stat. Ann. § 260.751–835.
51 *Id.* § 260.753.
52 *See* Adoptive Couple v. Baby Girl, 570 U.S. 637, 650 (2013); *see also* Matter of Adoption of B.B., 417 P.3d 1, 26 (Utah 2017).
53 *Compare* Minn. Stat. Ann. § 260.761(4) (West 2015) *with* 25 U.S.C. § 1912(a).
54 Minn. Stat. Ann. § 260.771(3) (West 2015).
55 Minn. Dept. of Human Servs., Indian Child Welfare Manual 1 (2016), www.dhs.state.mn.us.
56 Minnesota African American Family Preservation Act, S.F. 730, 91st Leg. (Minn. 2019). A previous version of this bill was also introduced in 2018. *See* Minnesota African American Family Preservation Act, H.F. 3973, 90th Leg. (Minn. 2018).
57 *Id.* § 2.
58 *Id.* §§ 3(2), 3(5).
59 *Id.* §§ 4–5(a).

PART II

Institutional Anchors in Civil Procedure

The chapters in Part II simultaneously describe and critique the fundamental premises of our civil justice system: due process, equality, access to courts, and the presence of neutral decision makers. These chapters contend that the playing field is tilted in favor of repeat players with money and power. In chapter 10, Norman Spaulding, Barbara Allen Babcock, and Toni Massaro describe the chasm between the idealized, Supreme Court–centric version of civil procedure taught in law school classrooms and the reality of civil litigation in the United States. While our attention is diverted by the Supreme Court, they contend ordinary people are shunted into mandatory arbitration, agency tribunals, or state courts—places where resources for plaintiffs are scarce and bias is rife. The chapters that follow also confront tensions between the ideal and the actual. A. Benjamin Spencer (chapter 11) contends that, while our federal civil justice system is premised on a liberal ethos marked by fairness and justice, a restrictive ethos—one aimed at weeding out the claims of out-groups in favor of dominant groups—is currently ascendant in civil procedure. The excerpt of Nancy Gertner's classic article "Loser's Rules" in chapter 12, drawn from her experience on the federal bench, explains how judges' tendency to write opinions when granting summary judgment—but not when denying summary judgment—has skewed federal discrimination doctrine in a way that is hostile to plaintiffs. Alexander Reinert in chapter 13, drawing on his own experience representing plaintiffs in civil rights litigation, makes the case that the norm of equality—which underpins and legitimizes the civil justice system—is eroding. And in chapter 14, Judith Resnik describes how economic class continues to be a barrier to the participatory parity that is key to the legitimacy of our civil justice system. Each of these authors seeks to re-center fairness, equality, and due process in our courts—not in an abstract and idealized way but in the lived experience of ordinary people.

In addition to questioning the fundamental norms of our civil justice system, Part II turns a critical eye on the two main sources of power in civil procedure: (1) the lawyers, academics, and judges who draft and amend the Federal Rules of Civil Procedure; and (2) the federal judges who interpret the Rules and create their own common law procedural rules. The Supreme Court is at the helm of both of these groups. As for the rule makers, Brooke Coleman's piece "#SoWhiteMale" (chapter 19) critiques the dominant presence of white men—and the complete lack of intersectional members such as Black women—on the Civil Rules Advisory Committee. The remaining chapters highlight the immense power of judges in determining the fate of parties and the law. An excerpt from Elizabeth Thornburg's contribution "(Un)Conscious Judging" (chapter 16) contends that judges—and not only juries—draw factual inferences that shape the course of litigation. Similarly, Victor Quintanilla in chapter 18 draws on Critical Race Theory and social psychology to argue that judges' decisions may reflect racist assumptions, and that judicial decisions may also elaborate and justify those assumptions, thereby embedding racism into precedent and doctrine. Myriam Gilles (chapter 17) shows how recent civil procedural decisions, including Supreme Court decisions as well as amendments to the Federal Rules, function to exclude poor people from the nation's courts. And, Brian Soucek (chapter 15) reflects on the interrelationship between judging and personal identity. He uses the debate over whether a gay judge should recuse himself from a decision regarding gay marriage as a springboard for critiquing the concept of judicial neutrality. The contributors identify problems inherent in a procedural system that accords power to an elite cadre of judges and rule makers, and each calls for the insiders in this system to become aware of—and empathetic to—people and groups outside their elite circle.

10

The Ideal and the Actual in Procedural Due Process

NORMAN W. SPAULDING, BARBARA ALLEN BABCOCK, AND TONI MASSARO

The field of procedure is in danger of slipping into a kind of formalist slumber. Most scholars who teach and write in the field consider ourselves, our classes, and our scholarship to be *quintessentially* realist—we seek to reveal the role of procedure in shaping substantive outcomes, and we insist on attending to the subtleties of facts and design choices in dispute resolution. And yet the procedural law we write about and teach is nothing like what most ordinary Americans experience when they step into court. Indeed, the evidence shows that most people in the US who have legal problems do not ever get to court or receive a meaningful alternative hearing. In this way, the discourse of procedure, even among those who see glaring problems of access to justice, is idealized, abstract, and ossified—unconnected to the actual. As the country has become increasingly diverse, wealth disparities more acute, and the economy declining, this inattention to the actual is dangerous—a threat to the legitimacy of the field.

Part of the problem is that analysis of what is actually happening outside the federal courts in the forums where most ordinary people in the US seek justice tends to begin and end with the study of a handful of canonical procedural due process cases from the so-called due process revolution of the 1960s and 1970s. Judge Friendly's landmark article in 1975 on procedural due process and the administrative state crystalized the spirit of these cases, insisting that adjudications in which most ordinary people in the US participate do not have to be—indeed, cannot be—designed like trials.[1] The highly decentralized, participatory, time-consuming, attorney-run traditions of adversary adjudication have their place, he allowed, but in a mass society there must be procedural tools for the mass processing of claims leavened by minimum guarantees of procedural due process—an impartial decision maker, the right to notice, and a meaningful opportunity to be heard.[2]

Academic and classroom discussions thus tend to gravitate around two issues: whether certain key features of adversarial justice (such as access to a lawyer) are constitutionally mandatory even though a full trial is not, and what exceptional government interests can justify dispensing with either notice or a hearing (or both). At the structural and normative levels, this framing invites comparison between administrative processes (where mass processing is the rule) and the judicial process (where it is supposed to be a closely regulated exception). It also invites either lamentation on the "vanishing trial"—the remarkable late-twentieth-century decline in the number of cases disposed of by trial[3]—or insistence on the imperatives of efficient administration of claims.

But in most procedure casebooks, as in the literature more broadly, analysis of what is actually happening outside the federal courts in the forums where most people in the US litigate is scant. The vanishing-trial theme continues through the study of the Federal Rules of Civil Procedure because many modern doctrines empower a judge to take cases away from juries and, increasingly, to dispose of cases before trial. Some of the challenges associated with mass processing of claims then resurface in the study of joinder and complex litigation. Remarkably, however, the study of how due process works outside the federal courts in the spaces where the vast majority of ordinary people encounter the administration of justice generally does not resurface.

This is a problem because what most people in the US experience is nothing like what the models of either administrative or judicial process describes. There is, in fact, alarming evidence of failure. The more marginal the relevant population of individual claimants, the more systemic the failure, the more inhumane the treatment of litigants appears to be, and the more demoralizing and compromising the position of judges and other decision makers. This chapter describes: the ideal/actual divide; the cognitive, doctrinal, and ideological effects of lingering on the ideal side of it; and the forms of subordination perpetuated on the actual side of both pedagogy and procedural reform from the perspective of the actual.

What Is Ideal Procedure?

Ideal procedure is an abstraction, divorced from the realities of litigation in the spaces most people in the US experience them. First and foremost, it is Olympian. Analysis generally begins with and concentrates (obsessively) on decisions emanating from the United States Supreme Court and amendments to the Federal Rules of Civil Procedure (FRCP) promulgated by the Advisory Committee on Rules of Civil Procedure—a committee staffed through appointments made by the Chief Justice. Both the selection and interpretation of lower federal court cases, administrative agency decisions, and alternative dispute resolution cases are filtered through the lens of Supreme Court precedent even though in every important respect the Supreme Court is the most distant supervisor of the discretionary decision-making and fact-finding of federal and state trial courts, administrative agencies, arbitral fora, and mediations. The administration of justice in the state courts, if it is studied at all, is usually read through the lens of federal procedure, which serves as an ideal type.

Second, although empirical work is burgeoning in the field of procedure, it paradoxically amplifies this top-down interpretive approach by concentrating almost exclusively on measuring the effects of Supreme Court decisions and amendments to the federal rules. Qualitative research is scarce.

Third, the discourse of due process, and therefore of procedure in general, is framed by the structure of an adversary trial even though trials occur in a vanishingly small number of cases—so few as to have rendered the state and federal constitutional right to a jury trial a dead letter for most litigants. Notwithstanding the centrality of the ideal of trial in the conceptualization of due process,[4] many judges have come to view their role as promoting, if not demanding, disposition before trial. As one federal judge famously observed "*a bad settlement is almost always better than a good trial*."[5] Notice the contradiction: The jury trial remains the gold standard of procedural due process, but it almost never happens, and judges believe they have succeeded in their role when trial is avoided. The important public purposes of trial are, as a practical matter, subordinated to the assumed benefits of private settlement and the efficiencies of pretrial disposition.[6] In this way, a jury trial is relegated to the purely ideal.

This is the height of procedural abstraction. We are all potential jurors, but only in trials we know will never happen.

There are, of course, practical reasons for this Olympian orientation. Most obviously, the bar exam tests federal procedure, so law students and law professors must attend to it at some level of specificity. Supreme Court decisions are controlling in federal courts and in the disposition of federal issues by state courts. With respect to the FRCP, as with all twentieth-century codification movements, the Advisory Committee for Civil Rules aspired from the very beginning to generate federal rules that would serve as standards for adoption in the states. The goal of all codification movements is to distill the "best" rules and universalize them in the name of uniformity, interpretive clarity, and predictability. But if there are egalitarian roots to this enterprise in the field of procedure (and there certainly are) there is also no mistaking the elements of centralized, elite, expert control—and these elements have permitted the egalitarianism of the rules to be undercut over time.

The Actual

The actual administration of justice plays out for the most part beyond the federal courts. In 2013, there were more than 16 million cases filed in state courts as compared to only 259,489 filed in federal district courts.[7] That means federal cases comprised *less than 2 percent of all civil cases in the United States*. Mandatory arbitration and agency adjudication compound the reality that federal courts are far from the actual.

State Courts

When we look to state courts, we see vast differences. A typical state court case is a fairly low monetary value dispute in which the defendant is unrepresented and the plaintiff secures a default judgment. Indeed, according to a study by the National Center for State Courts ("Landscape Study"), the "vast majority" are traffic, "debt collection, landlord/tenant, foreclosure, and small claims cases" in which the defendant is unrepresented.[8] Creditors, landlords, employers, and other people in positions of power are generally plaintiffs and prefer state courts "for the simple reason that in most jurisdictions state courts hold a monopoly on procedures to enforce judgments."[9] Moreover, securing judgments is a "mandatory first step to being able to initiate garnishment or asset seizure proceedings."[10] In sum, the state courts are operating primarily as accelerated debt collection courts.

There is generally no merits review or adjudication to speak of—not only no trial, but in the vast number of cases that default, no merits determination *whatsoever*. And there are strong incentives for plaintiff creditors, employers, and landlords to cut corners in giving notice because the likelihood that "gutter service" will be challenged is low. For all of these reasons, the "idealized picture of an adversarial system in which both parties . . . can assert all legitimate claims . . . *is an illusion*."[11]

Creditors who secure a state court judgment can also initiate court supervised "judgment debtor examinations" during which defendants are required to disclose information about their income and assets to satisfy the judgment. Failure to appear can have devastating consequences. An ACLU study found that, in forty-four states, judges "are allowed to issue arrest warrants for failure to appear at post-judgment proceedings or for failure to provide information about finances," and these warrants are issued "on the charge of contempt of court."[12] In this way, the body of the debtor is converted into a surety on the debt by the law of procedure. "Once arrested, debtors may languish in jail for days until they can arrange to pay the bail," in some cases up to two weeks.[13] And judges periodically set bail at the "exact amount of the judgment . . . [so that] the bail money is often turned over to the debt collector or creditor as payment against the judgment."[14] As a lawyer engaged in debt collection against student loan debtors in Texas nonchalantly observed, "*[i]t's easier to settle when the debtor is under arrest*."[15]

This is rough justice by any measure. Indeed, the ACLU report found that many of the people arrested for failure to appear at judgment debtor examinations "had no idea a warrant had been issued for their arrest."[16] And all too frequently the "people who are jailed or threatened with jail . . . are the most vulnerable Americans, living paycheck to paycheck, one emergency away from financial catastrophe."[17] Many already rely on some form of public assistance such as "Social Security, unemployment insurance, disability benefits, or veterans' benefits."[18]

In addition to these questionable collection practices for *private* debts, some state courts have become aggressive about enforcing *court-imposed* fines and fees. As we know from the Department of Justice's *Report on the Ferguson [Missouri] Police Department*, in at least some jurisdictions, overly coercive measures were vigorously pursued on terms that were also racially biased.[19] The municipal court not only failed to address stark racial disparities in policing; it imposed significant fees and other costs, and it regularly jailed city residents for failure to make payments when they did not have the means to pay, creating a vicious, racialized cycle of imprisonment for these debts.

If these and other failures of due process and equal protection seem more closely associated with criminal law than civil procedure, they should not. As the *Ferguson Report* emphasized, many of the underlying citations that initiated the cycle of fines, fees, warrants, and arrests were for noncriminal municipal code violations unconnected to threats to public safety. Moreover, there is evidence that judges on the municipal court treated debtors as a valuable revenue source. In this respect, Ferguson represents a particularly tragic example of municipal and judicial parasitism upon the very communities these institutions are supposed to serve—a perverse outcome of forcing state courts to operate on shoestring budgets.

As with the collection of private debts, a key procedural tool resulting in incarceration for failure to pay criminal or civil assessments in Ferguson and other cities is the use of civil contempt as the basis for issuing a warrant upon a resident's failure to appear. Some courts regularly fail to make the constitutionally required inquiry into a person's ability to pay before punishing failure to appear with arrest and jail time.[20] This specific due process violation became especially draconian in Jennings, Missouri, where the court conducted closed-door, off-the-record, mass hearings for primarily African American debtors. Court hearings for imprisoned debtors took place only once per week, forcing anyone who could not make payments to remain in custody without a constitutionally required inquiry into litigants' ability to pay. Debtors were forced to bid their way out of unconscionable conditions of confinement. The complaint described "overcrowded cells" in which

> impoverished people owing debts to the City . . . are denied toothbrushes, toothpaste, and soap; they are subjected to the stench of excrement and refuse in their congested cells; they are surrounded by walls smeared with mucus, blood, and feces; they are kept in the same clothes for weeks and without access to laundry . . . they step on top of other inmates whose bodies cover nearly the entire uncleaned cell floor, in order to access a single shared toilet that the City does not clean . . . they develop untreated illnesses and infections in open wounds that spread to other inmates . . . they endure days and weeks without being allowed to use the shower; women are not given adequate hygiene products for menstruation . . . they are routinely denied vital medical care and prescription medication . . . they are provided food so insufficient and lacking in nutrition that inmates are forced to compete to performing demeaning janitorial labor for extra food rations and exercise; and they must listen to the screams of other inmates being beaten or tased or in shrieking pain from unattended medical issues . . . [and] jail guards routinely taunt impoverished people when they are unable to pay for their release.[21]

This is "the actual." Justice is administered on terms that produce dehumanization, not a decision on the merits. Remarkably, the *same* court promptly vacated any arrest warrants and conducted its process like the casebooks teach: due process should work if the debtor could afford to retain counsel. These practices not only perpetuate racial subordination and drive people into poverty; they can cause "profound estrangement" in its victims, undermining faith in the rule of law.[22]

Arbitration

The Landscape Study found that "[i]n some instances, the costs of even initiating the lawsuit or making an appearance [in state court] as a defendant would exceed the value of the case."[23] Although arbitration has long been promoted as a more cost-effective procedure, the same problem arises there—boxing ordinary people out of both court and ADR. Plaintiffs frequently cannot afford to pursue their claims in arbitration individually because the money value of their individual claim is simply too small relative to the cost of arbitration. A *New York Times* investigation concluded that, by including contract clauses that ban class actions and mandate arbitration, "companies have essentially disabled consumer challenges to practices like predatory lending, wage theft and discrimination."[24]

In addition to the costs of arbitration, and the fact that consumers and employees are often bound to arbitrate by contracts of adhesion, there is evidence that arbitration procedures and adjudicators tend to favor the powerful companies that draft arbitration clauses into their contracts. Of 1,179 federal class actions filed between 2010 and 2014, which "companies sought to push into arbitration, *judges ruled in their favor in four out of every five cases*."[25] Other studies highlight that "arbitration is more common in low-wage workplaces. It is also more common in industries that are disproportionately composed of women workers and in industries that are disproportionately composed of African American workers."[26]

If there are advantages in an idealized conception of arbitration as compared to litigation (lower cost, faster disposition, direct participation), it matters that these advantages have not been realized in the actual experience of ordinary people. It also matters that the process defects fall disproportionately on already vulnerable and subordinated populations.

Administrative Adjudication

Litigation in court has been displaced not only by arbitration but also by the massive number of adjudications that take place before administrative agencies and never reach a court on appeal.[27] Although agencies enjoy enormous flexibility to permit them to balance enforcement priorities, resource constraints, and statutory mandates, evidence of both systemic bias and delay in flagship federal agencies is easy to find. "[A]berrations from adjudicatory neutrality" are not rare, and not merely "commonplace"; rather, they "represent the fundamental characteristics of the modern administrative process."[28] Critics insist there is "a built-in preference for the position taken by the very agency of which [the adjudicator] is a part."[29]

The administration of asylum and other immigration claims offers a sobering example of process defects with grave human consequences—indefinite detention, family separation, displacement outside the country during pending asylum litigation, judges pressured to rule against asylum claims, and "tent courts" that rely on patchy teleconferencing technology to connect to remotely located immigration judges and severely limit public access and participation by litigants.

With respect to delay, although agencies are touted for their superior efficiency relative to litigation in court, agency adjudication has become notoriously slow in agencies where ordinary people seek to secure public entitlements such as veterans and Social Security disability benefits.[30] People die waiting for resolution of their claims. Parallel problems of bias and delay can be found in state agencies.[31]

These and other data show that the most widely touted and used alternatives to trial are not functioning fairly.

Conclusion

If there was an actual revolution in procedural due process in the mid-twentieth century, it has been undermined by significant counterrevolutionary forces. No modern court system and no alternative adjudicative body appears to have the structure and capacity to efficiently, accurately, and fairly adjudicate the claims that regularly arise in the lives of ordinary people who appear before it. The values that animate procedural due process are not dead, but the divide between ideal and actual procedure today has become dangerously wide.

We believe that the concrete human effects of these forces need to be better understood, and not just within the traditional, relatively antiseptic framework of aggregate efficiency and accuracy. Ordinary people are being driven "to the wall."[32] Doctrinal and quantitative empirical research must therefore be complemented by rigorous qualitative work—"thick description" in the anthropological sense—to surface the social costs of procedural failure paid by those who suffer from it. And what we learn must be taught to law students, unblinkingly. Teaching procedural rules of decision divorced from the experience and testimony of those who have to live with them is trafficking in the very denial of a meaningful opportunity to be heard that due process is supposed to provide.

NOTES

Acknowledgment: This chapter is updated and adapted from the article Norman W. Spaulding, *The Ideal and the Actual in Procedural Due Process*, 48 Hast. Const. L.Q. 101 (2021).

1 Henry J. Friendly, *Some Kind of Hearing*, 123 U. Pa. L. Rev. 1267, 1268 (1975).
2 *See* Norman W. Spaulding, *Due Process Without Judicial Process? Antiadversarialism in American Legal Culture*, 85 Fordham L. Rev. 2249 (2017).
3 Marc Galanter, *The Vanishing Trial: An Examination of Trials and Related Matters in Federal and State Courts*, 1 J. Empirical Legal Stud. 459, 530 (2004); Norman W. Spaulding, *The Enclosure of Justice: Courthouse Architecture, Due Process, and the Dead Metaphor of Trial*, 24 Yale J.L. & Human. 311 (2012) (hereinafter *Enclosure*).
4 *See* Spaulding, *Enclosure*, *supra* note 3.
5 Stephen McG. Bundy, *The Policy in Favor of Settlement in an Adversary System*, 44 Hastings L.J. 1, 4 (1992) (emphasis added) (quoting In re Warner Commc'ns Sec. Litig., 618 F. Supp. 735, 740 (S.D.N.Y. 1985)).
6 *See* Owen M. Fiss, *Against Settlement*, 93 Yale L.J. 1073 (1984).
7 Nat'l Ctr. for State Courts, Civil Justice Initiative: The Landscape of Civil Litigation in State Courts 6 n.36 (2015), www.ncsc.org.
8 *Id.* at v.
9 *Id.*
10 *Id.* at iii–iv; *See also* Justin Weinstein-Tull, *The Structures of Local Courts*, 106 Va. L. Rev. 1031, 1042 (2020).
11 *Id.* (emphasis added).
12 American Civil Liberties Union, A Pound of Flesh: The Criminalization of Private Debt 4–6 (2018), www.aclu.org.
13 *Id.* at 6.
14 *Id.*
15 *Id.* at 7 (emphasis added).
16 *Id.* at 6.
17 *Id.* at 7.
18 *Id.*
19 C.R. Div., U.S. Dep't of Just., Investigation of the Ferguson Police Department (2015) (hereinafter Ferguson Report), https://www.justice.gov.
20 *See* Dan Kopf, *The Fining of Black America*, Priceonomics (June 24, 2016), https://priceonomics.com.
21 Plaintiffs Original Class Action Complaint at 1, 2, Jenkins v. City of Jennings, No. 4:15-cv-00252-CEJ (E.D. Mo. filed Feb. 6, 2015).
22 Monica C. Bell, *Police Reform and the Dismantling of Legal Estrangement*, 126 Yale L.J. 2054, 2057 (2017).
23 Landscape, *supra* note 7, at iv.
24 Jessica Silver-Greenberg & Robert Gebeloff, *Arbitration Everywhere, Stacking the Deck of Justice*, N.Y. Times (Oct. 31, 2015).

25 *Id.* (emphasis added).
26 Alexander J. S. Colvin, *The Growing Use of Mandatory Arbitration*, Econ. Pol'y Inst. (Apr. 6, 2018), https://www.epi.org.
27 Kent Barnett, *Against Administrative Judges*, 49 U.C. Davis L. Rev. 1643, 1652–53 (2016).
28 Martin H. Redish & Kristin McCall, *Due Process, Free Expression, and the Administrative State*, 94 Notre Dame L. Rev. 297, 298–99 (2018).
29 *Id.* at 299.
30 VA Office of Inspector Gen., Veterans Health Administration: Review of Alleged Mismanagement at the Health Eligibility Center 9 (2015), www.oversight.gov.
31 Michael Grabell & Howard Berkes, *The Demolition of Workers' Comp*, ProPublica (Mar. 4, 2015), https://www.propublica.org.
32 Sniadach v. Fam. Finance Corp., 395 U.S. 337, 342 (1969).

11

The Restrictive Ethos in Civil Procedure

A. BENJAMIN SPENCER

Those of us who study civil procedure are familiar with the notion that federal civil procedure under the 1938 Rules was generally characterized by a "liberal ethos," meaning that it was originally designed to promote open access to the courts and to facilitate a resolution of disputes on the merits.[1] Most of us are also aware of the fact that the reality of procedure is not always access-promoting or fixated on merits-based resolutions as a priority. Indeed, I would say that a "restrictive ethos" prevails in procedure today, with many rules being developed, interpreted, and applied in a manner that frustrates the ability of claimants to prosecute their claims and receive a decision on the merits in federal court.

* * *

There are two sides to civil procedure. The first is access-promoting and favors resolution of disputes on the merits. The other is more restrictive and cost-conscious, creating various doctrines that frustrate the assertion and prosecution of potentially meritorious claims. In other words, much of procedure is expressly directed not at the traditional goal of facilitating accurate outcomes but rather is designed and applied to frustrate or at least subordinate accuracy in certain contexts where efficiency of some sort or the interests of certain litigants are at stake.

These two sides of procedure coexist, although their opposing tendencies create a tension that cries for resolution. Resolution of this tension may be found in realizing that the liberal ethos and the restrictive ethos are dialectically related. That is, the basic thesis of procedure, its liberal ethos, yields its antithesis, the restrictive ethos, and the two can be reconciled through a synthesis that helps us understand how these seemingly contradictory attitudes cooperate toward a unified, more fundamental goal.

Professor Stephen Subrin has already demonstrated how the liberal aspects of civil procedure—which are primarily rooted in historical equity practices—resulted in a system that so favored access that certain observers felt the need to introduce the array of access-restricting reforms.[2] That is, the pursuit and realization of the liberal ethos is the very thing that generates its antithesis, the restrictive ethos; the goals promoted by the liberal ethos generate a systemic need for countervalues that can address the challenging or burdensome products of the liberal procedural ideal. Greater access to courts naturally increases the volume of litigation the system must handle and presents a greater opportunity to put forth claims asserting seemingly tenuous or disfavored rights. Seeking the resolution of disputes on their merits requires permitting parties a degree of freedom in asserting and establishing their claims that can subject adversaries and the courts to lengthy and expensive processes and proceedings. The costs and burdens seemingly imposed on courts and defending parties by the liberal ethos give rise to a collection of countervalues that seek to suppress the volume of claims and facilitate courts' ability to manage and dispose of claims sooner and more efficiently than a truly merits-centered system might allow.[3] In sum, access, simplicity, and affordability generate an overwhelming volume of (to some, undesirable) litigation activity[4] that restrictive values are designed to suppress.[5]

So on one level, the synthesis of the liberal ethos and the restrictive ethos might be in the nature of a checks-and-balances relationship: the restrictive ethos checks the excesses of the liberal ethos and vice versa. I believe, however, there is more to it than that. Although the checks-and-balances concept might accurately describe the relationship between the liberal and restrictive aspects of civil procedure in some respects, in reality it seems that the liberal ethos is in many respects overshadowed by the restrictive.[6] That is, although one can identify those liberal aspects of procedure in contemporary rules and doctrines, the restrictive ethos in procedure appears ascendant and poised for dominance. The United States Supreme Court's capitulation to defendant requests for more stringent pleading standards in *Bell Atlantic Corp. v. Twombly* and *Ashcroft v. Iqbal* is the clearest evidence of procedure's tilt toward restrictiveness. In *Twombly*, the Court was unashamed to cite discovery abuse as a ground for preventing plaintiffs from proceeding to discovery on the basis of equivocal pleading that might have satisfied *Conley v. Gibson*'s "no set of facts" standard.[7] In light of the zeal with which lower courts have embraced a restrictive interpretation of *Twombly*,[8] and the Court's reinforcement of restrictive pleading standards in *Iqbal*,[9] many litigants now face a potentially substantial obstacle to accessing the system to assert their claims. The Class Action Fairness Act, the narrow view of personal jurisdiction in the internet context, the discovery-scope amendment, and limitations on the discovery of burdensome electronically stored information all additionally evince the dominance of restrictiveness, and together these reflect the culmination of a move toward restrictiveness begun with the counterrevolutionary changes to Rule 16, Rule 11, and summary judgment that appeared only a generation ago.[10]

Given the simultaneous presence of a dominant restrictive ethos and the visible vestiges of the liberal ethos within civil procedure, I would describe the synthesis of the two not merely as a checks-and-balances relationship. Rather, the restrictive ethos enables the civil justice system to survive by reducing the number of disfavored actions that burden the system, while the more popularly known liberal ethos takes on the role of generating and sustaining the legitimacy of, and faith in, the civil justice system in the eyes of the public at large. In other words, procedure's central thesis (the liberal ethos) and antithesis (the restrictive ethos) can be synthesized into a concept I refer to as "ordered dominance": procedure's overarching, unified goal is to facilitate and validate the substantive outcomes desired by society's dominant interests; procedure's veneer of fairness and neutrality maintains support for the system, while its restrictive doctrines weed out disfavored actions asserted by members of social out-groups and ensure desired results.[11]

By "dominant interests" I mean the commercial class that uses the courts to litigate traditional claims such as contract or property disputes or who encounter the courts as civil defendants in all kinds of disputes. This group is important to the national economy and has the means and clout to influence policy makers at all levels of government. Civil procedure tends to favor the interests of these groups by keeping restrictive procedural doctrines (such as heightened pleading) from interfering with the resolution of ordinary commercial disputes[12] and by protecting commercial defendants against claims by members of various out-groups.

By "out-groups" I mean "those outside the political and cultural mainstream, particularly those challenging accepted legal principles and social norms. . . . [T]hose raising difficult and often tenuous claims that demand the reordering of established political, economic and social arrangements, that is, those at the system's and society's margins."[13] Dominant interests retain control over the mechanisms that control civil procedure, namely, the federal judiciary and derivatively the membership of the federal rulemaking committees.[14] In turn, those controlling the development of procedure since the 1970s have tended to prefer anti-access reforms that stymie the efforts of social out-groups to use the federal courts to vindicate their interests.[15] These anti-access reforms—particularly stricter pleading and looser summary judgment standards—favor pretrial dispositions that ultimately keep resolution of these claims out of the hands of representative juries and firmly within the control of judicial elites.

The idea of "disfavored actions" is already familiar. Allegations of fraud have been treated as disfavored for various reasons, and thus the Federal Rules have always required that such claims be pleaded with particularity.[16] Other actions have been disfavored as well; malicious prosecution, civil rights claims, securities claims, and antitrust claims have been treated by various courts throughout the history of the Federal Rules as disfavored and thus warranting a heightened pleading standard.[17] Such claims have been singled out for disproportionate scrutiny under Rule 11 as well.[18] Employment discrimination claims also seem to be disfavored given that summary judgment motions by defendants in such cases are relatively more likely to succeed.[19]

The idea of ordered dominance that I have described is certainly an oversimplification and likely fails to describe the whole of civil procedure accurately. However, it cannot be gainsaid that procedure today is recognized by all the relevant players—the rule makers, the judiciary, members of Congress, interested lobbyists—as being vitally connected with substantive policy interests and that some of those same players have consciously tinkered with (or manipulated) procedural rules or doctrines with a clear understanding of their likely impact on certain substantive policy ends.[20] Given that fact, it does not take much more investigation to reach the ordered-dominance thesis; none of the aforementioned players represent members of societal out-groups but rather are drawn from or represent privileged elites.[21] Although some among this group may fight for the interests of the out-groups when waging procedural battles, the restrictive regulatory and doctrinal outputs of procedural reform do not reveal much evidence in support of such a notion. To the contrary, modern procedural reforms, either through rulemaking, congressional intervention, or judicial interpretation, have bent toward the restrictive ethos, which undeniably has favored society's dominant interests as defined above.

* * *

Many may chafe at the idea of ordered dominance, given its seeming inconsistency with our traditional rhetoric of fair play, due process, and a day in court. Indeed, members of societal out-groups who are disadvantaged by the contemporary procedural regime may find the suggestion that civil procedure's restrictive ethos dominates its advertised liberal components particularly disheartening. But despondency is not the proper response to developing an understanding of the regime of ordered dominance revealed above. To the contrary, enlightenment is empowering; with a clear view of procedure one can articulate and advocate for appropriate reforms or, more likely, resist those reforms that are likely to further entrench the regime of ordered dominance.

Beyond enlightenment and empowerment, there is additional cause for hope. The concepts of access, fairness, and accuracy are powerful and deeply held ideals that likely enjoy universal public support. As long as these ideals remain part of the overall procedural scheme—whether as mere rhetoric or as actual working principles—there is a base from which more progressive reformers can argue that beneath the rhetoric of litigation abuses and explosions lay individual litigants with grievances that have a right to be heard. The US commitment to justice and fairness can form a wellspring of devotion to the ideal that those who have been wronged should have access to a system that will right those wrongs and the belief that substantive rights should not be smoldered simply by the conniving of procedure. The challenge is to translate these popular notions into procedural realities, particularly in the context of a court system that has limited time and resources to afford all civil disputants any and every procedural opportunity they might wish to enjoy. In time, perhaps, like all historical regimes, procedure's empire of ordered dominance too will come to an end.

NOTES

Acknowledgment: This chapter is updated and adapted from the article A. Benjamin Spencer, *The Restrictive Ethos in Civil Procedure*, 78 Geo. Wash. L. Rev. 353 (2010).

1 Richard L. Marcus, *The Revival of Fact Pleading Under the Federal Rules of Civil Procedure*, 86 Colum. L. Rev. 433, 439 (1986).

2 *See* Stephen N. Subrin, *How Equity Conquered Common Law: The Federal Rules of Civil Procedure in Historical Perspective*, 135 U. Pa. L. Rev. 909, 982 (1987).

3 *See, e.g.*, Jeffrey W. Stempel, *Politics and Sociology in Federal Civil Rulemaking: Errors of Scope*, 52 Ala. L. Rev. 529, 537–38 (2001).

4 Deborah R. Hensler, Nicholas M. Pace, Bonnie Dombey-Moore, Elizabeth Giddens, Jennifer Gross, Erik Moller, Rand Inst. for Civil Justice, Class Action Dilemmas: Pursuing Public Goals for Private Gain 49 (2000); Subrin, *supra* note 2, at 912, 944.

5 Professor Yamamoto described the obstructionist perspective on the suppression of undesirable litigation well when he wrote: "From a utilitarian perspective, some indignity suffered by a minority of the populace [denied access to the courts] is an unavoidable and tolerable result of system shrinkage in the interest of efficiency." Eric K. Yamamoto, *Efficiency's Threat to the Value of Accessible Courts for Minorities*, 25 Harv. C.R.-C.L. L. Rev. 341, 390 (1990).

6 This observation echoes that of Professor Walker, who recently opined that various common-law procedural doctrines, the so-called "Other Rules [of civil procedure] interact with the 1938 Rules in such a way as to counter the apparent progressive character of the 1938 Rules and produce a functioning system which is not progressive in reality but conservative." Laurens Walker, *The Other Federal Rules of Civil Procedure*, 25 Rev. Litig. 79, 80–81 (2006) (footnote omitted).

7 Bell Atl. Corp. v. Twombly, 550 U.S. 544, 559–563 (2007).

8 *See* A. Benjamin Spencer, *Pleading Civil Rights Claims in the Post-*Conley *Era*, 52 How. L.J. 99, 141–55 (2008).

9 Ashcroft v. Iqbal, 556 U.S. 662, 679 (2009).

10 Of course, restrictive impulses within the Federal Rules did not originate entirely within the past thirty years. The drafters were aware of the breadth of the system that they were creating and included measures such as the summary judgment device as one way to hold the line against the tenuous claims that their liberal pleading rules might allow. *See* Stephen B. Burbank, *Vanishing Trials and Summary Judgment in Federal Civil Cases: Drifting Toward Bethlehem or Gomorrah?*, 1 J. Empirical Legal Stud. 591, 603 (2004). By emphasizing the more recent developments in the direction of restrictiveness, I simply mean to suggest that explicit commitment to the restrictive ethos appears to have, over time, intensified, gained strength, and come to dominate those provisions that would otherwise be access-promoting in the Federal Rules.

11 As I explain below, I do not define the conflict between dominant interests and social out-groups in purely racialized, black-white terms, although others have

done so. *See, e.g.*, Roy L. Brooks, *Critical Race Theory: A Proposed Structure and Application to Federal Pleading*, 11 Harv. BlackLetter L.J. 85, 111 (1994) ("Society and its institutions, including its legal system, express a white world-view, a perspective that necessarily operates to the benefit of whites at the expense of people of color. The federal courts' treatment of civil rights claims, including Rule 11 sanctions, is merely further evidence of this built-in bias." [footnote omitted]). Racial minorities asserting certain claims certainly fit within the out-group category, but other groups, not defined simply by race (e.g., women, gay people, the elderly, consumers, small investors), fall within this category as well.

12 Yamamoto, *supra* note 5, at 345 ("[The] procedural system [is] hospitable to litigants with disputes involving well-settled legal principles.").

13 *Id.*

14 It is worth noting that since the appointment of Chief Justice Warren Burger in 1969, the Chief Justices—and thus the persons in control of the membership of the various rulemaking committees—have been appointed by Republican presidents, who have tended to support litigation-reform efforts more than the interests of pro-plaintiff trial attorneys and consumer groups. *See, e.g.*, Edward A. Purcell, Jr., *The Class Action Fairness Act in Perspective: The Old and the New in Federal Jurisdictional Reform*, 156 U. Pa. L. Rev. 1823, 1899 (2008) ("During Reagan's presidency, Republicans introduced 'tort reform' bills in Congress with increasing frequency. . . ."); Stephen Labaton, *Bush Calls for Change in Handling Asbestos Lawsuits*, N.Y. Times, Jan. 8, 2005, at A12. Professor Burbank points out that the Civil Rules Committee is dominated by judges rather than members of the bar, an imbalance that might put too heavy a thumb on the scale in favor of institutional interests that may favor only certain kinds of procedural reform. *See* Stephen B. Burbank, *Procedure, Politics and Power: The Role of Congress*, 79 Notre Dame L. Rev. 1677, 1714–15 (2004) ("Under Chief Justice Warren Burger, however, the Civil Rules Advisory Committee came to be heavily dominated by judges selected by the Chief Justice. This imbalance has continued. . . .").

15 Yamamoto, *supra* note 5, at 345 ("Reforms that discourage court access for minorities asserting 'marginal' rights claims reflect value judgments about the purposes of adjudication and the desirability of broad-based participation in the litigation process.").

16 Fed. R. Civ. P. 9(b); 5A Charles Alan Wright & Arthur R. Miller, Federal Practice & Procedure: Civil § 1296 (3d ed. 2004).

17 *See* Marcus, *supra* note 1, at 471–72.

18 Georgene M. Vairo, *Rule 11: A Critical Analysis*, 118 F.R.D. 189, 200 (1988) ("Rule 11 is being used disproportionately against plaintiffs, particularly in certain types of litigation such as civil rights [cases], employment discrimination [cases], securities fraud cases brought by investors, and antitrust cases brought by small companies.").

19 *See* Kevin M. Clermont & Stewart J. Schwab, *Employment Discrimination Plaintiffs in Federal Court: From Bad to Worse?*, 3 Harv. L. & Pol'y Rev. 103, 128

(2009) ("[P]retrial adjudication particularly disfavors employment discrimination plaintiffs."); *cf.* Joe S. Cecil, Rebecca N. Eyre, Dean Miletich & David Rindskopf, *A Quarter-Century of Summary Judgment Practice in Six Federal District Courts*, 4 J. Empirical Legal Stud. 861, 886–89 (2007) (noting the rise of summary judgment grants to defendants in civil rights cases, which presumably include employment discrimination claims).

20 *See* Burbank, *supra* note 14, at 1703–06 (2004) (describing Congress's increasing involvement in tinkering with civil procedure as it came to understand procedure's impact on its substantive policy goals); Richard L. Marcus, *Of Babies and Bathwater: The Prospects for Procedural Progress*, 59 Brook. L. Rev. 761, 771–76 (1993) (discussing politicization of procedure and the "hidden agendas" of some rule reformers who seek to further their own substantive interests through civil litigation reform).

21 For example, a cursory look at the membership of the current Advisory Committee on Civil Rules, which is available at www.uscourts.gov, reveals the presence of only one plaintiffs' attorney and one judge who was appointed to the bench by a Democrat. Defense lawyers, former prosecutors, and Republican-appointed judges (a good number of whom clerked for Chief Justice Rehnquist) dominate the committee.

12

Losers' Rules

NANCY GERTNER

Each year, the United States District Court for the District of Massachusetts holds an extraordinary panel. All active judges are present to answer questions from the bar. A lawyer's question one year was particularly provocative: "Why are the federal courts so hostile to discrimination claims?" One judge after another insisted that there was no hostility. All they were doing when they dismissed employment discrimination cases was following the law—nothing more, nothing less.

I disagreed. Federal courts, I believed, *were* hostile to discrimination cases. Although the judges may have thought *they* were entirely unbiased, the outcomes of those cases told a different story. The law judges felt "compelled" to apply had become increasingly problematic. Changes in substantive discrimination law since the passage of the Civil Rights Act of 1964[1] were tantamount to a virtual repeal. This was so not because of *Congress*; it was because of *judges*.

Decades ago, law-and-society scholars offered an explanation for that phenomenon, evaluating the structural forces at work in law-reform litigation that lead to one-sided judicial outcomes. Focusing on employment discrimination claims, Marc Galanter argued that, because employers are "repeat players" whereas individual plaintiffs are not, the repeat players have every incentive to settle the strong cases and litigate the weak ones.[2] Over time, strategic settlement practices produce judicial interpretations of rights that favor the repeat players' interests.[3] More recently, Catherine Albiston went further, identifying the specific opportunities for substantive rulemaking in this litigation—as in summary judgment and motions to dismiss—and how the repeat players take advantage of them.[4]

Drawing on my seventeen years on the federal bench, I attempt to provide a firsthand and more detailed account of employment discrimination law's skewed evolution—the phenomenon I call "Losers' Rules." I begin with a discussion of the wholly one-sided legal doctrines that characterize discrimination law. In effect, today's plaintiff stands to lose unless he or she can prove that the defendant had explicitly discriminatory policies in place or that the relevant actors were overtly biased. It is hard to imagine a higher bar or one less consistent with the legal standards developed after the passage of the Civil Rights Act, let alone with the way discrimination manifests itself in the twenty-first century. Although ideology may have something to do with these changes, I explore another explanation: asymmetric decision-making—where judges are encouraged to write detailed decisions *granting* summary judgment but not when *denying* it—fundamentally changes the lens through which employment cases are viewed, in two respects. First, it encourages judges to see employment discrimination cases as trivial or frivolous, as decision after decision details why the plaintiff loses. And second, it leads to the development of decision heuristics—the Losers' Rules—that serve to justify prodefendant outcomes and thereby exacerbate the one-sided development of the law.

The Skewed Evolution of Discrimination Law

Just as the social-psychological literature is exploding with studies about implicit race and gender bias,[5] federal discrimination law lurches in the opposite direction, often ignoring or trivializing evidence of explicit bias. And just as empirical studies highlight the stubborn persistence of discrimination at all levels of jobs and in salaries,[6] federal discrimination law assumes the opposite. In summary judgment decisions, judges search for explicitly discriminatory policies and rogue actors; failing to find them, they dismiss the cases. It is as if the bench is saying: "Discrimination is over. The market is bias-free. The law's task is to find the aberrant individual who just did not get the memo." Thus, the law reduces the complex phenomenon of discrimination into a simple paradigm of the errant discriminator or the explicitly biased policy, a paradigm that rarely matches the reality of discrimination in the twenty-first century.[7]

Even without the contrary insights of social psychologists, this development is curious. Discrimination cases are about intent—in the language of the statute, whether an action was taken "because of" race or gender bias.[8] Proof of intent is rarely direct. It is usually circumstantial, even multidetermined. In tort or contract cases, contests about intent require jury trials, because judges recognize that divining a person's intent is messy and complex and usually involves a material dispute of fact for a jury to decide. Employment discrimination cases, by contrast, are typically resolved on summary judgment,[9] although discriminatory intent may be even more difficult to identify on a cold record than is the intent of a contract's drafters or a putative tortfeasor's state of mind.

Is the explanation solely an ideological one—a more conservative bench, and in particular a more conservative United States Supreme Court, far less supportive of antidiscrimination laws than it was in the past? That is surely part of it. But these outcomes cut across the ideological spectrum, applying equally to judges who would describe themselves as sympathetic to discrimination claims. Judges, as the District of Massachusetts panel reflected, feel that the law "compels" them to decide cases as they do. But the "law" hardly compels anything in this context. Employment discrimination cases, after all, are factually complex, deal with state-of-mind issues, are typically proved circumstantially, and are rarely uncontested. The Supreme Court's legal standards for summary judgment are so general that, for the most part, they merely provide a way to organize the record and frame the issues but rarely mandate a result as would, for example, a statute of limitations or a failure to exhaust administrative remedies. Rather, the source of the law's "compulsion" is, at least in part, Losers' Rules.

The Role of Asymmetric Decision-making

When the defendant successfully moves for summary judgment in a discrimination case, the case is over. Under Rule 56 of the Federal Rules of Civil Procedure, the judge must "state on the record the reasons for granting or denying the motion."[10] But when the plaintiff prevails, the judge typically writes a single word of endorsement—"denied"—and the case moves on to trial. Of course, nothing prevents the judge from writing a formal decision, but given caseload pressures, few federal judges do.[11]

The result of this practice—written decisions only when plaintiffs lose—is the evolution of a one-sided body of law. Decision after decision grants summary judgment to the defendant or, on the heels of *Twombly*[12] and *Iqbal*,[13] dismisses the complaint. After the district court has described—cogently and persuasively, perhaps even for publication—why the plaintiff loses, the case may or may not be appealed. If it is not, it stands as yet another compelling account of a flawed discrimination claim. If it is appealed, the odds are good that on appeal the circuit court will affirm the district court's pessimistic assessment of the plaintiff's case.[14]

While the standard of review of summary judgment orders is *de novo*, appellate courts rarely reverse district courts' decisions.[15] It takes substantial work, not to mention a motivated decision maker, to dig into a voluminous summary judgment record and find a contested issue of fact. In my experience, few appellate court judges are so motivated. On the contrary, they are even more affected than are district court judges by the skewed pool of cases they see—the selection effects of reviewing appeal after appeal of plaintiffs' losses. They do not see the strong cases that settle. They may see appeals from successful plaintiffs' verdicts, but those appeals are few and far between. What they mainly see is a litany of losing cases, each resolved on summary judgment for the defendant.

Although judges do not publish all the opinions they write, the ones they do exacerbate the asymmetry. Advocates seeking authority for their positions will necessarily find many more published opinions in which courts granted summary judgment for the employer than for the employee. And although one would expect that plaintiffs would realize that their chances are slim and stop filing, dockets prove otherwise. Plaintiffs continue to believe in the fairness of the system, notwithstanding their odds, and flood the courts with claims.

But the problem is more than just the creation of one-sided precedent that other judges follow; the precedent also fundamentally changes the way judges view these cases. If case after case recites facts that do not amount to discrimination, it is no surprise that the decision makers have a hard time envisioning the facts that may well comprise discrimination. Worse, they may come to believe that most claims are trivial.

Statistics tell the story. A recent Federal Judicial Center report noted that roughly 60 percent of all summary judgment motions studied were granted in whole or in part, while more than 70 percent of such motions were granted in employment discrimination cases.[16] From 1994 to 1995, "employers prevailed in approximately 86% of published appellate opinions."[17]

One-Sided Heuristics: Losers' Rules

In addition to contributing to one-sided outcomes, the asymmetry of the decision-making process distorts the evolution of substantive legal standards. Losers' Rules evolve to justify the judicial analysis. Losers' Rules are heuristics, "simplistic, rule-like tests developed by the courts" to deal with otherwise complex cases in a more efficient manner.[18] They are particularly useful for organizing incomplete data,[19] such as those found in most summary judgment records. Although heuristics develop across many areas of the law and at many stages, the growing use of summary judgment in civil litigation in general,[20] and its increased use in employment discrimination cases in particular, make such "rule-like tests" all the more important. Thus, a pattern emerges. Courts create decision heuristics to enable them to quickly dispose of complex cases. They then write decisions employing the heuristics and publish their opinions. In short order, other courts rely on the heuristics, which become precedent, and the process is repeated over and over again.[21]

The problem with heuristics, however, is that they are subject to systematic errors in all directions.[22] In the context of employment discrimination cases, false positives occur when a court finds that there may have been discrimination when there was not, and false negatives occur when a court finds no discrimination when there was. When courts believe that most employment claims are without merit, as the decisional law suggests, they will be far more concerned with false positives than false negatives. One-sided heuristics—rules of thumb that oversimplify, dismiss, and often demean proof of discrimination—evolve. Sometimes their inculcation is explicit. At the start of my judicial career in 1994, the trainer teaching discrimination law to new judges announced, "Here's how to get rid of civil rights cases," then went on to recite a litany of Losers' Rules.

In *Iqbal* and *Twombly*, the Supreme Court effectively invited judges to use discrimination heuristics earlier in the litigation process than before, with far, far less information.[23] Both cases involved a motion to dismiss the complaint under Rule 12(b)(6). The *Iqbal* Court encouraged judges to use their "common sense" and "judicial experience" to determine when claims are "plausible,"[24] rather than to apply the far more objective notice pleading standards that predated these decisions.[25] Under notice pleading, courts asked whether any set of facts could be proven consistent with the allegations in the complaint.[26] Under *Iqbal* and *Twombly*, they are to determine whether alternative explanations for the events complained of are "more likely" than the allegations made by the plaintiff,[27] a probabilistic determination, despite the Court's disclaimer.

The Court's motivation could not have been clearer. It was concerned only about false positives, not false negatives that leave meritorious claims of discrimination unredressed. It focused expressly on the transaction costs to defendants that such claims engender, not the impact on the plaintiffs whose claims are given short shrift.[28] Its approach was compelled by the perception that case management, as the Court noted, had not been particularly effective in addressing the problem of insubstantial claims and had thus failed to control litigation expenses.[29]

But while it is one thing to be concerned about the limits of case management with respect to complex antitrust cases such as *Twombly*, it is another to be concerned in connection with civil rights cases such as *Iqbal*, where summary judgment has been wildly successful for employers and other defendants. *Iqbal* and *Twombly* have not yet produced wholesale dismissal of employment discrimination complaints,[30] but, given employment discrimination heuristics and precedent in other fields, that is a fair prediction.

More employment heuristics—more Losers' Rules—have evolved, the net effect of which has been to make summary judgment in the employer's favor increasingly likely.

Conclusion

Losers' Rules provide a blueprint for judges to grant defendants summary judgment or to dismiss complaints. Courts recite these "rules" in case after case, without regard to context and without examination. And, as did the judges in Massachusetts, judges truly believe that they are "just following the rules."

What to do about it? First, the problem has to be named: judges have made rules that have effectively gutted Title VII. These rules are not required by the statute, its legislative history, or the purposes of the Civil Rights Act. Second, the problem has to be addressed directly. Congress could, for example, amend Title VII to make its prohibitions more explicit. Alternatively, judicial education programs can train judges not on how to "get rid" of these cases, but rather on how to analyze the merits in a way that reminds the decision makers what the law was designed to reform in the first place. And finally, to address the asymmetry, courts must write decisions when they deny defendant motions for summary judgment—if only to show what counts as discrimination and not simply what does not.

NOTES

Acknowledgment: This chapter is updated and adapted from the article Nancy Gertner, *Losers' Rules*, 122 Yale L.J. Online 109 (2012):

1 Pub. L. No. 88–352, 78 Stat. 241 (codified as amended in scattered sections of 42 U.S.C.).

2 Marc Galanter, *Why the "Haves" Come Out Ahead: Speculations on the Limits of Legal Change*, 9 Law & Soc'y Rev. 95, 101 (1974).

3 *Id.* at 102.

4 Catherine Albiston, *The Rule of Law and the Litigation Process: The Paradox of Losing by Winning*, 33 Law & Soc'y Rev. 869, 877–86 (1999).

5 *See, e.g.*, John T. Jost, Laurie A. Rudman, Irene V. Blair, Dana R. Carney, Nilanjana Dasgupta, Jack Glaser & Curtis D. Hardin, *The Existence of Implicit Bias Is Beyond Reasonable Doubt: A Refutation of Ideological and Methodological Objections and Executive Summary of Ten Studies That No Manager Should Ignore*, 29 Res. Organizational Behav. 39 (2009); *see also* Anthony G. Greenwald & Linda Hamilton Krieger, *Implicit Bias: Scientific Foundations*, 94 Calif. L. Rev. 945, 946 (2006); Jonathan C. Ziegert & Paul J. Hanges, *Employment Discrimination: The Role of Implicit Attitudes, Motivation, and a Climate for Racial Bias*, 90 J. Applied Psych. 553 (2005).

6 *See, e.g.*, Majority Staff of Joint Econ. Comm., 111th Cong., Women And The Economy 2010: 25 Years Of Progress But Challenges Remain 1 (2010); Nathan Berg & Donald Lien, *Measuring the Effect of Sexual Orientation on Income: Evidence of Discrimination?*, 20 Contemp. Econ. Pol'y 394, 394 (2002); Marianne Bertrand & Sendhil Mullainathan, *Are Emily and Greg More Employable than Lakisha and Jamal? A Field Experiment on Labor Market Discrimination*, 94 Am. Econ. Rev. 991, 1006–07 (2004); Catherine Rampell, *Older Workers Without Jobs Face Longest Time Out of Work*, N.Y. Times: Economix (May 6, 2011, 6:27 PM), http://economix.blogs.nytimes.com.

7 *See* Elizabeth M. Schneider, *The Dangers of Summary Judgment: Gender and Federal Civil Litigation*, 59 Rutgers L. Rev. 705, 709 (2007); Michael J. Zimmer, *Slicing & Dicing of Individual Disparate Treatment Law*, 61 La. L. Rev. 577 (2001).

8 *See* 42 U.S.C. § 2000e-2(a)(1) (2006).
9 *See, e.g.*, Memorandum from Joe Cecil & George Cort, Fed. Judicial Ctr., to Judge Michael Baylson, U.S. Dist. Court for the E. Dist. of Pa. 7 tbl.4 (Nov. 2, 2007), www.fjc.gov.
10 Fed. R. Civ. P. 56(a).
11 During one case-management program in my district, the trainer, a senior judge, told the assembled judges, "If you write a decision, you have failed." The message was clear: you would write a decision only when you absolutely had to.
12 Bell Atl. Corp. v. Twombly, 550 U.S. 544, 570 (2007).
13 Ashcroft v. Iqbal, 556 U.S. 662, 678–83 (2009).
14 *See* Kevin M. Clermont, Theodore Eisenberg & Stewart J. Schwab, *How Employment-Discrimination Plaintiffs Fare in the Federal Courts of Appeals*, 7 Emp. Rts. & Emp. Pol'y J. 547, 553 (2003).
15 Richard L. Steagall, *The Recent Explosion in Summary Judgments Entered by the Federal Courts Has Eliminated the Jury from the Judicial Power*, 33 S. Ill. U. L.J. 469, 470 (2009); *see also* Ann C. McGinley, *Credulous Courts and the Tortured Trilogy: The Improper Use of Summary Judgment in Title VII and ADEA Cases*, 34 B.C. L. Rev. 203, 207 n.15 (1993).
16 Memorandum from Joe Cecil & George Cort, Fed. Judicial Ctr., to Judge Michael Baylson, U.S. Dist. Court for the E. Dist. of Pa. (rev. June 15, 2007), http://ftp.resource.org (reporting statistics for summary judgment in 78 jurisdictions).
17 Albiston, *supra* note 4, at 885.
18 Hillary A. Sale, *Judging Heuristics*, 35 U.C. Davis L. Rev. 903, 906 (2002).
19 *See* Amos Tversky & Daniel Kahneman, *Judgment Under Uncertainty: Heuristics and Biases*, 185 Science 4157 1124, 1124 (1974).
20 *See, e.g.*, Arthur R. Miller, *The Pretrial Rush to Judgment: Are the "Litigation Explosion," "Liability Crisis," and Efficiency Cliches Eroding Our Day in Court and Jury Trial Commitments?*, 78 N.Y.U. L. Rev. 982, 1048–50 (2003).
21 *See, e.g.*, Stephen M. Bainbridge & G. Mitu Gulati, *How Do Judges Maximize? (The Same Way Everybody Else Does—Boundedly): Rules of Thumb in Securities Fraud Opinions*, 51 Emory L.J. 83, 112–18 (2002) (complex securities litigation context).
22 *See* Tversky & Kahneman, *supra* note 19, at 1124; *see also* Sale, *supra* note 18, at 908 (PSLRA context).
23 Ashcroft v. Iqbal, 556 U.S. 662 (2009); Bell Atl. Corp. v. Twombly, 550 U.S. 544 (2007).
24 *Iqbal*, 556 U.S. at 679.
25 Conley v. Gibson, 355 U.S. 41, 45–48 (1957).
26 *Id.*
27 *Iqbal*, 556 U.S. at 680.
28 *See id.* at 684–85 (citing *Twombly*, 550 U.S. at 559).
29 *Twombly*, 550 U.S. at 559.
30 The courts are divided about the continued application of *Swierkiewicz v. Sorema N.A.*, 534 U.S. 506 (2002), which upheld notice pleading in employment cases.

13

Disruptors and Disruptions

Re-centering Procedural Narrative

ALEXANDER A. REINERT

It is common to hear of the "difficulty" of procedure, particularly for first-year law students. The difficulty arises among multiple axes. Sitting above everything is the tendency of first-year classes to be taught in silos, a problem that is challenging enough on its own before being magnified by the difficulty for students to see procedure in the context of substantive law. But even if we take procedure on its own terms, there is the language of procedure, because the colloquial meaning of certain words cannot be recognized when put into procedural context. There is the intellectual difficulty of the intersection of constitutional doctrine, statutory interpretation, and rulemaking that one must master. And there is the emotional challenge of looking at cases through the lens of procedure, looking for signs of justice in an unjust result. First-year students might credibly ask, "Is this really why I want to be a lawyer? To argue over the reasonableness of asserting personal jurisdiction over a particular defendant?"

But one of the most interesting challenges in both teaching and learning procedure goes beyond figuring out the *how* of procedure and turns toward the *why* of procedure. Why should I care whether there is a presumptive limit on the number of depositions or interrogatories? Why get exercised over whether federal courts may use their "judicial experience and common sense"[1] to evaluate pleadings? What is at stake when the United States Supreme Court elevates mandatory arbitration over class actions?

Procedure scholars and teachers often turn to the commonly understood interrelationship between substance and procedure to explain the *why* to their students. When we do so, we might have in mind the series of lectures given by Karl Llewellyn in the 1930s,[2] the "trans-substantive" dimension of federal procedural rules,[3] or critiques of substantive legal changes clothed in procedural garb.[4] These are all useful and important ways to consider the role that procedural rules play in achieving substantive goals. But for me and the clients I have served over the years, procedure has a different relationship to one substantive commitment in particular: equality.

My goal in this chapter is to shed more light on this substantive goal as it relates to the federal procedural rules. I hope to outline how the Federal Rules, even while motivated by a desire for uniformity, efficiency, and just resolution of controversies, also were premised on a norm of litigant equality. My students often ask me what I like so much about procedure—and eventually I come around to how procedural rules can accomplish a redistribution of power between parties, in a social context in which power, wealth, and legitimacy are maldistributed. In the work that I do, often on behalf of and in partnership with marginalized groups of people, procedural rules put them on an equal footing with those who exercise vast amounts of power.

Intervention in power dynamics of this kind was one of the achievements of the federal rules, but recent changes have challenged the extent to which the rules still serve that purpose. Whether through judicial interpretation or the rulemaking process, the equality intuition behind the original federal rules has given way to other maldistributive functions. Where once access to equal justice was a feature of federal courts that facilitated disruptions of the status quo, now those disruptions (and the attendant disruptors) are disfavored. Recognizing this attitudinal shift will sharpen the existing compelling critiques of recent federal procedural changes.

Equality Norms and Procedural Doctrine

> Regular procedure is necessary to secure equal treatment for all; it is necessary, too, for the quite as important factor of the *appearance* of equal treatment for all.[5]

Some years ago, when I was litigating civil rights cases full-time, one of my cases was a class action brought on behalf of people who used wheelchairs for mobility who were confined in New York State prisons. We were seeking to force the state of New York to use safety procedures and equipment that would prevent unnecessary injury while transporting them. During discovery, I was taking the deposition of the head of transportation for the New York state prison system. It quickly became clear to me that the deponent had never been presented with any of the evidence we had amassed regarding the significant safety issues presented by the department's practices of transporting people in wheelchairs without adequate restraints. Rather than an opportunity to discover information, the deposition was an opportunity for the plaintiffs to educate the defendant. I was the necessary intermediary, and the rules of procedure were the implements, but the process was one in which my clients were educating the state about the effects of its penal practices.

That dynamic cannot occur without the commitment to litigant equality that runs throughout federal procedure—the idea that each party is entitled to ask for and obligated to provide information to the other side, that each party is obliged to communicate in good faith with their opposition, and that the rules of procedure are tools that are indifferent to the social status of those who employ them. The premise of the system is that all parties have something necessary to contribute to the course of the litigation.

Equality norms inform and run throughout modern federal procedure. The radical concept that all litigants have access to compulsive discovery procedures, made uniform in federal court through the Federal Rules, is premised on disrupting unequal distribution of information that would otherwise systemically favor well-heeled interests over marginalized litigants.[6] Even as courts acknowledged early on that obligatory discovery imposed high costs, they recognized that "if rights are to be protected and wrongs righted, no system of justice can possibly permit the convenience of one from whom reparation is due to stand in the way of assuring it."[7]

Along similar lines, the Rules' commitment to trans-substantivity goes beyond the idea that courts should not be in the business of deciding which procedures should fit which kinds of claims; it also encompasses the notion that all kinds of claimants are equal in court. Implicit in this commitment to procedural equality is the additional notion that the tools of litigation are there for all to use. It would be naïve to pretend that those tools are equally available—no matter how fair a procedural system, law often reinforces power. But at least in principle trans-substantivity hands out swords and shields equally.

Equality itself, of course, can be cast in formal or substantive terms. Procedural rules may, on their face, appear to be limited to formal equality, but the Federal Rules, at least early on, also were premised on accomplishing substantive equality. Perhaps the best examples come from cases in the early 1940s involving claims, both individual and collective actions, concerning the Fair Labor Standards Act (FLSA), New Deal legislation enacted the same year as the Federal Rules (1938). In case after case, courts rejected arguments by defendants that plaintiffs needed to provide specific facts about their wages and hours, sometimes explicitly pointing to informational asymmetry as a reason to excuse detailed pleading.[8]

Even outside of FLSA cases, reference was often made to informational asymmetry, especially in cases that turned on the knowledge or state of mind of defendants.[9] This was repeated in other cases in which courts recognized that it would undermine the purposes of the Federal Rules to turn a blind eye to unequal access to resources. Leniency toward pro se (i.e., unrepresented) litigants, embraced early on by federal judges, is yet another such example.[10] Charles Clark, a member of the committee that drafted the original Federal Rules, was challenged with regard to the pleading standard by a lawyer who said, "Why, a sixteen-year-old boy could plead under these rules!"[11] In response, Clark stated, "[W]hy not, if he tells the court what his case is about? And that is what we are trying to ask the lawyers to do, and to do quite simply."[12]

As someone who has litigated for nearly two decades on behalf of people who have been more likely to have the law wielded against them than to use the law themselves, this equality norm in procedure was a refuge even when the substantive law was tilted against the clients I served. Even if the dispute at hand was rooted in other systemic inequality, knowing that my client and I had access to the same tools for vindicating rights as any other party provided opportunities for transformation.

One should not overstate the point: simplicity and efficiency were certainly main drivers of the Rules.[13] As David Marcus has described

Clark's pragmatic/realist approach to rules of procedure, they were tools that permitted a court to mete out justice "fairly and conveniently."[14] And one should always be mindful, as Stephen Subrin warned, that "[i]t can be misleading to look at a reform in hindsight" because the drafters of the Federal Rules might have been surprised at some of the consequences of their radical reform.[15] Neither should one ascribe to the drafters a uniform set of goals and substantive commitments, as some were surely driven by self-interest as much as any public-regarding principle.[16]

In particular, much of the procedural innovation was focused on giving *judges*, not necessarily litigants, more power to be flexible to achieve justice in a given case.[17] But even as the Rules gave more power to judges to employ equitable principles throughout litigation, judges were forced to grapple with, and respond to, the arguments raised by parties, who also were given more voice by the Rules.[18]

> In this sense open procedure is highly democratizing: the powerful cannot hide behind well-paid procedural sharps, but must stand before justice clothed only in the merits of their cases. The powerless can relieve at least some of their frustration with the thought that at least the courts remain equally open to them.[19]

An Emerging Procedural Narrative: Equality as Harm

In contrast to the positive account of litigant equality I have offered, recent procedural reform has been premised on something different. Highlights of procedural reform in the twenty-first century include limitations on class actions, heightened pleading, restrictions on discovery, and the rise of mandatory arbitration. These changes have been criticized on many accounts, and limitations of space prevent me from discussing them here. Taken together, they can be seen as an access to justice counterrevolution driven by powerful corporate and statist interests.

But I see them as premised on more than just the desire to make it harder for individual litigants to succeed against the powerful. They also accept a normatively negative account of litigant equality. In the new world of procedural reform, litigant equality imposes harms to our procedural systems that require turning our backs on some of the substantive commitments that generated the 1938 Rules. And those harms are seen in particular kinds of litigation (civil rights, employment discrimination, consumer rights, toxic torts)—unsurprisingly, litigation typically brought on behalf of people who systematically lack access to wealth and power.

In pleading doctrine and discovery, for example, an emerging narrative, typified by the Supreme Court's decisions in *Iqbal* and *Twombly*, is that liberal pleading doctrine too easily allows plaintiffs with insubstantial claims to wield the coercive power of expensive discovery to obtain settlements unrelated to the merits. In response, the Court's pleading doctrine requires more detail from plaintiffs at the outset of litigation, in cases in which much information rests in defendants' hands. In discovery, the Civil Rules Advisory Committee increased presumptive limits on discovery, scaled back the scope of discovery, and made considerations of "proportionality" central to obtaining discovery. On these accounts, the presumptions of litigant equality, both formal and substantive, have altered power dynamics toward individual litigants and away from institutional power, with changes to pleading and discovery considered necessary to reset the balance.

The class action—a device that has historically placed individual plaintiffs on equal footing with powerful corporate and governmental interests—also has been threatened by a narrative that such cases have become too "big" to provide procedural fairness to institutional defendants. At the same time, individual tort actions in certain cases are seen as threats that may overwhelm the judicial system, necessitating an expansion of Multi-District Litigation practice in which a plaintiff's ability to control her own cause is severely limited. The end result is a procedural amalgam that favors institutional interests over individual ones. Substantive litigant equality has been sacrificed at the altar of efficiency.

Conclusion: Re-centering the Narrative

In these changes, one can see an attempt to secure substantive goals in the world—to erode the power of certain classes of plaintiffs and enhance the power of certain entrenched interests. But my focus is on how the narrative and presuppositions that inform recent procedural reform run counter to the original premises of the Federal Rules. The equality fostered by the Federal Rules embraced disruptions to the status quo. Recent reforms look askance at the same dynamic. Perhaps most saliently, plaintiffs in particular are viewed as imposing harmful burdens on courts and defendants, necessitating an alteration of the substantive equality values embraced by the Federal Rules.

The recent trends are troubling, as is the characterization of those who initiate legal action—plaintiffs—as negative forces. Obscured is the central role that litigation has and can play in enforcing important rights. Left uninterrogated is the broader context of litigation. To view plaintiffs as the initiators of harm is to ignore the reality that litigation is often responsive to action in the world, to some disruption of the status quo by another party (i.e., the defendant). It may be that the defendant acted lawfully in so doing, but if the defendant harmed the plaintiff, even lawfully, then litigation is one attempt to restore the status quo. When one considers the additional fact that most people who have their rights violated do not, or are not able to, seek legal recourse, treating plaintiffs as the disruptors of a peaceful status quo is more problematic.

For students who are just learning procedure, my hope is that you will consider this chapter as a suggestion to think beyond what the Rules do in court, beyond what they ask of you as lawyers, to what they accomplish in the world and in particular whether they concentrate or disperse power and resources. I hope you will learn to recognize when the narrative of procedural reform obscures a subtext that is at war with the values you ascribe to a just procedural regime. The Federal Rules, as initially adopted, were one attempt to balance accuracy, fairness, efficiency, equality, and autonomy, among many important values. There is no one set of ideal procedural rules—every choice at every level requires balance and trade-offs. We can't begin to debate those choices, however, without being aware of all of the values that are at stake.

NOTES

1 Ashcroft v. Iqbal, 556 U.S. 662, 679 (2009).

2 Karl N. Llewellyn, *The Bramble Bush* 11 (2008) (advising students to "read each substantive course, so to speak, through the spectacles of the procedure. For what substantive law says should be means nothing except in terms of what procedure says that you can make real.").

3 *See, e.g.*, David Marcus, *Trans-Substantivity and the Processes of American Law*, 2013 BYU L. Rev. 1191, 1220–22 (2013) (discussing costs and benefits of trans-substantivity generally).

4 *See, e.g.*, Brooke D. Coleman, *One Percent Procedure*, 91 Wash. L. Rev. 1005 (2016) (criticizing outside power that elite interest groups have to pursue substantive ends through procedural reforms).

5 Charles E. Clark, *The Handmaid of Justice*, 23 Wash. U. L. Q. 297, 299 (1938).

6 Edson Sunderland, the primary drafter of the new discovery rules, openly acknowledged that the assortment of discovery devices provided under the Rules was bespoke. Stephen N. Subrin, *Fishing Expeditions Allowed: The Historical Background of the 1938 Federal Discovery Rules*, 39 B.C. L. Rev. 691, 719 (1998).

7 C. F. Simonin's Sons v. Am. Can Co., 30 F. Supp. 901, 901 (E.D. Pa. 1939).

8 *See, e.g.*, Winslow v. Nat'l Elec. Prods. Corp., 5 F.R.D. 126, 129 (W.D. Pa. 1946) (giving consideration "to the probability that the plaintiffs are without definite and exact knowledge of the hours and wages in controversy . . . [w]hereas, the defendants undoubtedly have full and complete records bearing on this matter."); Mitchell v. Brown, 2 F.R.D. 325, 327 (D. Neb. 1942) ("Nor should the court or the pleader neglect the relation of the parties to each other, or the nature and positions of the parties.").

9 *See, e.g.*, Makan Amusement Corp. v. Trenton-New Brunswick Theatres Co., 3 F.R.D. 429, 431 (D.N.J. 1944) (informational asymmetry in conspiracy cases); Mails v. Kansas City Pub. Serv. Co., 51 F. Supp. 562, 564–65 (W.D. Mo. 1943) (informational asymmetry in tort case).

10 *See, e.g.*, Dioguardi v. Durning, 139 F.2d 774 (2d Cir. 1944).

11 Sec. & Exch. Comm'n v. Timetrust, Inc., 28 F. Supp. 34, 41–42 (N.D. Cal. 1939).

12 *Id.*

13 *See, e.g.*, Edson R. Sunderland, *The New Federal Rules*, 45 W. Va. L. Q. 5, 26 (1938).

14 David Marcus, *The Federal Rules of Civil Procedure and Legal Realism as a Jurisprudence of Law Reform*, 44 Ga. L. Rev. 433, 486 (2010) (quoting Charles E. Clark, Commentary, *Pleading Negligence*, 32 Yale L.J. 483, 490 (1923)).

15 Subrin, *supra* note 6, at 743–44.

16 Judith Resnik, *Failing Faith: Adjudicatory Procedure in Decline*, 53 U. Chi. L. Rev. 494, 503–505 (1986) (describing varying agendas of rule makers).

17 Sunderland, *supra* note 13, at 7 ("I have before me . . . a list of forty express provisions by which various matters are left to the discretion of the judge.").

18 Owen M. Fiss, *Foreword: The Forms of Justice*, 93 Harv. L. Rev. 1, 13 (1979) ("Judges do not have full control over whom they must listen to. They are bound by rules requiring them to listen to a broad range of persons or spokesmen.").

19 Jack B. Weinstein, *After Fifty Years of the Federal Rules of Civil Procedure: Are the Barriers to Justice Being Raised?*, 137 U. Pa. L. Rev. 1901, 1920 (1989) (footnote omitted).

14

Class in Courts

Incomplete Equality's Challenges for the Legitimacy of Procedural Systems

JUDITH RESNIK

Courts are *services* that governments must provide to individuals. Because the ability to resolve disputes in accordance with the norms of a particular legal order is one mode of sustaining political power, governments rely on judges to enforce their laws and thereby legitimate the violence entailed in the enforcement of norms.[1]

Judiciaries are a long-standing feature of political entities (democratic or not), and governments' provisioning of courts (and of the related services of policing and prisons) often goes undiscussed.[2] But a sea change during the twentieth century in substantive legal entitlements raised the profile of and demand for adjudication. Through a mix of legislation and judicial decisions, courts became plausible sources of redress for a host of claimants, newly entitled to seek law's protection, such as tenants facing evictions, household members oppressed by their circumstances, mistreated prisoners, and many others.

This diversity of users, ushered in through legislative and constitutional innovations of the twentieth century, brought questions of court funding and user subsidies to the fore. When must, as a matter of constitutional law, governments waive entrance or other fees? Which litigants should be provided lawyers or experts? What procedural rules can be crafted to respond? And who pays for courts themselves?

These questions are at the core of twenty-first-century procedure, which has to take into account principles of equality and the political economy that produced contemporary conflicts about the values of and the resources needed to support adjudicatory systems. Class (as in economic capacity) and class (as in a mode of aggregation) are keys to courts. In this overview, I sketch the aspirations that emerged when diverse litigants came into courts, some of the doctrine and procedures that respond to asymmetries, and the barriers to participatory parity, which is a facet of courts requisite to the legitimacy of a judicial system.

* * *

As of 2020, more than 80 million cases were filed each year in the state courts. Most states devote 2 to 3 percent of their budgets to courts,[3] but demand outstrips supply. In the wake of the 2008 recession, some states closed their courthouses on certain days or furloughed judges. Judiciaries enlisted the bar and business communities to argue that courts were vital facets of economic and political life. In addition, many jurisdictions turned to users and imposed layers of fees, surcharges, and costs; such legal financial obligations can generate mounds of court-imposed debt.

The federal government does not have the constraints of many states, obliged to have balanced budgets. The United States can print money, and it runs a relatively small court system. About 325,000–350,000 civil and criminal cases are filed annually, plus bankruptcy filings. Between 1971 and 2005, the budget for the federal judiciary grew from less than one-tenth of a percent of the federal budget to two-tenths; in 1971, the federal judiciary was allotted $145 million and, by 2005, $5.7 billion dollars, and the federal courts' staff doubled from about 15,000 to more than 32,000, working in some 550 facilities around the country.[4]

Turn from the infrastructure to the individuals coming into court, both state and federal. In 2009, California's courts reported that 4.3 million people had come, without the assistance of lawyers, to seek remedies in civil cases;[5] New York counted 2.3 million civil litigants without lawyers—including almost all tenants in eviction cases, debtors in consumer credit cases, and 95 percent of parents in child support matters.[6] Many lawyerless litigants also come to federal court. From 2010 to 2020, about 25 percent of civil filings came from people without lawyers.[7] More than half of the cases before the federal appellate courts were brought by self-represented parties.[8]

The challenges of limited resources for those hoping to use courts are not new, even if the diversity and volume of claimants are. In the nineteenth century, Jeremey Bentham called filing fees a "tax on distress."[9] Nonetheless, a host of fees remain in place, and proceduralists in the United States today are accustomed to courts imposing an entrance fee for litigants who commence lawsuits. Less familiar is that some states (such as California and Illinois) charge defendants to respond.[10] Fees for other involuntary users cut across the litigation landscape. For example, California counties charged families tens of millions of dollars in fees when their children were taken into custody, and those charges pushed many households into debt and bankruptcy.[11]

A part of Bentham's proposed solution centuries ago was the creation of an "Equal Justice Fund," to be supported by "the fines imposed on wrongdoers" as well as by government and charities.[12] Bentham also wanted to subsidize legal assistance, the transport of witnesses, and the costs of producing other evidence. In addition, Bentham called for judges to be available "every hour on every day of the year" to hold one-day trials and to render immediate decisions.[13]

Bentham's recommendations echo in contemporary arguments for subsidies from the public and private sectors, for simplifying procedures, and for new technologies such as online dispute resolution. Yet adjudication's adversarial structure poses complex questions. Some litigants are criminal or civil defendants facing the state (whose litigation costs are paid by taxpayers), while other disputes involve private parties, often with vastly different access to resources. Asymmetries abound.

To borrow Ronald Dworkin's description of equality's entailments,[14] if governments seek to have their courts reflect "equal concern for the fate of every person over which it claims dominion," funds are needed to bring about a modicum of what the English call "equality of arms." Mechanisms for subsidies include waiving fees paid to courts (such as for filings, motions, and documents) and to third parties (including bail bondspersons, lawyers, experts, investigators, mediators and arbitrators, and probation officers) and changing the rules on ex post charges such as fines and restitution. Another way to ease burdens is to enable groups of people to join together to provide economies of scale. Aggregation mechanisms that have become familiar include class actions, the use (through a federal statute) of clumping pending cases in a multi-district litigation (MDL), and consolidations both formal and informal. Such techniques can generate intra-litigant cross-subsidies and incentives for lawyers to provide representation.

* * *

During the last several decades, responses in the United States to economic asymmetries in litigation have come through a mix of constitutional mandates and policy decisions in statutes and procedural rules. In the 1970s, a campaign aimed to convince the Supreme Court to recognize poverty as a "suspect" classification under the Equal Protection Clause; that effort lost in the context of school financing.[15] Yet some claims of unconstitutional wealth-based distinctions have generated positive rights to state-funded lawyers, to experts, and to fee waivers. Through reliance on the federal constitution's Sixth Amendment, its Petitioning Clause, and the alchemy of the Due Process and Equal Protection Clauses, judges have required funding in a few contexts.

The case law in such decisions generally focuses on the needs of the disputants. Yet, on occasion, courts recognize that the judiciary's legitimacy is at stake because courts seek to be perceived as open to all, regardless of economic wherewithal. Justice Harlan made that point when he explained in 1971, in *Boddie v. Connecticut,* that the state could not block access to divorce for people who lacked the means to pay the sixty dollars for filing and service.[16]

> Perhaps no characteristic of an organized and cohesive society is more fundamental than its erection and enforcement of a system of rules defining the various rights and duties of its members, enabling them to govern their affairs and definitely settle their differences in an orderly, predictable manner.[17]

In concluding that a fee waiver was essential, Justice Harlan drew on a 1956 decision that had addressed the problem of asymmetries *among* similarly situated criminal defendants, some of whom could afford to pay for transcripts required to appeal, while others could not. Requiring states to bridge that gap, Justice Black's plurality decision put forth a broad proposition: "There can be no equal justice where the kind of trial a man gets depends on the amount of money he has."[18]

Asymmetries between opponents came to the fore in the 1963 decision *Gideon v. Wainwright*,[19] which read the Sixth Amendment's "right to counsel" to require that states pay lawyers for indigent criminal defendants who face felony prosecutions; the current rule requires counsel if a criminal defendant faces imprisonment.[20] The Supreme Court relied on the Due Process Clause when requiring states to provide indigent criminal defendants on some occasions with experts, translators, and exculpatory information held by the prosecution.[21] Once again, the legitimacy of courts was part of the analysis: "Society wins not only when the guilty are convicted but when criminal trials are fair."[22]

In his 1971 *Boddie* opinion, Justice Harlan also linked litigant capacity to court legitimacy when he explained that the combination of "the basic position of the marriage relationship in this society's hierarchy of values and the state monopolization" of lawful dissolution meant that, as a matter of due process, Connecticut had to waive fees.[23] But, of course, access is not only a problem when divorce is the question. As Justice Brennan's concurrence argued, *Boddie* presented a "classic problem of equal protection"[24] on top of due process. In his view, the state's legal monopoly required access not only for family dissolution but for all lacking the means to "vindicate any . . . right arising under federal or state law."[25] That position, however, has not persuaded the Court to insist on fee waivers for many other civil litigants with limited resources, such as those who face bankruptcy or the denial of government benefits.[26]

Nevertheless, in the context of dissolving families, the Court has required a few subsidies in addition to filing fee waivers—albeit in an uneven pattern that reflects gendered household hierarchies. An indigent man defending against a paternity claim brought by a private party won state-funded testing because, as Chief Justice Burger explained in 1981, the "requirement of 'fundamental fairness' expressed by the Due Process Clause" would not otherwise be "satisfied."[27] Yet, in the same year, the Court concluded that state efforts to terminate the parental rights of an indigent woman did not create a per se right to counsel; instead a case-by-case analysis was required.[28] In 2011, the Court read narrowly the federal constitutional obligations to provide free counsel when it concluded that the Due Process Clause did not require a state-paid lawyer for an indigent man facing twelve months of detention for failure to pay child support to the family of the child's mother.[29] The Court did say that, when determining whether he was to be sent to jail, a state's procedures had to be fundamentally "fair," that equipping people with lawyers was one route to do so, and that other options included assistance from court personnel, including judges.[30]

The Court returned to the issue of the costs of transcripts in the context of terminations of parental rights.[31] After Melissa Lumpkin Brooks ("M.L.B.," as she was known in the Supreme Court) was divorced, her husband asked Mississippi to terminate her rights so that his new wife could adopt the two children. Ms. Brooks, who lost at trial, wanted to argue on appeal that the burden of proof—clear and convincing evidence that she had neglected or abandoned her children—had not been met. But she could not afford to pay the $2,352.36 for the trial transcript,[32] and Mississippi had no provision for transcript-fee waivers on appeal. The state argued that the three-day hearing provided all the process due, that Ms. Brooks could not prove Mississippi intended to discriminate, and that requiring a state to "subsidize" Ms. Brook's civil appeal would create a "new" and unfounded constitutional right.[33]

Writing for six members of the Court, Justice Ginsburg disagreed. Eschewing a resort to what she called "easy slogans or pigeonhole analysis,"[34] the Justice concluded that an amalgam of equal protection and due process required the state to fund the transcript on appeal. Equal protection, Justice Ginsburg wrote, related "to the legitimacy of fencing out would-be appellants based solely on their inability to pay core costs."[35] Due process spoke to the "essential fairness of the state-ordered proceedings."[36] The Court held that the fundamental nature of the right to parent, coupled with the absolutism of the termination order that was supposed to rest on clear and convincing evidence, meant that resource-limited litigants ought, like resourced litigants, to be able to appeal.[37] On remand, Ms. Brooks's visitation rights were restored. Yet this constitutional mandate has a narrow reach because parental termination proceedings are uncommon; between 1980 and 1996, a total of sixteen such appeals had made their way to the Mississippi Supreme Court.

The mix of equal protection and due process has also buffered individuals facing incarceration because of their inability to pay fines. In 1970, in *Williams v. Illinois*, Chief Justice Warren Burger wrote that the state could not extend a person's time of incarceration "beyond the maximum duration fixed by statute" based solely on the fact that a defendant was "financially unable to pay a fine."[38] The import of *Williams* and related decisions is the subject of contemporary litigation about the relationship of poverty to money bail and to the suspension of drivers' licenses and voting rights when fines and fees have not been paid. As of 2021, some state and federal courts have required judges to take into account ability to pay,[39] while others have concluded that the only trigger for constitutionally required ability-to-pay assessments is the threat of incarceration.[40]

This brief account of constitutional law in the United States is a small part of the problems that poverty poses for courts and of the governing legal regime, in which statutes and court rules play the dominant role. Moreover, as many have documented, an account of *principles* is not a description of *practices*. As illustrated by the United States Department of Justice's 2015 account of the municipal court in Ferguson, Missouri,[41] rather than "administering justice or protecting the rights of the accused," the local court's goal was "maximizing revenue" through "constitutionally deficient" procedures that had a racially biased impact.[42] Ferguson was not unique. Throughout the country, cycles of debt have generated a resurgence of "debtors' prisons," populated by individuals threatened with, or held in, contempt for failure to comply with payment orders.[43]

Research, litigation, and new statutes and practices aim to reduce legal financial obligations. The "Civil *Gideon*" movement focuses on funding lawyers to represent individuals in cases that relate to health, housing, and family life. Other efforts seek to lower the price of process and to provide new methods (such as "mental health courts") to meet the needs of subsets of litigants. In some jurisdictions, fees are no longer assessed and past debt is forgiven for certain kinds of litigants, even as in other places, legislatures and courts add assessments.[44] These many legislative, rule, and policy reforms interact with litigation that has an uneven track record in insulating litigants with limited wealth (disproportionately of color) from avoiding the extraction of resources *by* courts or obtaining less than they need by way of equipage *from* courts.

* * *

As I noted, one way to mitigate the costs of litigation is through collectivization. As courthouse doors were opening in the 1960s, the drafters of the Federal Rules of Civil Procedure rewrote the class action rule to expand its use.[45] In 1968, Congress authorized MDL to enhance economies of scale. Ben Kaplan—central to the 1966 revision of the federal class action rule—explained that aggregate litigation is key for subsidizing litigants who would otherwise have no effective way to come to court.[46]

And it had a major impact. Between 2010 and 2020, about 30 to 40 percent of pending federal civil cases were part of MDL, some of which included class actions. But as I, along with many others, have detailed, an assault on collective action is underway. A central example comes from the Supreme Court's reinterpretation of the 1925 Federal Arbitration Act. Since the 1980s, the Court has held that employers and service providers can require employees and consumers to waive all opportunities to use federal and state courts and to block collective action in arbitration as well. Claimants can proceed, if at all, single-file in closed arbitrations run by providers selected by the entities whose actions they contest.

Proponents generally offer two justifications: that the parties have signed a contract that binds them, and that arbitration's simplicity enables more people to pursue remedies. But as Arthur Leff explained, when a document is neither bargained for nor bargainable, it is a "thing" (to be regulated or not) rather than a contract.[47] Moreover, the mass production of arbitration clauses has not resulted in a massive number of arbitrations. Instead, the number of documented consumer arbitrations is startlingly small. For example, 134 individual claims (about twenty-seven per year) were filed against AT&T between 2009 and 2014. During that period, the estimated number of AT&T wireless customers rose from 85 million per year to 120 million, and lawsuits filed by the federal government charged the company with a range of legal breaches, including systematic overcharging for extra services and insufficient payments of refunds when customers complained.[48] In response, some consumers found routes by filing tens of hundreds of individual claims to create de facto class actions. Yet atop bans on class actions, companies have now tried to ward off such coordinated action through imposing nondisclosure requirements that aim to silence the very few who turn to arbitration.[49]

* * *

I have sketched just a few of the challenges that courts face—if they are committed to welcoming all persons as equal before the law. Likewise, I have highlighted some of the means to mitigate those problems, which are not unique to the United States. Indeed, courts in other countries have insisted on fee adjustments in light of litigant resources,[50] and many jurisdictions are turning toward collective redress.[51] Yet, as I have also shown, participatory parity is a problem that not all want to solve or mitigate.

This brief overview underscores that the institution of adjudication is both admired and under assault. Egalitarian norms have transformed courts and have challenged them. Conflicts over government regulation, subsidies, and support—vivid in the context of health care, education, and infrastructure—are likewise playing out in courts. In the judicial system, the question of participatory parity is entwined with the identity and the legitimacy of courts as well as of the governments of which they are a critical part.

NOTES

Acknowledgment: This chapter builds on several related articles, including *Representing What? Gender, Race, Class and the Struggle for the Identity and Legitimacy of Courts*, 15 Law & Ethics of Human Rights 1 (2021).

1 *See* Robert M. Cover, *Violence and the Word*, 95 Yale L.J. 1601 (1986).

2 *See generally* Judith Resnik, *Courts and Social Rights/Courts as Social Rights*, in Economic and Social Rights 259 (Katharine Young ed., 2018).

3 *See generally* National Center for State Courts, Budget Resource Center (2020), www.ncsc.org.

4 *See, e.g., Federal Judicial Caseload Statistics*, Admin. Off. of U.S. Courts (2020), www.uscourts.gov.

5 *See* Assemb. B. No. 590, 2009–2010 Leg., Reg. Sess. (Cal. 2009).

6 Jonathan Lippman, State of the Judiciary 2011: Pursuing Justice 4 (2011), *available at* www.courts.state.ny.us.

7 For the impact in state proceedings, see Anna E. Carpenter, Colleen F. Shanahan, Jessica K. Steinberg & Alys Mark, *Judges in Lawyerless Courts*, 110 Geo L.J. (forthcoming 2021).

8 *See, e.g., U.S. Courts of Appeal, Judicial Facts and Figures, Pro Se Cases Filed, By Nature of Proceeding*, tbl 2.4, U.S. Courts (Sept. 30, 2020), www.uscourts.gov.

9 Jeremy Bentham, *A Protest Against Law-Taxes: Showing the Peculiar Mischievousness of All Such Impositions as Add to the Expense of Appeal to Justice* (printed in 1793, first published in 1793), *in* 2 The Works of Jeremy Bentham 573, 582 (John Bowring ed., Edinburgh, Scot.: William Tait, 1843).

10 For details, *see* Judith Resnik, *A2J/A2K: Access to Justice, Access to Knowledge, and Economic Inequalities in Open Courts and Arbitration*, 96 N.C. L. Rev. 605 (2018).

11 *See* Jeffrey Selbin, *Juvenile Fee Abolition in California: Early Lessons and Challenges for the Debt Free Justice Movement*, 98 N.C. L. Rev. 401 (2020).

12 *See* Philip Schofield, Utility and Democracy: The Political Thought of Jeremy Bentham 310 (2006).
13 Thomas P. Peardon, *Bentham's Ideal Republic*, 17 Can. J. Econ. & Pol. Science 184, 196 (1951).
14 Ronald Dworkin, Justice for Hedgehogs 2 (2011).
15 *See* San Antonio Indep. Sch. Dist. v. Rodriguez, 411 U.S. 1, 18 (1973).
16 Boddie v. Connecticut, 401 U.S. 371, 372 (1971).
17 *Id.* at 374.
18 *See* Griffin v. Illinois, 351 U.S. 12, 19 (1956) (plurality opinion by Justice Black). *See also* Douglas v. California, 372 U.S. 353, 357 (1963).
19 372 U.S. 335 (1963).
20 Argersinger v. Hamlin, 407 U.S. 25 (1972); Scott v. Illinois, 440 U.S. 367, 373 (1979).
21 *See, e.g.*, Ake v. Oklahoma, 470 U.S. 68, 83 (1985). *But see* Dist. Attorney's Office v. Osborne, 129 S. Ct. 2308, 2319–20 (2009).
22 *See* Brady v. Maryland, 373 U.S. 83, 87 (1963).
23 *Boddie*, 401 U.S. at 374.
24 *Id.* at 388.
25 *Id.* at 387.
26 *See* United States v. Kras, 409 U.S. 434, 446–50 (1973) (rejecting subsidies for bankruptcy filings). *But see* Lindsey v. Normet, 405 U.S. 56 (1972), which struck down an Oregon statute that required tenants who appealed their eviction to post a bond of double the rent that would accrue during the appellate process.
27 Little v. Streater, 452 U.S. 1, 16 (1981).
28 Lassiter v. Dep't of Soc. Servs., 452 U.S. 18, 24 (1981).
29 Turner v. Rogers, 564 U.S. 431 (2011).
30 *Id.* at 435–44.
31 *See* M.L.B. v. S.L.J., 519 U.S. 102, 129 (1996).
32 *Id.* at 109.
33 Brief for Respondents at 14, *M.L.B.*, 519 U.S. 102 (1996) (No. 95-853), 1996 WL 365897 at *14.
34 *M.L.B.*, 519 U.S. at 104 (quoting *Bearden v. Georgia*, 461 U.S. 660, 666 (1983)).
35 *M.L.B.*, 519 U.S. at 120.
36 *Id.*
37 *Id.* at 107.
38 Williams v. Illinois, 399 U.S. 235, 243 (1970). *See* Judith Resnik, *(Un)constitutional Punishments: Eighth Amendment Silos, Penological Purposes, and People's "Ruin,"* 129 Yale L.J. F. 365 (2020). *See also* Beardon v. Georgia, 461 U.S. 660 (1983).
39 *See, e.g.*, ODonnell v. Harris Cty., 251 F. Supp. 3d 1052, 1135 (S.D. Tex. 2017), *aff'd in part and rev'd in part*, 892 F.3d 147 (5th Cir. 2018).
40 *See, e.g.*, Fowler v. Benson, 924 F.3d 247 (6th Cir. 2019).
41 Civ. Rights Div., *Investigation of the Ferguson Police Department*, U.S. Dep't Just. 42–62 (Mar. 4, 2015), www.justice.gov.
42 *Id.* at 42, 68–69.

43 *See, e.g.*, Alicia Bannon, Mitali Nagrecha & Rebekah Diller, Criminal Justice Debt: A Barrier to Reentry (2010).

44 *See generally* Fines and Fees Justice Center, https://finesandfeesjusticecenter.org (2020).

45 *See* Judith Resnik, *"Vital" State Interests: From Representative Actions for Fair Labor Standards to Pooled Trusts, Class Actions, and MDLs in the Federal Courts*, 165 U. Pa. L. Rev. 1765 (2017).

46 Benjamin Kaplan, *A Preparatory Note*, 10 B.C. Indus. & Com. L. Rev. 497, 497 (1969).

47 Arthur Leff, *The Contract as Thing*, 19 Am. Univ. L. Rev. 131 (1970).

48 Judith Resnik, *Diffusing Disputes: The Public in the Private of Arbitration, the Private in Courts, and the Erasure of Rights*, 124 Yale L.J. 2804 (2015).

49 Judith Resnik, Stephanie Garlock & Annie J. Wang, *Collective Preclusion and Inaccessible Arbitration: Data, Non-disclosure, and Public Knowledge*, 24 Lewis & Clark L. Rev. 611 (2020).

50 *See, e.g.*, R [on the application of UNISON] v. Lord Chancellor, [2017] UKSC 51; Trial Lawyers Association of British Columbia v. British Columbia (Attorney General) [2014] 3 S.C.R. 31.

51 *See Directive (EU) 2020/1828 of the European Parliament and of the Council*, EUR-Lex (Nov. 25, 2020) https://eur-lex.europa.eu.

15

Can a Gay Judge Judge a Gay Rights Case?

Thoughts on Judicial Neutrality

BRIAN SOUCEK

Procedural fairness and legitimacy require a judge who is neutral.[1] "To this end," the Supreme Court has said, in terms decidedly not (gender) neutral, "no man is permitted to try cases where he has an interest in the outcome."[2]

In 2010, a federal judge in California held a bench trial to determine whether the United States Constitution gives same-sex couples the right to marry. After siding with the same-sex couples, the judge acknowledged that he, too, was gay and had been in a relationship with another man for almost a decade. The losing side called for the judgment to be overturned, questioning the judge's neutrality, given his interest in the outcome.

This chapter takes their call seriously—in fact, critically. The point is less to decide whether the judge should have recused and more to show how much more complicated that question is than either side was willing to admit. To take a *critical* approach is to question what we mean when we talk about "neutrality," to examine what types of bias we're willing to discuss and prohibit, to destabilize the categories (gay/straight, white/black, male/female, married/unmarried) that these conversations often employ, and, finally, to see how thoroughly procedural questions intertwine with the substantive arguments that our "neutral" procedures are supposed to help us evaluate.

* * *

In 2008, the California Supreme Court held that California's statutory ban on same-sex marriage violated the state constitution.[3] But the victory for gay rights advocates was short-lived. The same election that made Barack Obama president also resulted in the passage of California's "Proposition 8" (Prop. 8), a ballot measure that amended the state constitution to say that "[o]nly marriage between a man and a woman is valid or recognized."[4]

Two couples filed suit in federal court in San Francisco in *Perry v. Schwarzenegger*,[5] claiming that Prop. 8 violated the federal constitution. Plaintiffs' lawyers were a legal celebrity odd couple: David Boies and Ted Olson, opposing counsel in the case that decided the 2000 election, *Bush v. Gore*.[6] California refused to defend Prop. 8, so the group that had put the measure on the ballot intervened. The *Perry* plaintiffs who wanted Prop. 8 struck down and same-sex marriage reinstated thus faced off against *Hollingsworth*, the proponents and now defendants of Prop. 8.

The case was randomly assigned to the district's chief judge, Vaughn Walker. Judge Walker is gay.

This wasn't universally known, though, when the case was filed or when Walker held the trial in January 2010. (At the time, only one federal judge in the entire country was openly gay.) It wasn't until the following month that a newspaper disclosed "the biggest open secret in the landmark trial over same-sex marriage."[7] And it wasn't until after Judge Walker ruled in plaintiffs' favor, struck down Prop. 8, and then, in 2011, stepped down from the bench, that Walker publicly acknowledged his "10-year relationship with a [male] physician."[8]

Defendants immediately asked the new judge assigned to the case to vacate Walker's decision. Walker should have recused himself, they said, because, as someone in a "committed, long-term, same-sex relationship," he had a "clear and direct stake in the outcome"—or at the very least, "his impartiality might reasonably have been questioned."[9]

Federal law requires a judge to "disqualify himself" if he knows he has a "financial interest in the subject matter in controversy . . . or any other interest that could be substantially affected by the outcome of the proceeding."[10] It also demands recusal "in any proceeding in which his impartiality might reasonably be questioned."[11]

Judge Walker hadn't stepped aside, he later said, because he and his partner had never discussed marriage and Walker didn't "want to suggest that a gay judge could not impartially judge gay issues."[12] Did he make the right decision? In place of an answer, the following passages offer a series of conflicting thoughts about what judicial neutrality might mean and require.

1.

The very suggestion that Judge Walker should have recused himself in *Perry* was "demeaning," "frivolous, offensive, and deeply unfortunate."[13] As plaintiffs' attorney argued, Prop. 8's defenders were "advocating a new standard that . . . would really do damage to the notion that our federal judges make their decisions based on the law, not on who they are, not on their personal beliefs."[14] This, to be clear, was a liberal take on the issue—*not* a critical one. It appeals to a particular vision of equality which insists that, beneath our personal interests, our divergent backgrounds, our racial, gender, and sexual identities, and differences in power stemming from class and social status, lies a neutral place (or "view from nowhere"[15]) from which we can judge without bias. Perhaps nothing is more fundamental to Critical Legal Theory than its rejection of all this—what Professor Kimberlé Crenshaw calls the "norm of perspectivelessness."[16]

Less naively aspirational was the argument from Kamala Harris, then California attorney general, who found the recusal motion "similar to long-discredited efforts to bar Black judges from adjudicating cases of race discrimination. Like race, gender, religion, and ethnicity," Harris argued, "sexual orientation is simply irrelevant to whether a judge is qualified to hear a case, regardless of the subject matter or the identity of the litigants."[17]

The court agreed. Distinguishing Judge Walker's situation from conflicts surrounding judges' particular financial interests, the court held that *everyone* has an interest in protecting civil rights and enforcing the Constitution. This idea is sometimes called the "Rule of Necessity": if all judges have an interest in a case, none should be disqualified, since it's necessary for someone to hear the case, after all.[18] The Rule of Necessity helps explain why it would be wrong to ask a Black woman such as Judge Constance Baker Motley to recuse herself from a case about race or gender discrimination. Asked to do so once, Judge Motley responded that every judge has a race or sex, so if those were reasons enough to recuse, all judges would have to step aside.[19]

After the district court refused to vacate Judge Walker's decision, the court of appeals went on to uphold Walker's decisions both on the merits and on recusal. In 2013, the United States Supreme Court determined that Prop. 8's proponents did not have standing to appeal the case. Since state officials had not appealed, Judge Walker's opinion became the last word. After almost five years, same-sex marriage returned to California.

2.

If Judge Walker's conflict of interest had involved one share of stock rather than his ability to wed his partner, he would have been forced to recuse. But who would ever care more about the former than the latter? Why does our recusal law fetishize financial conflicts over all the other ways that a judge's situation in the world could affect their decisions?

At common law, a judge's monetary interests were the only grounds for recusal. These days, cases where a judge's "impartiality might reasonably be questioned" can also lead to recusal.[20] But as to financial conflicts, federal law remains especially clear: *any* financial interest, "however small," requires a judge to step aside.[21]

Surely, it's overzealous to make judges recuse because of one share of stock. The rule is in place not because anyone thinks one share is likely to influence outcomes but in order to save judges, in closer cases, from having to make tough line-drawing decisions that litigants might then second-guess. Overemphasizing financial conflicts of interest, though, makes bias look like something personal or individualized rather than structural or group-based. This is the kind of individualistic notion of equality that the Supreme Court's conservative bloc has made dominant in contemporary Equal Protection doctrine.

Yet conflicts of interest are often not just individual, but they are shared across particular groups—not just minority groups, but majority groups too. Lesbian, gay, and bisexual (LGB) people may have had different interests at stake in same-sex marriage cases than their non-LGB counterparts. Refusing to ask that question (as the plaintiffs did in *Perry*) reinforces the fiction that personal financial interests are disqualifying, while group-based interests are nonexistent. The result: members of majority or socially dominant groups can promote their groups' interests without being questioned because recusal law makes the very possibility of such interests unspeakable.

3.

Gay rights advocates' outrage over the recusal motion was at odds with the substantive arguments they made during the trial. A partnered gay judge hearing a same-sex marriage case is *not* akin to African American or female judges interpreting antidiscrimination laws—*at least according to plaintiffs' arguments in the marriage cases.*

Recall that a crucial principle in the race and gender cases was the Rule of Necessity: if a case impacts every judge, none has to recuse. Most US antidiscrimination law (at least on the current Court's anticlassificationist understanding[22]) operates symmetrically: it applies equally to all races and genders. Thus, it is false to claim that people of any one race or gender have a unique stake in antidiscrimination cases. Accordingly, given the Rule of Necessity, no judge should be barred from hearing them.

Plaintiffs' argument in the Prop. 8 case was very different. They claimed that California's same-sex marriage ban imposed a harm specifically on same-sex couples. Extending marriage rights to same-sex couples would have *no effect* on opposite-sex[23] couples or the institution of marriage, they said. Judge Walker actually enshrined these arguments among his findings of fact after the trial.[24]

Unlike a typical antidiscrimination case, the outcome of which would affect all races or genders, the interests claimed in the Prop. 8 case were not symmetrical. The Prop. 8 plaintiffs were seeking a result that would affect only same-sex couples. As a member of a same-sex couple, Judge Walker thus stood to benefit in a way that a straight judge would not—at least on plaintiffs' theory of the case.

Plaintiffs' merits arguments were, therefore, at odds with their recusal argument, which treated Judge Walker as if he were situated no differently than his heterosexual colleagues. Given his findings of fact, Walker (and those opposing his recusal) should not have been able to rely on the Rule of Necessity.

To be sure, the other side was no more consistent. When seeking Judge Walker's recusal, defendants also seemed to forget their trial arguments. They had presented testimony about the so-called deinstitutionalization of marriage: allowing same-sex marriage, they said, would destabilize the institution, resulting in fewer marriages and higher rates of divorce. In short, the trial outcome would affect everyone: not just same-sex couples but also opposite-sex couples, whose marriages were at risk—according to the defendants—of becoming devalued. If everyone's interests were at issue in the Prop. 8 trial, as the defendants had suggested, the Rule of Necessity dictates that no judge should have to recuse.

4.

The inconsistency vanishes, at least on the plaintiffs' side, if we stop conceiving of the same-sex marriage fight in assimilationist terms.

When liberals and libertarians joined forces to fight for marriage equality, their emphasis was on equality as sameness. Their aim was to show how easily LGB couples would fit into a system that had been created by and for heterosexual couples. But this wasn't and isn't the only argument available. Consider what would happen were the liberal approach replaced by a more critical feminist or queer perspective on marriage.

Where the liberal approach insists that gay couples could be incorporated into the institution of marriage without disrupting it, a critical approach would emphasize and embrace the disruption. In fact, in this conception, what makes the old-fashioned institution of marriage ripe for constitutional challenge in the first place is its sex-discriminatory nature.[25]

The critical feminist/queer argument takes on the notion that gender differentiation and complementarity are essential to marriage. Traditionalists want to know "who wears the pants" in a family. Same-sex relationships challenge the necessity of these kinds of gendered roles—and hierarchies. The critical argument against same-sex marriage bans targets state-sanctioned gender policing as inconsistent with the Constitution's still unrealized guarantee of equality.

In the long legal fight over same-sex marriage, this argument was sometimes made but seldom emphasized, perhaps because it was so much more radical than those that did prevail. But the radicality of the argument is what leads to different implications for Judge Walker's recusal. By presenting same-sex couples as revolutionaries poised to make the institution of marriage something other—something fairer, less hierarchical—than it previously was, the radical argument shares a thought with conservatives: allowing same-sex couples to marry might fundamentally change the institution of marriage. (Whether for better or worse is where these two sides disagree.) In the context of judicial recusal, however, this means one thing: the Rule of Necessity is back! If everyone stands to be affected by the case, no judge needs to recuse.

The same would be true if plaintiffs had argued something even more critically queer, such as denying that the state should be in the business of endorsing certain intimate relationships over others.[26] That argument, too, would potentially affect all judges, triggering the Rule of Necessity once again.

Notice: we cannot evaluate the demands of judicial neutrality in a case such as this without considering the arguments being made on the merits. It is often thought that what counts as neutrality is something that can be judged in the abstract, from behind a veil of ignorance. Not so. Whether Judge Walker should have recused himself from the Prop. 8 case turns out to depend on what we think the Prop. 8 case is ultimately about.

5.

There is something deeply uncritical (and unqueer) about the framing of this whole discussion, starting with the chapter's title.

To ask whether a "gay" judge can judge a gay rights case is to ascribe judges a fixed sexual identity. Much of the argument over Judge Walker's recusal starts from this shared premise. A critical queer approach to these questions challenges fixed or essential categories such as these. The "born-this-way" narrative that has driven the incredible progress in LGB and trans rights within recent constitutional law is at odds with the boundary-blurring fluidity that characterizes many queer folks' experiences of sexuality and gender. And yet the immutability of sexual orientation was another of Judge Walker's findings of fact in the Prop. 8 trial.[27]

The only thing less critically queer than the liberal reliance on immutability is the insistence on an ideal of judicial neutrality unencumbered by any "personal information" about judges' sexual orientation or gender identity. Judge Walker's successor worried about judges disclosing "intimate, but irrelevant, details" about their personal lives.[28] But this is a double-edged sword. We might be wary of state-sanctioned intrusion into public employees' intimate affairs. But by calling attention to the sexual orientation of certain judges, litigants might come to realize that other judges, too, have a sexual orientation (and a race, and a gender, etc.).

What is truly offensive in the recusal motion, as in recusal requests in the race and gender cases of decades past, is the implication that *only* gay judges have a sexual orientation, that *only* minorities have a race, or that *only* women have a gender that potentially influences their views. The offensive implication is that the default or assumed majoritarian judicial identity (white, hetero, cis-gendered man) is a position of neutrality, which is to say, not an identity at all.

6.

What becomes of judicial neutrality if we accept that all judges have a race, a gender, and a sexual orientation, whether fixed or fluid? What happens when we acknowledge that all come to court with their own background, having grown up rich or poor, lived in a certain kind of neighborhood, attended a particular type of school, worked for the government, a business, or a public interest organization, been the prosecutor or victim of crime, navigated the world with a disability or health problem, experienced sexual harassment or inflicted it on others? Imagine if no single combination of these identities and backgrounds were treated as normal and thereby ignored in discussions of bias. What would become of neutrality if we acknowledged there is no disinterested, perspectiveless place from which to judge?

Rejecting perspectivelessness doesn't necessarily turn critical proceduralists into cynics who lump judges together as all equally and hopelessly biased. Rather than insisting, for the sake of judicial legitimacy, that everyone pretend judges don't have interests, critical proceduralists can ask instead that judges work to recognize interests beyond their own.

The view from nowhere might be a myth, but that doesn't mean that judicial empathy is similarly fictional or that judges can't and shouldn't prize virtues like what Professor Dan Kahan has referred to as aporetic judging: a style of reasoning and opinion writing that acknowledges the complexity of the issues judges must confront.[29] Aporetic judges refuse to write opinions that treat the outcome as obvious. They honor the genuine interests and values on both sides of the case and allow even the losing side to feel heard.[30] The difference between neutrality and empathy/aporia is the difference between a condition that is assumed versus a goal that looms ahead—a virtue that requires constant effort to attain.

Whether a gay judge can properly judge a gay rights case turns out to be a hard question. But that's not because "gay" judges are differently situated than any other judges: All have identities and backgrounds that shape their experience of the world; no position is neutral by default. We might just as well ask "Can a straight judge judge a gay rights case?" That question too is hard—because neutrality itself is hard, and hard work.

NOTES

1 *See* In re Murchison, 349 U.S. 133, 136 (1955).
2 *Id.*; *see also* The Federalist No. 10 (James Madison).
3 In re Marriage Cases, 183 P.3d 384 (Cal. 2008).
4 *See* Perry v. Schwarzenegger, 704 F. Supp. 2d 921, 927 (N.D. Cal. 2010).
5 *Id.*
6 531 U.S. 98 (2000).
7 Phillip Matier & Andrew Ross, *Judge Being Gay a Nonissue During Prop. 8 Trial*, S.F. Gate (Feb. 7, 2010), www.sfgate.com.
8 Dan Levine, *Gay Judge Never Thought to Drop Marriage Case*, Reuters (Apr. 6, 2011), www.reuters.com.
9 Defendant-Intervenors' Motion to Vacate Judgment at 2–3, Perry v. Brown, No. 09-CV-02292-JW (N.D. Cal. Apr. 25, 2011), ECF No. 768 (citing 28 U.S.C. § 455(b)(4) and § 455(a)).
10 28 U.S.C. § 455(b)(4) (2012).
11 28 U.S.C. § 455(a).
12 *See* Kenji Yoshino, *Speak Now: Marriage Equality on Trial* 240 (2015).
13 Hearing Transcript at 88, 59, Perry v. Brown, No. 09-CV-02292-JW (N.D. Cal. June 15, 2011), ECF No. 799.
14 *Id.* at 78.

15 *See* Thomas Nagel, *The View From Nowhere* (1987).

16 Kimberlé Williams Crenshaw, *Foreword: Toward a Race-Conscious Pedagogy in Legal Education*, 11 Nat'l Black L.J. 1, 2 (1988).

17 State Defendants' Opposition to Motion to Vacate Judgment at 1, Perry v. Brown, No. 09-CV-02292-JW (N.D. Cal. May 12, 2011), ECF No. 778.

18 *See* United States v. Will, 449 U.S. 200, 213–14 (1980).

19 Blank v. Sullivan & Cromwell, 418 F. Supp. 1, 4 (S.D.N.Y. 1975). An equally and justifiably famous response is Judge A. Leon Higginbotham's in *Pennsylvania v. Local Union 542*, 388 F. Supp. 155 (E.D. Pa. 1974).

20 28 U.S.C. § 455(a).

21 28 U.S.C. § 455(d)(4).

22 For an explanation of the difference between anti-classificationist and anti-subordinationist understandings of equal protection, *see, e.g.*, Reva B. Siegel, *From Colorblindness to Antibalkanization: An Emerging Ground of Decision in Race Equality Cases*, 120 Yale L.J. 1278 (2011). The latter allows for different treatment based on race to compensate for group subordination, while the former is symmetrical or "color-blind."

23 By its language, Prop 8 limited marriage not to heterosexual couples but to "a man and a woman," and the arguments made against it at the time mirrored these categories, focusing on same-sex couples and largely ignoring nonbinary people, who were also excluded under the law.

24 Perry v. Schwarzenegger, 704 F. Supp. 2d 921, 972, 978–79 (N.D. Cal. 2010) (findings of fact 55, 66–68).

25 I put aside a more pervasive line of thought within queer legal theory that litigation efforts should not be dedicated to promoting marriage at all. *See, e.g.*, Katherine Franke, Wedlocked: The Perils of Marriage Equality (2015); Michael Warner, The Trouble with Normal (1999).

26 Justice Kennedy's opinion in *Obergefell v. Hodges*, rooted primarily in fundamental due process rather than equal protection, took the opposite route. 135 S. Ct. 2584, 2608 (2015). Kennedy's valorization of marriage is one of the most controversial parts of his opinion among progressives.

27 *Perry*, 704 F. Supp. 2d at 964–67.

28 Perry v. Schwarzenegger, 790 F. Supp. 2d 1119, 1132 (N.D. Cal. 2011).

29 *See* Dan Kahan, *The Aporetic Judge*, The Cultural Cognition Project at Yale Law School (Oct. 2, 2012), www.culturalcognition.net.

30 For a critique of marriage equality cases in the United States, arguing that they ultimately failed to hear the arguments animating the losing side, *see* Brian Soucek, *Marriage, Morality, and Federalism: The USA and Europe Compared*, 15 Int'l J. of Const. L. 1098 (2018).

16

(Un)Conscious Judging

ELIZABETH THORNBURG

Inferences about facts are an integral and unavoidable part of civil litigation. As in life, much of what we *know* are conclusions, formed by drawing inferences from a collection of direct and circumstantial evidence. Juries, for example, are instructed that "[i]nferences are simply deductions or conclusions which reason and common sense lead the jury to draw from the evidence received in the case."[1] At trial, then, juries perform the intertwined functions of deciding what evidence to believe, what inferences to draw (and not draw), and how the law applies to the facts it has found.[2]

Trials, however, are not the only stage in which inferences play a role, and judges, rather than juries, consciously and unconsciously draw inferences that will shape the course of the litigation and the parties' likelihood of success. This has long been recognized in the context of the pivotal pretrial rulings that take the case away from the jury: dismissals on the pleadings and summary judgment. Less obvious are the many other ways in which judges make decisions based on facts during the pretrial period, as well as the ways in which they employ inferences in doing so. Although they do not technically end litigation, decisions about issues such as discovery, joinder of claims and parties, and class action status can have an enormous impact on the viability and scope of litigation. Even decisions that are labeled as exercises of discretion rather than as fact-finding are often undergirded by the judge's belief about facts, and those beliefs are formed after drawing inferences.

Defining "Inference" and Inference-Drawing

The kind of inferences and inference-drawing discussed in this chapter are what *Black's Law Dictionary* refers to as an "inferential fact"—a "fact established by conclusions drawn from other evidence rather than from direct testimony or evidence; a fact derived logically from other facts."[3] That derivation goes beyond the literal limits of the testimony. As Professor Dan Simon has pointed out, "[a]n inference is typically defined as any cognitive process of reasoning, in which a person goes beyond some known data to generate a new proposition. The result of an inference, then, is the addition of information to the person's mental representation of an issue."[4] For example, evidence might consist of a properly authenticated videotape of a bank robbery showing the robber wearing a yellow rain hat, along with testimony from a police officer that a search of the defendant's home produced a yellow rain hat (introducing into evidence the hat, which looks like the one on the video). An inference from that evidence might be that it is the same hat and, further, that the defendant robbed the bank.

* * *

Cognitive psychologists describe the fact-finding process, including inferences, as based on the construction of stories.[5] Their experiments show that jurors impose a narrative organization on trial evidence. The ways in which they do so require jurors to use their knowledge of the world—their generalizations—plus their knowledge about the expected structure of stories in reacting to trial evidence.[6] "Analyses of inference chains leading to story events reveal that intermediate conclusions are established by converging lines of reasoning which rely on deduction from world knowledge, analogies to experienced and hypothetical episodes, and reasoning by contradiction."[7]

The judicial system's confidence in generalizations is based on an assumption that judges and jurors share a body of knowledge that will make inferences fairly uniform. However, this assumption is problematic.

> This . . . is commonly described as "general experience," "background knowledge," "common sense," or "society's stock of knowledge." . . . [W]e need to ask, whose experience, sense, or knowledge? . . . The bases for such generalizations are as varied as the sources for the beliefs themselves—education, direct experience, the media, gossip, fiction, fantasy, speculation, prejudice, and so on.[8]

Judges, who like jurors operate by using human cognition, can be expected to use the same kind of evidence-generalization links to analyze inferences and to be similarly dependent on their own experiences in forming, using, and analyzing generalizations.[9] When judges draw inferences, or when they decide whether a reasonable jury could draw an inference, they are injecting not just logic but also their own store of generalizations into the mix. This is doubly important because the kind of reasoning involved in the inference process often operates intuitively. "The reasoner does not consciously identify the generalizations upon which her inferences depend."[10]

Implicit Bias

This subsection looks at heuristics' more insidious potential effects; they are the gateway to the operation of implicit biases based on factors such as race, gender, national origin, age, and religion. "Implicit biases are discriminatory biases based on implicit attitudes or implicit stereotypes."[11] We say that these attitudes and stereotypes are "implicit" when the person holding them is not intentional or even conscious of the bias. They can be especially difficult for the law to deal with, because implicit biases may be different from a person's conscious beliefs but nevertheless affect the person's actions.

One very common way to try to measure degrees of implicit associations between stereotypes and individual images is the Implicit Association Test (IAT), which is administered by Harvard University[12] and has been taken by millions of people over the years. The IAT is a sorting test in which the subject is asked to match categories and traits that are often associated with implicit biases—such as Male/Female sorted with Career/Family. It tends to take longer to tap the computer key that matches the categories with traits that are contrary to stereotypes.

* * *

There have been few experimental studies trying to assess judges' implicit bias. Many of the contemporary studies have been done by the trio of Professor Jeff Rachlinski, Professor Chris Guthrie, and US Magistrate Judge Andrew Wistrich (hereinafter "RGW group"). They did one test of black/white bias among generalist judges in criminal cases, using state court judges as subjects.[13] Their IAT results showed that judges, like most white people in the US, more closely associate African Americans than white people with negative concepts. The results of their experiments showed that those biases sometimes influenced judgments in hypothetical cases. It also showed, though, that in some instances—when the judges were aware of a need to monitor their own responses for the influence of implicit racial bias and motivated to suppress it—judges could focus more consciously on the issue of race and compensate for their implicit bias.

* * *

Absent the triggering and motivation, there are grounds to worry that judges are not sufficiently self-aware to correct for bias. The same researchers asked a group of judges to rate their ability to "avoid racial prejudice in decisionmaking"[14] relative to other judges attending the same conference. Thirty-five out of thirty-six (97 percent) of the judges rated themselves in the top half, and eighteen out of the thirty-six (50 percent) rated themselves in the top quarter of ability. The RGW group noted: "We worry that this result means that judges are overconfident in their ability to avoid the influence of race and hence fail to engage in corrective processes on all occasions."[15]

* * *

In observational studies examining the potential impact of judges' personal characteristics, including race and gender, patterns emerge in cases in which that characteristic might be salient, indicating that the judges' *experience* differs in ways that can affect outcomes.

* * *

One study is intriguing, supporting the possibility that the judge's experience, rather than sheer identity alone, can affect inferences.[16] Using a data set on judges' families and a data set of nearly a thousand gender-related cases, Professor Adam Glynn and Professor Maya Sen found that judges with at least one daughter vote in a more liberal fashion on gender issues than judges with no daughter. "The effect is robust and appears driven largely by male Republican appointees."[17] The most likely explanation: "[H]aving daughters leads judges to learn about issues that they ordinarily would not be exposed to—such as discrimination on the basis of pregnancy, Title IX, and reproductive rights issues."[18] In other words, having daughters can change the judges' experience and view of the world in ways that make inferences in favor of female litigants more plausible.

Federal judges in particular live in a somewhat rarified, elite environment in which they are isolated from both lawyers and the public, and they are treated with great deference. All of that can be a good thing when it comes to avoiding ethical conflicts and respecting the role of the courts, but it makes it even more challenging for them to have experiences that give them insights into the personal and professional experiences of everyday litigants. The judges' own experiences will predictably affect the generalizations they bring to inference-drawing, and their heuristics can amplify the biases that result.

How might heuristics and implicit bias show up in trial court inferences that matter? Their impact could show up in many places. Among the most common: They could affect whether a judge dismisses a case because the complaint is not "plausible"; they could affect whether a judge finds a discovery request sufficiently important to justify its expense; they could affect whether a judge believes that classwide statistical evidence would create a strong enough inference to meet the commonality requirement to allow class certification; and they could affect whether a judge believes that a reasonable jury could draw the inference needed to avoid summary judgment.

Judicial Demographics

Across the federal judiciary, the collective impact of heuristics would be somewhat less worrying if the judiciary was well-balanced in terms of professional and life experiences and cultural commitments. But is this the case?

The Congressional Research Service did a study of the demographics of the federal district and circuit courts as of June 2017.[19] Focusing on the district courts, where the bulk of the pretrial inferences are made, the data shows a group that is heavily white, male, and older. Of the 570 active district judges at that time, only 194 (34 percent) were women. In terms of race, 406 (71 percent) were white, 81 (14 percent) were African American, 58 (10 percent) were Hispanic, 16 (3 percent) were Asian American, 1 (.2 percent) was American Indian, and 8 (1.4 percent) were multiracial.[20]

It is likely that the percentage of white and male judges increased somewhat under former president Donald Trump. As of August 5, 2019, of his ninety-nine appointees to the federal district courts, he appointed sixty-four (64.6 percent) white male and nineteen (19.2 percent) white female district court judges (meaning that 83.8 percent of his appointees were white).[21]

Some research indicates that the presence of some nontraditional judges may help to broaden the perspective of other judges. One type of study focuses on the courts of appeal and looks at "panel effects," while others examine the possibility that a critical mass of nontraditional judges can make a difference.[22] In that regard, the federal district courts are a mixed bag. In June of 2017, there was at least one active female district judge in eighty of ninety-one district courts, but there were no women serving on eleven district courts.[23] Thirty-seven district courts had only one active female judge. Lack of racial minorities was even more dramatic. In June 2017, "there were African American judges serving on 44, or 48%, of the nation's 91 U.S. district courts; Hispanic judges serving on 24 (26%) of the courts; and Asian American judges serving on 12 (13%) of the courts."[24] Twenty-three of the district courts that did have an African American judge had only one. Only seven courts have at least one active district judge from all three of the groups counted ("i.e., there was at least one active African American, Hispanic, and Asian American judge serving on the court").[25]

From an income perspective, federal district judges are, by virtue of their salaries alone, in a place that makes them different from many litigants. For 2017, the annual salary of federal district judges was $205,100.[26] The US Census Bureau puts the 2017 median household income at $61,372, so judges are well above the median.[27] In fact, a 2018 Economic Policy Institute study showed that the district judge salary is comfortably in the average salary of the top 10 percent of earners for 2017.[28]

Taking all of this demographic information together, it seems possible that the experience of the federal district judges as a group may be skewed toward the experiences of the affluent, white, male majority.

While studies do not seem to show across-the-board differences between the decisions of male and female judges, or between white judges and judges of color, there is evidence of race and gender differences when race or gender is a salient issue in the case. Further studies, examining more fine-tuned heuristics, implicit biases, and cultural commitments, may find additional effects. In any case, conscious efforts to appoint a body of trial-level judges who are diverse across a number of measures would help to avoid overall tipping of inferences and even substantive law in favor of the experiences of a homogeneous group.

NOTES

Acknowledgment: This chapter is updated and adapted from the article Elizabeth Thornburg, *(Un)Conscious Judging*, 76 Wash. & Lee L. Rev. 1567 (2019).

1 Kevin O'Malley, Jay Grenig & William Lee, 1A Fed. Jury Prac. & Instr. § 12:05 (6th ed. 2019).

2 In doing so, they will apply the applicable standard of proof, generally "preponderance of the evidence" in civil cases.

3 *Inferential Fact*, Black's Law Dictionary (11th ed. 2019).

4 Dan Simon, *A Psychological Model of Judicial Decision Making*, 30 Rutgers L. J. 1, 42 (1998).

5 *See* Reid Hastie, *Introduction, in Inside the Juror: The Psychology of Juror Decisions Making* 3, 24 (Reid Hastie ed., 1993).

6 *See* Nancy Pennington & Reid Hastie, *A Cognitive Theory of Juror Decision Making: The Story Model*, 13 Cardozo L. Rev. 519, 525 (1991) ("Because all jurors hear the same evidence and have the same general knowledge about the expected structure of stories, differences in story construction must arise from differences in world knowledge."). Although it was developed in the context of criminal cases, the applicability of the story model in at least some civil cases has been demonstrated by later research. *See, e.g.*, Jill E. Huntley & Mark Costanzo, *Sexual Harassment Stories: Testing a Story-Mediated Model of Juror Decision-Making in Civil Litigation*, 27 L. & Hum. Behav. 29, 45 (2003) ("[I]n sexual harassment cases, the story model of juror decision-making appears to be useful."). For another examination of the story model, *see generally* Dominic Willmott, Danial Boduszek, Agata Debowska & Russell Woodfield, *Introduction and Validation of the Juror Decision Scale (JDS): An Empirical Investigation of the Story Model*, 57 J. Crim. Just. 26 (2018).

7 Pennington & Hastie, *supra* note 6, at 524.

8 *See* Terence Anderson, David Schum & William Twining, *Analysis of Evidence* 269 (William Twining & Christopher J. McCrudden eds., 2d ed. 2005).

9 *See* Chris Guthrie, Jeffrey J. Rachlinski & Andrew J. Wistrich, *Inside the Judicial Mind*, 86 Cornell L. Rev. 777, 821 (2001) ("Like the rest of us, [judges] use heuristics that can produce systematic errors in judgment.").

10 *See* Anderson, Schum & Twining, *supra* note 8, at 101.

11 Anthony G. Greenwald & Linda Hamilton Krieger, *Implicit Bias: Scientific Foundations*, 94 Cal. L. Rev. 945, 951 (2006).

12 *See Project Implicit*, Harv. Univ. (2011), https://implicit.harvard.edu (providing an online forum for users to discover their implicit associations).

13 Jeffrey J. Rachlinski, Sheri Lynn Johnson, Andrew J. Wistrich & Chris Guthrie, *Does Unconscious Racial Bias Affect Trial Judges?*, 84 Notre Dame L. Rev. 1205 (2009) (reporting results of "the first study of implicit racial bias among judges").

14 *Id.* at 1225.

15 *Id.* at 1226.

16 Adam N. Glynn & Maya Sen, *Identifying Judicial Empathy: Does Having Daughters Cause Judges to Rule for Women's Issues?*, 59 Am. J. Pol. Sci. 37, 37 (2015).

17 *Id.* at 38.

18 *Id.* at 51.

19 Barry J. McMillion, Cong. Research Serv., R43426, *U.S. Circuit and District Court Judges: Profile of Select Characteristics* (2017).

20 *Id.* at 17. When gender and race are combined, the data show that as of June 2017, 49.3 percent of federal district judges were white men, 21.9 percent were white women, 8.1 percent were African American men, 6.1 percent were African American women, 6.5 percent were Hispanic men, 3.7 percent were Hispanic women, 1.6 percent were Asian American men, and 1.2 percent were Asian American women. *Id.* at 19–20. The report noted that all categories other than white men are considered to be "nontraditional" and that 56.1 percent of the active nontraditional district judges had been appointed by President Obama. *Id.* at 21–22. Statistics on age show that the federal district judges skew older. In June 2017, the average age of a US district judge was 60.8 years (the median was 61.3). *Id.* at 23. The largest group (269 judges, or 47.2 percent) are between the ages of 60 and 69. *Id.* An additional 53 judges (9.3 percent) are 70 or older, making 56.5 percent of all federal district judges over 60 years of age. *Id.*

21 Calculations were made using the search tool *Biographical Directory of Article III Federal Judges, 1789-Present*, Federal Judicial Center, www.fjc.gov.

22 *See, e.g.*, Christina L. Boyd, Lee Epstein & Andrew D. Martin, *Untangling the Causal Effects of Sex on Judging*, 54 Am. J. Pol. Sci. 389, 406 (2010) ("For males at relatively average levels of ideology, the likelihood of a liberal, pro-plaintiff vote increases by almost 85% when sitting with a female judge."); Pat K. Chew, *Comparing the Effects of Judges' Gender and Arbitrators' Gender in Sex Discrimination Cases and Why It Matters*, 32 Ohio St. J. Disp. Resol. 195, 202 (2017) ("[E]vidence indicates that when groups are comprised of more diverse members, those members learn from each other and provide checks on the correctness of shared information, ultimately leading to more accurate decisionmaking."). *But cf.* Rachlinski et al., *supra* note 13, at 1227 (describing a study in which white judges, in a jurisdiction consisting of roughly half white and half black judges, still showed strong implicit biases and observing that "[e]xposure to a group of esteemed black

colleagues apparently is not enough to counteract the societal influences that lead to implicit biases").

23 McMillion, *supra* note 19, at 15.

24 *Id.* at 17.

25 *Id.*

26 *Judicial Salaries: U.S. District Court Judges*, Federal Judicial Center, www.fjc.gov.

27 Jonathan L. Rothbaum, U.S. Census Bureau, *Redesigned Questions May Contribute to Increase*, U.S. Census Bureau (Sept. 12, 2018), www.census.gov.

28 Lawrence Mishel & Julia Wolfe, *Top 1% Reaches Highest Wages Ever—Up 157% Since 1979*, Econ. Pol'y Inst. (Oct. 18, 2018, 11:49 AM), www.epi.org (*see* Table 1).

17

When Law Forsakes the Poor

MYRIAM GILLES

We live in a country riven by income and wealth disparities. Today, the richest 1 percent of people in the US possess more wealth than the bottom 90 percent.[1] This enormous concentration of economic power is the culmination of decades of significant income and wealth gains for the wealthy, combined with stagnant or decreasing growth for the majority. Indeed, since 1990, the top .01 percent of US families have been the beneficiaries of the greatest and most sustained growth in income and wealth ever recorded.[2]

Wealth disparities are projected in myriad ways across the contemporary socioeconomic landscape: fewer low-income families own their homes[3] or are even able to rent in neighborhoods with good schools, parks, and transportation options;[4] fewer have ready access to the internet, fresh food, green space, or adequate medical care;[5] fewer go to college and graduate;[6] fewer obtain stable, middle-class jobs;[7] and fewer live to old age.[8] But nowhere is the gap more glaring—or consequential—than the civil docket, where class actions brought by or on behalf of low-income consumers and employees are on the verge of disappearing.

Because individual lawsuits generally cost far more to adjudicate than the plaintiff stands to recover, class actions have historically provided an efficient procedural vehicle to aggregate individual, smaller-value claims for common litigation. For low-income groups in particular, aggregating claims has provided significant access to justice, as individual members of these groups are especially unlikely to "to seek legal redress, either because they do not know enough or because such redress is disproportionately expensive."[9] Equally important, class actions can secure forward-looking injunctive relief seldom available to individual litigants—remedies that are of critical importance to communities that are constantly confronted with nefarious business practices.

In prior eras, the class action device has been effectively employed to achieve important compensatory and deterrence goals. But in recent decades, judicial and legislative constraints have all but eliminated the availability of class and representative actions brought on behalf of low-income groups. These procedural rollbacks are disproportionately more harmful to members of low-income groups, who are more susceptible to the sorts of abusive practices enforceable via class and collective litigation. Moreover, members of low-income groups are disproportionately less able to achieve earnings mobility in their lifetimes. In other words, the poor in this country generally stay poor—sometimes for generations—and are therefore more likely to experience chronic instances of economic harm, recurring over the course of their lives and possibly the lives of their children.

As low-income plaintiffs find themselves blocked from bringing class actions, whole categories of legal claims are disappearing from the docket—private claims sounding in abusive debt collection, predatory lending, illegal foreclosures, unpaid wages, employment discrimination, and other areas that constitute "poverty law." These are the types of legal issues that economically vulnerable populations are likely to encounter; these are also the types of claims that have driven many important doctrinal and policy advances in consumer, employment, and other areas of law over the past half-century. Legal precedents in these disparate areas would ordinarily evolve in response to developments in the workplace, changing demographics, technology, and new theories of liability. But once the claims of low-income litigants disappear from the public justice system—save only for the stray public enforcement or nonprofit legal services case—common law development in these critical areas will simply cease, leaving judges a greatly-impoverished body of decisional law to draw upon.

Among the most alarming consequences of these doctrinal developments is that judges today preside over far fewer civil cases brought by or on behalf of poor people. And when judges are sporadically faced with the legal claims of low-income groups, it becomes harder to spot (or easier to ignore) patterns of exploitative, abusive conduct by corporate actors. As legal ethicist David Luban wrote, "[L]itigants serve as nerve endings registering the aches and pains of the body politic. . . . The law is a self-portrait of our politics, and adjudication is at once the interpretation and the refinement of the portrait."[10] Today, whole swaths of the population are glaringly absent from that self-portrait, and judicial "nerve endings" may well grow numb to their complaints.

Judicial Shortcomings

When judges are no longer confronted regularly with the civil claims of the poor, they become unversed in and desensitized to the underlying factual issues that affect lower-income groups.[11] This inexperience, in turn, may compound an existing, unconscious predisposition against lower-income claimants.[12] Over time, cultural and political distance between jurists and economically vulnerable groups may grow and solidify, eventually rendering judicial decisions exhibiting elements of classism altogether uncontroversial.

Many scholars have shown that deficiencies in judicial knowledge can have deleterious effects on the fair and just adjudication of claims. Professors Janet Cooper Alexander and Rhonda Wasserman have both suggested that, as more class actions are litigated only to the point of a class certification motion—depriving judges of substantive knowledge of the underlying facts that would be produced through discovery[13]—there is less law on the merits on which future judges may draw.[14]

The dearth of doctrine may hamper judges from accurately adjudging whether a proposed settlement is really fair to all affected parties. Indeed, Professor Alexander Reinert has observed that "federal judges have extremely limited judicial experience to apply to merits-based decisions" at the pleading stage, as required by the United States Supreme Court decisions in *Twombly* and *Iqbal*.[15] These "gaps in judicial experience," he asserts, can result in an "impoverished landscape of actual merits-based determinations."[16] And that is deeply problematic because:

> When we move away from public adjudication, we lose something important: information about how our justice system works to resolve disputes. This information, and the process by which it is divulged, is important not only for its own sake but also for reinforcing a democratic norm of equal accountability. What is sometimes overlooked, however, is that the information is important to ensuring legitimate and reliable future adjudication.[17]

As contemporary judges see fewer civil cases brought by or on behalf of poor people, they may grow further out of touch with and ill-equipped to manage these claims. Eventually, the inability to relate to these claimants and the systemic problems they face will reveal itself in decisions exuding a lack of empathy or understanding concerning the lives of the ninety million people in the US living in poverty.[18]

Examining Judicial Indifference

An example of judicial indifference to financial hardship is *United States v. Kras*,[19] where an indigent debtor filed for relief under the bankruptcy laws, but was unable to pay the $50 filing fee and was denied a hardship waiver.[20] The debtor then brought a constitutional challenge to the filing fee, relying on a series of Supreme Court precedents invalidating such administrative fees in divorce and other cases on due process/access to justice grounds.[21] But in *Kras*, a divided Court upheld the bankruptcy filing fee as constitutional.[22] In doing so, the majority engaged in a series of revealing observations concerning the debtor's financial circumstances and expressed its view that Kras ought to have been able to work (or talk) his way out of bankruptcy.

For example, Justice Blackmun's majority notes that the challenged filing fee—if it were paid in weekly installments of $1.92 over three months—represented "less than the price of a movie and little more than the cost of a pack or two of cigarettes,"[23] implying that the debtor was making deliberate choices about how to spend his capital. Of course, the more realistic take is that Kras simply had no money at all—whether to buy cigarettes or to pay a bankruptcy filing fee.[24] Wagging its finger, the majority next asserts that "if [Kras] really needs and desires [the bankruptcy] discharge, this much available revenue should be within his able-bodied reach."[25] Again, the scolding tone suggests that Kras had intentionally failed to secure full employment, rather than recognizing—as detailed in petitioner's briefs—that he had repeatedly sought and failed to find regular work.

And finally, the opinion patronizingly questions the very decision to file for bankruptcy, pondering why Kras—if he "really needs and desires the discharge"—didn't simply seek to "adjust his debts by negotiat[ing] with his creditors" so as to avoid involving the courts in the first place.[26]

Kras, who had little education and no funds to offer his creditors in settlement, could hardly be in a worse position to engage in the type of sophisticated dealmaking the justices appear to have in mind. Thoroughly out of touch with the petitioner and others like him, the *Kras* decision is striking for its insistence that poverty is a choice, full employment is readily available for anyone who seeks it, and creditors are interested in rational and collaborative cooperation with debtors.

Justice Marshall issued a strong dissent, chiding the *Kras* majority's insensitive and inaccurate understanding of the lives of the poor: "It may be easy for some people to think that weekly savings of less than $2 are no burden. But no one who has had close contact with poor people can fail to understand how close to the margin of survival many of them are."[27] For Marshall, the majority's "disgraceful" and "unfounded assumptions about how people live" were deeply consequential—he cited the 1970 census finding that 800,000 families lived on less than $20 per week—and went far beyond the specifics of this case.[28]

Kras was followed by numerous Supreme Court decisions exhibiting a cool detachment from the plight of the poor. In *Ortwein v. Schwab*,[29] for example, the majority upheld a $25 filing fee assessed to welfare applicants.[30] In his dissent, Justice Douglas angrily accused the majority of perpetuating a justice system that had become "the private preserve for the affluent."[31] As Professor Gene Nichol has powerfully argued, decisions such as *Kras* and *Ortwein* reveal the Court's willingness to retreat from "the core commitment" of meaningful access to justice in cases involving the poor.[32] The Court, and perhaps the rest of us as well, Nichol warns, "have become solidly comfortable with a scheme of civil justice that leaves millions out."[33] And comfort with this exclusion can easily develop into a stony disinterest in the underlying, systemic problems that face low-income groups.

The Ninth Circuit's 2010 decision in *United States v. Pineda-Moreno*[34] reveals the persistence of judicial indifference to the issues facing low-income litigants. There, the court upheld as permissible under the Fourth Amendment the Drug Enforcement Agency's placement of a GPS-tracking device on the defendant's car while it was parked outside his rented trailer home despite the government's concession that the car was "parked within the curtilage of [the defendant's] home."[35] For the chief judge of the Ninth Circuit, the panel's finding revealed the great gulf between federal judges and many of the litigants who come before them:

> There's been much talk about diversity on the bench, but there's one kind of diversity that doesn't exist: No truly poor people are appointed as federal judges, or as state judges for that matter. Judges, regardless of race, ethnicity or sex, are selected from the class of people who don't live in trailers or urban ghettos. The everyday problems of people who live in poverty are not close to our hearts and minds because that's not how we and our friends live. . . . When you glide your BMW into your underground garage or behind an electric gate, you don't need to worry that somebody might attach a tracking device to it while you sleep. But the Constitution doesn't prefer the rich over the poor; the man who parks his car next to his trailer is entitled to the same privacy and peace of mind as the man whose urban fortress is guarded by the Bel Air Patrol.[36]

This critique highlights the inability of many judges to empathize with poor people because they have never been poor and have had limited firsthand exposure to poor people. Indeed, the only reliable means by which judges are regularly exposed to marginalized groups—the poor, minorities, immigrants—is through the cases that appear by random assignment on their dockets. As many of these claims vanish from dockets, the cognitive, cultural, and political distance between jurists and economically vulnerable groups will only grow and harden. Eventually, judicial decisions exhibiting elements of classism, such as *Kras*, *Ortwein*, and *Pineda-Moreno*, may no longer seem so controversial—indeed, they may even issue without strong dissents. And, at some point in the not too distant future, the only cases in which judges will glimpse the lives of individuals living on the economic edge will be criminal cases such as *Pineda-Moreno*.

Much is lost when the legal system ignores the problems, situational facts, and voices of low-income litigants, rendering them invisible in law, as they are so often made invisible in modern life. If the point of procedural rules is to ensure that like cases are treated alike, then procedure's abandonment of low-income litigants is deeply disturbing. The refusal to hear the claims of the weakest among us reveals the fragility and political pliability not only of the rules but also of our own convictions about procedural justice, equality, and accountability under the law.

NOTES

Acknowledgment: This chapter is updated and adapted from the article Myriam Gilles, *Class Warfare: The Disappearance of Low-Income Litigants from the Civil Docket*, 65 Emory L. Rev. 1531 (2016).

1 *See* Jacob S. Hacker & Paul Pierson, *Winner-Take-All Politics: Public Policy, Political Organization, and the Precipitous Rise of Top Incomes in the United States*, 38 Pol. & Soc'y 152, 155–58, 163–64 (2010).
2 *Id.* at 155.
3 *See, e.g.*, Lisa Prevost, *Gap Persists in Homeownership*, N.Y. Times, Feb. 8, 2015.
4 *See, e.g.*, David Leonhardt, *Middle-Class Blacks in Poor Neighborhoods*, N.Y. Times, June 25, 2015.
5 *See, e.g.*, Tali Arbel, *FCC Head Unveils Proposal to Narrow 'Digital Divide'*, Associated Press, May 28, 2015.
6 *See, e.g.*, Susan Dynarski, *For Poor, Getting to College Is Only Half the Battle*, N.Y. Times, June 2, 2015.
7 *See, e.g.*, Greg J. Duncan & Richard J. Murnane, Restoring Opportunity: The Crisis of Inequality and the Challenge for American Education 19 (2014).
8 Sabrina Tavernise, *Life Spans of the Rich Leave the Poor Behind*, N.Y. Times, Feb. 13, 2016.
9 Helen Hershkoff, *Poverty Law and Civil Procedure: Rethinking the First-Year Course*, 34 Fordham Urb. L.J. 1325, 1347 (2007) (quoting Harry Kalven & Maurice Rosenfield, *The Contemporary Function of the Class Suit*, 8 U. Chi. L. Rev. 684, 686 (1941)).
10 David Luban, *Settlements and the Erosion of the Public Realm*, 83 Geo. L.J. 2619, 2638 (1995).
11 Further, if judicial experience with economically fragile communities becomes limited to criminal trials and sentencing, one might expect judges to grow more suspicious of civil claims brought by members of these groups. Michele Benedetto Neitz, *Socioeconomic Bias in the Judiciary*, 61 Clev. St. L. Rev. 137, 147 (2013).
12 Mitchell F. Crusto, *Empathetic Dialogue: From Formalism to Value Principles*, 65 SMU L. Rev. 845, 858 (2012).
13 Janet Cooper Alexander, *Do the Merits Matter? A Study of Settlements in Securities Class Actions*, 43 Stan. L. Rev. 497, 566 (1991); Rhonda Wasserman, *Secret Class Action Settlements*, 31 Rev. Litig. 889, 919–20 (2012).
14 Alexander, *supra* note 13, at 567.
15 Alexander A. Reinert, *The Burdens of Pleading*, 162 U. Pa. L. Rev. 1767, 1769, 1772 (2014).
16 *Id.* at 1769.
17 *Id.* at 1785 (footnotes omitted).

18 Gene R. Nichol, Jr., *Judicial Abdication and Equal Access to the Civil Justice System*, 60 Case W. Rsrv. L. Rev. 325, 330 (2010).

19 409 U.S. 434 (1973).

20 *Id.* at 437–38; *see also* Thomas Ross, *The Rhetoric of Poverty: Their Immorality, Our Helplessness*, 79 Geo. L.J. 1499, 1500 n.2 (1991) (quoting from Kras's affidavit: "Kras resides in a 2 1/2-room apartment with his wife, two children, ages 5 years and 8 months, his mother, and his mother's 6-year-old daughter. His younger child suffers from cystic fibrosis and is undergoing treatment in a medical center. . . . Kras [is] unemployed. . . . He has diligently sought steady employment. . . . The Kras household subsists entirely on . . . public assistance. . . . These benefits are all expended for rent and day-to-day necessities. . . .").

21 *Kras*, 409 U.S. at 444–45; *see, e.g.*, Boddie v. Connecticut, 401 U.S. 371, 382–83 (1971).

22 409 U.S. at 446–47; *Kras*, 409 U.S. at 450 (Burger, J., concurring); *Kras*, 409 U.S. at 451 (Stewart, J., dissenting).

23 *Kras*, 409 U.S. at 449.

24 *Id.* at 460 (Marshall, J., dissenting) ("A pack or two of cigarettes may be, for [the poor], not a routine purchase but a luxury indulged in only rarely. The desperately poor almost never go to see a movie, which the majority seems to believe is an almost weekly activity. They have more important things to do with what little money they have—like attempting to provide some comforts for a gravely ill child, as Kras must do.").

25 *Id.* at 449.

26 *Id.* at 445, 449.

27 *Id.* at 460 (Marshall, J., dissenting). Three other justices dissented. Justice Stewart wrote that the majority's decision denied justice "to those who need it most, to those who every day must live face-to-face with abject poverty—who cannot spare even $1.28 a week." *Id.* at 457 (Stewart, J., dissenting). Justice William O. Douglas, another of the four dissenters, wrote about the case some months later in his memoir, observing: "Never did I dream that I would live to see the day when a court held that a person could be too poor to get the benefits of bankruptcy." William O. Douglas, *Go East, Young Man: The Early Years* 175 (1974).

28 *Kras*, 409 U.S. at 459–60.

29 Ortwein v. Schwab, 410 U.S. 656 (1973) (per curiam).

30 *Id.* at 656, 661.

31 *Id.* at 661 (Douglas, J., dissenting) (quoting Meltzer v. C. Buck LeCraw & Co., 402 U.S. 954, 961 (1971) (opinion of Douglas, J.)).

32 Nichol, *supra* note 18, at 345 (citing Little v. Streater, 452 U.S. 1, 5–6 (1981)).

33 Nichol, *supra* note 18, at 349.

34 591 F.3d 1212 (9th Cir. 2010).

35 *Id.* at 1213, 1215, 1216–17.

36 United States v. Pineda-Moreno, 617 F.3d 1120, 1123 (9th Cir. 2010) (Kozinski, J., dissenting).

18

Doorways of Discretion

Psychological Science and the Legal Construction and Erasure of Racism

VICTOR D. QUINTANILLA

This chapter discusses two interconnected ways in which the Federal Rules of Civil Procedure intersect with race and racism, which are obscured from most Civil Procedure courses (and much Civil Procedure scholarship). First, the seemingly neutral and objective Federal Rules are permeated with *doorways of discretion*, particularly within rules and standards applying to pretrial case management. These doorways grant judges nearly unreviewable discretion; at the same time, judges are acculturated within a society with deeply rooted and permeating racist ideologies, societal inequalities, and racial subordination, one in which prejudice, stereotypes, and discrimination against people of color remain prevalent. Social psychological research reveals how these doorways of discretion intersect with the psychology of human decision-making to allow for prejudice against racial outsiders to emerge.

Second, these doorways of discretion interact with racializing societal and psychological processes in ways that lead to the *legal construction and erasure of racism*. Legal Realism, Critical Legal Studies, and Critical Race Theory have long discussed legal indeterminacy: given the gaps, ambiguities, and conflicts that exist within the subdoctrinal layers of law, judges must define and construct legal concepts when making legal decisions. Yet judges encounter factual indeterminacy in the civil justice system as well, especially when ruling on matters relating to unlawful discrimination. When justifying their pretrial decisions in these cases, judges elaborate legal concepts based on their understandings of race, racism, and what counts as discrimination. These legal constructions frequently elide or erase the lived experience of marginalized groups and reproduce and amplify societal inequality that undermines racial outsiders.

Doorways of Discretion

The Federal Rules are interpreted and applied by humans: judges and lawyers, who are themselves reared and socialized within a society that directs overt and subtle, structural and intrapersonal, and open and covert racism against racial outsiders. At the same time, the Rules are permeated with doorways of discretion, particularly in rules and standards that apply to pretrial case management. These doorways of discretion intersect with the social and cognitive psychology of judges and lawyers, thereby allowing societal prejudice, stereotypes, and racism to influence decision-making under the seemingly neutral and objective Federal Rules.[1]

Federal judges now devote the bulk of their time to pretrial management, including deciding dispositive motions, ruling on discovery matters, and conducting pretrial and settlement conferences. Indeed, for several decades the federal judicial role has shifted from a model in which judges serve as impartial arbiters over attorney-driven litigation to a model in which judges engage in active case management over discovery, class certification, and settlements followed by decision-making at key filtration points in litigation: Rule 12(b)(6), Rule 56, and Rule 50.[2] When ruling on such pretrial matters, the Rules afford federal judges considerable discretion and the constraints that circumscribe this power are largely absent.[3] At the same time, judges regularly experience pressure for efficiency, speed, reducing expenses, and peer comparisons in case disposition statistics, including when overseeing federal civil rights cases.[4]

To withstand a FRCP 12(b)(6) motion to dismiss, a complaint must now contain sufficient factual matter "to state a claim to relief that is plausible on its face."[5] When applying this new plausibility standard, a judge first separates legal conclusions from factual allegations, then determines whether the remaining factual allegations in the complaint state a claim to relief that is plausible on its face by drawing on their "experience and common sense."[6] In short, under *Ashcroft v. Iqbal*, federal courts must routinely decide whether members of stereotyped groups and racial outsiders have pleaded plausible federal claims, including claims of discrimination, by relying on their "experience and common sense," before evidence has been gathered in discovery.[7]

Implicit in this requirement is the epistemic assumption that judges are cold, deductive, color-blind beings who can neutrally and objectively draw on their "common sense" without the influence of cognitive schemas about race and racism, and without the pull of stereotypes, prejudice, and overt or implicit bias. This requirement also entails an ontological assumption that "common sense" about matters affecting stereotyped groups and racial outsiders is itself untainted by conscious, covert, or unconscious racism. Both of these assumptions are incorrect.

Social Psychological Research on Prejudice and Racism

Research amassed in the field of social psychology, especially in the area of intergroup relations, underscores that these doorways of discretion may allow racism to be expressed against members of subordinated groups.[8] In particular, social psychology research has found a disassociation between words and deeds toward racial outsiders.[9] Many White people in the US struggle with anti-Black attitudes. While many (not all) White people in the US reject overtly racist ideologies, many show deep ambivalence and feel a range of emotions including fear, anxiety, discomfort, and disgust toward racial outsiders. The societal prejudice that persists leads to harm, neglect, and decreased helping behavior and cooperation toward racial outsiders. At the same time, many majority group members like and trust other racial insiders, which leads them to facilitate and cooperate with others like them.[10]

Decades of well-designed psychological and behavioral experiments have been synthesized into a powerful conceptual model known as the Justification-Suppression Model of Prejudice, presented in figure 18.1.[11] This model offers a nuanced understanding of prejudice, which is sensitive to contexts and situations, and reveals the conditions under which prejudice and bias are most likely to harm racial outsiders within the civil justice system. This model is premised on the finding that majority-group members within our society have genuine prejudice toward racial

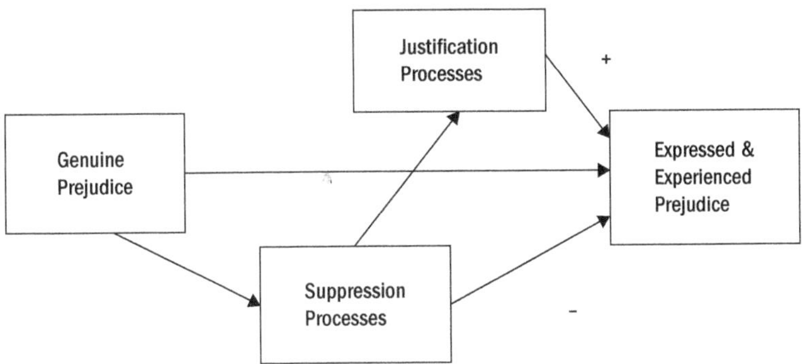

Figure 18.1. The justification–suppression model of prejudice.

outsiders. This prejudice is primary, primal, powerful, early-learned, automatic, cognitively simple, and relatively effortless.[12] This is, in part, because racism is woven into the structures, institutions, and minds constituting our society and has contemporary effects.[13] Under this model, situations and contexts alter the expression of prejudice, such that judges and lawyers will express prejudice depending on whether conditions of suppression or justification occur.[14] For example, the model predicts that judges and lawyers will behave in prejudiced ways when the norms in a situation are ambiguous and unclear, when a correct choice is uncertain, and when prejudice can be rationalized on some basis other than race.[15]

The justification-suppression model of prejudice has four elements: genuine prejudice, suppression, justification, and expressed prejudice. *Genuine prejudice* entails a negative feeling that is unadulterated and unmanaged that, while frequently not directly accessible, is nevertheless primary and powerful.[16] The second element is *suppression*. Other external forces and internal psychological factors suppress this genuine prejudice, and these external and internal factors may include egalitarian structures within environments, social norms, personal standards, beliefs, and values.[17] Judges and lawyers are more likely to suppress prejudice when externally motivated to do so (such as when egalitarian norms apply) or when internally motivated to do so (such as when judges adhere to humanitarian values, ant-racist commitments, or when they are personally committed to treating racial outsiders with dignity and compassion). The third element is *justification*, which prompts the expression of prejudice while providing cover, leaving a nonprejudiced and egalitarian self-image unimpaired by guilt or shame.[18] For example, ideologies, such as right-wing authoritarianism, social dominance, system justification, and color-blindness, may justify the expression of prejudice by labeling racist behavior as not racist. Moreover, perceived material and symbolic conflicts, such as anxiety created by demographic changes in the United States, release the expression of prejudice.[19] The final element is *expressed and experienced prejudice.*[20] Genuine prejudice is mediated and conditioned by these justification and suppression processes. When this prejudice is expressed, it may include overt expressions of prejudice or more covert and covered forms of discrimination in judicial decision-making.

Justification-Suppression in Pretrial Decision-making

In *Iqbal*, the Supreme Court requires federal judges to draw on their "experience and common sense" when deciding whether claims are sufficiently plausible to withstand dismissal.[21] This gatekeeping applies to all claims, including claims of discrimination brought by members of societally subordinated groups and racial outsiders. Yet as the research presented reveals, judges are humans who cannot draw on "common sense" without the influence of stereotypes, implicit bias, and prejudice toward racial outsiders, which contradicts the epistemic assumptions on which the plausibility pleading standard is based.

Moreover, doorways of discretion within the Federal Rules are troubling not only because they serve as conditions that allow prejudice to be expressed against racial outsiders but also because the judicial decisions that result are themselves important sites where the legal construction of racism takes root.[22] That is to say, judges not only make pretrial decisions; they *elaborate*, *rationalize*, and *justify* their decisions by developing legal concepts and patterns of reasoning that serve as heuristics for dealing with similar cases in the future.

For example, after the Supreme Court in *Iqbal* struck several allegations as legal conclusions not entitled to truth, it concluded that only two factual allegations remained. These two allegations were (1) that "the FBI, under the direction of Defendant Mueller, arrested and detained thousands of Arab Muslim men . . . as part of its investigation of the events of September 11"; and (2) that "[t]he policy of holding post-September-11th detainees in highly restrictive conditions of confinement until they were cleared by the FBI was approved by Defendants Ashcroft and Mueller in discussions in the weeks after September 11, 2001."[23] Drawing on its own experience and common sense, a 5–4 majority of the Supreme Court decided that, while these allegations were consistent with plaintiff's claim of purposeful discrimination, more "obvious alternative explanations" existed:

> The September 11 attacks were perpetrated by 19 Arab Muslim hijackers who counted themselves members in good standing of al Qaeda, an Islamic fundamentalist group. . . . It should come as no surprise that a legitimate policy directing law enforcement to arrest and detain individuals because of their suspected link to the attacks would produce a disparate, incidental impact on Arab Muslims, even though the purpose of the policy was to target neither Arabs nor Muslims. On the facts respondent alleges the arrests Mueller oversaw were likely lawful and justified by his nondiscriminatory intent to detain aliens who were illegally present in the United States and who had potential connections to those who committed terrorist acts.[24]

This "obvious alternative explanation," rendered plaintiff's claim of "purposeful, invidious discrimination . . . not a plausible conclusion."[25] The Court's theory appeared to be that "arrest[ing] and detain[ing] thousands of Arab Muslim men."[26] as part of a law enforcement investigation was not purposeful discrimination because, when policies have a disparate impact on communities of color, these policies are more likely to be motivated by neutral law enforcement reasons than institutional racism. The Court's analysis reveals the inadequacy of the ontological assumption that "common sense" is perspectiveless, inherently untainted, and unaffected by one's racial privilege and racial/ethnic group membership.[27] For example, communities of color with the lived experience of institutional racism believe it is "common sense" that police officers target their communities because of racist beliefs that associate their racial group membership with crime, rather than for neutral legitimate law enforcement reasons. The result is a pretrial device that erases racism as experienced and encountered in the everyday.[28]

Let us now return to the epistemic issue at hand. The central issue is whether, when ruling on motions to dismiss under Rule 12(b)(6), conditions will suppress this expression of prejudice or whether a doorway of discretion will unlock the expression of prejudice. All else being equal, this justification-suppression model of prejudice predicts that, while judges may seek to suppress their genuine prejudice toward racial outsiders, requiring them to make decisions based on their "common sense" will prompt and justify the release of prejudice, thereby resulting in the dismissal of claims by racial outsiders.

Empirical research bears this out. Since *Iqbal*, the rate of dismissal in federal courts has risen by approximately 10 percent across counseled cases and by 11 percent across cases filed by unrepresented (pro se) parties.[29] The dismissal rate in cases brought by Black plaintiffs who allege racial discrimination in the workplace has increased even more starkly. Indeed, the dismissal rate for these claims rose from 23.2 percent under *Conley v. Gibson*[30] to 53.2 percent under *Iqbal* and even more sharply for Black pro se claimants.[31] It is twice as likely that a judge will dismiss a Black plaintiff's legally sufficient claim of racial discrimination in the workplace under plausibility pleading than notice pleading.[32] What this means is that—when combining the rise in the percentage of cases challenged by Rule 12(b)(6) motions to dismiss and the increased dismissal rate in these cases—the overall percentage of Black plaintiffs' claims of race discrimination dismissed at the commencement of litigation has risen greatly. Moreover, while White and Black federal judges decided Black plaintiffs' claims of race discrimination comparably under notice pleading, it is twice as likely that a White judge will grant dismissal of a Black plaintiff's claim of race discrimination than a Black judge. This disparity turns largely on whether courts decided that these Black plaintiffs sufficiently pleaded prima facie cases of discrimination and plausible claims of discrimination.[33] Thus, the disparity centers on the legal construction of racism. Rule 12(b)(6) operates as a doorway of discretion through which prejudice, stereotypes, and discrimination shape judicial decision-making.

Conclusion

Ultimately, the seemingly neutral and objective Federal Rules of Civil Procedure are neither neutral in design nor in operation. Rather, the Federal Rules are interpreted in ways that privilege the views of powerful insiders and dominant commercial interests, routinely subordinating the perspectives of racial outsiders. The appearance of neutrality and objectivity in the Rules is a legitimizing fiction: they subtly tilt the balance of civil justice in ways that systematically disadvantage subordinated groups and racial outsiders. Not only are the Federal Rules askew but existing societal inequalities in the distribution of economic, social, and political power intersect with these seemingly neutral Rules to reproduce and amplify societal advantages, disadvantages, and inequalities, thereby undermining the interests of people of color. Nevertheless, legal scholars and law students who seek to achieve racial justice must embrace civil procedure as a tool necessary to advance racial justice while simultaneously using these two lessons to critique, deconstruct, and dismantle abuses of the civil justice system, and interpretations of the Rules that prevent subordinated groups from advancing visions of social equality and vindicating their civil and constitutional rights.

NOTES

1 *See* Jerry Kang, *Trojan Horses of Race*, 188 Harv. L. Rev. 1489 (2005); Linda Hamilton Krieger & Susan T. Fiske, *Behavioral Realism in Employment Discrimination Law: Implicit Bias and Disparate Treatment*, 96 Calif. L. Rev. 997 (2006); Roy L. Brooks, Critical Procedure (1998); Charles R. Lawrence III, *The Id, the Ego, and Equal Protection: Reckoning with Unconscious Racism*, 39 Stan. L. Rev. 317 (1987).

2 *See* A. Benjamin Spencer, *The Restrictive Ethos in Civil Procedure*, 78 Geo. Wash. L. Rev. 353 (2010); Suja A. Thomas, *The New Summary Judgment Motion: The Motion to Dismiss under Iqbal and Twombly*, 14 Lewis & Clark L. Rev. 15 (2010).

3 *See* Judith Resnik, *Managerial Judges*, 96 Harv. L. Rev. 374 (1982).

4 *See* Laura Beth Nielsen & Robert L. Nelson, *Scaling the Pyramid: A Sociolegal Model of Employment Discrimination Litigation*, *in* Handbook of Research on Employment Discrimination 3, 3–34 (Laura Beth Nielsen & Robert L. Nelson eds., 2008).

5 Ashcroft v. Iqbal, 556 U.S. 662, 678.

6 *Id.* at 679.

7 *Id.*

8 *See* John F. Dovidio & Sam L. Gaertner, *The Effect of Race, Status, and Ability on Helping Behavior*, 44 Soc. Sci. Q. 192 (1981).

9 *See* John F. Dovidio & Sam L. Gaertner, *On the Nature of Contemporary Prejudice: The Causes, Consequences, and Challenges of Aversive Racism*, *in* Confronting Racism: The Problem and the Response 3, 5–6 (Jennifer L. Eberhardt & Susan T. Fiske eds., 1998).

10 *Id.* at 25–26.

11 Christian S. Crandall & Amy Eshleman, *The Justification-Suppression Model of Prejudice: An Approach to the History of Prejudice Research*, *in* Social Psychology of Prejudice: Historical and Contemporary Issues 237 (Christian S. Crandall & Mark Schaller eds., 2004).

12 *See id.* at 241.

13 *See* Devon W. Carbado & Daria Roithmayr, *Critical Race Theory Meets Social Science*, 10 Ann. Rev. L. & Soc. Sci. 149 (2014).

14 Crandall & Eshleman, Social Psychology of Prejudice, *supra* note 11, at 240–42.

15 *See* Dovidio & Gaertner, Confronting Racism, *supra* note 9, at 4–8.

16 Crandall & Eshleman, Social Psychology of Prejudice, *supra* note 11, at 238.

17 *Id.* 241.

18 *Id.*

19 *See* Maureen A. Craig & Jennifer A. Richeson, *Coalition or Derogation? How Perceived Discrimination Influences Intraminority Intergroup Relations*, 102 J. Pers. & Soc. Psych. 759 (2012).

20 Crandall & Eshleman, Social Psychology of Prejudice, *supra* note 11, at 257.

21 Ashcroft v. Iqbal, 556 U.S. 662, 679 (2009).

22 *See* Ian F. Haney Lopez, *The Social Construction of Race: Some Observations on Illusion, Fabrication, and Choice*, 29 Harv. Civ. Rts.–Civ. Liberties L. Rev. 1 (1994).

23 *Iqbal*, 556 U.S. at 681.

24 *Id.* at 682.

25 *Id.*

26 *Id.* at 662. For a discussion revealing that the majority of those arrested were not immigrants from Arab Muslim countries (e.g., Pakistani men) and, thus, that the Court constructed and applied this mistaken category when reasoning based on "common sense," *see* Shirin Sinnar, *The Lost Story of* Iqbal, 105 Geo. L.J. 379, 440 (2017).

27 There is no inherent, fixed, perspective-free definition of what racism and discrimination are. *See* Samuel R. Sommers & Michael I. Norton, *Lay Theories About White Racists: What Constitutes Racism (and What Doesn't)*, 9 Grp. Processes & Intergroup Rel. 117, 131–32 (2006). For example, the concept of racism may be understood broadly or narrowly or accessed from the perspective of victim or perpetrator and turns on the lay theory applied. *See* Kimberle W. Crenshaw, *Race, Reform, and Retrenchment: Transformation and Legitimation in Antidiscrimination Law*, 101 Harv. L. Rev. 1331 (1988).

28 *See* Anne E. Ralph, *Narrative-Erasing Procedure*, 18 Nev. L.J. 573, 628 (2018). For example, many people of color may experience racism in intersectional ways, as double-binds that require identity performances, as all too common microaggressions, as the denial that race matters, or as within–racial group prejudice affecting those perceived as more stereotypically Black. *See* Devon W. Carbado & Mitu Gulati, Acting White? Rethinking Race in "Post-Racial" America (2013).

29 *See* Alexander Reinert, *Measuring the Impact of Plausibility Pleading*, 101 Va. L. Rev. 2117, 2143–44 (2015).

30 Conley v. Gibson, 355 U.S. 41 (2007).

31 Victor D. Quintanilla, *Critical Race Empiricism: A New Means to Measure Civil Procedure*, 3 U.C. Irvine L. Rev. 187, 206 (2013).

32 Victor D. Quintanilla, *Beyond Common Sense: A Social-Psychological Study of* Iqbal*'s Effect on Claims of Race Discrimination*, 17 Mich. J. Race & L. 1, 40, n.238 (2011).

33 *See id.*; Quintanilla, *Critical Race Empiricism*, *supra* note 30.

19

#SoWhiteMale

Federal Civil Rulemaking

BROOKE COLEMAN

The Civil Rules Committee drafts and amends the Federal Rules of Civil Procedure, a responsibility that exerts a vast impact on the civil justice system. It has existed for more than eighty years. During that time, of the 136 individuals who have served on the Civil Rules Committee, 116 are white men, 15 are white women, and five are men of color. Of the current fourteen members on the committee, nine are white men, four are white women, and one is a black man. In other words, since the Civil Rules Committee was established in 1934, the gender and racial identity of committee members has remained static. The committee has been and remains #SoWhiteMale.

One deflection of this critique is that the rules are too technical—too boring, frankly—to be tainted by misogyny or racism. Courts and many commentators, including the rule makers themselves, argue that the rulemaking process is technocratic; thus, it is ostensibly neutral and apolitical. Indeed, a primary reason the United States Supreme Court delegated its rulemaking authority to a committee was to ensure that litigation experts, not Congress, would create and monitor the Civil Rules. Yet when it comes to rulemaking, there is no clean line between expertise and politics. Ideology, politics, and identity all inform how the civil rulemaking committee members approach their work.

In addition, while the Rules may be dry and technical, they are a foundational mechanism for regulating the legal profession, which excluded men of color and all women for centuries and still struggles to empower anyone other than white men. Because of, and in spite of, that history, legal institutions should aggressively pursue equalizing measures. This effort includes creating a rulemaking committee that reflects the greater population. Putting an end to a #SoWhiteMale rulemaking committee would help break down the inequalities entrenched in the legal profession and civil justice system.

#SoWhiteMale Civil Rules Committee

The Civil Rules Committee, which has primary responsibility for drafting the Federal Rules of Civil Procedure, has been in place since 1934 with only a two-year hiatus (1956–1958). It consists of fifteen people, including a chairperson, a reporter, and a member of the Department of Justice, most often an assistant attorney general, who sits ex officio. Between 1934 and 2018, 136 individuals have served on the committee. Of the 136 individuals who have served on the committee, 116 are white men, 16 are white women, 4 are black men, and 1 is a Latino/Hispanic man. The committee composition by race and gender is set forth in Figures 19.1–19.5.

There are several caveats to consider when breaking down the racial and gender composition of the committee. With respect to racial identity, I used the US Census Bureau racial designations. Distilling identity down to a single categorical description, the Census Bureau oversimplifies personal identity and perpetuates categories that have their origins in oppression and racism.[1] At the same time, categorical labels are required to describe and define the lack of diversity on the committee (and beyond). To that end, I use the Census Bureau's racial descriptors, but not without trepidation.[2]

With respect to gender, the terminology refers to "men" and "women." These terms are also problematic. They wrongly presume that gender is binary, and the term "woman/women" erases the intersectionality that differently impacts women of different races, sexual orientation, class, or other factors. Where possible—and where the statistics are available—this chapter presents information about women divided at the very least along racial lines. As the figures show, the committee's historical gender composition is 89 percent men and 11 percent women. In terms of race and gender, the historical composition of the committee is 85 percent white men, 3 percent black men, 0.7 percent Latino/Hispanic men, and 11 percent white women. No people of color or women served on the committee

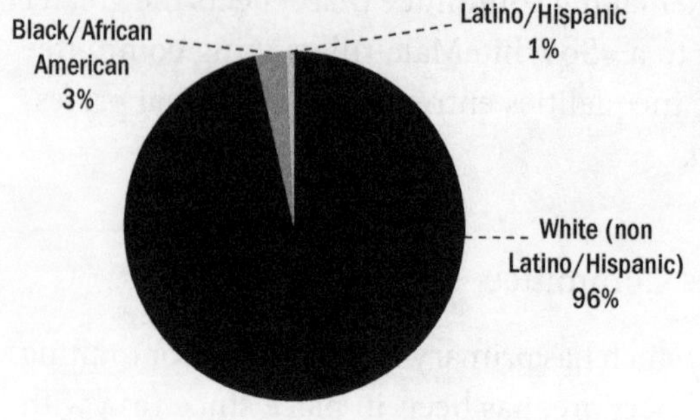

Figure 19.1. Racial composition of Civil Rules Committee, 1934–2018.

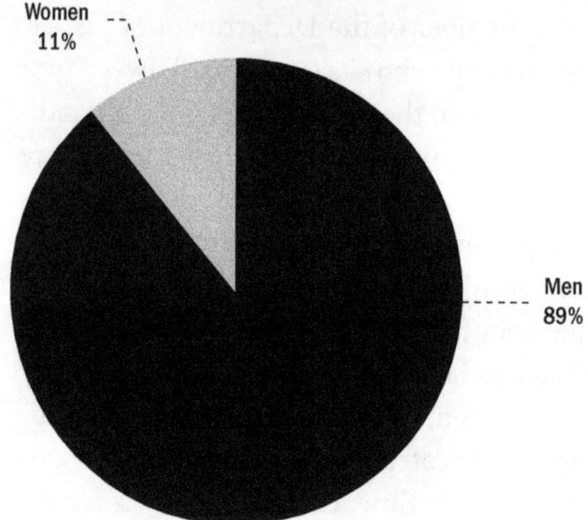

Figure 19.2. Gender composition of Civil Rules Committee, 1934–2018.

during four decades of the committee's existence. In the other five decades, people of color have served in severely disproportionate numbers compared to white individuals. Only five men of color have served—four black men and one Latino/Hispanic man. This amounts to approximately one person of color on the fifteen-member rules committee each decade. White women have had greater representation than men of color, but their representation still falls far short of equipoise.

To further put these stark numbers into context, table 19.1 compares the racial composition of the committee to the racial composition of the United States as reported by the Census Bureau (as of July 2019), followed by the racial composition of lawyers and federal district court judges in the United States—the groups from which committee members are drawn.

Table 19.1 shows that white men—both historically and currently—dominate the committee's composition. This is true with respect to every metric: general population, legal practice, and federal district court judges. Conversely, every racial designation is underrepresented on the committee on every count. For example, while Latino/Hispanic individuals hold 14 percent of federal district court judgeships and make up about 5 percent of the Bar, they have made up less than 1 percent of the Rules Committee over time. The story is roughly the same for other people of color. For instance, while black individuals hold 14 percent of federal district court judgeships, no black federal judges serve on the committee. The only person of color serving on the committee currently is a black male law professor appointed in 2017.

Gender composition of the committee is no different. Women hold 34 percent of federal district court judgeships and make up 36 percent of practicing lawyers, yet they have held only 11 percent of the committee seats over time. Four women have served on the committee in recent years, making up 28 percent of its composition. This is certainly progress, but again, these women are all white, although women of color hold 11.9 percent of federal judgeships[3] and make up 14.5 percent of practicing lawyers.[4]

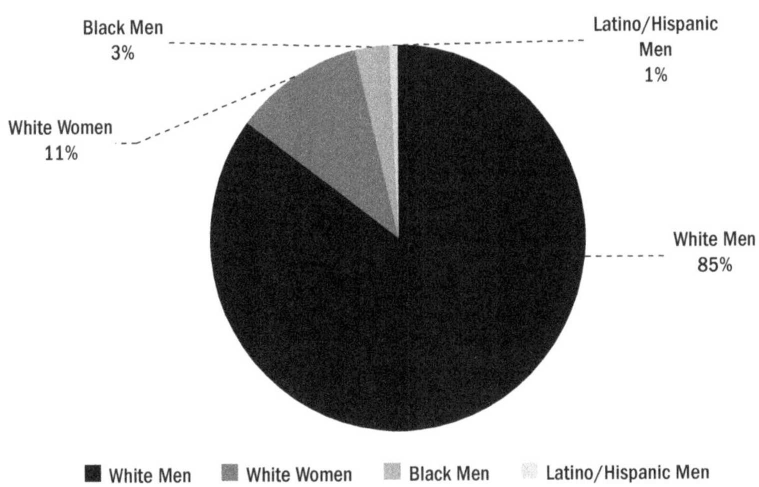

Figure 19.3. Racial and gender composition of Civil Rules Committee, 1934–2018.

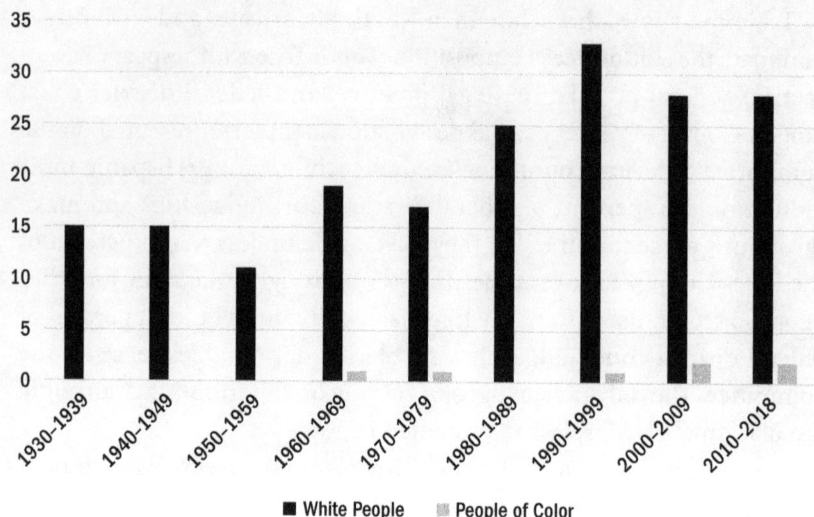

Figure 19.4. Racial composition of Civil Rules Committee for each decade since 1930.

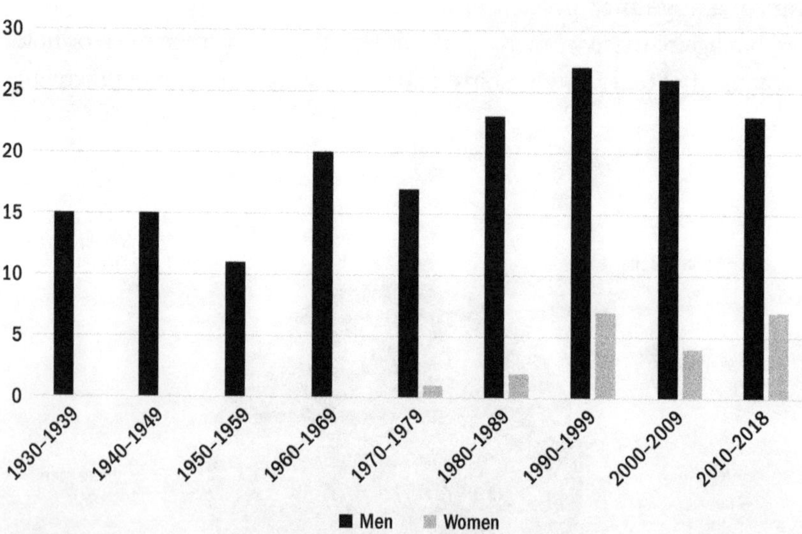

Figure 19.5. Gender composition of Civil Rules Committee for each decade since 1930.

The homogeneity of the committee membership is even more prominent when looking at committee leadership. The two key roles on the committee are the chair and the reporter. All but one of the fifteen committee chairs—the Honorable Lee Rosenthal, a white woman—has been a white man. And every single one of the nine reporters has been a white man. In other words, like the committee's membership, the committee's leadership is #SoWhiteMale.

Identity Matters

The identity of the rulemaking committee is homogeneous—that much is clear. The question is whether that homogeneity should matter. The answer is yes.

Some committee members and scholars assert that the committee is an apolitical body engaging in neutral, expert-driven work. It is true

TABLE 19.1. Committee membership racial identity compared to general population, law practice population, and judiciary

Race	Committee membership (1934–2018)	Current committee membership	US population (Census)[i]	Legal practice[ii]	Federal district court judges[iii]
White (non-Latino/Hispanic)	96%	94%	60.7%	85.5%	71%
Latino/Hispanic	0.7%	0%	18.1%	5.1%	10%
Black/ African American	2.9%	7%	13.4%	4.6%	14%
American Indian or Alaska Native	0.0%	0%	1.3%	**	**
Asian	0.0%	0%	5.8%	4.8%	3%
Native Hawaiian or Other Pacific Islander	0.0%	0%	0.2%	**	**

** The data provided in the *IILP Review 2017* (see citation ii below), did not break down percentages in these two categories.

[i] *Quick Facts: United States*, U.S. Census Bureau, www.census.gov (estimates as of July 1, 2019).

[ii] Institute for Inclusion in the Legal Profession, *IILP Review 2017: The State of Diversity and Inclusion in the Legal Profession* 18 (2017), www.theiilp.com/. Numbers reflect data for 2015.

[iii] Erin Duffin, *Percentage of Active U.S. District Court Judges as of August 2017, by Race and Hispanic Origin*, Statista (Feb. 17, 2021), www.statista.com. The categories are slightly different than what is presented in this table because the statistics account for "multi-racial," with 8% of federal district court judges falling into that category.

TABLE 19.2. Committee membership gender identity compared to general population, law practice population, and judiciary

Gender	Committee membership (1943-2018)	Current committee membership	US population (Census)[i]	Legal practice[ii]	Federal district court judges[iii]
Male	89%	72%	49.2%	64%	66%
Female	11%	28%	50.8%	36%	34%

[i] *Quick Facts: United States*, U.S. Census Bureau, www.census.gov (estimates as of July 1, 2019).
[ii] Institute for Inclusion in the Legal Profession, *IILP Review 2017: The State of Diversity and Inclusion in the Legal Profession* 18 (2017), www.theiilp.com, at 18.
[iii] Barry J. McMillion, Cong. Rsch. Serv., *U.S. Circuit and District Court Judges: Profile of Select Characteristics* 15 (2017), https://fas.org.

that in civil rulemaking pure politics is not front and center. The Chief Justice of the United States Supreme Court, an unelected member of the judicial branch, appoints the committee members, many of whom are judges themselves whose day job is based on their ability to be neutral and objective. Yet—as recent battles over judicial nominations have brought to light—both the Chief Justice and the committee members he appoints possess biases and experiences that inform how they view the world and, more narrowly, civil litigation.

Finally, almost every rule amendment reflects the committee members' normative judgment about what litigation values should be elevated. For example, Rule 26(b)(1) was amended in 2015 to require that discovery be "proportional to the needs of the case." This rule amendment reflected a normative judgment that discovery under the prior iteration of the rule created unnecessary costs in time and money. The new rule encourages judges to restrict discovery—even if those restrictions mean that some plaintiffs with valid claims will be unable to get the information they need to win their cases. This judgment contrasted with previous committee members' value judgment that discovery should be expansive (even at the expense of some delay).

In addition, the rulemaking committee is a deliberative body that depends on thoughtful consideration by its members. Social science studies repeatedly demonstrate that diverse perspectives in decision-making bodies improve the product. For example, a recent study of jury deliberations determined that the ethnically diverse group of jurors was significantly more likely than the all-white group of jurors to notice missing evidence, ask better questions, and make accurate decisions.[5]

In rulemaking too, a more representative rulemaking body might produce different, and perhaps better, rules. When people work with individuals who are different from themselves, they tend to ask better questions and think harder about issues.[6] That is because it creates what researchers call "friction."[7] Friction "can increase conflict in some group settings," but it can also inspire group members to ask better questions, think more deeply about problems, and actively participate in the proceedings.[8] According to researchers, for this kind of decision-making, "vigilant skepticism is beneficial; overreliance on others' decisions is risky."[9] Heterogeneity in group decision-making may not lead to a smooth, conflict-free decision-making process, but it will lead group members to "sharpen" their thinking and make better decisions.[10] In other words, in a context such as federal civil rulemaking, diverse decision-making bodies are "smarter."[11]

For example, when the modern class action rule (Rule 23) was adopted in 1966, the committee was an all–white male body.[12] Yet Rule 23(b)(2), the class action injunction rule, was adopted in response to the school desegregation cases of the 1950s and 1960s. Benjamin Kaplan and Albert Sacks, the committee members who spearheaded the adoption of Rule 23(b)(2), were both active in the civil rights movement, and the remaining committee members, while white, male, and elite, were exceedingly progressive.[13] The committee designed a procedural tool to eradicate a systemic wrong.

Imagine if a woman served on this committee—a person steeped in the challenges for women in the workplace. Would the rule have developed differently if the committee members had considered other types of institutional reform litigation, such as gender discrimination or sexual harassment? For example, might Rule 23(b)(2) have expressly allowed for the recovery of certain kinds of monetary relief such as back pay along with the injunctive relief? In *Wal-Mart Stores, Inc. v. Dukes*,[14] the Supreme Court held that the individualized back pay sought by the plaintiffs was not permitted in a Rule 23(b)(2) class action. A rule that specifically allowed for this relief and anticipated future structural reform would have put this question to bed. It is at least possible that a committee with different membership would have produced a better rule.

In summary, the federal civil rulemaking process relies on expertise—and rightfully so. Yet, that expertise does not eliminate the potential for bias in decision-making. A committee that is more representative of men of color and of women of all colors would not only mitigate these biases but also likely produce rules that reflect a variety of diverse perspectives and consider issues that other members may have overlooked.

The history of exclusion in the legal profession is a second important reason to pursue greater diversity on the rulemaking committee. As a body that represents the most elite members of the legal community, the committee should endeavor to actively right the wrongs of this past.[15] The Chief Justice must prioritize appointing more men of color and women of all colors to the committee; however, this will not happen without the insistence of the greater judiciary, lawyers, and members of the legal academy.

The committee cannot remediate the inevitable results of the exclusion of whole categories of individuals overnight, but diversifying membership is a step in the right direction. A more diverse committee will have concrete benefits for the rulemaking process and the rules themselves, and it will contribute to what should be a professional commitment to correcting the legal profession's history of excluding so many qualified individuals based on identity alone.

Conclusion

#SoWhiteMale should not describe the federal civil rulemaking process or the Federal Rules of Civil Procedure. In the first survey of its kind, this chapter evaluates the gender and racial compositions of the rulemaking committee over its eighty-year-plus tenure and finds that, historically, white men have disproportionately served on the committee to the exclusion of men of color and women of all colors. There are also clear disadvantages to excluding diverse individuals from the rulemaking committee. Social science studies show that diverse perspectives can help mollify members' potential biases, identify details other members may miss, and encourage deeper thinking about complex problems. While the committee has made progress in including white women and men of color in the last few decades, no women of color have ever been appointed to the committee, and white men continue to be appointed in overwhelming numbers.

Moreover, the underrepresentation of men of color and women of all colors on the committee reflects the dearth of diverse voices and perspectives within the legal profession itself. Prioritizing the diversification of the rulemaking committee is a small step in correcting the systematic exclusion of diverse individuals in the legal profession.

The time has come for the Chief Justice to commit to ensuring that the rulemaking committee's racial and gender composition is more representative. The evidence of imbalance is clear, and the action to be taken is quite simple. Judges, attorneys, and academics must now demand change.

NOTES

Acknowledgment: This chapter is updated and adapted from the article Brooke D. Coleman, *#SoWhiteMale: Federal Civil Rulemaking*, 113 Nw. U. L. Rev. 407 (2018).

1 Janet E. Helms, *Introduction: Review of Racial Identity Terminology*, in *Black and White Racial Identity: Theory, Research, and Practice* 3, 3 (Janet E. Helms ed., 1990) (stating that "the term 'racial identity' actually refers to a sense of group or collective identity based on one's *perception* that he or she shares a common racial heritage with a particular racial group").

2 *See* Kenneth Prewitt, *Fix the Census' Archaic Racial Categories*, N.Y. Times, Aug. 22, 2013, at A27 (critiquing current designations and calling for a new approach to collecting census data).

3 Barry J. McMillion, Cong. Res. Serv., U.S. Circuit & District Court Judges: Profile of Select Characteristics 20, fig. 12 (2017), sgp.fas.org.

4 *IILP Review 2017: The State of Diversity and Inclusion in the Legal Profession* 18 (2017), www.theiilp.com.

5 Samuel R. Sommers, *On Racial Diversity and Group Decision Making: Identifying Multiple Effects of Racial Composition on Jury Deliberations*, 90 J. Personality & Soc. Psych. 597, 605–06 (2006).

6 *Id.*

7 Sheen S. Levine, Evan P. Apfelbaum, Mark Bernard, Valerie L. Bartelt, Edward J. Zajac & David Stark, *Ethnic Diversity Deflates Price Bubbles*, 111 Proc. Nat'l Acad. Scis. 18,524, 18,525 (2014).

8 *Id.*

9 *Id.*

10 Daniel Rock & Heidi Grant, *Why Diverse Teams Are Smarter*, Harv. Bus. Rev. (Nov. 4, 2016), https://hbr.org/2016/11/why-diverse-teams-are-smarter.

11 *Id.*

12 David Marcus, *Flawed but Noble: Desegregation Litigation and Its Implications for the Modern Class Action*, 63 Fla. L. Rev. 657, 709 (2011).

13 *Id.* at 702–05.

14 564 U.S. 338 (2011).

15 In response to past critiques, the Chief Justice's appointments to the committee have become more geographically varied and included some variety of practice types (smaller firms, for example). Peter G. McCabe, *Renewal of the Federal Rulemaking Process*, 44 Am. U. L. Rev. 1655, 1666 (1995). Yet, gender and race have not been prioritized.

PART III

Constitutional Procedure

Due Process and Jurisdiction

Students and professors of civil procedure spend a lot of time studying and teaching jurisdiction. Part III challenges us to think about why that is, as well as to consider what we might be missing. Together these chapters reveal the degree to which persistent narratives about the doctrines of personal jurisdiction and notice mislead. Charlton Copeland in chapter 20 takes on the notion that robust personal jurisdiction doctrines harm some business interests by showing how larger companies hide behind a false narrative of small businesses suffering. The effect is that large businesses are able to shield themselves from liability, while small businesses reap little benefit, especially if they wish to litigate against a larger corporate defendant. Robin Effron (chapter 21) breaks down standard assumptions about who our modern notice regime actually protects by unpacking how state and federal courts differ so deeply in the kind of cases they see and the lineup of the litigants who use them. These chapters challenge the standard tropes of personal jurisdiction and notice and invite readers to think more deeply about how these doctrines are contributing to a system of less—not more—justice.

The chapters on subject matter jurisdiction and choice of law once again illuminate how the US civil litigation system is not one of idealized courts. In an idealized court system, courts applying the same law to similar parties and legal questions would reach the same result. This is the calling-balls-and-strikes theory of judicial decision-making: the objective court reaches an objective result. Yet these chapters show us how this is not reality. Elizabeth McCuskey in chapter 22 challenges the superiority premise of federal courts. Through an application of convergence theory, McCuskey questions whether the homogeneous federal bench is really any better than state courts. Angelique EagleWoman in chapter 23 describes the existence and operation of Tribal Courts and critiques the

United States Supreme Court's interference with those courts' ability to resolve disputes within tribal lands. David Marcus (chapter 24), using a case study of Congress's jurisdiction-channeling immigration legislation, demonstrates how federal appellate courts effectively sidestep their obligation to mete out justice by reading such legislation as a limitation on their authority. Finally, Briana Rosenbaum (chapter 25) explores how juvenile transgender defendants are sometimes unable to raise their protections under Title IX simply because of the adjudicatory forum in which they find themselves. Rosenbaum's chapter reminds us that, even if the law is favorable to a party, the result still depends on who is doing the interpreting. Together these chapters dissect the differences among—and justifications for—variant court systems.

20

Building a Litigation Coalition

Business Interests and the Transformation of Personal Jurisdiction

CHARLTON COPELAND

Prior studies of reduced access to litigation have largely focused on conservative, business-oriented partisan influence on rulemaking and on enhancing the federal pleading requirements. This chapter expands on this critique to include jurisdictional challenges to litigation, on both the federal and state court levels. More specifically, this chapter sheds a critical light on a network of anti-litigation movements within elite legal and policy circles[1] that are transforming personal jurisdiction to erect barriers to litigation.

Given the nature of the US state's aversion to strong, centralized, bureaucratically oriented policy-making, private litigation performs important regulatory and redistributive functions. The rise of the so-called litigation state has been necessary given the harsh realities of a free market, which rewards individual entrepreneurialism and risk-taking. As such, the twentieth century saw the rise of an ecology supportive of litigation, including the expansion of states' capacity to vindicate the interests of their citizens injured as a result of out-of-state actors. The transformation of personal jurisdiction jurisprudence in the middle of the twentieth century was marked in 1945 by *International Shoe v. Washington*'s[2] recognition of the realities of the then-modern world, as well as the necessity to empower states with adjudicatory capacity to meet their obligations to their citizens.[3]

The framework built by *International Shoe* and its progeny has been challenged by businesses that argue against broad state adjudicatory authority because it undermines their capacity to coordinate relationships with states and to control potential liability in multiple jurisdictions.

Critics of liberal state authority contend that the framework gives rise to forum shopping, which places defendants at a disadvantage.

This chapter relies on ClassCrit theory to show how corporate power and conservative ideological organizations have combined to establish a near-uniform voice opposed to state assertion of adjudicatory authority over out-of-state defendants.[4] ClassCrit theory highlights the ways that entrepreneurial litigators mask distinctions among "business" interests by arguing that expansive state jurisdiction over defendants is always bad. Given that one of the first objectives of ClassCrit scholarship is to make class visible, this objective is an important aspect of challenging the seemingly unified business voice in arguments before appellate tribunals.[5] To this extent, this chapter calls attention to the rhetoric of litigation used to constrain state adjudicatory authority.

There is a cadre of elite repeat players who file amicus briefs in cases involving specific and general in personam jurisdiction, in addition to domestic and foreign defendants who urge courts to restrain state adjudicatory authority. This chapter focuses on the most frequent actors in personal jurisdiction appellate litigation. Among the most dominant voices are the United States Chamber of Commerce (US Chamber) and the Product Liability Advisory Council.[6] In briefs filed before the United States Supreme Court, these organizations advance arguments that bridge the interests of domestic and foreign business entities and aggregate the interests of small and large businesses. In short, these organizations have broken down barriers among business entities in order to erect them between litigants and the courts.

Commentators have noted how the rise of a politically mobilized business establishment has had to overcome differences among small and large businesses that represent the much discussed "Main Street/Wall Street" divide. From a ClassCrit perspective, the elite business establishment's blindness to the distinctions between their interests and those of other types of business enterprises is analogous to the larger project of hiding class.[7] If large businesses are able to ally themselves with smaller businesses, they are better able to hide the class distinctions implicit in the different corporate structures.

But this unified business voice—one that is intentionally blind to class divisions—is a recent phenomenon in the personal jurisdiction context.

Asahi Metal v. Superior Court of California,[8] the most significant pre–Roberts Court era personal jurisdiction decision, provides a ready example of how business interests diverged in their personal jurisdiction advocacy. As *Asahi* evidenced a developing ideological divide between conservative and liberal justices on the Court, it also exposed a divide between domestic and foreign corporate interests.

Asahi addressed whether an international parts manufacturer could be sued in a California court resulting from an accident involving the finished product. The Court divided along lines of how much awareness was required by a defendant before a state could assert jurisdiction over the defendant. Justice O'Connor, joined by Chief Justice Rehnquist and Justices Powell and Scalia, asserted that the defendant's "mere foreseeability or awareness" that its product was sold in a particular state was insufficient to establish the contacts necessary to assert adjudicatory authority over the defendant.[9] The "liberal" justices—Justices Brennan, White, Marshall, and Blackmun—rejected the higher bar the other justices attempted to establish. Justice Stevens wrote separately, also rejecting the higher standard. Despite the disagreement on the issue of sufficient contacts to establish jurisdiction, the Court unanimously decided that California could not assert jurisdiction over the foreign defendant on the ground that this would violate the Due Process Clause because of the burden this would place on the defendant.

Asahi is notable because it was the first decision that marked disagreement across the Court's ideological wings. Up to that point, much of the disagreement in personal jurisdiction jurisprudence was as likely to come within ideological camps as across them.

Asahi is also notable as the first of the then-contemporary line of personal jurisdiction cases to attract the attention of amici.[10] The only brief in support of the defendant's position was by the American Chamber of Commerce in the United Kingdom (U.K. Chamber) and the Confederation of British Industry (CBI). The U.K. Chamber described itself as a nonprofit "founded in 1916 to promote and develop trade between the United States and Great Britain."[11] The CBI described itself as a nonprofit that "exists primarily to inform governments on the needs of British business."[12] The amici filed a brief because "some of the international concerns expressed [by the parties] have not been adequately addressed by the parties."[13] The amici argued in favor of the foreign defendant's position that California's assertion of adjudicatory authority "threatens important and legitimate interests of their member enterprises and the international business community generally."[14]

While the British business community weighed in on the side of the defendants, the US business community, to the extent it weighed in at all, supported California's assertion of authority over the foreign defendant.[15] The California Manufacturers Association (CMA) described itself as an organization that represented "approximately 70 percent of California's industrial workforce, and company sizes range from the smallest business to the largest, multi-national corporations in the world."[16] In supporting California's assertion of adjudicatory authority, the CMA's brief argued: "A reversal of the California court's holding may jeopardize the lives, safety and health of California consumers, businesses and manufacturers, by providing another barrier which increases the difficulty an individual or company presently confronts when seeking a legitimate and lawful solution to the assignment of responsibility."[17] Further, the brief asserted: "[A reversal of the California court decision] could be devastating to the manufacturers represented by CMA, as well as to the consumers who purchase their products."[18]

In the period between the decision in *Asahi* in 1987 and *J. McIntyre Machinery v. Nicastro*[19] in 2011, the ideological fault lines about what constitutes sufficiently purposeful activity by the defendant remained. In *Nicastro*, as in *Asahi*, there was a clear distinction between the conservative and liberal members of the Court. According to the conservative members of the Court, a defendant had to do more than merely seek to serve a national commercial network before being subjected to a state's adjudicatory authority. The conservative plurality held that a state's assertion of authority would not be consistent with due process unless a defendant directed its actions to the specific forum. By contrast, the liberal position—represented by Justices Ginsburg, Sotomayor, and Kagan—sustained the liberal position in *Asahi*. They asserted that New Jersey's assertion of adjudicatory authority was consistent with due process because the defendant's action evidenced a purpose to serve a national commercial network, without any particular concern as to the state with which the defendant made contact. That, the minority argued, was all that was required. In the middle, Justices Breyer and Alito sided with the liberal minority with respect to the appropriate doctrinal framework but agreed with the plurality that the defendant's actions did not meet the standard to justify jurisdiction.

But something had changed in the intervening period with respect to how businesses viewed personal jurisdiction. Nearly twenty-five years earlier, as evidenced by the amicus briefs filed, the business community was divided along domestic and international lines. By 2011, this division evaporated. The US Chamber found its voice and described itself as representing "three-hundred thousand direct members and indirectly [] an underlying membership of more than three million US businesses and professional organizations of every size and in every sector and geographic region of the country."[20] The US Chamber argued in favor of more stringent requirements, asserting that the "more relaxed stream-of-commerce test" "has deleterious consequences for the US economy and US business. That requirement cripples interstate and foreign commerce, much like a state statute designed to undermine the flow of goods into the state."[21] The US Chamber's *Nicastro* brief emphasized the adverse impact that liberal state authority to adjudicate would have on small businesses and component parts manufacturers. The brief also dismissed any distinctions between domestic and foreign defendants. The US Chamber's brief emphasized the impact that broad adjudicatory authority would have on the actions of plaintiffs, who "will exploit the [expense of jurisdictional discovery]."[22]

In addition, the Product Liability Advisory Council (PLAC), which describes itself as a "non-profit corporation with 100 corporate members representing a broad cross-section of American industry," comprising automobile, aircraft, electronics, chemical, and pharmaceutical industries,[23] weighed in in *Nicastro*. The PLAC argued in favor of the O'Connor plurality in *Asahi*. Its amicus brief argued that "the changing nature of modern commerce has altered and augmented the traditional manufacturer-distributor paradigm. Now, any individual or company can readily purchase goods and resell them via novel internet-based distribution networks, thereby becoming *bona fide* resellers in their own right."[24] This "new reality,"[25] PLAC argued, justified a heightened (not lessened) scrutiny of state assertions of adjudicatory authority. Like the

US Chamber, PLAC emphasized that transformations in distribution networks—via Amazon and other web-based platforms—would ensnare small businesses and even individuals. PLAC argued that under these new circumstances anyone can become a distributor of a good manufactured by another. In its view, a manufacturer, if not protected against broad state adjudicatory authority, would be liable for suit in far-flung jurisdictions.[26]

The arguments in the briefs paint a picture of a unified business community whose interests and risks are aligned in a globally competitive world. But these arguments are decidedly different from those advanced by the California business community in *Asahi*. As stated above, in its amicus brief, the CMA tied domestic business interests to the interests of injured consumer plaintiffs. In seeing themselves as potential plaintiffs who would be left holding the bag in cases where foreign component parts manufacturers are virtually immune from suit in the United States, the domestic manufacturers argued that the defendant's sale of more than 1.3 million component parts to the plaintiff did not constitute unilateral activity on the part of the purchaser but was the sort of activity that ought to give rise to sufficient contacts to establish jurisdiction. In fact, the California manufacturers appeared to contend that the very fact of selling even a component part in "a variety of international markets" constituted more than "unilateral" activity.[27] In other words, the California manufacturers saw their interests as aligned with manufacturers who employ parts made as part of a global supply chain, and who would be left holding the proverbial bag of liability if foreign parts manufacturers eluded US courts.

Yet mere decades later, in *Nicastro*, business interests—as represented by their amici briefs—have aligned themselves with one another. Again, ClassCrit theory offers a framework for understanding why elite business enterprises seek to cloak themselves as aligned with smaller, mom-and-pop business interests.[28] First, these businesses display the rugged individualism that appeals to conservative justices by behaving as if they are in common cause with mom-and-pop businesses. Second, courts welcome corporate interests that speak with one strong voice; it is hard to deny the appeal of simplicity when applying a fractured and confusing doctrine such as personal jurisdiction. And finally, all businesses—large and small—are the benefactors of a contracted personal jurisdiction doctrine because in essence it immunizes many businesses from liability. But missing is any sense that the interests of smaller business enterprises are ever at odds with those of larger businesses. Indeed, the issues in *Asahi* raised exactly this conflict. A generation of conservative legal and political institution-building has rendered these conflicts invisible. Indeed, the success of this movement is parasitic upon maintaining such invisibility.

By combining forces in their personal jurisdiction advocacy, business interests reap a collective benefit. This explains why institutional resources aimed at challenging state adjudicatory authority have increased. The US Chamber established the National Chamber Litigation Center (NCLC) as the organization's litigation arm to challenge the increased regulatory activity of the federal government, "including class actions and arbitration, labor and employment, energy and environment, securities and corporate governance, financial regulation, free speech, preemption, government contracts, and criminal law."[29] Notably, its focus on procedural and jurisdictional issues has increased substantially in the last several years. A review of the NCLC's website reveals that the NCLC's litigation in personal jurisdiction was basically nonexistent as early as 2010, before which it reports having filed no amicus briefs on the subject.[30] Starting with its amicus brief urging the Court to grant certiorari in *Goodyear Dunlop Tires Operations, S.A. v. Brown* in 2010, the NCLC has filed an amicus brief challenging the exercise of personal jurisdiction every year since.[31] In 2019 alone, the Center filed amicus briefs in nine different lawsuits challenging personal jurisdiction.[32]

In sum, through the concerted effort of elite business interests, the doctrine of personal jurisdiction has been transformed. Despite the size of the company immediately before them, courts tend to focus on how the smallest business might fare in too-robust a personal jurisdiction regime. That is no accident. By aligning themselves with smaller businesses, elite corporate interests have leveraged small business's interests to their advantage. Similarly, smaller businesses have benefited by riding big-business's coattails into increased immunity from suit. This clever alliance renders invisible class differentials in litigation between potential plaintiffs and business defendants. ClassCrit theory teaches that such a result is shamelessly by design.

NOTES

1 *See, e.g.*, Steven M. Teles, *The Rise of the Conservative Legal Movement: The Battle for Control of the Law* (2008).

2 International Shoe Co. v. Washington, 326 U.S. 310 (1945).

3 *See* Harold L. Korn, *The Choice-of-Law Revolution: A Critique*, 83 Colum. L. Rev. 772, 833 (1983).

4 *See* Arthur R. Miller, *McIntyre in Context: A Very Personal Perspective*, 63 S.C. L. Rev. 465, 480 (2012) (noting people have remarked to the author: "The Chamber of Commerce seems to have a seat on the Supreme Court.").

5 *See* Athena D. Mutua, *Introducing ClassCrits: From Class Blindness to Critical Legal Analysis of Economic Inequality*, 56 Buff. L. Rev. 859 (2008).

6 For other scholars' attention to the role of organized business interests in procedural litigation, *see* Joanna C. Schwartz, *The Cost of Suing Business*, 65 DePaul L. Rev. 655 (2016).

7 One need only look at the beneficiaries of the Paycheck Protection Program, enacted to combat the economic consequences of the COVID-19 pandemic, to see the extent to which a "class-blindness" to the differences among small businesses results in less access to financial resources for small and medium-size businesses. *See* Danielle Kurtzleben, *Not-So-Small Businesses Continue to Benefit from PPP Loans*, NPR (May 4, 2020, 5:51 PM), www.npr.org.

8 Asahi Metal v. Superior Court of California, 480 U.S. 102 (1987).

9 *Id.* at 111.

10 A Westlaw search of the three cases that were decided closest in time to *Asahi* show no amici briefs filed in any of the cases: Kulko v. Superior Court of California, 436 U.S. 84 (1978); World-Wide Volkswagen Corp. v. Woodson, 444 U.S. 286 (1980); and Burger King Corp. v. Rudzewicz, 471 U.S. 462 (1985).

11 Brief of the Am. Chamber of Commerce in the U.K. and the Confederation of Bus. Indus. as Amici Curiae in Support of Petitioner at 2, *Asahi*, 480 U.S. 102 (1987) (No. 85-693), 1986 WL 727584.

12 *Id.*

13 *Id.*

14 *Id.* at 1.

15 Brief of Amicus Curiae Cal. Mfrs. Ass'n in Support of Respondent, *Asahi*, 480 U.S. 102 (No. 85-693), 1986 WL 727586.

16 *Id.* at 2.

17 *Id.* at 3.

18 *Id.*

19 564 U.S. 873 (2011).

20 Brief of the Chamber of Com. of the U.S. as Amicus Curiae Support of Petitioner at 1–2, *Nicastro*, 564 U.S. 873 (2011), No. 09-1343, 2010 WL 4803147.

21 *Id.* at 3–4.

22 *Id.* at 17. The United States Chamber further emphasized that jurisdictional discovery is one-sided, which represents an especially powerful weapon in a plaintiff's arsenal for piling on costs and can "push cost-conscious defendants to settle even anemic cases before reaching those proceedings." *Id.* (citing Bell Atlantic Corp. v. Twombly, 550 U.S. 544, 559 (2007)).

23 Brief of the Prod. Liab. Advisory Council, Inc. as Amicus Curiae in Support of Petitioner at 1, *Nicastro*, 564 U.S. 873 (2011), No. 09–1343, 2010 WL 4717267.

24 *Id.* at 10.

25 *Id.* at 7.

26 *Id.* at 31–32.

27 Brief of Amicus Curiae Cal. Mfrs. Ass'n in Support of Respondent at 22, Asahi Metal Indus. v. Superior Ct. of Cal., 480 U.S. 102 (No. 85–693), 1986 WL 727586. The California manufacturers' attempt to distinguish themselves from foreign manufacturers was a reasonable response according to leading commentators. In criticizing *Nicastro*, Paul Carrington has argued that the Chamber's advocacy for the foreign manufacturer put domestic manufacturers at a comparative disadvantage. *See* Paul D. Carrington, *Business Interests and the Long Arm in 2011*, 63 S.C. L. Rev. 637 (2012).

28 *See* Athena Mutua, *Framing Elite Consensus, Ideology and Theory & a ClassCrits Response*, 44 Sw. L. Rev. 635 (2015).

29 *See Who We Are*, U.S. Chamber Litigation Center, www.chamberlitigation.com.

30 *See Recent Activity: Jurisdiction & Procedure, Personal Jurisdiction*, U.S. Chamber Litigation Center, www.chamberlitigation.com.

31 *See id.*

32 *Id.*

21

Notice and the Narratives of Court Access

ROBIN J. EFFRON

Notice and the opportunity to be heard are fundamental rights, not only in litigation but also in any other governmental proceeding for which a constitutionally protected interest is at stake. The ability to defend oneself against a potential deprivation—liability on a judgment, eviction, repossession of one's vehicle, to name a few—hinges on knowledge of the existence of an impending proceeding and sufficient information about it to begin to prepare a defense. This proposition is so uncontroversial as to be relatively unremarkable in modern discourse. Yet notice, despite its centrality to due process, is a dusty little corner of civil procedure,[1] confined to a due process footnote adjacent to longer treatments of personal jurisdiction or a dull lecture on the mechanics of service of process. Notice may seem to be too ministerial to be problematic. Most ordinary questions about service of process skate below *Mullane*'s[2] constitutional radar and below the radar of scholars and advocates.

This complacency is unjustified. Examining the due process right of notice through a critical lens reveals why it has been, well, so unnoticed. The law of notice reinforces structural inequalities that benefit property owners and institutional defendants at the expense of our most vulnerable populations. A serious reckoning with the normative assumptions underlying notice and service of process raises uncomfortable truths about the narratives of court access that progressive scholars and advocates take for granted when discussing procedural justice.

Notice rules are not one-size-fits-all. Certain types of defendants have received heightened notice protections, while other defendants get short shrift. Unsurprisingly, these distinctions tend to fall along lines of race and class.

The United States Supreme Court is the most solicitous toward owners of real property,[3] and it should give us pause that this is a specially recognized group. After all, real property is typically owned by those who already have some degree of wealth in society. Moreover, we have an uncomfortable history of exhibiting special solicitude to the landed class at the expense of other groups, some of whom experienced centuries of de jure and de facto barriers to property ownership.

In contrast, consider those most likely to be affected by poor notice and service of process: incarcerated persons, persons without a stable residence, persons for whom the English language (or literacy more broadly) is a barrier, persons who mask their whereabouts due to fears surrounding immigration status, or absent claimants whose only meaningful avenue for redress is a class action trial or settlement. For these people, the constitutional and statutory jurisprudence is spotty. Often, the Court has expressed concern about their circumstances but stopped short of offering a workable remedy.[4] Throughout time—including up to today—certain institutional actors have pushed, often successfully, for streamlined proceedings, with minimal notice. These supposed efficiencies often come at the expense of vulnerable populations and everyday consumers. Yet these instances of unjust notice have not provoked scholarly interest or outrage.

Take, for example, the problem of "sewer service," wherein low-income defendants are victims of poor or even semifraudulent service of process.[5] It is far from a sporadic or theoretical problem, and investigative reporting from as recently as 2020 has uncovered widespread problems of falsification of service affidavits by process servers, many of which resulted in default judgment and eviction of low-income tenants.[6] Scant attention has been paid to the needs of persons who lack a permanent address or for whom understanding a summons requires the aid of a translator.

Owners of small businesses often operate on tight margins and, as sole proprietors or owners of family businesses, are frequently indistinguishable from ordinary consumers. Yet in several states, they are capable of waiving their constitutional right of notice altogether via a "cognovit note" or confession of judgment clause. Once signed, the creditor, upon a predetermined event such as nonpayment, can proceed straight to court and obtain a default judgment without ever serving process on the defendant. While the Court has indicated that this doctrine is somewhat narrower than, say, the ability to agree to a forum selection clause or arbitration clause, it is still a strikingly broad power of creditors that can be used against defendants, some of whom are genuinely vulnerable. Yet, with narrow exceptions, scholars and advocates have overlooked these pervasive but technical violations of due process, even though confession of judgment clauses—just like mandatory arbitration clauses—remove whole categories of claims from the courts.

The systemic problems with notice are also endemic in class actions. Notice—a due process right—is a core requirement of class adjudication. Notice enables participation, objection, or total exit by class members. The theory of notice also undergirds the legitimacy of the whole concept of class actions. Here, too, however, notice doctrine has often evolved to protect parties along lines of class. Notice in class actions is big business. Literally.

The mechanics of class action notice have evolved in the digital era. However, the notices themselves have not necessarily evolved. They are still often boilerplate legalese printed in tiny font. Even with the modest attention paid to reaching more class members via digital means, response rates are often dismal, either because they do not reach some class members at all or because they appear to be spam.[7] The reality is that suboptimal notice in class actions is so widely accepted that it is baked in to class settlements.

Having established that notice is worth more attention than it has received, I turn to the next question: Why such inattention? In progressive legal circles, the conventional court access story is one in which marginalized and underrepresented groups are most likely to be plaintiffs, who need liberal access to courts (especially federal courts) in order to vindicate existing rights and create expanded rights. The underlying premise is that lawyers and commentators must exercise vigilance to protect court access from further erosion and engage in vigorous advocacy to restore the broader court access that claimants have, at various points in the past century, enjoyed in public tribunals.

There is, of course, nothing wrong with this narrative in and of itself. Courts have been and continue to be undeniably important sites for the protection and expansion of substantive rights and remedies. The fight to retain public forums for vindicating these rights can feel daunting, as court access seems to be constantly under threat from all directions, whether it be jurisdictional barriers, heightened pleading standards, or the enforceability of arbitration clauses. Even those plaintiffs who make it past the courts' initial access gates must then navigate more court gauntlets restricting access, such as restrictive discovery rules or aggressive summary judgment standards, meant to weed out so-called frivolous cases. Given these challenges, it is no surprise that progressive advocates and commentators have devoted significant time and energy to protecting plaintiffs' access to courts.

While these are all serious concerns, this narrative has focused progressive efforts more heavily on plaintiffs than on defendants. Defendants are not a monolithic group of privileged cisgender heterosexual white men; neither are they always faceless monied corporations. Defendants, like plaintiffs, can come from the ranks of the disadvantaged and underrepresented and tend to be overrepresented in certain categories of cases, for example, in debt collection actions.[8] Service of process rules should not be a zero-sum game in which gains to defendants as a group necessarily entails losses or restrictions to plaintiffs. "Court access" is frequently invoked as a plaintiff-centric buzzword, but defendants too have access issues. Perhaps this idea seems a bit counterintuitive. After all, a defendant, almost by definition, is a party who is made to come to court, not a party who, by various doctrines, might be blocked at the courthouse steps. And while defendants might have access to *justice* problems (such as the inability to afford counsel or foot other litigation costs), these are not technically court *access* problems. But notice *is* a court access problem: if the defendant does not know of a proceeding, she can't show up to defend herself.

Notice and service of process should be taken seriously and should be addressed as social justice issues. But such scholarly endeavors lead to a "court access conundrum" for commentators who wish to advocate for stronger notice procedures. The unspoken fear is perhaps that sustained inquiries into notice have led to reforms that, in other contexts, leave progressive attorneys with lingering discomfort: namely, doctrines that throw up hurdles in the path of plaintiffs. This is because most solutions to issues of notice in adversarial litigation come in the form of additional requirements of the opposing party. Notice must be "reasonably calculated under all the circumstances." In the US legal system, the tacit understanding is that those "circumstances" are shaped, in large part, by the resource constraints of the notifying party.[9]

The natural result of the court access conundrum has been a shyness on the part of progressive activists to take up inequities in notice and service of process doctrines with the same rigor and zeal with which we have approached countless other procedural doctrines. But we may fairly ask: Why has the scholarly establishment passively accepted a legal framework that essentially pits the court access needs of plaintiffs against the court access needs of defendants when it is possible to identify vulnerable populations in both camps? Why must we accept this framing of the right of notice and opportunity to be heard as the correct framework at all?

I believe that most courts and commentators have accepted the "circumstances" as being what they have always been: notice is provided, funded, and executed largely by the parties (with limited exceptions for situations where the US marshals or equivalent state agencies may serve process).[10] Why must these be the circumstances? Perhaps there is room for some more fundamental thinking about what the right of notice is and should be, as well as how it can be reframed in a manner that avoids the court access conundrum and makes room for robust progressive advocacy.

There are a few avenues for escaping the conceptual and structural deadlock. The first is to engage in a critical rereading of *Mullane* and courts' subsequent notice jurisprudence. The constitutional standard for notice under *Mullane* consists of an inquiry of what sort of notice is reasonable under the circumstances. For nearly seven decades, courts and commentators have understood the circumstances as a fixed state of affairs that one must accept as a part of notice analysis. This might seem a little strange—after all, the purpose of the *Mullane* standard is to create a flexible standard under which judges can make a fact-specific, case-by-case inquiry into the differing circumstances of unique plaintiffs and defendants. But the background circumstances regarding litigation and notice should not be taken for granted. Some of these circumstances are not static facts about the world, but are, instead, circumstances of our own creation that we should feel empowered to challenge and change.

Mullane was part of a procedural revolution that was driven, in large part, by changed circumstances. The old *Pennoyer* regime,[11] in which both personal jurisdiction and notice were driven by strict territorial rules and the primacy of in-hand personal service, had become untenable in a new world of fast-paced interstate commerce conducted over great distances. In *International Shoe*, the Supreme Court let go of the need to establish that the defendant have some sort of physical presence in the forum as a prerequisite to the exercise of in personam jurisdiction.[12] Five years later in *Mullane*, the Court used the temporally and geographically dispersed beneficiaries of the trust to demonstrate that there are some actions for which individualized notice (let alone in-hand service) are simply not reasonable given the realities of modern financial instruments and the complex actions needed to adjudicate their status or litigate alleged wrongdoings.

Although the worlds of *International Shoe* and *Mullane* looked quite different from the world of *Pennoyer*, our twenty-first century reality looks yet different from that of the midcentury procedural revolution from which our current standards emerged. Despite tremendous changes in technology (and the concomitant changes in how people live their lives), we seem to be stuck in a mindset of the primacy of first-class mail that parallels the paradigm of in-hand personal service that had long become stale by the time of *Mullane* and *International Shoe*. No one has questioned, for example, why nearly every jurisdiction has created networked systems for the electronic *filing* of cases and service of documents in ongoing litigation, while virtually no jurisdictions have enabled universally accessible and inexpensive systems for electronic *notice* of the commencement of an action or of the pendency of class action certification or settlement.

Many people are easily reachable by email or other electronic means. In fact, for many people, an email address is a far more durable means of identification and communication than is first-class mail. At the very least, recent reporting and scholarship suggest that the assumption that first-class mail can and does reach most people demands serious rethinking.[13] To assume that circumstances have not really changed is to assume that the old way of doing things is the standard and that new ways of being and living are different or deviations from an imaginary norm, even if it turns out that vast numbers of people conform more to a new model than the old. This is law's conservatism at its worst. And it hides most easily behind a supposedly flexible standard such as *Mullane* because that flexibility gives judges too much leeway to see the world as they believe it always has been, rather than how it actually is.

When it comes to other forms of notice, such as class action notices, we must adapt to a new circumstance of the marketplace for attention. While litigants might possess valid contact information (such as an email or residential address), these notices are received in a very different information environment in which people are bombarded with daily emails, texts, and "junk" mail, making it difficult to discern real or important messages from the daily barrage of advertisements and communications. Targeted technology that uses social media and advertising can go hand-in-glove with traditional notice practices to direct people's attention to important communications. This might, somewhat ironically, be the moment to revive and update older and disfavored doctrines such as notice by publication.

Publication is no longer confined to paper journals with local or limited (or perhaps national but diffuse) circulation. Instead, online publication can be distributed through a complex network of algorithms that have been engineered to reach precise demographics and to do so with astonishing accuracy and efficiency. It might be time to realize that the algorithms that drive social media networks and search engines are actually capable of *better* individualized targeting than using lists of names, phone numbers, residential addresses, and even email addresses that might be inaccurate or out of date. We are living in an era where notice by publication *very well might be* individual notice, even though it does not look like the personal in-hand service of process that was once the poster child for gold-standard service.

Modernizing notice and equipping service of process procedures for the modern era will not be easy. It will require hard work in fixing the inequities of how notice is received and comprehended by vulnerable communities—a problem that cannot be fixed by simply moving the old analog procedures to an online interface. It will involve harnessing the possibilities for inexpensive and accurate ways of reaching the right people with the serious privacy and safety concerns of using data, algorithms, and private channels of internet communication. And it will necessitate constant attention to the fundamental court access conundrum—how progressive advocates can ensure meaningful court access for parties on *both* sides of the proverbial adversarial "v."

NOTES

1 This chapter focuses on the due process right of notice as it applies to adversarial litigation in American courts. Notice, of course, has a much broader application, as the Fifth and Fourteenth Amendments and *Mullane* standard apply to a wide variety of situations in which a government action might deprive a person of a protected interest.

2 Mullane v. Cent. Hanover Bank & Tr., 339 U.S. 306 (1950).

3 Jones v. Flowers, 547 U.S. 220 (2006); Mennonite Bd. of Missions v. Adams, 462 U.S. 791 (1983).

4 Dusenbery v. United States, 534 U.S. 161 (2002). Note that in *Dusenbery*, the Court upheld service by certified mail even though the prisoner claimed he did not receive *actual* notice.

5 The term comes from the practice of tossing process in the sewer and then submitting a falsified affidavit or affirmation that process had, indeed, been served. *See* Adrian Gottshall, *Solving Sewer Service: Fighting Fraud with Technology*, 70 Ark. L. Rev. 813, 818 (2018).

6 *See* Josh Kaplan, *Thousands of D.C. Renters Are Evicted Every Year. Do They All Know to Show Up to Court?*, DCist (Oct. 5, 2020, 1:43PM), https://dcist.com.

7 Brian T. Fitzpatrick & Robert C. Gilbert, *An Empirical Look at Compensation in Consumer Class Actions*, 11 N.Y.U. J. L. & Bus. 767, 777 (2015) (describing participation rates as low as .000006 percent and as high as more than 90 percent). Note that I disagree with their characterization of some of these success rates as successful.

8 *See How Debt Collectors Are Transforming the Business of State Courts*, Pew Charitable Tr. (May 6, 2020), www.pewtrusts.org.

9 This has created particularly thorny problems when it comes to class action notices, although this is also a realm in which litigants have been the most successful in harnessing new technologies to deliver notice. How successful these notification efforts actually are is another question entirely.

10 I explore this idea in depth in *The Invisible Circumstances of Notice*. Robin J. Effron, *The Invisible Circumstances of Notice*, 99 N.C. L. Rev. (forthcoming 2021).

11 Pennoyer v. Neff, 95 U.S. 714 (1878).

12 Of course, we have seen a return to territoriality and sovereignty as dominant concepts in personal jurisdiction. These cases notwithstanding, the minimum contacts test from *International Shoe* persists as the touchstone for personal jurisdiction.

13 *See* William Crozier, Brandon L. Garrett & Karima Modjadidi, *Undeliverable: Suspended Driver's Licenses and the Problem of Notice*, 4 UCLA Crim. Just. L. Rev. 185 (2020); Markian Hawryluk, *Return to Sender? Just One Missed Letter Can Be Enough to End Medicaid Benefits*, NPR (Nov. 1, 2019, 5:00AM), www.npr.org.

22

Subject Matter Jurisdiction

The Interests of Power and the Power of Interests

ELIZABETH MCCUSKEY

Jurisdiction is power. Subject matter jurisdiction provides the source of courts' power to adjudicate disputes and thereby establish precedent for posterity. In the United States, federal and state courts share this power unevenly. The limited nature of federal courts' subject matter jurisdiction rests on theoretical assumptions about the superiority of the federal judiciary—namely, that federal courts offer a superior degree of neutrality, expertise, and uniformity than state courts do.[1] This superiority premise often is invoked to justify the authorization or denial of federal subject matter jurisdiction, based on value judgments about which kinds of disputes deserve the option of adjudication in the superior system.[2]

As a doctrine allocating power, subject matter jurisdiction sits squarely in the path of critical legal theory, which asks whether and how law subordinates outsiders and how we might address that subordination.[3] Critical theory supplies tools to interrogate both the superiority premises and related value judgments for their roles in oppression or empowerment.

Viewed with a critical lens, the evolution of diversity and federal question jurisdiction reveals the abiding interests of powerful commercial parties in the federal courts, as well as the federal courts' duality as both protectors and frustraters of subordinated groups' rights. This evolution complicates prevailing notions about federal courts' superiority by illustrating ways in which federal jurisdiction serves hegemonic interests. The institutional features of life tenure, salary protection, and selection process are supposed to make federal judges less susceptible to bias and more attentive to federal law.[4] But these institutional features also serve to entrench the interests and biases of dominant groups that are historically and currently overrepresented in the federal judiciary—namely, white men of privileged socioeconomic class.

The interest-convergence principle from Critical Race Theory interrogates the consequences that flow from the allocation of subject matter to the federal courts based on the interests represented there. Interest convergence poses that law will accommodate the interests of subordinated groups only when those interests converge with the interests of dominant groups in power.[5] From an interest-convergence perspective, the federal judiciary's claims to superiority over state courts on metrics of bias and solicitude for federal law fall short when measured with reference to subordinated groups' rights.

The disproportionately white maleness of the federal judiciary thus undermines a central premise of federal courts' subject matter jurisdiction and, ultimately, their legitimacy. Interest convergence exposes this weakness by revealing the interests of power and the power of interests in ways that the formalism of jurisdiction doctrine often conceals.

The Interests of Power in Federal Jurisdiction

Federal subject matter jurisdiction is treated as precious and prestigious. In the conventional account, federal courts are supposed to achieve relative superiority over state courts in *neutrality*, *expertise*, and *uniformity* through their judiciary's life tenure, salary protection, selection process, federal structure, and unitary procedural rules. Life tenure protects federal judges from the parochial and popular biases that elected state judges might face, while salary protection insulates federal judges from punitive budgeting by the legislative and executive branches. Selective appointment through Senate confirmation is supposed to put more highly qualified jurists on the federal bench, while life tenure provides them decades over which to hone their expertise in federal law.

In light of these premises, bestowing federal jurisdiction represents a valuation that certain cases deserve a superior adjudicatory forum than state courts might provide. This valuation has economic and social dimensions, primarily benefitting two different categories of litigants: sophisticated commercial parties and individuals denied the full expression of citizenship due to discrimination. Federal courts are thought to benefit commercial parties by offering a national adjudication system that breeds confidence in interstate commerce. And federal courts are supposed to benefit individuals seeking to enforce federal rights when state actors may be hostile to those rights.

These bias/expertise/uniformity premises and value judgments have driven the evolution of federal jurisdiction. They also signal the interests that federal subject matter jurisdiction grants are most apt to serve: the economic and social interests of dominant groups.

Diversity Jurisdiction

The federal courts began as business-friendly courts. When Congress established the federal district courts in 1789, it gave them jurisdiction over diversity suits between "citizens of different States"[6] to protect interstate commercial interests from state judicial biases. The bias of concern to Congress members was not the bias of dominant groups against minority ones but rather the framers' distrust of rural judges and the perceived threat that state judges would favor fellow state residents over out-of-state parties and would favor debtors' interests over creditors.[7] Diversity jurisdiction responds to class bias by favoring the dominant socioeconomic class.

Diversity jurisdiction also contributed to the subordination of racial minorities and women. Diversity jurisdiction in the founding era of the federal courts categorically excluded most nonwhite, nonmales. The status of state "citizen" prerequisite to diversity jurisdiction was reserved for white men for the first 75 years of diversity jurisdiction. Before the Civil War, the United States Supreme Court recognized corporations' citizenship for diversity purposes[8] but famously denied that status to natural persons who were Black in the 1856 *Dred Scott* decision.[9]

Similar "legal disabilities" restricted women's participation as citizens and litigants.[10] The all-white male Supreme Court in 1858 created the "domestic relations exception," which refuses diversity jurisdiction over divorce, alimony, child support, and other "domestic" matters.[11] Feminist critiques of this judicially crafted exception describe how it devalues these disputes and perpetuates the subordination of women.[12]

The interests of state "citizen" litigants thus reflected the hegemonic economic and cultural interests of the group exclusively permitted to hold that status as parties, as well as judges: white men. Those economic interests included the maintenance of a white supremacist racial order on which the institution of slavery depended.[13] The neutrality premise underlying diversity jurisdiction at the outset held little or no value for the groups most subordinated by actual biases and prejudices: racial minorities, women, and the poor.[14]

Federal Question Jurisdiction

Federal question jurisdiction rests on a different version of the bias premise: concern that state courts would be hostile to and unfamiliar with federal law. The Judiciary Act of 1789 eliminated federal question jurisdiction from its initial grant to appease slave-state legislators who resisted the notion of federal judicial power to enforce federal law,[15] especially federal laws that slave owners perceived as threats to racial supremacy and the economy founded on it.[16]

Congress provided a federal forum to enforce the expanding body of federal law only after the Civil War. The Reconstruction Amendments prohibited the denial of rights based on race and required states to respect those rights with due process and equal protection, while the Ku Klux Klan Act of 1871 created a federal remedy against states for violating those federal rights.[17] Both had to be litigated in state courts until Congress granted federal question jurisdiction in 1875. Federal question jurisdiction opened the federal courts for protection of Unionists and newly freed Black citizens in former Confederate states, as well as to deal with an explosion of interstate commerce.[18]

The grant of federal question jurisdiction directly responded to Confederacy states' overt hostility toward federal laws. The enduring narrative that the federal judiciary is more solicitous of federal *rights*,[19] however, is complicated by the federal courts' retrenchment on the enforcement of rights provided by Congress.[20]

The laws of racial freedom and equality Congress passed during Reconstruction collided with opposing interests ensconced in the federal judiciary, and "[a]s a practical matter . . . federal courts were usually forums of disappointment" in the administration of this new legal freedom.[21] Though more solicitous of federal law than some state courts, federal courts "were not emancipatory forums" during the eras of slavery or Reconstruction.[22] Instead, federal courts "operated primarily to produce order and serve populations who held power—economic, political, cultural, social, and racial."[23] While the Supreme Court eventually struck down racial segregation in *Brown v. Board of Education*, the federal courts' broader recalcitrance in enforcing federal laws of equality in citizenship diminish their claim to superior solicitude.[24]

Confronted with the realities of desegregation and expansion of federal civil rights after *Brown*, white majorities perceived the enforcement of minority rights as threatening their status, prompting strident conservative backlash.[25] Where conservative executive and legislative efforts at retracting substantive rights had only limited success, efforts to "weaken the infrastructure" for enforcing those rights "flourished in the federal courts."[26] Those judicial efforts include interpretive interventions like implementing desegregation with "all deliberate speed," expanding qualified immunity defenses, curtailing private rights of action and standing, and diluting incentives for private enforcement. Federal courts' retrenchment on enforcing federal laws against discrimination by states is particularly striking because these are the disputes in which the "probability" of state judicial bias "seems the greatest."[27]

The Power of Interests

From an interest-convergence perspective, the overrepresentation of white men and socioeconomic elites on the federal bench helps explain federal courts' protection of wealth and recalcitrance on effectuating the federal rights of subordinated groups. Derrick Bell's explication of *Brown v. Board of Education* illustrates this principle: before *Brown*, courts had innumerable opportunities to invalidate racial segregation and definitively refused to do so.[28] Bell identifies the about-face in 1954 as prompted by new political and economic advantages of desegregation for whites, rather than segregation's moral injustice for Blacks.[29] These advantages included gaining international credibility in "America's struggle with Communist countries to win [] hearts and minds," mitigating domestic disillusionment and anger among Black veterans who returned from World War II to face violent inequality at home, and eliminating segregation as a barrier to economic growth and industrialization in the South.[30]

The bias/expertise/uniformity premises for federal subject matter jurisdiction are relative metrics, not absolutes, prompting the question whether federal courts are still better than state courts. For representing of subordinated groups' interests, the answer is "not really." The federal judiciary underrepresents subordinated groups by an even greater margin than state judiciaries do, faring slightly worse than state courts on gender representation[31] and representation of nonwhite populations.[32] The intersection of race and gender then amplifies this underrepresentation.[33]

Since the 1980s, the federal judiciary has sluggishly diversified. Former president Donald Trump, however, reversed even that modest progress. His judicial appointments were 84 percent white and 76 percent male, and he appointed a larger share of white judges than any president in the previous 27 years while simultaneously managing to appoint zero LGBTQ+ jurists.[34] Should that regression persist, state courts may widen their advantage over federal courts. The lack of representation in both judicial systems means that, from an interest-convergence standpoint, "the[ir] similarities overwhelm the[ir] differences."[35] Interests within demographic groups are not homogenous, and thus achieving demographic representation will not automatically represent any unitary or "essential" set of interests.[36] Still, from an interest-convergence standpoint, the predominance of white men in the judiciary suggests that dominant group interests vastly overwhelm those of subordinate groups on the courts.

The institutional features of the federal judiciary also seem inadequate to support the premise of superiority over state courts on biases. Life tenure, expertise, and the selection process may entrench biases rather than remove them. Life tenure insulates Article III judges from majoritarian pressures but does not alone assure their solicitude toward the interests of outsider litigants—from other states or from subordinated social groups. Instead, life tenure impedes efforts at correcting the historical exclusion of women and minorities by preventing turnover on the federal bench. Salary protection likewise insulates federal judges from the punitive influences of the executive and legislative branches; it also stifles turnover by deterring judges from retiring.

The expertise, solicitude, and professionalism with which federal judges are thought to approach federal law also cut different ways, depending on the interests served by different federal laws. For example, federal courts have used their solicitude for federal commercial laws to expand the preemption of state remedies, while using their facility with federal law and procedure to curtail federal civil rights remedies. The formalist conceit of neutrality obscures the retrenchment of rights, as "restrictive jurisdictional practices may substitute for a value judgment that if articulated would reflect hostility to civil liberties cases on the merits."[37] The neutrality and expertise premises thus reinforce the formalist mystique of jurisdiction[38] and vice versa.

The professionalism and expertise values placed on the federal judiciary, to the extent that they overlap with the overrepresentation of wealthy and privileged backgrounds, amplify federal courts' biases in favor of wealthy litigants and against impoverished ones.[39] The appointment and confirmation processes that are supposed to recruit this higher caliber of jurists to the federal courts have spread to state courts, too, with many states now using executive appointment for their judiciaries, and several even giving life-tenure to some judges.[40]

* * *

On closer inspection, the preciousness of federal subject matter jurisdiction based on the bias/expertise/uniformity premises does not hold consistently for subordinated groups. As Roy Brooks observed, the federal court "is a more prestigious court in our culture," enhanced by "[c]onsiderations of professionalism and procedural innovation," which "add to the superiority of the federal forum."[41] This perceived superiority suggests that "the choice between a state and federal court is not outcome-neutral,"[42] and the decision to bestow or withhold federal jurisdiction remains consequential. Whether those consequences perpetuate subordination bears on the legitimacy of the federal courts' power.[43]

Interest convergence questions the premise that federal courts are less susceptible to race, gender, sexual orientation, and class biases than state courts and thereby questions a core justification for federal courts' precious and prestigious subject matter jurisdiction. Viewed in this light, diversification of the federal judiciary acquires an existential urgency.

NOTES

1 *See generally* Roy L. Brooks, Critical Procedure 68–69 (1998).

2 *See, e.g.*, Grable & Sons Metal Prods., Inc. v. Darue Eng'g & Mfg., 545 U.S. 308, 312 (2005). *But see, e.g.*, Martha Field, *The Uncertain Nature of Federal Jurisdiction*, 22 Wm. & Mary L. Rev. 683, 684 (1981); Amanda Frost, *Overvaluing Uniformity*, 94 Va. L. Rev. 1567 (2008); Pamela S. Karlan, *Two Concepts of Judicial Independence*, 72 S. Cal. L. Rev. 535 (1999).

3 *See generally* Brooks, *supra* note 1, at xxiv–xxv; Angela P. Harris, *Race and Essentialism in Feminist Legal Theory*, 42 Stan. L. Rev. 581 (1990).

4 This chapter focuses on the life-tenured Article III judiciary central to this longstanding premise, but it also recognizes that an array of untenured and adjunct jurists play directive roles in adjudication. *See* Judith Resnik, *Rereading "The Federal Courts": Revising the Domain of Federal Courts Jurisprudence at the End of the Twentieth Century*, 47 Vand. L. Rev. 1021, 1036–37 (1994).

5 *See* Derrick A. Bell, Jr., Brown v. Board of Education *and the Interest-Convergence Dilemma*, 93 Harv. L. Rev. 518, 523–24 (1980).

6 28 U.S.C. § 1332(a) (2018).

7 *See* Russell R. Wheeler & Cynthia Harrison, Creating the Federal Judicial System 8 (1989); Debra Lynn Bassett, *The Hidden Bias in Diversity Jurisdiction*, 81 Wash. U. L. Q. 119 (2003).

8 *See* Hertz Corp. v. Friend, 559 U.S. 77, 85–88 (2010).

9 Dred Scott v. Sanford, 60 U.S. 393 (1857). *See* Kevin R. Johnson, *Integrating Racial Justice Into the Civil Procedure Survey Course*, 54 J. Legal Educ. 242, 246 (2004).

10 *See* Judith Resnik, *"Naturally" Without Gender: Women, Jurisdiction, and the Federal Courts*, 66 N.Y.U. L. Rev. 1682, 1736–39 (1991).

11 *See, e.g.*, Emily J. Sack, *The Domestic Relations Exception, Domestic Violence, and Equal Access to Federal Courts*, 84 Wash. U. L. Rev. 1441, 1466–73 (2006);

12 *E.g.*, Resnik, *supra* note 10.

13 *See generally* Aaron Hall, *Slavery and Emancipation in the Federal Courts*, *in* Approaches to Federal Judicial History 54–55 (Gautham Rao, Winston Bowman & Clara Altman eds., 2020).

14 *Compare* Edward A. Purcell, Jr., *Litigation and Inequality: Federal Diversity Jurisdiction in Industrial America*, 1870–1958 (1992).

15 *See* Charles Warren, *New Light on the History of the Federal Judiciary Act of 1789*, 37 Harv. L. Rev. 49, 62 (1923).

16 *See, e.g.*, Hall, *supra* note 13.

17 42 U.S.C. § 1983 (2018).

18 *See* Wheeler & Harrison, *supra* note 7, at 18.

19 *E.g.*, Bert Neuborne, *The Myth of Parity*, 90 Harv. L. Rev. 1105 (1977).

20 *E.g.*, William B. Rubenstein, *The Myth of Superiority*, 16 Const. Commentary 599 (1999).

21 Hall, *supra* note 13, at 59.

22 *Id.* at 64.

23 *Id.*

24 *See* Resnik, *supra* note 10; Rubenstein, *supra* note 20.

25 *See* Angela Onwuachi-Willig, *For Whom Does the Bell Toll: The Bell Tolls for* Brown?, 103 Mich. L. Rev. 1507, 1519 (2005).

26 Stephen B. Burbank & Sean Farhang, *Rights and Retrenchment in the Trump Era*, 87 Fordham L. Rev. 37, 37 (2018).

27 Field, *supra* note 2, at 724.

28 *E.g.*, Plessy v. Ferguson, 163 U.S. 537 (1896).
29 Bell, Jr., *supra* note 5, at 524.
30 *Id.* at 524–25.
31 In 2017, women comprised only 26 percent of Article III federal judges. *Demography of Article III Judges, 1789–2020*, Fed. Jud. Ctr., www.fjc.gov. In 2018, women comprised only 33 percent of state court judges nationwide. *See 2018 US State Court Women Judges*, Nat'l Ass'n of Women Judges, www.nawj.org.
32 Racial minorities comprised less than 20 percent of state judiciaries as of 2014, with "dramatically" more pronounced underrepresentation in the states in the South and West. Tracey E. George & Albert H. Yoon, The Gavel Gap: Who Sits in Judgment on State Courts? 9–10 (2017). In the federal courts, as of the same year, nonwhite judges comprised only 18.8 percent of the Article III judiciary, increasing only to 19.6 percent by 2017. *FJC Judges*, *supra* note 31.
33 Women of color represent 20 percent of the population but only 8 percent of state trial and appellate court judges; men of color comprise 19 percent of the population but only 9 percent of state trial court judges and 12 percent of state appellate court judges; and white women comprise 31 percent of the population but only 26 percent of state trial court judges and 22 percent of state appellate court judges. Meanwhile, white men comprise 30 percent of the population but make up almost double that share (57 percent and 58 percent) of state trial and appellate court judges. George & Yoon, *supra* note 32, at 7.
34 John Gramlich, *How Trump Compares With Other Recent Presidents in Appointing Federal Judges*, Pew Rsch. Ctr. (Jan. 13, 2021), www.pewresearch.org; Carl Tobias, *Appointing Lesbian, Gay, Bisexual, Transgender and Queer Judges in the Trump Administration*, 96 Wash. U. L. Rev. Online 11, 11 (2018).
35 Richard Delgado, *Rodrigo's Thirteenth Chronicle: Legal Formalism and Law's Discontents*, 95 Mich. L. Rev. 1105, 1132 (1997).
36 Harris, *supra* note 3, at 585 (critiquing reliance on the notion of "a unitary, 'essential' women's experience [that] can be isolated and described independently of race, class, sexual orientation, and other realities of experience").
37 Field, *supra* note 2, at 724.
38 *See e.g.*, Roy L. Brooks, Structures of Judicial Decision Making from Legal Formalism to Critical Theory 37–47 (2d ed. 2005).
39 This extends to the federal judiciary's selection of law clerks with similarly unrepresentative pedigrees.
40 *See* U.S. Dep't of Just., Bureau of Just. Stats., Special Report: State Court Organization, 2011 (Nov. 2013).
41 Brooks, *supra* note 1, at 68.
42 *Id.* at 69.
43 *E.g.*, Nancy Scherer, *Diversifying the Federal Bench: Is Universal Legitimacy for the U.S. Justice System Possible?*, 105 Nw. U. L. Rev. 587 (2011).

23

Jurisprudence and Recommendations for Tribal Court Authority Due to Imposition of US Limitations

ANGELIQUE EAGLEWOMAN (*WAMBDI A. WAS'TEWINYAN*)

There are more than 570 federally recognized Tribal Nations in the United States and more than 330 tribal courts serving as the judicial branch of those nations. Yet, there is little mention of the existence of tribal courts in most mainstream civil procedure courses taught in the 200-plus law schools across the country. To gain any knowledge as to the existence of these courts, law students must take a course on federal Indian law, which is not available in most law schools. In fact, less than twenty law schools offer a series of courses forming an Indian law program.[1] Thus, the invisibility of tribal courts is perpetuated through curriculum omission in mainstream civil procedure courses and rarely remedied through offering a stand-alone course on federal Indian law. Tribal Nations have existed from time immemorial with their own laws, dispute resolution systems, and governing structures. This lack of attention and suppression of information serves only to reinforce colonizing ideas of subsuming tribal governance into the forums set up by the United States.

An Overview of Tribal Courts

Tribal Nations are preconstitutional and indigenous to North America. Within these societies, dispute resolution processes were developed and followed to maintain harmony and balance for social functioning.

Customary/Traditional Law in Tribal Courts

Customary legal principles and norms have been taught through generations based on accounts and stories expressing both socially acceptable behaviors and the disapproval of unacceptable behaviors. Thus, children received this behavioral training early on to shape their understanding of proper ethical, legal, and social standards. In contemporary tribal courts, judges may take judicial notice of customary legal principles, receive expert testimony from qualified cultural knowledge holders, or follow precedent in decisions detailing the appropriate customary law for that particular tribal society. Court decisions and customary legal principles compose the common law of tribal courts.

One of the most prominent traditional customary law practices is found in the Navajo Nation Peacemaker Court and program, which has been the subject of study by legal scholars throughout the world. In explaining the concept of horizontal justice in the Navajo mindset, Chief Justice Emeritus Robert Yazzie distinguishes the Anglo view of vertical justice as the adversarial system with judges as decision makers through power over the parties:

> Navajo justice is a sophisticated system of egalitarian relationships where group solidarity takes the place of force and coercion. In it, humans are not in ranks or status classifications from top to bottom. Instead, all humans are equals and make decisions as a group. The process—which we call "peacemaking" in English—is a system of relationships where there is no need for force, coercion or control. There are no plaintiffs or defendants; no "good guy" or "bad guy." These labels are irrelevant. "Equal justice" and "equality before the law" mean precisely what they say. As Navajos, we do not think of equality as treating people equal *before* the law; they are equal *in* it. Again our Navajo language points this out in practical terms.[2]

Cases are initiated in Peacemaker Court by the parties to the dispute or through referrals by courts, government agencies, or schools.[3] Participating in the peacemaking program is always voluntary. Once the case is filed, a well-respected community peacemaker is assigned; the peacemaker is responsible for gathering interested individuals to facilitate the ceremonial stages of the process. Components of the resolution process include prayers, every person contributing to both speaking and listening, the ability of family members to respond to excuses, teachings by the peacemaker appropriate to the situation, and a closing with a meal.

Tribal governments may codify traditional law, incorporate specific legal processes, or acknowledge adversarial proceedings as applicable law in modern tribal courts. By drawing upon cultural principles, customs, and traditional legal concepts, tribal courts working within tribal communities are reinvigorating the values and standards that provide tribal cohesion. But they do so in the face of strong United States government forces that undermine their work and tribal sovereignty.

The Code of Federal Regulations Courts

For thousands of years, Tribal peoples had governed their own societies with laws and dispute resolution processes across the Western Hemisphere. In the 1880s, the US government had asserted control over Indian reservations and employed US Indian agents to do so. As tools of oppression, the first judicial forums established on American Indian reservations by the Indian agents were the Code of Indian Offenses Courts, or the Code of Federal Regulations Courts (CFR Courts).[4] The Indian Reorganization Act of 1934 (IRA)[5] signaled a shift in policy, which provided for the adoption of tribal constitutions.[6] Under the Department of the Interior, Bureau of Indian Affairs (BIA) personnel developed boilerplate constitutions for adoption by Tribal Nations.[7] These constitutions often included provisions for the establishment of tribal courts.

Even with this less than ideal governance structure, the provisions of the IRA signaled a return to self-government for Tribal Nations and the relaxing of the grip of federal authority by US Indian agents in tribal communities. The shift in US policy from military control to the recognition of tribal authority to self-govern was heartily embraced by Tribal Nations.

The Operation of Tribal Courts

After the 1934 Indian Reorganization Act, tribes have taken different approaches to operating their tribal courts. First, a majority of Tribal Nations reestablished tribal dispute resolution or court systems that provide law and order functions, decision-making for civil matters, and the handling of family law cases.[8] Customary or traditional laws may be employed in tribal judicial opinions alongside tribal statutes and other legal sources. These self-government-era tribal courts replaced the former Courts of Indian Offenses and have the authorization of inherent tribal sovereignty legitimizing the forums. Tribal court systems handle both civil and criminal cases for matters impacting the tribal citizenry and government. Tribal courts review Tribal Council actions for conformity with the relevant tribal constitutions, resolve disputes in the commercial realm, and provide remedies in tort law.

Second, Tribal Nations rejecting the boilerplate constitutions had similar opportunities to benefit from the Indian Reorganization Act and assert tribal governmental powers under both the federal law and the reassertion of tribal sovereignty. For example, the Navajo Nation has developed district courts and a Navajo Supreme Court. A separate Peacemaker Court completes the judicial system. The Navajo Nation did not adopt an IRA constitution and does not operate under a written constitution.

For various reasons, a third approach has been for a small number of tribal governments to use the CFR Courts.[9] Unlike tribal courts, these courts operate under the BIA's authority and are circumscribed by federal regulations on civil and criminal jurisdiction. A benefit of operating under the BIA is funding. Yet, some commentators criticize CFR Courts because they inhibit the development of tribal law and application of customary law.[10]

Finally, tribal governments may retain judicial authority in the Tribal Council. The entanglement between politics and judicial neutrality does not make this a best practice in tribal communities. As entities with sovereignty within their territorial boundaries, Tribal Nations have choices in the structuring of court systems and dispute resolution practices.

Tribal Appellate Courts

Tribal governments have options in creating the appellate process of tribal courts. The first option enables a tribal government to form an appellate court under its own laws. Another option is for a tribal government to enter into a regional appellate court system. The Tribal Council, exercising discretionary authority to hear appeals from the tribal district court(s), may also retain jurisdiction over the appellate process. The right of appeal is recognized across the spectrum of appellate court fora for tribal jurisdictions and contemplated by tribal government in mandating the appropriate appeal process.

United States Restriction of Tribal Court Civil Jurisdiction

The civil jurisdiction of tribal courts is governed by the tribal laws establishing the court systems. For most governments, their court systems assert jurisdiction over claims arising from conduct within the government's territory. For example, the government of Greece may apply its laws to the full extent throughout its territorial boundaries, and the Greek courts may resolve any and all criminal and civil cases arising within those same boundaries. In contrast, both the United States Congress and the United States Supreme Court have sought to restrict the full extent of tribal governmental authority within the tribal territory.

* * *

Tribal governments have established courts as forums for any type of civil action based on legislative authority, whether involving commercial disputes, domestic issues, personal injury actions, or governmental administrative matters, to name a few areas. In general, tribal courts follow civil procedure requirements for adjudicative authority based on the Federal Rules of Civil Procedure with more emphasis on due process rights than on enforcing strict adherence to procedural standards.

Public Law 280 and Effects on Tribal Courts

The enactment of Public Law 280[11] during the termination era of US Indian policy has impacted the operation of tribal courts. One aspect of the enactment of Public Law 280 was to open the state courts as alternative forums for civil actions involving Indians that arise in tribal territories. This civil law component of Public Law 280 was initially enacted to apply in Alaska, California, Minnesota (except on the Red Lake Band of Chippewa Reservation), Nebraska, Oregon (except the Warm Springs Reservation), and Wisconsin.[12] The nine states currently operating with optional Public Law 280 jurisdiction are Arizona, Florida, Idaho, Iowa, Montana, Nevada, North Dakota, Utah, and Washington.[13]

Civil actions filed in state court must involve at least one reservation Indian party under this federal grant of authority for an action arising within a tribal territory.

By allowing civil actions involving Indians as private persons that arise in tribal territories to be heard in either state or tribal court, the exercise of state court jurisdiction undermines tribal courts. Legal jurisprudence is developed by the consideration of issues over time with judicial decisions building on rationales and strengthening bodies of interpretative law. When state forums hear civil cases arising within tribal lands, it is to the detriment of tribal courts and their ability to develop tribal law for civil causes of action.

US Supreme Court Jurisprudence Regarding the Civil Jurisdiction of Tribal Courts

Tribal Nations have been labeled the "third sovereign" in the United States along with the federal and state governments. However, tribal governments do not neatly fit within the US constitutional framework. Moreover, the United States Supreme Court has inconsistently respected the sovereignty of Tribal Nations. The Court has unevenly followed the current overarching US Indian policy of self-determination since the late 1960s, which was intended to support tribal legislative and adjudicatory authority within tribal territories. Further, the civil jurisdiction of tribal courts has been subject to narrowing by Supreme Court decisions based on whether the defendant is a non-Indian or a nonmember and whether the cause of action is based on federal law.

Reservation lands allotted to tribal peoples were held in trust status by the US government and were acknowledged as within the tribal jurisdiction.[14] Fee lands are parcels that private parties purchased on a reservation or within a tribal community boundary. Today, fee lands, and the jurisdiction of the fee lands, remain complicated based on the type of jurisdiction asserted. Thus, jurisdiction on reservations is labeled a "crazy quilt" of tribal, federal, and state jurisdiction.[15]

The 1981 Supreme Court decision in *Montana v. United States*[16] provides the starting point for the Court's incursion into tribal jurisdiction. When the Crow Tribal Council attempted to prevent non-Indians from hunting within reservation boundaries, Montana disputed the tribal authority and licensed hunting on fee lands within the reservation. The Court upheld Montana's licensure. The Court set out a two-part test for determining when a tribal government had the power to exercise jurisdiction on fee lands within tribal boundaries over nonmembers. First, under the consensual relations prong, "[a] tribe may regulate, through taxation, licensing, or other means" commercial agreements between nonmembers and members.[17] Second, under the direct effects prong, "[a] tribe may also retain inherent power to exercise civil authority over the conduct of non-Indians on fee lands . . . when that conduct threatens or has some direct effect on the political integrity, the economic security, or the health or welfare of the tribe."[18] Applying this test, the Court opined that the tribal government lacked jurisdiction to regulate hunting on fee lands owned by non-Indians within the reservation.[19]

Following *Montana*, several non-Indian civil defendants invoked federal court authority to override tribal court adjudications. In *National Farmers Union Insurance Companies. v. Crow Tribe of Indians*,[20] the defendants went to federal court to enjoin a lawsuit, which arose from a negligence action on the reservation, from proceeding in tribal court. The Court applied federal question jurisdiction, holding that "all civil actions arising under the Constitution, laws, or treaties of the United States"[21] included the Court's common law regarding tribal court jurisdiction. The Court upheld jurisdiction to review whether a tribal court properly asserted its jurisdiction over nonmember defendants in civil actions.[22]

The Court also articulated an abstention doctrine for federal courts, requiring them to stay their decision until a civil defendant exhausts tribal remedies—through every level of the tribal court system—prior to making a federal determination on tribal jurisdiction.[23] In a footnote, the Court detailed three exceptions to the exhaustion requirement. First, where the assertion of tribal court jurisdiction stems from an intent to harass or is conducted in bad faith; second, where the action is "patently violative of express jurisdictional prohibitions"; or third, where exhaustion would be futile.[24]

Through these decisions, the Supreme Court has announced limitations previously unknown to tribal court authority and sought to base its reasoning on the status of parcels of land within reservation boundaries and circular ideas concerning federal question and diversity of citizenship jurisdiction under the US Constitution. By instituting a process of federal court analysis of cases originating in tribal courts, the Court has created disincentives for the filing of lawsuits in tribal courts. The potential for the civil defendant to litigate through every level of the tribal court system and then seek review of the tribal court's jurisdiction in federal court is much too costly and inefficient. In addition, tribal courts are deemed as administrative bodies, forced to explain the grounds for tribal court jurisdiction for the benefit of a federal court down the line. Finally, in response to these Supreme Court decisions and their jurisdictional overreach, federal courts are left to engage in mental gymnastics to find subject matter jurisdiction to preside over tribal enforcement actions against no-members.

Questioning the Legal Basis for Federal Court Review of Tribal Jurisdiction

In examining Supreme Court decisions limiting tribal court authority, the first question is: By what authority does the Court oversee tribal court jurisdiction? In *Nevada v. Hicks*,[25] the Court correctly noted that Article III in the US Constitution does not mention tribal governments or tribal courts.[26] The Constitution under Article 1, Section 8 references tribal governments in relation to Congress: "To regulate commerce with foreign nations, among the several states, and with the Indian Tribes."[27] Tribal Nations are extraconstitutional and are not bound or otherwise within the jurisdiction of the Constitution, as acknowledged by the Supreme Court in 1896.[28]

In justifying the ability of federal courts to review tribal jurisdiction, two federal statutes are used: 28 U.S.C. § 1331 and 28 U.S.C. § 1362. Both are inapposite. First, section 1331, the federal question statute, does not authorize federal review of tribal governmental authority or courts; rather, it is the enactment of the US Constitution's Article III provisions for federal court jurisdiction.[29] Yet, in *National Farmers Union Insurance Companies v. Crow Tribe*,[30] the Court engaged in the following circular reasoning: since the Court's decisions have limited tribal jurisdiction, an analysis of federal common law is required to determine whether the tribal court is properly applying tribal jurisdiction. This reasoning completely fails to acknowledge that tribal governments exist independently of, and existed prior to, the US government and its judiciary. Tribal governmental laws defining the civil jurisdiction of tribal courts are not derived from federal law and, thus, are not within federal courts' federal question jurisdiction.[31]

Second, section 1362 provides that federal courts "have original jurisdiction of all civil actions brought by any Indian tribe or band with a governing body duly recognized by the Secretary of the Interior, wherein the matter in controversy arises under the Constitution, laws, or treaties of the United States."[32] This law allows federal courts to hear claims brought by tribal governments, but it does not provide for federal review of cases originating in tribal courts. Rather, the statute clarifies § 1331 federal question jurisdiction to expressly include federal question cases brought by tribal governments in federal courts.

The Supreme Court's default justification for curtailing tribal sovereign authority to adjudicate civil claims in tribal forums is the judicially announced "plenary power" doctrine exercised by Congress and the Court's common law authority. Neither of these announced powers are authorized by the US Constitution or consented to by Tribal Nations. Indian law scholar Robert Clinton has aptly explained that "there is no acceptable, historically-derived, textual constitutional explanation for the exercise of any federal authority over Indian tribes without their consent manifested through treaty. . . . [N]either Congress nor the federal courts legitimately can unilaterally adopt binding legal principles for the tribes without their consent."[33]

Two Paths Forward or One Step Back?

Through the circular reasoning of the so-called plenary power, the federal courts continue to overreach into tribal jurisdictions by crafting common law doctrine ungrounded in legal authority. US courts have the authority to regulate governmental authority within the bounds of the US Constitution. The entire line of cases surrounding tribal civil jurisdiction is outside those bounds and sets the course of the US Supreme Court on a legislative, rather than judicial, track.[34]

If the US government and courts continue coercing tribal courts into lesser authority and eventually seek to subsume these courts, that would be to take one step backward—an act of returning to colonization. These colonizing ideas of supplanting Indigenous legal systems with the surrounding European-based systems would swing the pendulum of US Indian policy toward the negation of tribal governance. The pseudo-anthropological spectrum of human evolution with American Indians depicted on the "primitive" end of the spectrum is a relic of a racist, colonizing past and should be put to rest once and for all.

During the negotiations at the Treaty of Niagara in 1764, the two rows wampum belt was exchanged, denoting parallel governments in alliance: one row representing the British government and the other representing Indigenous Nations.[35] As Chief Justice John Marshall asserted in *Johnson v. M'Intosh*,[36] the United States, as the successor government to Great Britain, entered into a relationship with Tribal Nations. Thus, the two paths forward would continue to allow tribal governments, through tribal court systems, to provide dispute resolution in harmony with tribal values, laws, and ideals. The United States, as an ally to Tribal Nations, would restrain impulses to pressure tribal court systems to replicate Anglo-Saxon norms and laws. Rather, as allies on shared lands, the federal and state court systems would respect the legal processes of tribal courts. This may lead to consensual agreements regarding adjudicatory authority and an adherence to principles of comity and full faith and credit for tribal court decisions.

Rather than allow the Supreme Court to create from whole cloth common law doctrines extending federal jurisdiction ungrounded in the Constitution or federal law, the treatymaking authority of the United States would be an appropriate alternative to realign the governmental understandings involving tribal court and federal court jurisdiction. By reengaging the treatymaking process, the federal courts' overreach and the uncertainty around enforcement of tribal court judgments in those same courts would be settled through sovereign consent.

As an initial matter in such a treaty process, the Supreme Court should abandon the circular reasoning it previously used to limit the civil jurisdiction of tribal courts. Tribal civil jurisdiction should extend to the limits of the tribal territorial boundaries and be fairly applicable to all who enter the tribal territory. In recognizing the competency and cultural importance of tribal court jurisprudence, the US government, as a treaty partner, has an obligation to join together with Tribal Nations for the benefit of justice throughout mid–North America.

NOTES

Acknowledgment: This chapter is updated and adapted from Angelique EagleWoman, *Jurisprudence and Recommendations for Tribal Court Authority Due to Imposition of U.S. Limitations*, 47 Mitchell Hamline L. Rev. 342 (2021).

1 *See The State of Indian Law at ABA-Accredited Law Schools*, Nat'l Native Am. Bar Ass'n (2019), www.nativeamericanbar.org (listing 16 certificate Indian law programs and 31 law schools offering more than one Indian law course at ABA-accredited law schools).

2 Robert Yazzie, *"Life Comes From It": Navajo Justice Concepts*, *in* Navajo Nation Peacemaking: Living Traditional Justice, 47 (Marianne O. Nielsen & James W. Zion eds., 2005).

3 *See Navajo Nation Peacemaking Program*, Tribal Access to Justice Innovation, www.tribaljustice.org.

4 *See* Cohen's Handbook of Federal Indian Law § 4.04[3][c][iv][B], at 266–67 (Nell Jessup Newton ed., 2012).

5 25 U.S.C. §§ 5101–5144.

6 *See generally* Indian Reorganization Act of 1934, Pub. L. No. 73–383, 48 Stat. 984, 25 U.S.C. § 5101 et seq. (originally 25 U.S.C. § 461 et seq.).

7 *Id.* at § 5123.

8 *See generally Tribal Court Clearinghouse*, Tribal Law and Pol'y Inst., www.tribal-institute.org.

9 *See Court of Indian Offenses*, U.S. Dept. of the Interior: Indian Affs., www.bia.gov.

10 *See* Gavin Clarkson, *Reclaiming Jurisprudential Sovereignty: A Tribal Judiciary Analysis*, 50 U. Kan. L. Rev. 473, 489–90 (2002).

11 18 U.S.C. § 1162.

12 28 U.S.C. § 1360(a).

13 *See* Carole Goldberg & Heather Valdez Singleton, *Research Priorities: Law Enforcement in Public Law 280 States*, 2 n.4 (2005),www.ncjrs.gov (noting that North Dakota required tribal consent to assert jurisdiction but has not gained that consent).

14 Law of Feb. 8, 1887, ch. 119, 24 Stat. 388 (repealed 1934); *see also* Francis Paul Prucha, Extract from the Annual Report of the Commissioner of Indian Affairs Oct. 10, 1882, in *Documents of United States Policy*, 170–73 (Univ. of Neb. Press, 3rd ed., 2000).

15 *See* Gloria Valencia-Weber, *Tribal Courts: Custom and Innovative Law*, 24 N.M. L. Rev. 225, 234 (1994).

16 450 U.S. 544 (1981).

17 *Id.* at 565.

18 *Id.* at 566.

19 *Id.* at 566–67.

20 471 U.S. 845 (1985).

21 28 U.S.C. § 1331.

22 471 U.S. at 850–53.

23 *Id.* at 857.

24 *Id.* at 856, n.21. The Court has similarly held that diversity jurisdiction suits under 28 U.S.C. § 1332 require abstention by federal courts and exhaustion of tribal remedies. *See* Iowa Mutual Ins. Co. v. LaPlante, 480 U.S. 9 (1987).

25 *Nevada v. Hicks*, 533 U.S. 353 (2001).

26 *Id.* at 366–67.

27 U.S. Const. art. I, § 8.

28 Talton v. Mayes, 163 U.S. 376 (1896).

29 Likewise, 28 U.S.C. § 1738 (1948) State and Territorial statutes and judicial proceedings, full faith and credit has not been interpreted to include Indian tribes.

30 471 U.S. 845, 852–53 (1985).

31 Relatedly, tribal governments are not diverse citizens and have sovereign immunity from suit in federal forums. Thus, the application of 28 U.S.C. § 1332 diversity jurisdiction to tribal governments is also inapplicable, contrary to the holding in *Iowa Mutual Insurance Company v. LaPlante*. 480 U.S. 9, 18–20 (1987).

32 28 U.S.C. § 1362 (2018).

33 Robert N. Clinton, *There is No Federal Supremacy Clause for Indian Tribes*, 34 Ariz. St. L. J. 113, 115–16 (2002).

34 Angelique EagleWoman, *A Constitutional Crisis When the U.S. Supreme Court Acts in a Legislative Manner? An Essay Offering a Perspective on Judicial Activism in Federal Indian Law and Federal Civil Procedure Pleading Standards*, 114 Penn. St. L. Rev. 41, 42 (2010).

35 John Borrows, *Wampum at Niagara: The Royal Proclamation, Canadian Legal History, and Self-Government*, Aboriginal and Treaty Rights in Canada: Essays on Law, Equality, and Respect for Difference, 155, 169 (Michael Esh ed., 1997).

36 21 U.S. 543, 584 (1823).

24

How Jurisdiction-Channeling Erodes Rights

DAVID MARCUS

Congress can use its power over the federal courts' subject matter jurisdiction to erode rights.[1] Targeting disfavored causes and politically vulnerable groups, it can entrench systemic injustice through jurisdictional regulation in at least two ways. First, Congress can close the federal courthouse doors altogether. Numerous proposals over the decades would have ended federal court involvement with plaintiffs' efforts to desegregate schools, win marriage equality, and protect abortion rights. But these attempts usually fail as structural and political barriers often block proposed jurisdiction-stripping legislation.[2] Skeptical federal courts use "clear statement" requirements to interpret and defang the rare provisions that get passed.[3] The erosion of rights through jurisdiction-stripping, it seems, is just too brazen. This type of jurisdictional regulation gives marginalized litigants little to fear.

But Congress can also narrow the path for civil lights litigants in a second, more subtle, manner by channeling cases to certain federal courts. A "channeling" provision of this sort does not bar litigants from court altogether. Thus, it faces fewer barriers to passage and less judicial skepticism once enacted. But jurisdictional channeling can "define" a case by limiting its procedural form, cabining its remedial potential, and constraining its evidentiary horizons. These more subtle effects can leave rights just as functionally toothless as jurisdiction-stripping can. The failure of a litigation campaign to get counsel for immigrant children illustrates how judicial tolerance for the insidious effects of jurisdiction-channeling, intended by Congress to thwart rights vindication, deepens systemic injustice.

Lawyers in Immigration Adjudication

Immigrants challenging efforts to deport them often appear before immigration judges (IJs), agency adjudicators whom the Attorney General supervises. Members of an "irredeemably dysfunctional" adjudication system,[4] IJs have grown increasingly hostile to immigrants since January 2017, an attitude reflected in the historic collapse of the rate at which immigrants win in removal proceedings.[5] If an immigrant loses before an IJ, she can appeal to the Board of Immigration Appeals, an overburdened entity that offers little succor.[6] The immigrant's case eventually enters the federal judiciary through a petition for review filed with a US Circuit Court of Appeals.[7]

The substance and procedure of immigration adjudication are remarkably complex,[8] and unrepresented immigrants have almost no chance to prevail.[9] Immigrants with financial means can hire lawyers.[10] But because removal proceedings are technically civil and not criminal, indigent immigrants—that is, the vast majority of immigrants in removal proceedings—have no right to appointed counsel.[11] This situation makes an obvious mockery of due process, given the complexity of immigration adjudication and the deep harm an erroneous decision causes a deported immigrant. The affront is undeniable when the unrepresented immigrant is a child.

Jurisdiction-Channeling and Immigration Litigation

Congress has a lengthy history of manipulating judicial review of immigration orders. Concerned by "the 'flagrant abuse of judicial review' by 'aliens, mostly subversives, gangsters, immoral, or narcotic peddlers,'" Congress in 1961 laid the foundation for today's jurisdictional regime. It cut district judges out of the review of deportation orders and required immigrants to petition for review in courts of appeals instead.[12] This channeling provision, however, did not apply when cases targeted an aspect of immigration enforcement "collateral" or "ancillary" to a deportation order.[13] Such instances included challenges to the practices or customs immigration authorities use to administer policy.[14]

McNary v. Haitian Refugee Center, Inc., decided in 1991, embraced this impact-litigation exception to jurisdiction-channeling.[15] As the

Supreme Court explained, systemic claims require evidence more extensive than what the adjudication of an individual petition for review encompasses. A court of appeals relies on the record assembled before the agency, and it lacks a district court's "fact-finding and record-developing capabilities."[16] By defining a case as an individual petition, the jurisdiction-channeling provision would render systemic challenges to the administration of immigration policy functionally impossible—"the practical equivalent of a total denial of judicial review."[17] *McNary* demanded a clearer statement of congressional intent before it would let jurisdictional regulation degrade judicial capacity to protect immigrants' rights.[18]

Impact litigators in the 1980s and 1990s took advantage of this exception to attempt to "end . . . widespread INS illegalities" in immigration enforcement.[19] Congressional immigration skeptics took note. When these legislators sought harsh substantive changes to immigration laws in the mid-1990s, they also proposed jurisdictional restrictions to make court access "extraordinary."[20] Lobbying against the legislation, immigrants' advocates largely focused on the substantive proposals. They conceded the jurisdictional changes, which got enacted when Congress passed the Illegal Immigration and Immigrant Responsibility Act (IIRIRA) in 1996. Among others, these provisions include § 1252(a)(5), which deems "a petition for review filed with an appropriate court of appeals" to "be the sole and exclusive means for judicial review of an order of removal." Another provision, § 1252(b)(9), provides that "[j]udicial review of all questions of law and fact . . . arising from any action taken or proceeding brought to remove an alien . . . shall be available only in judicial review of a final order."

Because appellate courts do not certify classes and cannot supervise discovery, IIRIRA's confinement of judicial review to appellate consideration of individual removal orders placed a formidable barrier in the way of impact litigation. But exactly what jurisdictional residue §§ 1252(a)(5) and (b)(9) left in the district courts to entertain systemic challenges remained uncertain after IIRIRA's passage. Sometimes the provisions derailed class actions,[21] but other courts found sufficient ambiguity in the statute to permit class actions to proceed. One district court, for example, refused to dismiss a case vindicating a statutory right to appointed counsel for "mentally disabled immigrant detainees" in removal proceedings.[22] The class members did not seek relief from removal per se—a remedy that only the courts of appeals could provide—but sought only to enforce their right to counsel. Thus, the court held, IIRIRA's provisions did not prevent merits adjudication.[23]

A Case-Defining Dismissal

Seeking similar jurisdictional favor, a class action alleging a right to counsel for all immigrant children began in 2014, a year during which 19,676 of the 58,721 juveniles in removal proceedings lacked lawyers.[24] A district court denied the government's motion to dismiss. Invoking *McNary*, the court noted that, because IJs cannot decide constitutional challenges to immigration court proceedings, any administrative record compiled on the issue would be too sparse to permit meaningful review by a court of appeals.[25] Sections 1252(a)(5) and (b)(9) did not apply because the right-to-counsel issue is "collateral to the substance of the underlying removal proceedings."[26]

The case proceeded as a class action, so the plaintiffs' due process claim turned on the needs of children generally, not specific individuals. Evidence-gathering in discovery focused on matters such as the psychological and intellectual barriers that make children unable to represent themselves and the astonishing rate at which IJs order unrepresented children removed. Discovery also yielded damning deposition testimony that betrayed systemic disregard of children's capacities by IJs. One IJ notoriously testified that he had "taught immigration law literally to three-year-olds and four-year-olds."[27] "It takes a lot of time. It takes a lot of patience," the IJ continued, denying that any child is too young to represent herself in court: "They get it. It's not the most efficient, but it can be done."[28]

Evidence of this sort gave plaintiffs a powerful case for a categorical right to counsel for all immigrant children. But the Ninth Circuit, deciding an interlocutory appeal, ordered the case dismissed on jurisdictional grounds. The court held that §§ 1252(a)(5) and (b)(9) applied because right-to-counsel claims are "an inextricable part of the administrative process."[29] Thus children could bring right-to-counsel claims to federal court only in individual petitions for review filed with courts of appeals. Citing *McNary*, plaintiffs insisted that jurisdiction-channeling denied the right-to-counsel claim a meaningful day in court. But

IIRIRA disavowed *McNary*, the Ninth Circuit ruled. No statutory text or legislative history supports the court's determination.[30] But no "clear statement" rule applies, the Ninth Circuit insisted, because IIRIRA had not "foreclose[d] *all* judicial review."[31] All its provisions do is "limit *how* immigrants can challenge their removal proceedings" by "channel[ing] judicial review."[32] Neither the institutional limitations of appellate courts nor longstanding jurisdictional solicitude for impact litigation could justify infidelity to "an unambiguous statute."[33]

The Failed Petition for Review

The Ninth Circuit ordered the government to help class counsel find an individual petition for review to use as a vehicle for the right-to-counsel claim. The parties identified the case of "C.J.," a thirteen-year-old boy who fled Honduras after a gang member threatened to kill him and his family.[34] After the IJ denied his asylum claim, C.J. argued the right-to-counsel issue before the BIA, then petitioned the Ninth Circuit for review.[35]

The Ninth Circuit rejected C.J.'s claim in a rambling, sometimes incoherent opinion. Applying the *Mathews v. Eldridge* balancing test, the court conceded that one of its factors favored C.J. because his wrongful removal threatened his "liberty—indeed . . . his very life."[36] But the rest of the due process calculus tilted "strongly" toward the government.[37] Most important, the court held that the existing procedures—a hearing before an IJ without counsel—did not risk an erroneous deprivation of C.J.'s right to stay in the country.

The court acknowledged that immigration law is complex and that unrepresented children as a general matter suffer dramatically poor outcomes. The class action had developed evidence to this effect, and it would have turned on these sorts of generalized determinations. But IIRIRA's jurisdiction-channeling provisions gave the Ninth Circuit cover to dodge the general question of whether children can possibly represent themselves fairly before IJs. The court instead cast the relevant issue as whether the record in C.J.'s case, developed without counsel, sufficiently supported the asylum denial. In effect, the Ninth Circuit reviewed the IJ's decision on the merits and found it sufficient. The existing procedure did not risk an erroneous deprivation of C.J.'s right to remain, the Ninth Circuit concluded, because the IJ did not *in this instance* err.

This reasoning is exactly backward. *Mathews* is based on the premise that, without adequate procedural protections, a proceeding cannot generate a record sufficient to support an acceptably accurate decision.[38] The Ninth Circuit instead considered the record, determined that C.J. had no case, and only then concluded that a lawyer would not have made a difference.

The decision did not survive en banc reconsideration.[39] But the en banc majority avoided the right-to-counsel issue. Instead, it remanded CJ's case because the IJ failed to advise him of his potential eligibility for alternate relief. One Ninth Circuit judge captured what had happened. The jurisdictional dismissal "shut one door to the courthouse on the promise of keeping another open" to the due process claim. But then the court "duck[ed] out of that door . . . as well."[40]

Jurisdiction, Case Definition, and Rights Degradation

As Hiroshi Motomura observes, "[a] reviewing court may have a cramped or even distorted view of the controversy if it examines only one person's case in isolation."[41] IIRIRA's jurisdiction-channeling provisions have created these cramped and isolating conditions. The class action asked whether children need lawyers to make removal proceedings fundamentally fair. Evidence of psychological and intellectual limitations in juveniles and the miserable rate at which unrepresented children win relief would have weighed heavily in the due process balance had the case, defined in these systemic terms, proceeded to the merits. The individual petition for review, by contrast, defined the case narrowly. Focusing myopically, the Ninth Circuit could ignore overwhelming evidence of systemic injustice and simply ask whether a lawyer could have helped C.J.

Nothing in IIRIRA's jurisdiction-channeling provisions formally prohibits a reviewing court from deciding the right to counsel claim in a petition for review on general, not individualized, grounds. But the likelihood that an individual petition will buck IIRIRA's case-defining effects is remote. Few unrepresented children can possibly navigate the process from an IJ's courtroom to a court of appeals, preserving the right-to-counsel claim all along.[42] Moreover, a reviewing court would have to conclude that the child's lack of counsel violated due process even though the IJ made no reversible error. Otherwise, if the IJ's decision-making was subpar in any other respect, the court—obliged to avoid constitutional questions—would remand on the statutory basis, as the en banc panel did in C.J.'s case. A court of appeals can decide the due process claim only in a case the IJ otherwise handled acceptably—hardly the most propitious factual context for a landmark step in due process jurisprudence.

IIRIRA's case-defining effects have contributed to an epic human rights catastrophe. Each week in 2019 the United States commenced removal proceedings against more children than it did in all of 2009. Of the 479,083 children who found themselves before IJs in 2019, nearly 70 percent lacked lawyers.[43] Perhaps the government would have won the right-to-counsel class action in the district court. Perhaps the Ninth Circuit would have reversed a plaintiff's verdict. A Supreme Court hostile to new procedural rights would have had the final say. But the class action would have forced courts bent on denying children lawyers to justify the unjustifiable: that unrepresented children as young as three or four, speaking no English, often on their own, facing removal to gang-ridden, violent countries, can have fundamentally fair proceedings before overworked, hostile IJs. The Ninth Circuit's crabbed interpretation of IIRIRA defined the case to let the federal courts off the hook.[44]

Real rights vindication requires more than just one open courthouse door, as the tragedy of immigrant children and their quest for counsel show. Jurisdiction-channeling can degrade rights through subtle—and for that reason insidious—means. Brazen attempts to deny rights vindication to politically vulnerable groups through jurisdiction-stripping may fail. But courts have blessed jurisdiction-channeling provisions, even as they lead to the same result.[45] Immigrant children have suffered deeply from the degrading case-defining effects of jurisdictional regulation. They are not alone.[46]

NOTES

1 *E.g.*, Martin H. Redish, *Same-Sex Marriage, the Constitution, and Congressional Power to Control Federal Jurisdiction: Be Careful What You Wish For*, 9 Lewis & Clark L. Rev. 363, 364–365 (2005).

2 Tara Leigh Grove, *The Structural Safeguards of Federal Jurisdiction*, 124 Harv. L. Rev. 869 (2011); Tara Leigh Grove, *The Article II Safeguards of Federal Jurisdiction*, 112 Colum. L. Rev. 250 (2012).

3 *E.g.*, Grove, *supra* note 2, at 929–930.

4 1 Am. Bar Ass'n, 2019 Update Report: Reforming the Immigration System: Proposals to Promote Independence, Fairness, Efficiency, and Professionalism in the Adjudication of Removal Cases ES-15 (2019).
5 Catherine Y. Kim & Amy Semet, *An Empirical Study of Political Control over Immigration Adjudication*, 108 Geo. L.J. 575, 625–26 (2020); Innovation L. Lab & S. Poverty L. Ctr., The Attorney General's Judges: How the U.S. Immigration Courts Became a Deportation Tool 21 (2019); Exec. Off. for Immigr. Rev., Adjudication Statistics: Asylum Decision Rates (2020), www.justice.gov.
6 *E.g.*, Innovation L. Lab & S. Poverty L Ctr., *supra* note 5, at 17.
7 8 U.S.C. § 1252(a)(5).
8 *E.g.*, Balthazar-Alcazar v. INS., 386 F.3d 940, 948 (9th Cir. 2004).
9 Karen Berberich & Nina Siulc, Vera Inst. of Just., Why Does Representation Matter? The Impact of Legal Representation in Immigration Court 1 (2018).
10 8 U.S.C. § 1362.
11 Trench v. INS, 783 F.2d 181, 183 (10th Cir. 1986).
12 Dastmalchi v. INS, 660 F.2d 880, 884 (3d Cir. 1981).
13 Orantes-Hernandez v. Smith, 541 F. Supp. 351, 364–366 (C.D. Cal. 1982).
14 *E.g.*, Haitian Refugee Ctr v. Smith, 676 F.2d 1023, 1026–27 (5th Cir. Unit B 1982); Jean v. Nelson, 727 F.2d 957, 980 (11th Cir. 1984) (en banc).
15 McNary v. Haitian Refugee Ctr, Inc., 498 U.S. 479, 497 (1991).
16 *Id.* at 497.
17 *Id.*
18 *Id.* at 496.
19 Lucas Guttentag, *Immigration Legislation and Due Process: The Forgotten Issue*, *in* 19 In Defense of the Alien 25, 33 (1996).
20 Lamar Smith & Edward R. Grant, *Immigration Reform: Seeking the Right Reasons*, 28 St. Mary's L.J. 883, 918 (1997).
21 *E.g.*, Aguilar v. U.S. Immigr. & Customs Enf't Div., 510 F.3d 1, 9 (1st Cir. 2007).
22 Franco-Gonzales v. Holder, 767 F. Supp. 2d 1034, 1038 (N.D. Cal. 2010).
23 *Id.* at 1045.
24 *Juveniles—Immigration Court Deportation Proceedings*, TRAC Immigr., https://trac.syr.edu.
25 J.E.F.M. v. Holder, 107 F. Supp. 3d 1119, 1131 (W.D. Wash. 2015).
26 *Id.*
27 Deposition of Honorable Jack H. Weil at 69–70, J.E.F.M. v. Lynch, 107 F. Supp. 3d 1119 (W.D. Wash. 2015) (No. 2:14-cv-01026).
28 *Id.* at 69–70.
29 J.E.F.M. v. Lynch, 837 F.3d 1026, 1033 (9th Cir. 1033).
30 The court did not cite any such evidence of legislative intent. A search for "McNary" in IIRIRA's legislative history in the Proquest Congressional database yields no results.
31 837 F.3d at 1031.
32 *Id.*

33 *Id.* at 1036, 1038.
34 C.J.L.G. v. Sessions, 880 F.3d 1122, 1129–31 (9th Cir. 2018).
35 *Id.* at 1131–1132.
36 *Id.* at 1137.
37 *Id.* at 1145.
38 Addington v. Texas, 441 U.S. 418, 425 (1979).
39 C.J.L.G. v. Barr, 923 F.3d 622 (9th Cir. 2019).
40 *Id.* at 640 (Berzon, J., concurring).
41 Hiroshi Motomura, *Judicial Review in Immigration Cases After* AADC: *Lessons from Civil Procedure*, 14 Geo. Immigr. L.J. 385, 386 (2000).
42 Between 2005 and 2016, only three children navigated the review process from an IJ's chambers to a circuit court even partially on their own. Plaintiffs-Appellees'/Cross-Appellants' Reply Brief at 6–8, J.E.F.M. v. Lynch, 837 F.3d 1026 (9th Cir. 2016) (Nos. 15-35738, 15-35739).
43 *Juveniles—Immigration Court Deportation Proceedings*, *supra* note 24.
44 For a less crabbed interpretation of § 1252(b)(9), *see* Jennings v. Rodriguez, 138 S. Ct. 830, 840 (2018); Las Americas Immigrant Advoc. Ctr. v. Trump, Civ. No. 3:19-cv-02051, 2020 WL 4431682, at *7 (D. Or. July 31, 2020).
45 *E.g.*, Elgin v. Dep't of Treasury, 567 U.S. 1, 10 (2012); Shalala v. Ill. Council on Long Term Care, Inc., 529 U.S. 1, 19 (2000).
46 *E.g.*, Veterans for Common Sense v. Shinseki, 678 F.3d 1013, 1028–29 (9th Cir. 2012) (invoking a jurisdiction-channeling provision to dismiss a class action challenging delays in the veterans' benefits system).

25

Procedural Barriers to the Use of Title IX as a Defense for Transgender Students in State Juvenile Justice Proceedings

BRIANA ROSENBAUM

State courts must follow valid federal constitutional and statutory law. This is a basic constitutional principle grounded in the Supremacy Clause.[1] For transgender children in places such as Tennessee, situated in the Sixth Circuit Court of Appeals, this should be excellent news. Since 2016, the Sixth Circuit has followed the majority of lower federal courts in interpreting "sex discrimination" in Title IX of the Education Amendments of 1972[2] to prohibit discrimination and harassment in schools on the basis of transgender status.[3] Even more promising, the United States Supreme Court has recently signaled strong support for the Sixth Circuit's interpretation of Title IX. In *Bostock v. Clayton County*, the Court interpreted Title VII of the Civil Rights Act of 1964 to prohibit discrimination against transgender employees. As the Court held, "discrimination based on homosexuality or transgender status necessarily entails discrimination based on sex."[4]

Following this precedent, public schools in Tennessee should be: allowing students to use the bathrooms corresponding with their gender identity; allowing students to self-identify, including by using their preferred name; and protecting students from harassment due to their transgender status. But the on-the-ground experiences of transgender students and their families show that this is not the reality. Many transgender children in public schools in Tennessee have been forced to use bathrooms that do not align with their identified genders, have not been called their preferred name or gender pronoun, and have been subjected to routine harassment and bullying with little institutional support.[5] Transgender students who experience harassment and bullying based on their LGBTQ+ status are more likely to experience "academic underachievement, increased truancy, and higher dropout rates"[6] and are therefore more likely to interact with the state juvenile justice system.[7]

This chapter illustrates how federal question jurisdiction and choice of law can impact the enforcement of Title IX, particularly in state truancy proceedings—which are a predictable result of transgender students avoiding school.[8] The experiences of transgender children in Tennessee confirm the complexity of raising federal civil rights claims or defenses in state courts. A student in a truancy proceeding might have a valid Title IX claim based on the discrimination and harassment she experienced in school. However, any lawyer representing such a student in a state truancy proceeding would have to consider a number of potential procedural factors before deciding to raise such a defense. In short, the path from Supreme Court precedent to actually having an effect on a person's life is not always clear.

In order to show how federalism and federal procedure impede enforcement of Title IX, the first section considers a hypothetical case of a transgender student going through the state truancy process after having experienced harassment and discrimination in school; the second section considers the jurisdictional issues raised when considering how to articulate and define a potential federal harassment and discrimination defense in a state court proceeding; and the third section addresses the *Erie*[9] question of what law controls when potential federal civil rights defenses are raised in state truancy proceedings.

The Case

Consider the following hypothetical experience of a student, Tania, in Knoxville, Tennessee. Assume for the moment that Tania's school has referred her to court based on truancy charges for ten days of "unjustified" school absences. Tania is now before a state juvenile justice court defending herself against a charge of "chronic truancy."[10] Tania concedes that she missed school, a violation of Tennessee's compulsory education law, Tenn. Code Ann. § 49-6-3001. However, she says that she missed school to avoid the harassment and discrimination she experienced there due to her transgender status. School administration forced her to either use the male bathroom or conspicuously request a key for the faculty bathroom (leading to more taunting by her peers). Her teachers and peers continued to call her by her birth name, Matt, a name incongruous with her gender identity and clothing choice. Further, despite complaining to teachers and the principal, other students constantly harassed her, including by calling her derogatory names such as "he/she."

Tania has hired a lawyer, who is considering arguing that, because the harassment and discrimination Tania experienced violates Title IX, her absences are "justified" and she should not be found truant. As the following makes clear, jurisdictional and choice of law problems complicate this decision.

Nature of the Action

The first thing that Tania might consider is to file a Title IX action in federal court. A federal suit could seek relief against the school as well as a declaratory judgment preventing the state district attorney from prosecuting the truancy proceeding against her. Based on the facts of her case, Tania has a viable Title IX case. The kind of conduct that Tania has been experiencing—deadnaming, discriminatory bathroom access, and harassment due to transgender status—is unlawful in Tennessee under the Sixth Circuit's 2016 decision in *Dodds v. US Department of Education.*[11] The court in *Dodds* held that "settled law" prohibits "[s]ex stereotyping based on a person's gender non-conforming behavior" and noted that "[t]he weight of authority establishes that discrimination based on transgender status is already prohibited by the language of federal civil rights statutes."[12] The Supreme Court in *Bostock* signaled support for *Dodds* when it held that, under Title VII, "discrimination based on homosexuality or transgender status necessarily entails discrimination based on sex."[13] Lower courts traditionally rely on the Supreme Court's interpretations of Title VII to inform their interpretation of Title IX, especially when determining who is encompassed by the term sex discrimination.[14]

Despite the positive outlook for any case filed in federal court against the school district, the federal suit is unlikely to have any practical effect on Tania's state truancy proceeding. Although federal courts have some powers to stay state proceedings, those powers are quite limited.[15]

Thus, Tania will have to raise the Title IX as a "defense" to the truancy charge. She and her lawyer might think about trying to remove her case to federal court under 28 U.S. Code § 1441. But this tactic, too, is destined to fail. Removal under § 1441 is limited to "civil actions," and truancy proceedings have been characterized as quasicriminal due to their potentially harsh direct and indirect penalties.[16] Even if removal were possible, Tania cannot remove her case to federal court under the well-pleaded complaint rule. The federal issue, Title IX, is raised by a "defense" and therefore could not establish federal court jurisdiction.[17] Instead, Tania must proceed through the state truancy process, ensuring that the harassment/failure to correct defense will be heard by the local state juvenile court judge.

Erie, Reverse-*Erie*, and What Law Controls?

Since Tania's harassment/discrimination defense will be heard by the state juvenile court, the next question is: What law will control her defense? This "choice of law" question invokes two issues central to the viability of Tania's defense. First, in evaluating Tania's harassment defense, does the state juvenile court judge have to apply federal law? Or can she apply some other source of law, such as state harassment law? And second, even if the juvenile court recognizes Tania's Title IX defense, is it bound by the Sixth Circuit's expansive interpretation of "sex discrimination" under Title IX?

First, can the juvenile justice court reject the application of Title IX altogether and instead apply a state-law definition of harassment? You bet. A state judge wishing to do this might characterize Tania's truancy defense as one of state statutory law, not federal law. This sounds contentious, even obstructionist, because a state court is obliged to apply valid federal statutory law—here, Title IX. Furthermore, state courts must apply federal law even when there is seemingly conflicting state law on point.[18]

However, in this case, the state truancy law and Title IX are not conflicting but potentially complementary. In Tennessee, just as in many other states, the state must prove that a students' absences were "without justification" to bring a successful truancy action. As part of that process, the student can raise defenses,[19] including by arguing that bullying and harassment justified the truancy.[20] There is little precedent in Tennessee on the meaning of "without justification," but certainly the definition of "justified" is a matter of state law.

Thus, a state juvenile court may use its own common law definition of harassment—ungrounded in Title IX principles—to determine whether there was enough "justification" in a particular case to support a student's defense. Should the state court in Tania's case follow this approach, even a direct Supreme Court decision interpreting Title IX would not assist her. This is so *even if* such harassment would be deemed actionable discrimination under Title IX by a district court sitting across the street, or even by the Supreme Court.

But a state court could also reasonably interpret the phrase "without justification" to include violations of Title IX. In that event, the court would incorporate federal law into the state law. That's the ideal approach from Tania's perspective, as the federal precedent is strongly in her favor. But this leads to the second choice of law question: If the juvenile court does follow federal law and recognizes her Title IX defense as a "justification," is the court obligated to follow the Sixth Circuit's expansive interpretation of "sex discrimination" under Title IX?

The answer is no. Because this involves a question of how a court of one sovereign (Tennessee) must apply the law of another (the United States), it raises a choice of law issue under the doctrine of *Erie R. Co. v. Tompkins*.[21] The basic *Erie* principle requires that federal courts defer to state court precedent when applying state substantive law.[22] A related principle, often referred to as "reverse *Erie*," governs the deference state courts must give to federal precedent.[23]

The majority view among state courts—and the view in Tennessee—is that federal trial or appellate court decisions interpreting law are not binding on state courts. Instead, such precedents are merely "persuasive authority."[24] Therefore, our juvenile court judge will not be bound by the Sixth Circuit's interpretation of Title IX. He may consider it persuasive, but then again he may not, choosing instead to rely on common law precedents in Tennessee. The same goes for the Supreme Court's recent decision in *Bostock*; because the Court in that decision was analyzing Title VII, there is nothing formally stopping the state court from coming to a different conclusion about Title IX.[25] Although this potential split between federal and state courts on the meaning of a federal law may seem odd at first to law students who have studied *Erie*, a number of jurists celebrate it.[26] To quote Justice O'Connor, we should encourage "dialogue among different jurists . . . [t]he benefits of [which] can, for at least a limited time, outweigh the immediate need for uniformity."[27]

Conclusion

State juvenile courts have considerable leeway to recognize—or not recognize—defenses of bullying and harassment of transgender students. Until the United States Supreme Court directly decides the issue, local courts remain unbound by federal precedent on the issue. And even a direct Supreme Court precedent might not be enough: state courts may rely on their own definitions of what is "justified." In short, even if a student's Title IX defense has merit, as a practical matter, choice of law and jurisdictional limitations might impede her ability to enforce her federal statutory civil rights in state courts. The federalist institutional structure of our judicial system empowers local state courts to make idiosyncratic decisions such as these.

This is disturbing. By either failing to recognize the federal law as controlling, or by failing to recognize an issue as implicating federal law, state courts can undermine the enforcement of federal civil rights protections for transgender people and other vulnerable populations. Court decisions such as *Bostock* and *Dodds* are vitally important, but vulnerable populations may spend years attempting, unsuccessfully, to have these rights recognized in hostile state forums—including in state courts and schools. And, although the Supreme Court can theoretically step in to resolve conflicts among the courts, the Court rarely does so. Transgender students do not have the luxury of waiting calmly for "dialogue among different jurists." Every day counts. Wait-and-see is not an option.

NOTES

1 U.S. Const. art. VI § 2. *See* Felder v. Casey, 487 U.S. 131, 151 (1988).

2 20 U.S.C. §§ 1681–1688.

3 Dodds v. United States Dep't of Educ., 845 F.3d 217, 222 (6th Cir. 2016).

4 Bostock v. Clayton County, 140 S. Ct. 1731, 1747 (2020).

5 For a comprehensive view of the experiences of LGBTQ+ children in American schools, see Human Rights Watch, *Hatred in the Hallways: Violence and*

Discrimination Against Lesbian, Gay, Bisexual, and Transgender Students in U.S. Schools (2001), www.hrw.org (May 2010); Joseph G. Kosciw, Emily A. Greytak, Adrian D. Zongrone, Caitlin M. Clark & Nhan L. Truong, GLSEN, *The 2017 National School Climate Survey: The Experiences of Lesbian, Gay, Bisexual, Transgender, and Queer Youth in Our Nation's Schools*, www.glsen.org (2018); National Center for Transgender Equality, *2015 U.S. Transgender Survey, Tennessee State Report* (2015), www.transequality.org (Oct. 2010).

6 Note, Jason Lee, *Too Cruel for School: LGBT Bullying, Noncognitive Skill Development, and the Educational Rights of Students*, 49 Harv. C.R.-C.L. L. Rev. 261, 288 (2014) (citing Harper ex rel. Harper v. Poway Unified Sch. Dist., 445 F.3d 1166, 1178–79 (9th Cir. 2006), *vacated as moot*, 549 U.S. 1262 (2007)).

7 Billie Gastic, *School Truancy and the Disciplinary Problems of Bullying Victims*, 60 Educ. Rev. 391, 397 (2008); Rudy Estrada & Jody Marksamer, *Lesbian, Gay, Bisexual, and Transgender Young People in State Custody: Making the Child Welfare and Juvenile Justice Systems Safe for All Youth Through Litigation, Advocacy, and Education*, 79 Temp. L. Rev. 415, 420 (2006). Regarding the difficulty of determine the precise number LGBTQ+ children in the justice system, see Randi Feinstein, Andrea Greenblatt, Lauren Hass, Sally Kohn & Julianna Rana, Urban Justice Center, *Justice for All? A Report on Lesbian, Gay, Bisexual, and Transgendered Youth in the Juvenile Justice System*, at 26–27, https://files.eric.ed.gov (2001).

8 As this chapter is limited in scope, it will not cover other potential procedural barriers to federal civil rights enforcements, such as issue preclusion.

9 Referring to the landmark case Erie R.R. Co. v. Tompkins, discussed in the third section.

10 For further background on the truancy process see Dean Hill Rivkin, *Truancy Prosecutions of Students and the Right [to] Education*, 3 Duke F. for L. & Soc. Change 139 (2011); Ashley Goins, *Justice for Juveniles: The Importance of Immediately Appointing Counsel to Cases Involving Status Offenses and Engaging in Holistic Representation of Juveniles in All Cases*, 2 The Forum: A Tennessee Student Legal Journal 33 (2015).

11 *Dodds*, 845 F.3d at 221.

12 *Id.* (quoting G.G. ex rel. Grimm v. Gloucester Cty. Sch. Bd., 822 F.3d 709, 729 (4th Cir.) (Davis, J., concurring), *vacated and remanded*, ___ U.S. ___, 137 S. Ct. 1239, 197 L.Ed.2d 460 (2017)). *See also* EEOC v. v. R.G. &. G.R. Harris Funeral Homes, Inc., 884 F.3d 560, 568 (6th Cir. 2018), *cert. granted in part sub nom.* R.G. & G.R. Harris Funeral Homes, Inc. v. E.E.O.C., 139 S. Ct. 1599, 203 L. Ed. 2d 754 (2019), and *aff'd sub nom.* Bostock v. Clayton Cty., Georgia, 140 S. Ct. 1731 (2020).

13 *Bostock*, 140 S. Ct. at 1747.

14 *See, e.g.*, Preston v. Com. of Va. ex rel. New River Cmty. Coll., 31 F.3d 203, 206 (4th Cir. 1994); *see also* Grimm v. Gloucester Cty. Sch. Bd., No. 19–1953, slip op. at 52 (4th Cir. Aug. 26, 2020).

15 *See, e.g.*, D.T. by and through B.K.T. v. Sumner Cty. Sch., No. 3:18-CV-00388, 2018 WL 4776080, at *2 (M.D. Tenn. Oct. 3, 2018).

16 Goins, *supra* note 10, at 27–28.
17 *See* Arthur R. Miller, *Artful Pleading: A Doctrine in Search of Definition*, 76 Tex. L. Rev. 1781, 1782 (1998).
18 Free v. Bland, 369 U.S. 663, 666 (1962).
19 *See* Goins, *supra* note 10, at 34 (citing Tenn. Code Ann. § 37-1-102(b)(23)(A) (2014)).
20 *See* Jason B. Langberg & Barbara A. Fedders, *How Juvenile Defenders Can Help Dismantle the School-to-Prison Pipeline*, 42 J.L. & Educ. 653, 679 (2013); Rivkin, *supra* note 10, at 12.
21 Erie R.R. Co. v. Tompkins, 304 U.S. 64 (1938).
22 *See* Suzanna Sherry, *Wrong, Out of Step, and Pernicious: Erie As the Worst Decision of All Time*, 39 Pepp. L. Rev. 129, 141 (2011); John Hart Ely, *The Irrepressible Myth of Erie*, 87 Harv. L. Rev. 693, 722–23 (1974).
23 For thorough discussions of the reverse-*Erie* doctrine see Amanda Frost, *Inferiority Complex: Should State Courts Follow Lower Federal Court Precedent on the Meaning of Federal Law?*, 68 Vand. L. Rev. 53, 55 (2015); Kevin M. Clermont, *Reverse-Erie*, 82 Notre Dame L. Rev. 1, 20 (2006); Donald H. Zeigler, *Gazing Into the Crystal Ball: Reflections on the Standards State Judges Should Use to Ascertain Federal Law*, 40 Wm. & Mary L. Rev. 1143, 1177 (1999); Colin E. Wrabley, *Applying Federal Court of Appeals' Precedent: Contrasting Approaches to Applying Court of Appeals' Federal Law Holdings and Erie State Law Predictions*, 3 Seton Hall Circuit Rev. 1, 16–28 (2006).
24 Frost, *supra* note 23, at 62; State v. Carruthers, 35 S.W. 3d 516, 561 n.45 (Tenn. 2000). For minority state approaches to the reverse-Erie doctrine, see Frost, *supra* note 23, at 63.
25 For a discussion on state court powers to hear federal claims, see Josh Blackman, *State Judicial Sovereignty*, 2016 U. Ill. L. Rev. 2033, 2039 (2016).
26 *See, e.g.*, Sandra Day O'Connor, *Proceedings of the Middle Atlantic State-Federal Judicial Relationships Conference*, 162 F.R.D. 173, 181–82 (1994); David L. Shapiro, *State Courts and Federal Declaratory Judgments*, 74 NW. U. L. Rev. 759, 771 (1979). For a contrary view, see Frost, *supra* note 23.
27 O'Connor, *Proceedings*, *supra* note 26, at 181–82.

PART IV

The Process of Litigation

The ability of marginalized people to tell their story and assert their rights in the civil litigation system is precarious and fragile. This is the theme of Part IV. We're often told that the plaintiff is the "master of their complaint," but the chapters in this section paint a starkly different picture. Deseriee Kennedy (chapter 26), challenges the myth of plaintiff empowerment by showing how the Supreme Court has created a new and heightened pleading requirement for civil rights claimants in § 1981 suits—a standard that she critiques as out of step with our modern understanding of how subtle forms of discrimination oppress people within systems. Andrew Hammond (chapter 27) explains that, in a society rife with economic inequalities, pleading requirements often function as barriers excluding pro se plaintiffs from the courts. Pleading burdens fall especially hard on undocumented immigrants, as Stephen Lee shares in chapter 28. Fear of having one's immigration status revealed in the discovery process has left undocumented immigrants especially vulnerable to the intimidation tactics of their employers in wage theft and dangerous and abusive working conditions cases. Seth Katsuya Endo (chapter 29) reminds us that transgender plaintiffs are another group vulnerable in a discovery process whereby defendants can use intrusive discovery as a sword against an opponent. Together these chapters urge judges—who exercise even more discretion in the pleadings and discovery arenas today—to use that discretion in a way that considers the life experiences of outsiders and marginalized groups.

Another set of contributors challenges summary judgment, a core procedural mechanism that defendants often use to prevent litigation from reaching a jury. Jasmine Gonzales Rose in chapter 30 explains how a mostly white federal bench impermissibly considers race in negatively assessing the victim's character and positively assessing the perpetrator's actions in police brutality cases. Similarly, Elizabeth Schneider (chapter 31) challenges how summary judgment has been used to defeat gender bias claims when a predominantly male judiciary can assess what behavior is reasonable based on a paper record that is bereft of a woman's particular experience. Suja Thomas in chapter 32 notes the disproportionate summary judgment grant rates in employment discrimination cases and broadens the scope of our inquiry into the procedural device by questioning its constitutionality. And while we might lament that summary judgment often takes viable cases away from jury deliberation, Kevin Johnson (chapter 33) reminds us that, even when cases survive a motion for summary judgment, juror eligibility requirements disproportionately exclude broad swaths of marginalized people, including immigrants, non–English speakers, people with felony convictions, and people with disabilities, from jury service.

26

Pleading and Antiracism

DESERIEE KENNEDY

Despite the persistence of US racism, African Americans consistently have pursued the promise of equality through the courts.[1] However, calls for equality have increasingly been supplemented by demands for antiracist policies and institutions. Antiracism goes beyond focusing on intentional bad behavior and requires reckoning with how institutions and policies help maintain White supremacy and contribute to passive racism. *Passive racism* is "an apathy toward systems of racial advantage or denial that those systems exist."[2] This evolution in thought is occurring at the same time that federal courts are raising the bar for plaintiffs. Recent United States Supreme Court decisions on how to sufficiently establish discrimination claims raise questions about the role federal courts play in the pursuit of racial justice and antiracist institutions.

Section 1981 and the Right to Contract

It is significant that, after the Constitution was amended to end slavery, the right to contract freely was the first civil right recognized by Congress. The Civil Rights Act of 1866 was enacted even before the grant of citizenship to people of African descent through the Fourteenth Amendment's ratification. That act, now codified in Title 42 of the United States Code § 1981, provides that "[a]ll persons within the jurisdiction of the United States shall have the same right . . . to make and enforce contracts . . . as is enjoyed by white citizens."[3] The Civil Rights statute was a response to Blacks' formal and informal exclusions from public life. At the time, state laws termed "Black Codes" restricted Blacks' rights to own property, work, contract, and move freely through society. These provisions restricted Blacks' freedom through acts of public and private violence designed to maintain a system of White supremacy.

This racial caste system, which placed those considered a member of the "White race" at the top of the hierarchy and those considered Black at the bottom, is US slavery's most enduring legacy. Thus, although the Civil War and the Thirteenth Amendment ended slavery in many forms, they did little to address White supremacy. The passing of the Civil Rights Act in 1866 is seen by many as the Reconstruction Congress's acknowledgment of the role that denying Blacks the same right to make contracts, sue, be parties, and give evidence as Whites had in reinforcing racial hierarchies.

The Civil Rights Act still plays a significant role in dismantling the racial caste system imposed by governments and private individuals. However, the act's effectiveness at disrupting racial exclusion and hierarchy depends directly on the ability of those aggrieved to access courts to obtain relief.

The New Pleading Hurdle in Section 1981 Suits

In a series of recent decisions, the Supreme Court has narrowed the right to relief for discrimination plaintiffs by layering a tort standard onto pleading requirements in discrimination claims.[4] This is a noteworthy change for § 1981 suits. Under § 1981, plaintiffs must assert that they suffered discrimination in the "making, performance, modification, and termination of contracts, and the enjoyment of all benefits, privileges, terms, and conditions of the contractual relationship."[5] Plaintiffs must plead and later prove that defendants "intentionally and purposefully discriminated against them" based on race.

In *Comcast Corp. v. Nat'l Ass'n of African Am.-Owned Media* (*NAAOM*),[6] the Court held that, to survive a motion to dismiss, plaintiffs must allege discrimination is the "but for" cause of the disparate treatment or outcome in § 1981 claims. The plaintiff was Entertainment Studios Network (ESN), a Black-owned television network operator founded in 1993. ESN produces more than 60 syndicated television shows and owns eight channels, including The Weather Channel and Local Now. According to the complaint, Comcast repeatedly refused to contract with ESN, even though it launched multiple White-owned networks during the same period. ESN asserted that a Comcast executive, during the negotiations period, stated that Comcast was not "trying to create any more Bob Johnsons," a remark that ESN took to reference Robert Johnson, the African American founder of Black Entertainment Network. ESN alleged that defendants refused to contract with it because of race and that ESN was not given the same right to contract as White-owned media companies. Comcast responded that it had legitimate business reasons for refusing to contract with ESN and filed a motion to dismiss for failure to state a claim under § 1981.

Dismissal at the pleading stage turned on whether plaintiffs were obligated to allege that discriminatory intent was the "but-for cause" or simply a "motivating factor" in the refusal to contract. The district court took the position that the complaint did not plead discriminatory intent as the but-for cause of Comcast's refusal to enter into a contract with ESN. The district court dismissed ESN's complaint because it failed to "undercut" Comcast's "alternative explanation" for refusing to contract with the plaintiff. It opined that the complaint "did not exclude" the possibility that Comcast's refusal to contract "was based on legitimate business reasons."[7]

The Ninth Circuit reversed, reasoning that "[p]laintiffs need only to plausibly allege that discriminatory intent was a factor in Comcast's refusal to contract." According to the circuit court, "a plaintiff must only plead facts plausibly showing that race played 'some role' in the defendant's decision-making process."[8] The appellate court noted that it could plausibly infer that ESN "experienced disparate treatment due to race and was thus denied the same right to contract as a white-owned company."[9] The court found that plaintiffs alleged sufficient facts to suggest race played a role in the case.

In a unanimous opinion, the Supreme Court reversed the Ninth Circuit, concluding that alleging race as a "motivating factor" is insufficient to survive a motion to dismiss for failure to state a claim in a § 1981 suit. The Court stated that plaintiffs are required to allege that race was a but-for cause of the alleged discrimination.[10] This but-for pleading standard is inconsistent with the purpose of the Civil Rights statute, which was designed to level the playing field for citizens divided along racial fault lines created by hundreds of years of enslavement and marginalization. A pleading standard that requires plaintiffs to allege more than race as a motivating factor neutralizes the effect of the Civil Rights Act of 1866 and dulls its ability to root out discrimination in contracting.[11]

The Court's approach also leaves open for interpretation precisely what is required of plaintiffs to allege but-for discrimination.[12] Even though judges, when ruling on a motion to dismiss for failure to state a claim, must view the allegations as true and draw inferences in favor of the nonmoving party, the but-for standard increases judicial discretion. Some judges may allow plaintiffs to move forward with their litigation if race is one of many factors affecting a decision whether to contract. However, *NAAOM*'s but-for standard invites judges to mandate that plaintiffs allege discrimination as the sole motivating cause of defendant's actions. Unsurprisingly, the decision was feted by employers' counsel and large corporations.

This more stringent and less forgiving but-for pleading standard ignores policy and purpose distinctions between tort and discrimination law in a manner that undermines discrimination law.[13] In his dissent in the age discrimination case *Gross v FBL Financial Services, Inc.*, Justice Breyer succinctly notes the discordance in applying tort causation in discrimination claims, stating "it is an entirely different matter to determine a 'but-for' relation when we consider, not physical forces, but the mind-related characterizations that constitute motive."[14]

The opinion reflects a view of racism out of step with the scientific understanding of how subtle forms of discrimination manifest in systems that maintain the racial hierarchy that the Civil Rights Act of 1866 was designed to help dismantle. Requiring but-for causation allegations in complaints privileges an antiquated view of human behavior and racism as primarily an overt dislike or mistreatment of others because of race. However, racism is more aptly described as a system of advantage based on race that segregates and excludes, advantaging some over others.[15] In this light, the "causation" the Supreme Court asks plaintiffs to allege in the pleadings also fails to take note of the reality that race-neutral justifications for a defendant's behavior do not demonstrate an absence of racist intent or discriminatory conduct.

Neither does the requirement to plead race as a sole or even principal factor reflect the complex role that race may play in decision-making. Marketplace discrimination against consumers of color that evidences an undervaluation of these consumers has been well documented.[16] Suppose a refusal to contract is based in part on a reluctance to increase a Black customer base or a fear of alienating coveted White customers.

In those instances, the plaintiff should be able to take its case beyond the pleading stage of litigation. Yet the Court's decision in *NAAOM* may cut off such cases at the outset, thereby diminishing efforts to correct disparities such as the racial wealth gap, which has not improved since 1968, exists at all income and education levels, and reveals that White families hold eight times the wealth than Black families.[17]

Raising the pleading standard for § 1981 suits is likely to make it more challenging to address these and other racial disparities such as the ownership of small businesses, the number of large corporation executive officers, and media company ownership. Business-savvy defendants are unlikely to display overt racial bias. Studies about implicit bias make it clear that humans often harbor unconscious biases based on race that they may act on and may affect decision-making. Moreover, studies show "the human tendency to offer compelling explanations for one's own behavior even when such explanations have little to do with the real reasons behind that behavior."[18] Implicit bias can even cause decision makers to "subtly adjust criteria in real time to modify their judgments of merit" and influence behavior.[19]

Judges may also rely on unconscious bias about race and the rationality of business decisions that contrast with a plaintiff's allegations of discriminatory conduct on the part of the defendant. In his coauthored article "Implicit Bias in the Courtroom," Jerry Kang reasons that the plausibility standard in federal pleading allows the judging of plaintiff's claim "on minimal facts," which opens the door for judges to rely on "schemas," presumptions, or stereotypes about the parties.[20] The lack of racial diversity on the federal bench heightens these concerns about the impact of implicit bias on decision-making. According to the Federal Judicial Center, in 2017 the overwhelming majority of Article III judges were White, and the committee that devises the rules lacked representative diversity.[21]

The Supreme Court's but-for pleading requirement can result in unnecessary early dismissals of legitimate claims of discrimination, resulting in restricted access to federal courts. It is noteworthy that, before *NAAOM* was decided, research revealed that post-*Iqbal* discrimination complaints were being dismissed at higher rates than other claims. Patricia Hatamayar found an increase in dismissal rates in Title VII employment discrimination cases after *Iqbal* that was not found in contract cases.[22] Similarly, Victor Quintanilla found a similar increase in dismissals in all federal employment discrimination cases.[23]

The Supreme Court's ruling in *NAAOM* raises the bar yet again on pleading and disadvantages plaintiffs. The but-for standard requires greater knowledge of a defendant's business operations and decision-making strategy than is typically available to plaintiffs before discovery, mainly since the facts necessary to support these allegations generally are in the defendant's control. Moreover, the standard requires plaintiffs to expend resources very early in the litigation, collecting the data necessary to meet the plausible but-for standard without the benefit of discovery. Plaintiffs are then forced to reveal to defendants details about their case, including exposing which facts the plaintiff is aware of and may provide early clues as to the witnesses and other sources of the plaintiff's information in its complaint. This early revelation of the plaintiff's litigation strategy may place plaintiffs at a disadvantage in the pursuit of justice. Thus, even plaintiffs who successfully defend Rule 12(b)(6) motions to dismiss are disadvantaged.

One rationale for raising the pleading standard is fear of opening the floodgates and unnecessarily extending litigation. These concerns are overblown: plaintiffs must still meet the stringent plausibility requirement in pleading a motivating factor. In addition, summary judgment remains a barrier to lawsuits that lack merit after an opportunity for discovery.[24]

The but-for pleading standard articulated in *NAAOM* has wide-ranging effects and is not of interest only to large companies. It impacts anyone seeking to enter into contracts, including consumers experiencing racially charged interactions in stores and employment relationships.[25] More important, the pleading standard applied to § 1981 claims sends a chilling message about the courts' commitment to the struggle to dismantle racial hierarchies.

Procedural rules restricting access to courts are an integral part of a "legal process [that] has always acted as an expression of social control," advantaging some groups while disadvantaging others.[26] Therefore, it is not surprising that Blacks, as a group, have far less confidence in the fairness of courts than do Whites.[27] The layering effect of high barriers to entry and the imposition of pleading standards in discrimination cases that seem to benefit defendants over plaintiffs may be helping to fuel those differences. A Supreme Court opinion about pleading claims under a civil rights statute designed to help dismantle a system of White supremacy that does not mention racism or White supremacy, and instead analogizes discrimination claims to torts, is part of the problem.[28] To construe the pleading rules "to do justice," it is not enough to assess whether they are fair in an abstract sense. Rather, it is essential to assess whether they create racially disparate impacts and are antiracist as a crucial part of the struggle for racial justice.

NOTES

1 Melisa Milewski, *From Slave to Litigant: African Americans in Court in the Postwar South, 1865–1920*, 30 Law & Hist. Rev. 723, 764 (2012).

2 Steven O. Roberts & Michael T. Rizzo, *The Psychology of American Racism*, American Psychologist (June 25, 2020), http://dx.doi.org/10.1037/amp0000642.

3 42 U.S.C. § 1981(a); McDonald v. Sante Fe Trail Transp. Co., 427 U.S. 273 (1976) (holding that statute protects all races).

4 *See* Univ. of Tex. Sw. Med. Ctr. v. Nassar, 570 U.S. 338 (2013) (finding plaintiffs must show "but for" causation to establish a Title VII retaliation claim); Gross v. FBL Fin. Servs., Inc., 557 U.S. 167 (2009) (finding plaintiffs are required to establish "but for" cause under the Age Discrimination in Employment Act).

5 42 U.S.C. § 1981(b).

6 140 S. Ct. 1009 (2020).

7 Nat'l Ass'n of Afr.-Am. Owned Media v. Comcast Corp., No. CV151239TJH-MANX, 2016 WL 11652073, at *1 (C.D. Cal. Oct. 5, 2016), *rev'd and remanded*, 743 F. App'x 106 (9th Cir. 2018), *vacated and remanded*, 140 S. Ct. 1009 (2020), vacated and remanded, 804 F. App'x 709 (9th Cir. 2020).

8 Comcast Corp., 140 S. Ct. at 1013.

9 Nat'l Ass'n of Afr. Am.-Owned Media, 743 F. App'x at 107.

10 *See* Univ. of Tex. Sw. Med. Ctr., 570 U.S. at 364, (Ginsburg, J., dissenting) (requiring plaintiffs satisfy a "but-for" rather than a "mixed motive" standard for Title VII retaliation claims imposes a "stricter standard").

11 *Civil Rights Act of 1866—Antidiscrimination Law—Pleading Standards*—Comcast Corp. v. National Ass'n of African American-Owned Media, 134 Harv. L. Rev. 580, 588 (2020).

12 Comcast Corp., 140 S. Ct. at 1013; Nat'l Ass'n of African-Am. Owned Media v. Charter Commc'ns, Inc., No. 2:16-cv-00609-GW-(FFMx) (C.D. Cal. Oct. 24, 2016); Tentative Ruling on Renewed Motion to Dismiss Plaintiffs' Second Amended Complaint, Nat'l Ass'n of African-Am. Owned Media, No. 2:16-cv-00609-GW-(FFMx) (C.D. Cal. Aug. 27, 2020); Defendant Charter Communications Inc.'s Renewed Motion to Dismiss Plaintiffs' Second Amended Complaint, Nat'l Ass'n of African-Am. Owned Media, No. 2:16-cv-00609-GW-(FFMx) (C.D. Cal. June 29, 2020).

13 *See* Sandra F. Sperino, *The Emerging Statutory Proximate Cause Doctrine*, 99 Neb. L. Rev. 285, 286 (2020); Sandra F. Sperino, *Discrimination Law: The New Franken-Tort*, 65 DePaul L. Rev. 721, 722 (2016) (critiquing the "tortification" of discrimination law); Sandra F. Sperino, *Discrimination Statutes, the Common Law, and Proximate Cause*, 2013 U. Ill. L. Rev. 1; Sandra F. Sperino, *The Tort Label*, 66 Fla. L. Rev. 1051 (2014).

14 Gross v. FBL Fin. Servs., Inc., 557 U.S. 167, 190 (2009) (Breyer, J., dissenting) (finding mixed-motives jury instruction is never proper in an ADEA case).

15 Roberts & Rizzo, *supra* note 2 (identifying seven factors contributing to American racism: categories, factions, segregation, hierarchy, power, media, and passivism).

16 *See, e.g.*, Anne-Marie G. Harris, Geraldine R Henderson & Jerome D. Williams, *Courting Customers: Assessing Consumer Racial Profiling and Other Marketplace Discrimination*, 24 J. of Pub. Policy & Mktg. 163 (2005).

17 Neil Bhutta, Andrew C. Chang, Lisa J. Dettling & Joanne W. Hsu, *Disparities in Wealth by Race and Ethnicity in the 2019 Survey of Consumer Finances*, Federal Reserve Board of Governors, FEDs notes, Sept. 28, 2020, https://doi.org; Moritz Kuhn, Mortiz Schularick & Ulrike I. Steins, *Income and Wealth Inequality in America, 1949–2016*, 128 J. of Pol. Econ. 3469 (2020); William Darity, Jr., Darrick Hamilton, Mark Paul, Alan Aja, Anne Price, Antonio Moore & Caterina Chiopris, Samuel Dubois Cook Ctr. of Soc. Equity, Insight Ctr. for Cmty. Econ. Dev., *What We Get Wrong About Closing the Racial Wealth Gap*, 6 (2018), https://socialequity.duke.edu.

18 Michael I. Norton, Samuel R. Sommers, Joseph A. Vandello & John M. Darley, *Mixed Motives and Racial Bias: The Impact of Legitimate and Illegitimate Criteria on Decision Making*, 12 Psychol., Pub. Policy, and Law 36, 39 (2006).

19 Jerry Kang, Judge Mark Bennett, Devon Carbado, Pam Casey, Nilanjana Dasgupta, David Faigman, Rachel Godsil, Anthony G. Greenwald, Justin Levinson & Jennifer Mnookin, *Implicit Bias in the Courtroom*, 59 UCLA L. Rev. 1124, 1159 (2012).

20 *Id.* at 1161–62 (discussing "social judgeability").

21 Demography of Article III Judges, 1789–2020, Federal Judicial Center, www.fjc.gov; Brooke D. Coleman, *#SoWhiteMale: Federal Civil Rulemaking*, 113 Nw. U. L. Rev. 407, 421 (2018).

22 Patricia W. Hatamyar, *The Tao of Pleading: Do* Twombly *and* Iqbal *Matter Empirically?*, 59 Am. U. L. Rev. 553, 597 (2010).

23 Victor D. Quintanilla, *Beyond Common Sense: A Social Psychological Study of* Iqbal*'s Effect on Claims of Race Discrimination*, 17 Mich. J. Race & L. 1 (2011).

24 Fed. R. Civ. P. 56; *see* Celotex Corp. v. Catrett, 477 U.S. 317 (1986).

25 Title VII allows an employee to allege the protected characteristic as a "motivating factor" in the decision.

26 A. Leon Higginbotham, Jr., In the Matter of Color: Race and the American Legal Process 13 (1978).

27 Richard R. W. Brooks & Haekyung Jeon-Slaughter, *Race, Income, and Perceptions of the U.S. Court System*, 19 Behav. Sci. & L. 249, 256 (2001); *see also* Model Rules of Prof'l Conduct Preamble ¶ 6 (Am. Bar Ass'n 1983).

28 Alexandra D. Lahav, *Why Justice Gorsuch Was Wrong About Causation in* Comcast, 23 Green Bag 2d 205, 209 (2020); Sperino, *The Emerging Statutory Proximate Cause Doctrine*, *supra* note 13, at 305.

27

The Master of the Complaint?

Pleadings in Our Inegalitarian Age

ANDREW HAMMOND

Federal and state court judges often describe the plaintiff as "the master of the complaint."[1] This chapter uses that image as a jumping-off point to explore how the procedural rules that govern pleadings should be understood in the context of unyielding economic inequality.[2] To say the plaintiff is the "master of the complaint" implies a few oft-stated understandings of civil procedure. The first is that plaintiffs enjoy a good degree of control over their case, particularly at the beginning of the litigation.[3] After all, plaintiffs name defendants. A plaintiff in a police misconduct case can choose to plead a claim against the individual officer, or the police department, or both.[4] Also, by pleading certain claims, a plaintiff characterizes the nature of the harm. A plaintiff in an employment discrimination case can include claims of disparate treatment as well as harassment or retaliation. Plaintiffs can select which remedies to include in their prayer for relief. And, often, plaintiffs can initially choose the forum by filing in federal or state court. That's why some lawyers lament that defendants do not get to pick where or when they are sued. It is the plaintiff who has chosen to haul the defendant into court. And as a result, there is a belief among the US bench and bar that plaintiffs, if they fail to exercise that control wisely, have only themselves to blame. In dismissing individual claims or the plaintiff's entire case, a court will sometimes characterize its act as simply a recognition of the plaintiff's failings: a plaintiff has pled herself out of court.

But this metaphor obscures some uncomfortable realities of civil justice in the United States. The plaintiff may exercise control over the complaint when she drafts it, but once filed, the complaint takes on a life of its own. It is visible to the court and other parties (and, almost always, the public). The court can dismiss the complaint for want of jurisdiction, for failure to state a claim, or for other reasons.[5] The judge sometimes needs a corresponding motion from an adverse party to do so but often can do so sua sponte (on her own). Of course, the plaintiff can amend the complaint, but not always unilaterally. Sometimes, the plaintiff will need the defendant's or the judge's consent. Furthermore, defendants, like plaintiffs, are empowered to plead various claims and defenses "alternatively or hypothetically" and "regardless of consistency."[6]

More broadly, this idea of mastery implies that a plaintiff has the tools to fashion a complaint that is sufficient not only to begin litigation but also perhaps to prevail. Yet, that notion betrays the court's assumption that it is the plaintiff's attorney who often drafts the complaint. A plaintiff, in most cases a person with no formal legal training, ultimately must decide to file a case, but it is her lawyer who drafts the pleading itself.

This chapter suggests that we should not assume mastery—either in terms of craft or control—in a system where many people litigate without the benefit of counsel. In 2019, more than 10 percent of federal nonprisoner civil cases were pro se (without attorney representation).[7] That national percentage masks variation across the 94 federal district courts. Some district courts have much higher percentages of pro se filings, exceeding 25 percent.[8] For many state court systems, unrepresented litigants are the modal parties.[9]

The extent of the justice gap is not surprising when we remember that economic inequality, by many measures, increasingly defines US society—and with it the courts. Social science metrics such as the Gini coefficient are one way to understand this unyielding social and political phenomenon.[10] Other indicators that are more intelligible to Americans point in the same direction. For example, Americans entering the labor market today are much less likely to move up the economic ladder than they were 50 years ago.[11] Wages for the average American have not risen in 40 years.[12] And yet, 40 years ago, CEOs made roughly 30 times more than their average worker; today, CEOs make 320 times more.[13]

Beyond the numbers, episodes in the twenty-first century suggest a society defined by accumulated advantage and opulence for the few and economic insecurity for everyone else. The earth-shattering 2008 financial crisis and the ensuing recession—the deepest economic downturn since the Great Depression—are still reverberating here and abroad.

And in response, the Barack Obama administration's modest financial regulation gave way to a swift deregulatory swerve by the Donald Trump administration. The only major legislation passed by the 115th Congress and signed by President Trump was the Tax Cuts and Jobs Act of 2017, which tax experts and citizens understand to be windfall tax cuts for corporations and the wealthiest people in the US.[14] Meanwhile, the COVID-19 pandemic continues to impact the country as of publication, further exacerbating deep divisions in US society. Even the celebrity obsessions and scandals that dominate the media are symptomatic of this inegalitarian era.[15] When people in the US look at their own economic status, they are far from comforted.[16] All contribute to a sense that ours is a new Gilded Age.

What does this pervasive economic inequality mean for the procedure of pleadings? The Federal Rules of Civil Procedure require that a plaintiff's complaint contain "a short and plain statement of the claim showing that the pleader is entitled to relief."[17] This "notice pleading" standard required only that the pleading give the defendant notice of the plaintiff's grievance.[18] However, the United States Supreme Court in *Bell Atlantic Corp. v. Twombly*[19] and *Ashcroft v. Iqbal*[20] ushered in a new and uncertain era of plausibility pleading—one that is now in its second decade.

In *Twombly*, plaintiffs brought a class action against telecommunications companies for antitrust violations. No one doubted that the plaintiffs' pleadings gave the corporate defendants adequate notice of the nature of the claim, and the complaint was legally sufficient under federal antitrust law. But the Court held that the plaintiffs did not plead sufficient facts, which if assumed to be true, would "nudge[] their claims across the line from conceivable to plausible," and that the complaint should have been dismissed.[21] While some thought *Twombly*'s holding might be restricted to antitrust suits, the Supreme Court held in *Iqbal* that this new plausibility standard applies to all federal pleadings. As the Court explained, determining a complaint's plausibility will be "a context-specific task that requires the reviewing court to draw on its judicial experience and common sense."[22]

What the Supreme Court understood in *Twombly* and *Iqbal* is that a notice-pleading regime relies largely on a discovery process to test the strength of pleadings. Thus, the Supreme Court believed a tougher pleading standard would curb discovery abuse. Both cases would have involved extensive discovery, for the telecommunications companies in *Twombly* and then–Attorney General John Ashcroft and then–FBI Director Robert Mueller in *Iqbal*. Indeed, *Twombly* and *Iqbal* are part of a larger effort by the Supreme Court to shape civil procedure by deciding cases rather than, as Congress intended, by making rules. Like *J. McIntyre Machinery, Ltd. v. Nicastro* in the personal jurisdiction context or *Wal-Mart Stores v. Dukes* for class actions, *Twombly* and *Iqbal* evince a preoccupation by the Supreme Court to limit the exposure of corporate defendants to civil litigation.

Following *Twombly* and *Iqbal*, federal judges may now draw on their "judicial experience and common sense" to evaluate the plausibility of pleadings.[23] When so much of federal civil litigation turns on people experiencing discrimination (Title VII claims), misconduct by police and other officers (section 1983 claims), and disability (Social Security Act claims), Twombly and Iqbal counsel judges and defendants to screen implausible pleadings.[24] And yet, the circumstances of a dangerous encounter with a police officer or the workplace harassment of an employer may seem less plausible to a lawyer or judge who has not experienced that conduct himself.[25] Under this new regime, defendants can brief a motion to dismiss along these lines and convince a judge of the implausibility of a plaintiff's case and, as a result, obtain a favorable decision. If judges are gatekeepers of what is plausible in civil litigation and which cases should proceed, then it matters how judges respond (or don't respond) to this era of inequality. Perhaps, judges can rise above their personal experience, the people they interact with, and what they read, but any account of a justice system is better off assuming judges are human, not heroic.

Do *Twombly* and *Iqbal* represent the twilight of a more liberal system of pleading? Or do they stand for a revolution that wasn't? The empirical research is decidedly mixed.[26] But while plausibility pleading certainly could have troubling consequences for low-income litigants, we should not let the shift from notice to plausibility pleading obscure two features of pleadings that predate *Twombly* and *Iqbal*: the expectation that self-represented litigants draft legal documents, and the commitment that plaintiffs can determine whom to sue, for what, and where. Indeed, these two features—the ubiquity of self-representation and the plaintiff's initial control—will persist. Until we reckon with how the courts exist apart, along, and against our increasingly unequal society, we will continue to expect litigants, regardless of financial circumstances, to square off against deep-pocketed parties.

How are self-represented (pro se) litigants equipped to respond to this development? Some research suggests that these litigants are outmatched by their represented adversaries in this new era of plausibility pleading.[27] Plaintiffs may need to make their complaints more specific, but that might in turn limit discovery. That might have been the Supreme Court's animating purpose in raising the bar from notice to plausibility pleading. And this specter of increased screening comes at a time when the Judicial Conference has recently scrapped all but two of the forms that provided a kind of instructive appendix to the Federal Rules of Civil Procedure.[28]

To understand why so many litigants are going without lawyers requires understanding how lawyers are hired. There are multiple ways to pay for litigation. The parties can pay for the lawsuit themselves or rely on a third party. Insurers, federal and state governments, and nonprofit organizations all fund attorneys in various civil lawsuits. However, for people at the bottom of the income distribution, few will be able to pay lawyers by the hour. Courts and commentators often point to the fact that the "American rule," whereby each party pays its own fees, is a pro-plaintiff rule compared to other litigation systems in which the loser pays the winner's fees. But access to affordable legal services is as much a function of geography as it is cost. Unless there are local attorneys who will take cases on a contingency fee basis, the 39 percent of people in the US who report being unable to cover a $400 emergency will also not be able to hire counsel.[29]

While legal aid could potentially fill this justice gap, federal legal aid funding has fallen precipitously. Adjusted for inflation, the federal government funded $1 billion worth of legal aid in 1979.[30] In 2019, it funded $415 million.[31] In 1979, 11.6 percent of the country (roughly 26 million people in the US) were officially poor.[32] In 2019, 10.5 percent (more than 34 million) were officially poor.[33] A snapshot of US legal aid is incomplete without an accounting of state government funding (typically minimal), pro bono representation by private firm attorneys, and law school clinics. However, it is certain that even though fewer people in the US can afford legal services, there is less federal legal aid funding available to low-income people in the US than there was 40 years ago.

If litigants cannot find counsel, they might rely on court staff, materials in a public or court library, or whatever is on the internet. They might ask for help from others in their lives who may be familiar with court systems. The fact that several federal district courts have created pro se help desks, pro bono panels, and other resources suggest that there is demand for such assistance. Or a litigant may hope that, when the case is initially filed, a judge may appoint counsel through a formal program with the trial bar or the judge's informal network.

This lack of representation also creates challenges for judges. Judges may be skeptical of a complaint simply because a pro se litigant drafted it. Because judges are aware of the American rule and fee-shifting for civil rights claims, a judge might conclude that a self-represented litigant betrays the fact that several attorneys have passed on taking her case.[34] Indeed, in many motions for in forma pauperis status and for appointment of counsel, self-represented litigants must list the lawyers they have approached—both whom and how many.[35] Driven by a "justice gap" of people who cannot afford legal services, the rise of self-representation sits uncomfortably beside the rise of plausibility pleading.

A notice-pleading system offers litigants with less resources the chance, through discovery, to build the record they need to vindicate their claims. Notice pleading also affords judges the clarification that comes with such a record, before evaluating the merits of any particular claim. With plausibility, an unrepresented litigant's pleading is assumed defective because she is making allegations before a judge who knows she has no formal training in doing so. Until we recognize that people in the US who litigate do so from a weaker position relative to their banks, employers, and government, we will fail to understand the distributive consequences of our pleading system.

Despite these troubling developments and the unyielding inequality of contemporary US society, civil litigation remains a system of private enforcement of legal rights and duties. As such, civil justice represents a forum and therefore a promise for those who are marginalized by our winner-take-all economy and our plutocratic politics. Pleadings do not simply put defendants on notice and permit judges to screen meritless litigation. Pleadings frame the action. That latent, even subversive, potential of pleadings empowers people with fewer resources and lower socioeconomic status to assert their rights in court. These people may be incarcerated or in low-wage work. They may be navigating vast bureaucracies to obtain basic assistance or challenging arbitration agreements that deny them financial relief. The power to claim their own worth as a rights-holder enhances their dignity—and not just in the courtroom. Pleadings promise a way for people to put into their own words the harm they experienced, the rights they bear, and the relief they deserve. In doing so, pleadings allow a person, regardless of status in society, to challenge the illegal actions of officials and institutions accustomed to getting their way.

NOTES

1 *See, e.g.*, Utah Stream Access Coal. v. VR Acquisitions, LLC, 2019 UT 7, ¶¶ 36, 41, 439 P.3d. 593, 601 (2019) (describing "the notion that the plaintiff is the master of the complaint" as "a core component of our adversary system").

2 Complaints are not the only pleadings. Pleadings include a defendant's answer, which may include responses to the plaintiff's claims or identify new claims ("counterclaims"). *See* Fed. R. Civ. P. 7(a). The Federal Rules distinguish between these "pleadings" and "motions," which include any other "request for a court order." *See* Fed. R. Civ. P. 7(a)–(b). This bright-line division is muddled in practice because many lawyers and judges refer to this stage of the litigation, before discovery and preparation for trial, as the "pleadings stage."

3 *See* Fed. R. Civ. P. 3.

4 *See, e.g.*, Wright v. Cleburne Cty. Hosp., 255 So. 3d 186, 192 (Ala. 2017) ("And, of course, it is the plaintiff who is 'the master of his complaint.'").

5 *See* Fed. R. Civ. P. 12(b).

6 Fed. R. Civ. P. 8(d).

7 U.S. Courts, Table C-13 U.S. District Courts—Civil Pro Se and Non-Pro Se Filings, by District, During the 12-Month Period Ending September 30, 2019 1 (2019), www.uscourts.gov.

8 Those districts include the Middle District of Alabama (25 percent), the District of Hawaii (26 percent), the Southern District of Indiana (31 percent), and the District of South Dakota (25 percent). *See id.* at 2–4.

9 Anna E. Carpenter, Jessica K. Steinberg, Colleen F. Shanahan & Alyx Mark, *Studying the "New" Civil Judges*, 2018 Wis. L. Rev. 249, 258–59 (describing how the "state civil justice caseload [is] primarily concerned with relatively low-value (in monetary terms) contract and family law disputes" where "lack of representation is the norm").

10 *See* Org. for Econ. Co-op. & Dev., Income Inequality, https://data.oecd.org (showing that the United States is more unequal, as measured by its Gini coefficient, than 32 of the 36 other OECD member countries).

11 *See* Raj Chetty, David Grusky, Maximilian Hell, Nathaniel Hendren, Robert Manduca & Jimmy Narang, *The Fading American Dream: Trends in Absolute Income Mobility Since 1940*, 356 Science 398, 405 (Apr. 2017).

12 *See* Drew Desilver, *For Most U.S. Workers, Real Wages Have Barely Budged in Decades*, Pew Rchs. Ctr. (Aug. 7, 2018), www.pewresearch.org.

13 Lawrence Mishel & Jessica Schneider, Econ. Pol'y Inst., CEO Compensation Surged 14 percent in 2019 to $21.3 Million 13–16 (2020).

14 *See* Ben Steverman, Dave Merrill & Jeremy C. F. Lin, *A Year After the Middle Class Tax Cut, the Rich Are Winning*, Bloomberg (Dec. 18, 2018), www.bloomberg.com.

15 *See* Richard J. Reddick, *The "Opportunity Hoarding" Behind the College Admissions Scandal*, Hous. Chron., (Mar. 18, 2019), www.houstonchronicle.com.

16 *See* Bd. of Governors of the Fed. Rsrv. Sys., Report on the Economic Well-Being of U.S. Households in 2018 5–7, (2019) [hereinafter Fed. Rsrv., Report on Economic Well-Being].

17 Fed. R. Civ. P. 8(a)(2).

18 Conley v. Gibson, 355 U.S. 41, 48 (1957).

19 550 U.S. 544 (2007).

20 556 U.S. 662 (2009).

21 *Twombly*, 550 U.S. at 570.

22 *Iqbal*, 556 U.S. at 679.

23 *Id.* at 679.

24 *See, e.g.*, Elizabeth M. Schneider, *The Changing Shape of Federal Civil Pretrial Practice: The Disparate Impact on Civil Rights and Employment Discrimination Cases*, 158 U. Pa. L. Rev. 517, 532–36 (2010).

25 Victor D. Quintanilla, *Beyond Common Sense: A Social Psychological Study of* Iqbal*'s Effect on Claims of Race Discrimination*, 17 Mich. J. Race & L. 1, 2–3 (2011).

26 *See, e.g.*, David Freeman Engstrom, *The* Twiqbal *Puzzle and Empirical Study of Civil Procedure*, 65 Stan. L. Rev. 1203, 1207–08 (2013); Jonah B. Gelbach, *Material Facts in the Debate over* Twombly *and* Iqbal, 68 Stan. L. Rev. 369, 369–70 (2016).

27 Brooke D. Coleman, *The Efficiency Norm*, 56 B.C. L. Rev. 1777, 1822–23 (2015); William H. J. Hubbard, *The Effects of* Twombly *and* Iqbal, 14 J. of Empirical Legal Stud. 474, 510–12 (2017).

28 *See* Fed. R. Civ. P. 84 (2014) (abrogated 2015).

29 *See* Fed. Rsrv., Report on Economic Well-Being, *supra* note 16, at 2.

30 David Reich, *Additional Funding Needed for Legal Service Corporation, Center on Budget and Policy Priorities* (Feb. 1, 2021, 2:15 PM), www.cbpp.org.

31 *Legal Services Corporation*, Am. Bar Ass'n, www.americanbar.org.

32 U.S. Census Bureau, Rep. No. P60–125, Money Income and Poverty Status of Families and Persons in the United States: 1979 (Advance Report) 1 (1980).

33 Jessica Semega, Melissa Kollar, Emily A. Shrider, and John F. Creamer, U.S. Census Bureau, Rep. No. P60–270, Income and Poverty in the United States: 2019 1 (2020).

34 *Cf.* Victor D. Quintanilla, Rachel Allen & Edward Hirt, *The Signaling Effect of Pro Se Status*, 42 Law & Soc. Inquiry 1091, 1107 (2016) (finding that law students and lawyers' views on the settlement value of Title VII cases decreased substantially if they were first told the claimant was pro se).

35 Andrew Hammond, *Pleading Poverty in Federal Court*, 128 Yale L.J. 1478, 1499 (2019).

28

Undocumented Civil Procedure

STEPHEN LEE

The federal courts serve as an important guardian of individual rights. Nowhere is this dynamic more pronounced than when courts rule on claims advanced by undocumented plaintiffs. Nearly one-quarter of the national foreign-born population lacks authorization to remain or work in the United States, yet despite this marginalized status, a host of laws confers on these noncitizens a variety of rights and benefits. Federal and state antidiscrimination, labor and employment, and education laws create individual rights that are not contingent on lawful immigrant status. As a formal matter, undocumented status poses no barrier to the pursuit of claims in federal court, but of course the reality is much more complicated. Many undocumented plaintiffs are understandably reluctant to even file an initial complaint without knowing whether they will be forced to divulge their immigration status in downstream discovery proceedings. Even significant monetary gains may not be worth it if the cost of winning is removal from this country.

This chapter centers the experiences of undocumented plaintiffs—undocumented migrants who live and work under legally vulnerable conditions, thereby complicating their ability to pursue otherwise enforceable legal rights. Courts play an important role in protecting these legally vulnerable communities, but the rules governing civil claims can inhibit court access. This chapter focuses on how discovery rules are used to regulate that access.

Who Are Undocumented Plaintiffs?

Who are undocumented plaintiffs? And how are they different from the kinds of foreign or noncitizen plaintiffs who usually appear within civil procedure scholarship? The foreign-born population in the United

States hovers around 44 million people.[1] This large group comprises individuals with a heterogeneous range of legal statuses; some, such as naturalized citizens, face virtually no threat of deportation, whereas others, such as undocumented immigrants, toil under a constant cloud of uncertainty. In this chapter, I focus largely on the undocumented community because of the particular legal vulnerabilities that segment of the foreign-born population faces. The experiences of the undocumented community force us to grapple with broader questions about the rules of procedure and the courts that construe and apply these rules. What does it mean, for example, for a court to craft procedural orders when the mere fact of asserting legal claims in such a public forum risks long-term or even permanent expulsion from the United States?

In a statement meant to describe the legal importance of citizenship, Chief Justice Earl Warren in 1958 famously described citizenship as the "right to have rights."[2] This sentiment often leads people to erroneously assume the truth of the inverse—namely, that *not* having citizenship means having no rights. In reality, a wide range of laws creates protections that apply to parties irrespective of immigration status. This is true in the K–12 education context,[3] in governing and regulating the terms and conditions of work,[4] and in guarding against discrimination in many social and economic settings.[5] Thus, several federal and state laws reduce barriers for undocumented migrants to access our court system despite the many barriers preventing them from otherwise moving freely through other social, economic, and political spaces. Whatever harms, slights, or setbacks an undocumented migrant might experience as a worker, a student, or community member, these substantive laws enable these migrants to assert their rights as plaintiffs.

Undocumented plaintiffs face challenges in realizing the full benefits of these substantive rights. Migrants who work within the informal economy often perform low-wage work, making any recovery a less-than-lucrative investment of time for an individual attorney. Thus, plaintiffs pursuing these kinds of claims often must turn to nonprofit organizations or law-school clinics, which can provide excellent services but are in short supply. Alternatively, undocumented plaintiffs must hope that a lawyer can see a larger pattern or practice of violations, which might support an aggregated-claims (and therefore more lucrative) lawsuit. Litigation realities therefore can sometimes create access-to-justice problems.

These economic realities mean that undocumented plaintiffs bear little resemblance to the foreign plaintiffs who typically appear within the pages of the Federal Reporter and the United States Reports and attract the attention of most civil procedure scholars. A significant strand of civil procedure scholarship highlights the challenges that foreign plaintiffs can pose in the context of doctrines such as forum non conveniens and broader issues related to transnational litigation.[6] The undocumented plaintiffs pursuing claims related to labor, employment, educational, and civil rights laws reflect characteristics that are different in at least two significant ways.

First, undocumented plaintiffs tend to have deeper connections to the United States. On the whole, the pool of undocumented immigrants in the United States reflects a longer period of residence than in years past.[7] And for those asserting violations of labor and employment laws, and asserting civil rights more generally, their complaints will involve something that happened within the United States.[8] For this reason, most of the threshold questions that animate our civil justice system, such as jurisdiction and venue and overarching principles of due process, will be answered in different ways than for the more familiar issues that arise in transnational litigation.

Second and related, undocumented plaintiffs tend to have limited choices in selecting a forum for pursuing claims. They often assert claims seeking recovery of unpaid wages and challenging dangerous working conditions, neither of which tends to yield huge payouts for lawyers who take on such cases. Thus, even where a defendant has some plausible connections to the foreign venue and plaintiffs have an interest in litigating there, moving a case overseas increases the costs. Unless the ultimate recovery in the case is significant enough to outweigh the added costs, undocumented plaintiffs have little choice but to pursue claims within the United States.

Moreover, even putting aside the cost-benefit realities of litigation, undocumented plaintiffs simply do not have anything close to resembling the kind of freedom of movement necessary to pursue claims in a foreign venue. In the context of transnational litigation, the underlying assumption is that the parties, and especially the plaintiffs, have a choice in forum. This is certainly the case among and between sophisticated and well-resourced parties,[9] but this is also true of relatively powerless parties who can find ways to aggregate their claims.[10] Central to this story is the ability of parties to enter and leave the United States with minimal intrusion. This is not the case for undocumented plaintiffs. For the most part, undocumented migrants are trapped here. Antiimmigrant advocates and nativists often argue that migrants are "free to go" if migrants find conditions in the United States to be unbearable.[11] Many of these migrants might leave at least temporarily if the costs of reentering at some future data was not so steep.[12] Thus, the best and often only chance that undocumented plaintiffs have for recovery is through the pursuit of claims within US courts.

Discovery and Immigration Status

If undocumented plaintiffs can secure representation, their primary hurdle once proceedings begin is the discovery process. Traditionally, the Federal Rules of Civil Procedure conceived judges as passive managers in an information exchange process that was largely self-executing. Any information that was "relevant" to the underlying subject matter of the suit in the possession of each party was considered subject to disclosure and exchange. Over the years, changes to the rules governing discovery have given judges greater discretion over the information exchange between the parties and thereby increased the role of judges in the process. At the same time, lawsuits have been increasingly disposed of through settlements or dispositive pretrial motions, such as for summary judgment; this makes the information produced through discovery crucial to determining the parameters for settlement negotiations and the likelihood of success in a summary judgment motion. These trends have given judges greater influence over the stage of litigation that was most likely to inform the terms of recovery.

As has been well documented and persuasively argued, these changes have tended to favor defendants. In response to defense lawyers' complaints that discovery enabled plaintiffs to engage in fishing expeditions, the Rules Committee in 2000 and 2015 issued amendments that narrowed the scope of discovery. Legal scholars have mostly critiqued these amendments, arguing that these changes give more discretion to judges and arguably make it harder for plaintiffs to get important information.[13] At the same time, for undocumented plaintiffs, these discovery amendments empowered judges to take a more proactive role in managing the discovery process. Judges—if they choose to—could exercise their discretion in ways that protected vulnerable populations against defendant discovery requests designed to reveal the vulnerable status of undocumented plaintiffs and thereby increase chances of their deportation. Specifically, judges could manage the discovery process and protect undocumented plaintiffs against intimidation tactics through the issuance of protective orders.

For example, *Rivera v. NIBCO*[14] provides helpful guidance on crafting protective orders in cases involving undocumented plaintiffs. A core purpose of the rules of discovery is to facilitate production of information relevant to resolving claims and defenses. In establishing support for a claim, a plaintiff's informational needs are straightforward. A restaurant worker, for example, who alleges that an employer had misclassified workers to avoid greater wage obligations would almost certainly seek an employer's payroll information, tax documents, and employee logs. Workers at a manufacturing plant who claim that an employer's use of an English proficiency test discriminated on the basis of race and national origin would likely request documents related to communications among and between management, submit interrogatories, and conduct depositions focusing on exchanges that reflect on the employer's motivation in setting such a policy. All of these are standard discovery requests.

For their part, defendants would seek information from plaintiffs that might show some other cause for an adverse employment action related to acts of incompetence or abusive behavior or any other neutral ground for termination. Importantly, defendants typically do not argue that information related to a plaintiffs' immigration status is relevant for purposes of contesting liability. Rather, they often seek such information to assert a defense at the remedy stage. Asserting claims in many cases does not require establishing lawful immigration or work-authorized status, thereby rendering those kinds of discovery requests irrelevant. Rather, in many cases, a plaintiff's immigration status informs the scope of remedies a plaintiff might be able to secure should she prevail.[15]

Rivera v. NIBCO clarified how to resolve discovery disputes that arise with undocumented plaintiffs. As with many discovery cases, *Rivera* took a pragmatic approach weighing the benefits versus the burdens of forcing the plaintiffs to disclose information related to their immigration status. The district court had issued a protective order against the compelled disclosure of immigration-related information and the Ninth Circuit affirmed, explaining that such a request would pose an "'undue burden' on the plaintiffs."[16] Importantly, the Ninth Circuit's affirmation relied on the enforcement realities governing an employer's hiring practices:

> Regrettably, many employers turn a blind eye to immigration status during the hiring process; their aim is to assemble a workforce that is both cheap to employ and that minimizes their risk of being reported for violations of statutory rights. Therefore, employers have a perverse incentive to ignore immigration laws at the time of hiring but insist upon their enforcement when their employees complain.[17]

Rivera has proven to be a widely influential decision, what one legal scholar calls the "gold standard in protective order litigation for unauthorized immigrants."[18] This decision has informed district court opinions both within and outside the Ninth Circuit.[19] Within the context of a set of rules that are generally subject to a case-by-case analysis, the *Rivera* decisions set something close to a categorical rule against the disclosure of information related to a plaintiff's immigration status in federal employment discrimination cases.

An equally important "undocumented discovery decision," also from a circuit court, is *Cazorla v. Koch Foods of Mississippi*.[20] In that case, several poultry-processing plant workers complained to the Equal Employment Opportunity Commission (EEOC) of discriminatory abuse and harassment by Koch Foods. Several of the plaintiffs were undocumented, leading them to apply for a "U visa," which is a temporary visa designated for those who can assist in the investigation and prosecution of criminal violations. The EEOC eventually filed its own suit on behalf of Koch workers. Koch claimed that the plaintiffs had an incentive to fabricate or exaggerate claims to qualify for immigration benefits and for this reason requested access to the plaintiffs' U visa applications.[21]

As the court did in *Rivera*, the Fifth Circuit in *Cazorla* focused on whether inquiring into the plaintiffs' immigration status could amount to an "undue burden." Calling U visa applications "novel and significant impeachment evidence," the Fifth Circuit permitted some discovery of those materials but instructed the district court to anonymize the materials through the liability phase of litigation.[22] The identities of the workers could be revealed, if at all, for purposes of determining damages.[23] The Fifth Circuit remanded with these instructions, and the case eventually settled in 2018.[24]

As a discovery case, *Cazorla* stands apart for clarifying and sketching out the kinds of structural conditions district courts ought to consider when crafting protective orders. For one thing, the Fifth Circuit explained that the district court erred by failing to consider how a protective order might affect nonclaimants in the lawsuit. The court pointed to how "this high-profile case will undermine the spirit[] if not the letter" of the U visa statutory scheme, "deterring immigrant victims of abuse—many of whom already mistrust the government—from stepping forward and thereby frustrating Congress's intent in enacting the U visa program."[25]

Moreover, the court recognized the broader and very complicated information economy in which public enforcement agencies operate. It rejected the employer's argument that the plaintiffs had little reason to fear the consequences of discovery because they had already outed themselves as undocumented to EEOC officials. But the Fifth Circuit explained that the U visa application process requires disclosure only to certain officials whose purpose is to process these applications. Legal scholars have long recognized the importance of striking the right conditions of confidentiality to ensure that immigrants can reveal sensitive information without fear of reprisal.

As these cases show, defendants can use discovery as a weapon of intimidation against undocumented plaintiffs. To mitigate this risk, attorneys can request, and judges can issue, protective orders. Current discovery rules provide judges with ample discretion to protect these migrants, a class of plaintiffs that already faces significant hurdles to enforcing their rights. While discretionary legal tools inevitably introduce a degree of uncertainty and unpredictability into the process of resolving claims, protective orders create the possibility that discretion can be exercised in a meaningful way—in ways that narrow rather than widen the access-to-justice gaps undocumented migrants must face in an already daunting legal process.

Conclusion

The set of rules and doctrines composing the field of Civil Procedure provides an effective way to teach students about inequality. Specifically, this area of law helps students appreciate how broadly applicable, neutral, and trans-substantive rules—while conceptualized as tools for inclusion—can be applied in ways that thwart the efforts of politically vulnerable individuals to assert their rights. Focusing the attention of first-year students on the relationship between the rules of discovery and undocumented plaintiffs provides a useful starting point to help students understand that trans-substantive rules grounded in principles of fairness do not by themselves reach and protect legally vulnerable communities. A fair amount of work and coordination among several parties is required, which is a lesson that will continue to reward students even as they move beyond their first year.

NOTES

1 Jeanne Batalova & Elijah Alperin, *Immigrants in the U.S. States with the Fastest-Growing Foreign-Born Populations*, Migration Policy Institute, (Jul. 10, 2018), www.migrationpolicy.org.

2 Perez v. Brownell, 356 U.S. 44, 64 (1958) (Warren, C.J., dissenting).

3 Plyler v. Doe, 457 U.S. 202 (1982).

4 *See* Fair Labor Standards Act; National Labor Relations Act.

5 *See* Title VII of the Civil Rights Act and various state law equivalents.

6 *See, e.g.*, Christopher A. Whytock & Cassandra Burke Robertson, *Forum Non Conveniens and the Enforcement of Foreign Judgments*, 111 Colum. L. Rev. 1444 (2011).

7 Stephen Lee, *Family Separation as Slow Death*, 119 Colum. L. Rev. 2319, 2352 (2019).

8 A key driver of undocumented litigation in the federal courts is economic insecurity. *See* V.B. Dubal, *Wage Slave or Entrepreneur? Contesting the Dualism of Legal Worker Identities*, 105 Calif. L. Rev. 101 (2017); David Weil, *Crafting a Progressive Workplace Regulatory Policy: Why Enforcement Matters*, 28 Comp. Lab. L. & Pol'y J. 125 (2006).

9 *See* The Bremen v. Zapata Off-Shore Co., 407 U.S. 1 (1972).

10 *See* Doe I v. Unocal Corp., 395 F.3d 932 (9th Cir. 2002).

11 Indeed, this is the point with certain laws. K-Sue Park, *Self-Deportation Nation*, 132 Harv. L. Rev. 1878, 1881–83 (2019).

12 Lee, *supra* note 7, at 2323.

13 *See* Morgan Cloud, *The 2000 Amendments to the Federal Discovery Rules and the Future of Adversarial Pretrial Litigation*, 74 Temp. L. Rev. 27, 45–47 (2001); Patricia W. Hatamyar Moore, *The Anti-Plaintiff Pending Amendments to the Federal Rules of Civil Procedure and the Pro-Defendant Composition of the Federal Rulemaking Committees*, 83 U. Cin. L. Rev. 1083, 1110–20 (2015).

14 Rivera v. NIBCO, 384 F.3d 822 (9th Cir. 2004).

15 Legal scholars often cite the Supreme Court's decision in *Hoffman Plastics Compounds v. Nat'l Lab. Rels. Bd.*, which excluded undocumented immigrants from key remedies under the National Labor Relations Act, as a key turning point for these expansive discovery practices. Robert I. Correales, *Did Hoffman Plastic Compounds, Inc., Produce Disposable Workers*, 14 Berkeley La Raza L.J. 103, 128 (2003).

16 Rivera, 364 F.3d at 1074.

17 *Id.* at 1072.

18 Keith Cunningham-Parmeter, *Fear of Discovery: Immigrant Workers and the Fifth Amendment*, 41 Cornell Int'l L. J. 27, 51 (2008).

19 *See, e.g.*, Equal Emp. Opportunity Comm'n v. Signal Int'l, No. CIV.A. 12–557, 2013 WL 4854136 (E.D. La. Sept. 10, 2013); Equal Emp. Opportunity Comm'n v. Restaurant Co., 448 F. Supp. 2d 1085 (D. Minn. 2006); Equal Emp. Opportunity Comm'n v. Bice of Chi., 229 F.R.D. 581 (N.D. Ill. 2005); Galaviz-Zamora v. Brady Farms, 230 F.R.D. 499 (W.D. Mich. 2005).

20 Cazorla v. Koch Foods of Miss., 838 F.3d 540 (5th Cir. 2016).

21 *Id.* at 546.

22 *Id.* at 562.

23 *Id.* at 564.

24 Press Release, Equal Emp. Opportunity Comm'n, Koch Foods Settles EEOC Harassment, National Origin and Race Bias Suit (Aug. 1, 2018), www1.eeoc.gov.

25 *Cazorla*, 838 F.3d at 562–63.

29

Privilege and Voice in Discovery

SETH KATSUYA ENDO

After six years of working as a funeral director and embalmer at Harris Funeral Homes, Aimee Stephens wrote a letter to her colleagues:

> I have known many of you for some time now, and I count you all as my friends. What I must tell you is very difficult for me and is taking all the courage I can muster. . . . I intend to have sex reassignment surgery. . . . At the end of my vacation on August 26, 2013, I will return to work as my true self, Aimee Australia Stephens, in appropriate business attire.[1]

Two weeks later, the funeral homeowner described Ms. Stephens's decision to dress as a woman as "unacceptable" and fired her.[2] Ms. Stephens rejected a proposed separation agreement that included a confidentiality clause.[3] Instead, she filed a discrimination charge with the Equal Employment Opportunity Commission, alleging that firing her for being transgender, her transition from male to female, and because she did not conform to sex- or gender-based stereotypes violated Title VII of the Civil Rights Act of 1964.[4]

Ultimately, Ms. Stephens and other transgender plaintiffs prevailed at the United States Supreme Court. In *Bostock v. Clayton County*, the Court held that Title VII's language barring discrimination "because of . . . sex" includes discrimination against employees on the basis of their being transgender or gay.[5] But the early stages of the case brought up important legal issues about how identity and voice are privileged in civil litigation.

After Harris Funeral Homes's motion to dismiss was denied, it propounded more than a dozen discovery requests seeking information about the state of Ms. Stephens's sexual anatomy, her marital status, other familial background and relationships, any medical or psychological records related to the progress of her gender transition, and other intimate details of her life.[6] Ms. Stephens sought a protective order from the court, contending that the requested information was irrelevant, annoying, embarrassing, and oppressive.[7]

The district court held that the status of Ms. Stephens's transition—including the state of her genitalia—and familial relationships were irrelevant because the question of liability turned on whether Harris Funeral Homes terminated Stephens because she exhibited characteristics or behaviors that her supervisors perceived to be inconsistent with the male gender.[8] Counsel for Harris Funeral Homes admitted that he could not articulate how the requested information would bear materially on any fact at issue in the gender stereotyping claim, effectively ceding its irrelevance.[9] Although the court's decision formally turned on relevance, it highlighted that "[s]uch information is of the most intimate and private nature, and it would be harassing and oppressive to require its disclosure."[10]

The discovery dispute in Ms. Stephens's case was resolved to protect the vulnerable party. But that is not always the outcome. Defendants in discrimination cases can use discovery as a shield that prevents disclosure of information indicating wrongdoing and as a sword to pierce into private aspects of plaintiffs' lives. And much of this flies below the radar: the importance of discovery is not always made apparent in law school and is rarely addressed in published opinions that invite scrutiny.

Despite being frequently overlooked by scholars and appellate courts, discovery's value should be easy to understand: in a notice-pleading system, parties might not have all of the information necessary to prosecute or defend a claim at the start of the case.[11] As such, a judicial decision resolving a discovery dispute can have an outcome-dispositive impact.[12] And, in a world in which civil cases rarely proceed to trial,[13] discovery disputes take on even greater importance[14] because parties will rely on facts uncovered during discovery in their dispositive motions and settlement negotiations without the opportunity to put witnesses before fact finders.[15]

Discovery can also amplify the voice of litigants even when it does not impact the outcome of a case.[16] By allowing parties to tell their stories and to learn more from their adversaries, discovery affords dignity to litigants and acknowledges the worth of an affected party's voice.[17]

The exchange of information may even lead to rapprochement between the parties if, for example, plaintiffs learn about weaknesses in their cases or the defenses' strengths.[18] From a critical approach, discovery can develop and shape a narrative that impacts how the court, public, and even the parties themselves understand the case.[19]

Narrative storytelling brings in voices that are not otherwise privileged or well represented in the judiciary.[20] But a critical approach to discovery primarily reveals how discovery can subordinate the interests of individuals who belong to minority or other structurally disempowered groups. For example, Federal Rule of Civil Procedure 26(b)(1) permits parties to obtain "any nonprivileged matter that is relevant to any party's claim or defense and proportional to the needs of the case."[21] Rule 26(b)(1)'s ambit is the focus of many discovery fights, particularly over whether a requested form of discovery is "relevant" or "proportional."[22] Rule makers added this language in 2015, in response to assertions that the scope and cost of discovery was out of control.[23] Prior versions had permitted the court to order discovery "of any matter relevant to the subject matter involved in the action."[24] This provision was deleted, suggesting a shift toward a narrower conception of discovery.[25] And the change raises concerns that large defendants will analogize to the restrictive *Iqbal* pleading standard to block discovery into discriminatory intent or other areas that are in the control of the alleged wrongdoer.[26]

Rule 26's more stringent relevance requirement also might harm minorities by permitting judges to define relevance through the lens of their individual intuitions and implicit biases.[27] To adapt an example from Catharine MacKinnon, a heterosexual male judge might "find it credible that homosexual advances are unwanted, unsolicited, and coercive, and blame the perpetrator instead of the victim, while women are widely supposed to 'want' heterosexual relationships which they reject."[28] These same biases may control discovery dispute outcomes that turn on whether a plaintiff's sexual history is relevant to a harassment claim.

In *Weiss v. Amoco Oil Co.*, for example, Arnold Weiss sued Amoco for wrongful termination after having been dismissed from his position based on allegations of sexual harassment.[29] Weiss sought to obtain discovery from Steebin, the sexual harassment complainant and a nonparty witness, about her past sexual relationships with other Amoco employees, arguing that such relationships could show that Weiss's actions were neither offensive nor unwelcome.[30] The court agreed, permitting discovery,[31] reading earlier cases as holding that a complainant's sexual history is relevant to a sexual harassment claim if it has any connection to the employment context.[32] But in the precedent cases, the requested information involved behavior between the complainant and the defendant or conduct that actually happened at the workplace.[33] In contrast, there was no indication that Steebin's sexual relationships with coworkers either took take place at work or involved Weiss. The scope of discovery is meant to be paired with Rule 26(c)(1)'s protections against unreasonably burdensome or intrusive discovery.[34] And courts can—and do—apply those protections even when the subject of the requests are nonparties.[35] But the *Weiss* court failed to take Rule 26(c) into account despite the intensely private nature of the discovery request.[36]

The decision in *Weiss* stands in contrast to the outcome in *A. W. v. I.B. Corp.*, in which a male supervisor accused of sexual harassment sought discovery about the male complainant's sexual history for the same purpose.[37] In *A. W.*, the court found most of the requests irrelevant and blocked the discovery requests.[38] In contrast to *Weiss*, the *A. W.* court carefully balanced the probative value of the requested information with the prejudice and harm that might occur, ultimately prohibiting any inquiry into nonworkplace, off-duty sexual behavior.[39]

In addition to restricting relevance, the 2015 Rule 26(b)(1) amendments integrated a proportionality requirement.[40] Courts already could limit discovery by balancing the costs and benefits of a request. But this balancing is now part of the very definition of "scope."[41] And while Rule 26 lists a number of factors to be considered,[42] the inquiry often functionally turns on a narrow conception of efficiency.[43] In other words, monetary considerations crowd out other concerns, including the participation element of legal process that ensures everybody's voice is heard.[44] This myopic, cost-centered approach has particularly problematic implications for employment discrimination and other civil rights cases that often involve claimants who belong to historically disempowered groups.[45] An all-too-common example is that racial minorities and women generally make less money than white men, which depresses their potential damages and leads to a harsher proportionality inquiry.[46] Courts can deny plaintiffs' requested discovery about broader corporate practices to uncover reliable statistical evidence of discrimination due to this cost-benefit analysis.[47] Thus, the law governing the scope of discovery is used as a shield to protect the interests of structurally powerful actors like large corporations against litigation efforts by members of historically disempowered groups.

These concerns about the subordination of minority interests in the creation and application of the law governing the scope of discovery have several likely causes. First, as Victor Quintanilla explains, judges' broad discretion to manage discovery effectively insulates them from meaningful oversight.[48] Second, discovery decisions typically are the product of a single district court or magistrate judge. And judges, as a group, are disproportionately likely to share demographic characteristics of structurally powerful groups (economically well off, white, male, heterosexual, cisgender, etc.).[49] Such individuals' intuitions about the expansiveness of a claim might very well differ from that held by litigants who are not in positions of structural privilege.[50] This permits traits associated with a narrow but dominant group to appear as the neutral default.[51] And the combination of a single decision maker and a lack of diversity among the decision makers means there is no opportunity for robust discussion that would encourage judges to examine their mental shortcuts, which might rely on stereotypes or other assumptions.[52] Third, the rules themselves are the product of a committee that is disproportionately white and male.[53] Accordingly, it is unsurprising that they do not reflect the concerns of minority communities.[54]

Civil discovery is at an important moment of flux as court decisions give on-the-ground meaning to the amended Rule 26(b)(1). This chapter's critical approach seeks to highlight how the rules, doctrine, and application of discovery in civil litigation make it so that "we do not all suffer the civil rules equally."[55]

NOTES

1 Brief for Respondent Aimee Stephens at 8, R.G. & G.R. Harris Funeral Homes, Inc. v. Equal Emp. Opportunity Comm'n & Aimee Stephens, (No. 18–107), 2019 WL 2745392, www.aclu.org [hereinafter Brief].

2 Equal Emp. Opportunity Comm'n v. R.G. & G.R. Harris Funeral Homes, Inc., No. CV 14–13710, 2015 WL 9700656, at *1 (E.D. Mich. Sept. 24, 2015), *objections overruled*, No. 14–13710, 2015 WL 7567503 (E.D. Mich. Nov. 25, 2015).

3 Donna Stephens, *We Need the Courage of Aimee Stephens to Win LGBTQ Rights Fight*, Detroit Free Press, June 28, 2020, at A23.

4 *Id.*; Brief at 11–12.

5 Bostock v. Clayton Cty., Georgia, 140 S. Ct. 1731 (2020) (*consolidated with* R.G.& G.R. Harris Fun. Hones, Inc. v. Equal Emp. Opportunity Comm'n).

6 *R.G. & G.R. Harris Funeral Homes*, 2015 WL 9700656 at *1.

7 *Id.*

8 *Id.* at *3–4.

9 *Id.* at *3.

10 *Id.*

11 *See, e.g.*, Norman W. Spaulding, *The Rule of Law in Action: A Defense of Adversary System Values*, 93 Cornell L. Rev. 1377, 1406 (2008).

12 Cine Forty-Second St. Theatre Corp. v. Allied Artists Pictures Corp., 602 F.2d 1062, 1064 (2d Cir. 1979).

13 John H. Langbein, *The Disappearance of Civil Trial in the United States*, 122 Yale L.J. 522, 524 (2012).

14 Michael Moffitt, *Three Things to Be Against ("Settlement" Not Included)*, 78 Fordham L. Rev. 1203, 1221–22 (2009); Richard D. Freer, *Exodus From and Transformation of American Civil Litigation*, 65 Emory L.J. 1491, 1512 (2016).

15 Omri Ben-Shahar & Lisa Bernstein, *The Secrecy Interest in Contract Law*, 109 Yale L.J. 1885, 1920 (2000).

16 Rebecca Hollander-Blumoff, *The Psychology of Procedural Justice in the Federal Courts*, 63 Hastings L.J. 127, 154 (2011).

17 Martin H. Redish, *Procedural Due Process and Aggregation Devices in Mass Tort Litigation*, 63 Def. Couns. J. 18, 21 (1996).

18 *Cf.* In re: FEMA Trailer Formaldehyde Products Liability Litig., No. 09-31131 (5th Cir. Dec. 14, 2010).

19 Eric K. Yamamoto, Moses Haia & Donna Kalama, *Courts and the Cultural Performance: Native Hawaiians' Uncertain Federal and State Law Rights to Sue*, 16 U. Haw. L. Rev. 1, 19 (1994).

20 Anne E. Ralph, *Not the Same Old Story: Using Narrative Theory to Understand and Overcome the Plausibility Pleading Standard*, 26 Yale J.L. & Human. 1 (2014); George A. Martinez, *Philosophical Considerations and the Use of Narrative in Law*, 30 Rutgers L.J. 683, 684 (1999).

21 Fed. R. Civ. P. 26(b)(1).

22 Black v. Buffalo Meat Serv., Inc., No. 15CV49S, 2016 WL 4363506, at *6 (W.D.N.Y. Aug. 16, 2016).

23 Fed. R. Civ. P. 26 advisory committee's note to 2015 amendment.

24 Fed. R. Civ. P. 26 (2014), available at www.uscourts.gov.

25 Fed. R. Civ. P. 26 advisory committee's note to 2015 amendment.

26 Elizabeth Thornburg, *Cognitive Bias, the "Band of Experts," and the Anti-Litigation Narrative*, 65 DePaul L. Rev. 755, 762–64 (2016); Elizabeth M. Schneider, *The*

Changing Shape of Federal Civil Pretrial Practice: The Disparate Impact on Civil Rights and Employment Discrimination Cases, 158 U. Pa. L. Rev. 517, 519 (2010).

27 Judge Dana Leigh Marks, *Who, Me? Am I Guilty of Implicit Bias?*, Judges' J. (Fall 2015), at 22; *see also* Paul Stancil, *Discovery and the Social Benefits of Private Litigation*, 71 Vand. L. Rev. 2171, 2196 (2018); Jerry Kang, Mark Bennett, Devon Carbado, Pam Casey, Nilanjana Dasgupta, David Faigman, Rachel Godsil, Anthony G. Greenwald, Justin Levinson & Jennifer Mnookin, *Implicit Bias in the Courtroom*, 59 UCLA L. Rev. 1124, 1160 (2012).

28 Catharine A. MacKinnon, Sexual Harassment of Working Women: A Case of Sex Discrimination 205 (1979).

29 142 F.R.D. 311, 312 (S.D. Iowa 1992).

30 *Id.* at 312–13.

31 *Id.* at 317.

32 142 F.R.D. at 315–17 (discussing Meritor Savings v. Vinson, 477 U.S. 57 (1986); Mitchell v. Hutchings, 116 F.R.D. 481 (D. Utah 2019).

33 *Meritor Savings*, 477 U.S. at 68–69 (permitting inquiries into workplace dress and discussion of sexual fantasies at the workplace); *Mitchell*, 116 F.R.D. at 485–86 (permitting inquiries into behavior that either directly involved the defendants or took place at work).

34 Paul W. Grimm & David S. Yellin, *A Pragmatic Approach to Discovery Reform: How Small Changes Can Make a Big Difference in Civil Discovery*, 64 S.C. L. Rev. 495, 515 (2013).

35 *See, e.g.*, Green v. Seattle Art Museum, No. C07–58MJP, 2007 WL 4561168, at *4 (W.D. Wash. Dec. 21, 2007) (rejecting discovery request seeking contact information of nonparties); Elite Lighting v. DMF, Inc., No. CV 13–1920 JC, 2013 WL 12142840, at *3 (C.D. Cal. May 6, 2013) (noting that defendants might be unduly embarrassed and annoyed by discovery requests of the defendants' independent contractors).

36 One sees the barest of nods toward this in a footnote that limits the discovery request to only relationships known to Weiss, as though that would somehow protect Steebin's privacy. 142 F.R.D. at 317 n.8.

37 A.W. v. I.B. Corp., 224 F.R.D. 20, 27 (D. Me. 2004).

38 *Id.*

39 *Id.* at 26–27.

40 *See* Fed. R. Civ. P. 26 advisory committee's note to 2015 amendment.

41 *Id.*

42 Fed. R. Civ. P. 26(b)(1) (listing "the importance of the issues at stake in the action, the amount in controversy, the parties' relative access to relevant information, the parties' resources, the importance of the discovery in resolving the issues, and whether the burden or expense of the proposed discovery outweighs its likely benefit").

43 Brooke D. Coleman, *The Efficiency Norm*, 56 B.C. L. Rev. 1777 (2015).

44 Brooke D. Coleman, *One Percent Procedure*, 91 Wash. L. Rev. 1005 (2016).

45 *See, e.g.*, United States v. Lake Cty. Bd. of Comm'rs, 233 F.R.D. 523, 529 (N.D. Ind. 2005); *see also* Suzette Malveaux, *A Diamond in the Rough: Trans-Substantivity of the Federal Rules of Civil Procedure and Its Detrimental Impact on Civil Rights*, 92 Wash. U. L. Rev. 455, 517–18 (2014); Elizabeth M. Schneider, *The Changing Shape of Federal Civil Pretrial Practice: The Disparate Impact on Civil Rights and Employment Discrimination Cases*, 158 U. Pa. L. Rev. 517, 520 (2010).

46 *See generally* Andrew W. Jurs & Scott DeVito, *A Tale of Two Dauberts: Discriminatory Effects of Scientific Reliability Screening*, 79 Ohio St. L.J. 1107, 1112 (2018).

47 *See, e.g.*, Solorzano v. Shell Chem Co., No. 00-31191, 2001 WL 564154, at *8 n.13 (5th Cir. May 18, 2001) n.13 (5th Cir. 2001); *see generally* Angela D. Morrison, *Duke-Ing Out Pattern or Practice After Wal-Mart: The EEOC As Fist*, 63 Am. U. L. Rev. 87, 105–06 (2013); *cf.* Duke v. Univ. of Texas at El Paso, 729 F.2d 994, 996 (5th Cir. 1984) (reversing district court's denial of discovery); Trevino v. Celanese Corp., 701 F.2d 397, 406 (5th Cir. 1983) (same).

48 Victor Quintanilla, *Doorways of Discretion: Psychological Science and the Legal Construction and Erasure of Racism* (chapter 18 in this volume); *see also* Crawford-El v. Britton, 523 U.S. 574, 598 (1998) ("Rule 26 vests the trial judge with broad discretion to tailor discovery narrowly and to dictate the sequence of discovery.").

49 Jonathan K. Stubbs, *A Demographic History of Federal Judicial Appointments by Sex and Race: 1789–2016*, 26 Berkeley La Raza L.J. 92, 113 (2016).

50 Elizabeth Thornburg, *(Un)conscious Judging*, 76 Wash. & Lee L. Rev. 1567, 1578–79 (2019); Elizabeth Thornburg, *(Un)conscious Judging* (chapter 16 in this volume).

51 Sumi Cho, *"Unwise," "Untimely," and "Extreme": Redefining Collegial Culture in the Workplace and Revaluing the Role of Social Change*, 39 U.C. Davis L. Rev. 805, 809 (2006); Nancy S. Ehrenreich, *Pluralist Myths and Powerless Men: The Ideology of Reasonableness in Sexual Harassment Law*, 99 Yale L.J. 1177, 1207 (1990).

52 Helen Hershkoff, *Some Questions About #MeToo and Judicial Decision Making*, 43 Harbinger 128, 137–38 (2019).

53 Brooke D. Coleman, *#SoWhiteMale: Federal Civil Rulemaking*, 113 Nw. U. L. Rev. 407, 408 (2018).

54 *See, e.g.*, Patricia W. Hatamyar Moore, *The Anti-Plaintiff Pending Amendments to the Federal Rules of Civil Procedure and the Pro-Defendant Composition of the Federal Rulemaking Committees*, 83 U. Cin. L. Rev. 1083, 1112–13 (2015); Adam N. Steinman, *The End of an Era? Federal Civil Procedure After the 2015 Amendments*, 66 Emory L.J. 1, 36–37 (2016); Stephen N. Subrin & Thomas O. Main, *The Fourth Era of American Civil Procedure*, 162 U. Pa. L. Rev. 1839, 1850–51 (2014).

55 Judith Resnik, *The Domain of Courts*, 137 U. Pa. L. Rev. 2219, 2219–20 (1989).

30

Civil Rights Summarily Denied

Race, Evidence, and Summary Judgment in Police Brutality Cases

JASMINE GONZALES ROSE

Within seconds of arriving to conduct a mental health wellness check, white police officers from Dallas, Texas, shot Jason Harrison, a 39-year-old Black man, and let him die on the ground.[1] The officers claimed that the victim had lunged at them with a screwdriver.[2] The victim's mother, an eyewitness and plaintiff in the ensuing § 1983 action, claimed otherwise.[3] The district court—relying on the Supreme Court case *Scott v. Harris*[4]—found that a body camera video[5] spoke for itself, and it granted summary judgment for the police defendants.[6]

Harrison's case is but one example of the tripartite system of racialized police violence in the United States. First are the officers on the ground who directly enact violence on people of color. They are backed up by the police departments, which may try to cover up or otherwise shield the officer and themselves from prosecution and liability.[7] Second are prosecutors who are reluctant to prosecute officers for on-duty killings and brutality.[8] In light of the lack of prosecution and their own losses, surviving victims' and families' only recourse is the civil justice system. Enter the third level of this system of injustice: the judiciary. Here, summary judgment motions on qualified immunity present the opportunity for institutional racial insiders to maintain racial order.

Because the judiciary is disproportionately white when compared to jury pools, summary judgment, as a procedural device, is a racialized one.[9] When judges use videos as evidence in summary judgment decisions, they compound the racial implications and injustice. In this context, Dan Kahan has demonstrated that judges suffer from "cognitive illiberalism."[10] In other words, judges are not the neutral, unbiased adjudicators they believe themselves to be. When viewing judicial cognitive illiberalism under the lens of Critical Race Theory, the problem intensifies. This chapter situates the phenomena of cognitive illiberalism into the system of racial stratification and racism in the United States by examining judicial reliance on "racial character evidence."

Racial character evidence is "the way a person's race is used as de facto proof of his or her character."[11] At summary judgment, reliance on racist stereotypes to justify police killing or injuring community members of color is not merely racial bias. It constitutes reliance on impermissible racial character evidence that allows for racist fear and othering of people of color to combine with reverence for police both as white individuals and as members of white institutions. White judges viewing video evidence often see Black victims as dangerous and violent. This is true even when the evidence is ambiguous or portrays the contrary. Racist stereotypes about people of color's supposed dangerousness become faux expert witness evidence, creating an unfounded belief that the victim posed such a danger that deadly or other force was warranted and that no other interpretation of the facts could be reasonable.

The lawsuit challenging the police shooting death of Jason Harrison provides a prime example. On the morning of June 14, 2014, Harrison's mother, Shirley Harrison, dialed 9-1-1 asking for assistance because her son, who had been diagnosed with schizophrenia, was incoherent due to not taking his medication and needed help getting to a hospital.[12] She repeatedly requested, and the 9-1-1 operator reassured her, that the responders would be trained in working with people experiencing mental illness crises. The operator provided information about Harrison to police dispatchers who, in turn, dispatched Officers Hutchins and Rogers to help. Officers from this department had responded to Ms. Harrison numerous times before to transport her son to the hospital without incident.

The officers knocked on the front door and Harrison's mother calmly exited, ready to head to the hospital.[13] She identified her son and told them about his mental illness. Harrison stood in the front doorway, absent-mindedly twiddling a small screwdriver in his hands. The officers abruptly began shouting "drop it" but did not specify what "it" was. Harrison, possibly startled, darted out of the doorway. During Harrison's movement, the video provides only a partial view of Harrison's body from his upper ribcage to lower hip. Harrison's path and arm positions are not clearly visible. The officers immediately opened fire, unloading a total of five shots at Harrison. Approximately six seconds elapsed from the officers seeing Harrison to them opening fire. Harrison then lay on the ground for nine minutes while the officers did not provide him any medical aid or comfort, despite observing aloud that he was still moving. His mother wailed "You killed my child!" repeatedly in the background. Harrison died on the ground from gunshot wounds.

The video is shocking, disturbing, and heartbreaking. The former commander of the New Orleans Police Department's Crisis Intervention Team summed it up when she said, "It's the worst thing I've ever seen in my life," and she emphasized that the officers should have deescalated the situation rather than immediately shouting and drawing their guns.[14] Despite evidence that the officers' actions were highly unreasonable—if not egregious—a grand jury failed to criminally indict the officers, which is sadly not unusual in police killing cases.[15]

Harrison's parents filed suit under § 1983 for violations of their son's constitutional rights, among other claims. In response, the officers moved for summary judgment on the ground of qualified immunity.[16] The district court granted the summary judgment motions, finding that the officers did not violate Harrison's constitutional rights.[17] Relying wholly on the body camera footage, the trial court determined that "[d]ispositions of the motions begins and ends with . . . the Video." The judge found that while "[t]he viewing angle was not always ideal[,] . . . the Video clearly shows the salient fact: before the Officers fired, Harrison lunged at them from close range with a seven inch long screwdriver in his hand."[18] Harrison's mother disputed this fact, and the court responded by echoing *Scott v. Harris*'s proposition that "'[w]hen opposing parties tell two different stories, one of which is blatantly contradicted by the record, so that no reasonable jury could believe it, a court should not adopt that version of the facts for purposes of ruling on a motion for summary judgment.'"[19]

In *Harrison*, the trial judge viewed the video as irrefutable evidence that Harrison was dangerous and aggressive toward the officers. This echoed how the officers themselves viewed the scene. The defendant officers and the trial judge did not see Harrison as a vulnerable community member needing transportation to a hospital—who also happened to be fidgeting with a small tool in his hands. They did not see him as a person in a mental health crisis who bolted in panic after the defendants yelled and pointed guns at him. The judge and defendants viewed him as someone very dangerous: someone of such physical strength and deadly ability that he could transform a small household tool into lethal weaponry and pose imminent mortal harm to two trained, armed, fully outfitted police officers who had unobstructed exits if any actual danger arose.

Watching the video of the shooting, this perception seems inexplicable until we consider the role of racist stereotypes of Black people. Unjustifiably, long-standing racial stereotypes persist today that Black people are "brutes" or "thugs,"[20] extraordinarily large and strong,[21] and even superhuman.[22] White police officers then—often unconsciously—misperceive Black people as so dangerous that they need to use extreme force to defuse the danger. Belief in these racist stereotypes serves to justify police killings of Black people as reasonable. Under such racist beliefs, everyday objects become deadly weapons, failure to immediately comply with unreasonable and unclear commands is a death-eligible offense, and firing multiple bullets into an innocent human being is acceptable. In Harrison's case, while we cannot know for certain the officers' and trial judge's thoughts, the shooting itself and the judge's exoneration of the officers afterward comport with the all-too-recurrent racist trope of the big Black brute victimizing blameless white people.

In addition to using racial character evidence against victims of color such as Harrison, judges also impermissibly consider racial character evidence *in favor* of white police defendants at summary judgment by viewing white people as safer and more trustworthy. The majority of police officers, generally, and those who perpetuate force on people of color, specifically, are white.[23] Thus, there is a risk that jurists consider a defendant's whiteness as de facto evidence that he behaved reasonably. Moreover, white people are the racial group most likely to have confidence in the police.[24] Therefore, white judges, when compared to a diverse jury of community members, are statistically more likely to trust police defendants.

Reliance on racial character evidence to grant summary judgment in police violence cases is unacceptable. At summary judgment, the judge must view facts in the light most favorable to the nonmoving party,[25] here the § 1983 plaintiffs. Relying on racial character evidence against a victim and for a defendant is the converse. Further, judges are not permitted to make credibility determinations at summary judgment.[26] However, in these instances, judges make credibility determinations based on race. The court may consider only evidence that could be admissible at trial,[27] and racial character evidence is never admissible.[28] Moreover, pseudo-expert evidence in the form of a judge's own racial stereotypes and bias—whether against the victim or in favor of the defendant—is prohibited, if not deplorable.

Judges' reliance on video evidence in police brutality cases to foreclose the opportunity for a jury trial (or a settlement prompted by the possibility of jury trial) contributes to and reinforces systemic racism. Police killings are not only a contemporary racial justice issue; they are state violence[29] with roots in history. Modern policing originated with slave patrols and continued with the enforcement of Jim Crow laws, mass beatings of civil rights protesters, and continued brutality and killing of people of color.[30] Policing has been utilized for centuries to oppress people of color and maintain white superiority.[31] In both the overrepresentation of white persons employed[32] and law enforcement agencies' implicit institutionalized purpose of racial order,[33] police departments are white institutions. Police killings and police violence against people of color are some of the most profound acts of state-perpetuated and -sanctioned racism in the United States.[34] Incidents of racial prejudice and racially motivated discrimination and violence by private citizens are negligible compared to police killings and violence because the latter is perpetrated by agents of the state and then affirmed by state institutions: the courts.[35]

Summary judgment in police brutality cases forecloses accountability, deterrence, and legal acknowledgment that the Constitution, as well as Black and Brown lives, matter. Through video-reliant summary judgment rulings using racial character evidence, courts ensure racial subordination. Law enforcement agents—and the culture of policing—continue to terrorize communities of color and serve to deny people of color their basic civil rights. And the state works as a unified system to maintain a racial hierarchy that deems Black and Brown people disposable—where being the "wrong" color, in the "wrong" neighborhood, not abiding by an officer's commands, and fleeing to save your life or protect your body or livelihood can result in a swift sentence of injury or death.

Civil juries are necessary checks on the ruling classes, especially the ruling *racial* class. While a judge must provide the law, a jury determines the facts based on the "commonsense judgment of the community."[36] Fact finders' perceptions of race heavily influence their perceptions of facts. Studies have revealed that racially diverse juries deliberate more thoroughly, consider more-varied perspectives, commit fewer errors, and express less racism than homogenously white fact finders.[37] Thus, fairly selected juries are an important safeguard to ensure that substantive constitutional rights—such as the Fourth Amendment right to not be unjustifiably beaten and killed by police—are enforced. Although most legal professionals view summary judgment as a race-neutral procedural mechanism, it is not. The disposal of civil rights claims based on racially biased perspectives of the evidence at summary judgment is a civil procedural obstruction to substantive civil justice.

NOTES

1 Plaintiff's Original Complaint at 5, Harrison v. City of Dallas, No. 3:14-CV-3585-N (N.D. Tex. filed Oct. 3, 2014).

2 Defendants Andrew Hutchins and John Rogers' Joint Motion for Summary Judgment on Qualified Immunity as to the Claims by Plaintiff David Harrison at 8, *Harrison*, No. 3:14-CV-3585-N (N.D. Tex. filed Apr. 7, 2015).

3 Plaintiffs Shirley Marshall Harrison and David Sean Harrison's Amended Complaint at 4, *Harrison*, No. 3:14-CV-3585-N (N.D. Tex. filed Mar. 19, 2015).

4 550 U.S. 372 (2007).

5 Gunscom, *RAW BODY CAM: Dallas Police Officers Shoot Mentally-Ill Jason Harrison Holding Screwdriver*, YouTube (Mar. 18 2015) [hereinafter *Jason Harrison Video*], https://youtube.com.

6 Order, *Harrison*, No. 3:14-CV-3585-N (N.D. Tex. Mar. 14, 2016).

7 Vida B. Johnson, *Bias in Blue: Instructing Jurors to Consider the Testimony of Police Officer Witnesses with Caution*, 44 Pepp. L. Rev. 245, 266, 278–80 (2017).

8 *See* Jonathan Witmer-Rich, *Restoring Independence to the Grand Jury: A Victim Advocate for Police Use of Force Cases*, 65 Clev. St. L. Rev. 535, 538 (2017); Kimberly Kindy & Kimbriell Kelly, *Thousands Dead, Few Prosecuted*, Wash. Post, Apr. 12, 2015, at A1.

9 State trial and appellate judges are 83 percent and 80 percent white, respectively. Tracey E. George & Albert H. Yoon, Am. Const. Soc'y, *The Gavel Gap: Who Sits in Judgment on State Courts?* 1, 7, http://gavelgap.org. Additionally, "[o]f the 1,352 . . . federal judges, 60 percent are white men, while only 11 percent are black and 7 percent are Latino." Michele L. Jawando & Allie Anderson, *Racial and Gender Diversity Sorely Lacking in America's Courts*, Ctr. for Am. Progress (Sept. 15, 2016, 9:00 AM), www.americanprogress.org. White men make up only

about 37.5 percent of the US population, which is 76.3 percent white, 18.5 percent Latinx, and 13.4 percent Black. *Quick Facts: United States*, U.S. Census Bureau, www.census.gov.

10 Dan M. Kahan, David A. Hoffman & Donald Braman, *Whose Eyes Are You Going to Believe?* Scott v. Harris *and the Perils of Cognitive Illiberalism*, 122 Harv. L. Rev. 837 (2009).

11 Jasmine B. Gonzales Rose, *Racial Character Evidence in Police Killing Cases*, 2018 Wis. L. Rev. 369, 371 (2018).

12 Plaintiffs Shirley Harrison and David Harrison's Amended Complaint, *supra* note 3, at 2–3.

13 *Jason Harrison Video*, *supra* note 5.

14 *Experts Clash Over Video of Dallas Police Shooting Mentally Ill Man*, Dallas Morning News (Mar. 17, 2015, 10:49 PM), www.dallasnews.com.

15 James C. McKinley Jr. & Al Baker, *A System, With Exceptions, That Favors Police in Fatalities*, N.Y. Times, Dec. 8, 2014, at A1.

16 Defendants Andrew Hutchins and John Rogers' Joint Motion for Summary Judgment on Qualified Immunity, *supra* note 2, at 1–30.

17 Order, *supra* note 6, at 8.

18 The seven inches included the handle. *See id.* at 5.

19 *Id.* (quoting Scott v. Harris, 550 U.S. 372. 380 (2007)).

20 Ryan Patrick Alford, *Appellate Review of Racist Summations: Redeeming the Promise of Searching Analysis*, 11 Mich. J. Race & L. 325, 346 (2006); Calvin John Smiley & David Fakunle, *From "Brute" to "Thug": The Demonization and Criminalization of Unarmed Black Male Victims in America*, 26 J. Hum. Behav. Soc. Env't 350, 350–51 (2016).

21 *See* Ben Guarino, *People See Black Men as Larger and Stronger Than White Men—Even When They're Not, Study Says*, Wash. Post (Mar. 14, 2017, 7:08 AM), www.washingtonpost.com.

22 J.C. Sevcik, *Study Shows Whites Think Blacks Are Superhuman, Magical*, United Press Int'l (Nov. 14, 2014, 8:27 PM), www.upi.com (discussing Adam Waytz, Kelly Marie Hoffman & Sophie Trawalter, *A Superhumanization Bias in Whites' Perceptions of Blacks*, 6 Soc. Pysch. & Personality Sci. 352 (2014)).

23 Charles E. Menifield, Geiguen Shin & Logan Strother, *Do White Law Enforcement Officers Target Minority Suspects?*, Pub. Admin. Rev. 56, 60 (2019); Jeremy Ashkenas & Haeyoun Park, *The Race Gap in America's Police Departments*, N.Y. Times (Apr. 8, 2015), www.nytimes.com.

24 Bruce Drake, *Divide Between Blacks and Whites on Police Runs Deep*, Pew Rsch. Ctr.: FactTank (Apr. 28, 2015), www.pewresearch.org/; Mark Hugo Lopez & Gretchen Livingston, *Hispanics and the Criminal Justice System: Low Confidence, High Exposure*, Pew Rsch. Ctr. (Apr. 7, 2009), www.pewresearch.org.

25 Reeves v. Sanderson Plumbing Prods., Inc., 530 U.S. 133, 149–50 (2000).

26 Anderson v. Liberty Lobby, Inc., 477 U.S. 242, 253, 255 (1986).

27 Cairel v. Alderden, 821 F.3d 823, 830 (7th Cir. 2016).

28 Jasmine B. Gonzales Rose, *Toward a Critical Race Theory of Evidence*, 101 Minn. L. Rev. 2243, 2264 (2017).

29 *See* Jeremy I. Levitt, *"Fuck Your Breath": Black Men and Youth, State Violence, and Human Rights in the 21st Century*, 49 Wash. U. J.L. & Pol'y 87, 113 (2015); Mary Romero, *State Violence, and the Social and Legal Construction of Latino Criminality: From El Bandido to Gang Member*, 78 Denv. U. L. Rev. 1081 (2001).

30 *See, e.g.*, Norm Stamper, To Protect and Serve: How to Fix America's Police (2016).

31 Amna A. Akbar, *Toward a Radical Imagination of Law*, 93 N.Y.U. L. Rev. 405, 478 (2018).

32 Menifield, Shin & Strother, *Do White Law Enforcement Officers Target Minority Suspects?, supra* note 23; Ashkenas & Park, *The Race Gap, supra* note 23.

33 Paul Butler, *The System Is Working the Way It Is Supposed To: The Limits of Criminal Justice Reform*, 104 Geo. L.J. 1419, 1425 (2016).

34 Thus, these acts of violence were the impetus for the formation of the Black Lives Matter movement. *Herstory*, Black Lives Matter, https://blacklivesmatter.com.

35 V. Noah Gimbel & Craig Muhammad, *Are Police Obsolete? Breaking Cycles of Violence Through Abolition Democracy*, 40 Cardozo L. Rev. 1453, 1459–60 (2019).

36 Lockhart v. McCree, 476 U.S. 162, 174–75 (1986) (quoting Taylor v. Louisiana, 419 U.S. 522, 530 (1975)).

37 Edie Greene & Kirk Heilbrun, Wrightsman's Psychology and the Legal System 305 (6th ed. 2007); Bruce Evan Blaine, Understanding the Psychology of Diversity 101–04 (2d ed. 2012); Neil Vidmar, *The North Carolina Racial Justice Act: An Essay on Substantive and Procedural Fairness in Death Penalty Litigation*, 97 Iowa L. Rev. 1969, 1980 (2012).

31

Gender and Summary Judgment

ELIZABETH M. SCHNEIDER

Procedure is widely viewed as a technical and neutral area of the law. The Federal Rules that govern US procedure are intentionally trans-substantive, cutting across all areas of civil substantive law. Yet the premise of this book is that procedure is not neutral and is often interpreted in ways that manifest racial bias, gender bias, and bias against poor people, immigrants, and other marginalized groups. Every chapter in this volume is a testament to the ways that procedure can impact marginalized groups in deleterious ways and the need for critical perspectives on procedure that highlight and address these biases.

The ways in which gender bias can impact procedure has been widely recognized. Gender Bias Task Force Reports in many states and federal circuits that began in the 1980s uncovered problems of bias by judges in both substantive and procedural issues.[1] These Reports examined the ways in which male judges and lawyers treated women lawyers and litigants and expressed stereotypical attitudes about women. Burgeoning feminist analysis led to the pathbreaking Association of American Law Schools Program on Gender and Civil Procedure at the annual meeting in 1991 and the publication of the first law-review symposium on feminism and procedure in the *Cincinnati Law Review* in 1993.[2] It included a wide range of topics: the state and federal Task Force reports, discrimination on juries, and essays by many eminent scholars in civil procedure and jurists, including Barbara Babcock,[3] Shirley Abrahamson,[4] and Harold Koh.[5] Since then, wide-ranging aspects of civil procedure have been the subject of scholarly writing and judicial opinions, summary judgment,[6] class actions,[7] pleading standards in cases involving gender,[8] gender and judging,[9] the experiences of women judges,[10] the impact of intersectionality,[11] the composition of federal rulemaking committees,[12] and the demographics of the judiciary.[13] Most recently, investigation and sanctioning of federal judges for sexual harassment of judicial law clerks has led to revisions of the judicial codes of conduct governing federal district and appellate court judges.[14] Shocking disclosures about federal judges revealed deep sexism in the federal judiciary. Just as with racial bias, gender bias has to be closely examined in procedure for the way it can operate in a discriminatory manner.[15]

In this chapter, I explore the role gender plays in cases involving summary judgment in federal court. Since the mid-1980s, the practice of liberally granting summary judgment—often known as the "federal summary judgment industry"[16]—has taken flight largely at the expense of civil rights plaintiffs. In 1986, the Supreme Court decided the infamous summary judgment trilogy of *Matsushita*,[17] *Liberty Lobby*,[18] and *Celotex*.[19] The trilogy of rulings marked a dramatic shift from the traditional way courts decided summary judgment motions. Posttrilogy, courts have become very inclined to grant summary judgment for reasons such as docket-clearing and preservation of federal court resources. And the deprivation of reasonable juries faced by civil rights plaintiffs has played a major role in blocking their access to justice.

I do not suggest that cases involving women plaintiffs are the only, or even the worst, problems with summary judgment. Cases involving issues of gender underscore the problems of summary judgment in other contexts. These cases inevitably involve judicial evaluation of credibility, which many social science studies and Gender Bias Task Force Reports have identified as a serious problem for women litigants, particularly women plaintiffs (as well as women witnesses, expert witnesses, and lawyers).[20] They also involve judicial assessment of controversial or innovative claims. In ruling on summary judgment, judges frequently slice and dice law and fact in a technical and mechanistic way without evaluating the broader context on an arid record, a record that is limited to discovery.[21]

Judicial Assessment of Reasonableness

In order for a district court to conclude that a case is inappropriate for summary judgment, the court must decide that a "reasonable juror" could find for the plaintiff. Thus, a district court's assessment of what would be reasonable for a juror to find is crucial. In "maternal wall" or "sex-plus" cases, in which there are allegations of caregiver discrimination, this "reasonable juror" determination has posed a problem.

In *Back v. Hastings on Hudson Union Free School District*,[22] Elana Back, an elementary-school psychologist, brought suit under 42 U.S.C. § 1983, claiming that she was denied equal protection when her superiors campaigned to deny her tenure. They questioned her commitment to the job when she returned to work after having a baby, despite the fact that she had received outstanding performance reviews before and after giving birth. She alleged that as her tenure review approached in 2000, two superiors repeatedly questioned whether she would be able to work a full day. One allegedly said "she did not know how she could perform [her] job with little ones"[23] and it was "not possible for [her] to be a good mother and have this job."[24] Her bosses also questioned whether she would show the same level of commitment once she had tenure, given that she was raising a family. She alleged that they encouraged parents who had complained about her in the past to put their complaints in writing, and also that she began getting negative evaluations of her performance, which she argued were a pretext for discrimination. District Judge Charles L. Brieant granted summary judgment for the defendants, finding in part that the superiors' comments were "stray remarks" that were not evidence of sex discrimination and that Back had failed to prove that the reasons given for denying her tenure were pretextual.[25]

The Second Circuit reversed. Judge Calabresi noted that the case presented "a crucial question: What constitutes a 'gender-based stereotype'?"[26] He stated that "it takes no special training to discern stereotyping in the view that a woman cannot 'be a good mother' and have a job that requires long hours."[27] The appellate court ruled that there was sufficient evidence in the record to show intentional discrimination on the part of her direct supervisors and remanded the case for trial.

Slicing and Dicing

Jennings v. University of North Carolina at Chapel Hill[28] involved Title IX and § 1983 claims brought by two former University of North Carolina (UNC) varsity women's soccer players against the women's soccer coach, Anson Dorrance, and other UNC employees.[29] At 45 years old, Dorrance was the most powerful intercollegiate women's soccer coach in the United States (because UNC was one of the best teams in the country at the time).[30] He asked the plaintiffs "Who are you f***ing?" and made comments to them regarding sexual partners.[31] He touched team members frequently[32] and made comments suggesting inappropriate interest in their sexual lives.[33] Despite a detailed record of truly shocking statements, the district court granted the defendant's motion for summary judgment.[34] The Fourth Circuit first affirmed the grant of summary judgment, over a strong dissent by Judge M. Blane Michael.[35] After rehearing en banc, in a decision written by Judge Michael, the Fourth Circuit vacated the district court's grant of summary judgment on the Title IX claim and on the § 1983 claims against Dorrance and other defendants.[36]

Jennings is a classic example of courts taking a slice-and-dice approach to summary judgment. The initial majority opinion analyzes each part of the plaintiffs' claims but does not look at the evidence in a holistic way. Instead, it focuses on the fact that Dorrance did not have a sexual relationship with the individual plaintiffs, and that it was important to differentiate comments that are "merely vulgar and mildly offensive" from those that are "deeply offensive and sexually harassing."[37] Yet the majority clearly recognized that the coach's comments were more than "mildly offensive"; rather than quote the coach's actual words, the opinion disguises them with a series of asterisks.[38]

In contrast, the en banc court quotes the coach's comments in full from the record: His unflattering comments about the players' physical appearances, his views of their sex appeal, and his comments concerning his sexual fantasies about them.[39] The en banc decision highlights the players' dependence on Dorrance for any future career in soccer.[40] Relying on that stark evidence, it concluded that a reasonable juror could find sexual harassment and gender discrimination on the record presented.

In another slice-and-dice case, *Williams v. General Motors*,[41] a Sixth Circuit opinion reversing summary judgment in a hostile work environment case, Judge Martha Daughtrey used the phrase "impermissible disaggregation of the incidents" to describe the district court's reversable error.[42] She argued that the district judge had isolated aspects of evidence of "hostile environment" rather than looking at the evidence in light of the "totality of the circumstances."[43]

Summary Judgment "On the Law"

There are many gender cases in which district courts grant summary judgment as a matter of law, ruling that there really were no "legal" claims. In many of these cases, district courts' finding that plaintiffs had no cognizable claim as a matter of law is based on a very narrow interpretation of the governing law.

One example of this is *Jespersen v. Harrah's Operating Co.*,[44] wherein the Ninth Circuit, sitting en banc, reversed a district court ruling granting summary judgment.[45] Darlene Jespersen claimed that a Harrah's Casino policy, which required female, but not male, bartenders to wear makeup, violated Title VII.[46] The Ninth Circuit ruled that the relevant legal standard was whether the makeup policy created an unequal burden because of the plaintiff's gender and held that the plaintiff had failed to present sufficient evidence of such an unequal burden. This is an example of summary judgment "on the law," in which a district court and the circuit court clarify legal standards in a controversial and developing area of the law.[47]

Another example is *EEOC v. National Education Ass'n, Alaska*,[48] a Title VII action on behalf of three women employees alleging that the employer created a sex-based hostile work environment and constructively discharged one of the employees.[49] The supervisor was shouting and using foul language toward the plaintiffs, though the behavior was not explicitly sex- or gender-related. The district court found that the Equal Opportunity Employment Commission "presented substantial evidence that Harvey is rude, overbearing, obnoxious, loud, vulgar, and generally unpleasant" but nonetheless ruled for the defendant, finding that, because "there is no evidence that any of the exchanges . . . were motivated by lust" or by "sexual animus toward women as women," his conduct was not discriminatory.[50]

The Ninth Circuit reversed, holding as a matter of law that "differences in subjective effects (along with, of course, evidence of differences in objective quality and quantity) is relevant to determining whether or not men and women were treated differently, even where the conduct is not facially sex- or gender-specific."[51] The court found that the record revealed "a debatable question as to the objective differences in treatment of male and female employees, and strongly suggests that differences in subjective effects were very different for men and women."[52] It concluded that the facts presented a triable issue as to whether the work environment that Harvey created was sufficiently severe to constitute an illegal hostile work environment on the basis of sex under Title VII.

Implications for Summary Judgment

Although there is more quantitative and qualitative research to undertake on the interrelationship of gender and summary judgment presented in this chapter, the gender cases suggest that summary judgment can be "dangerous" and is likely to be more "dangerous" in particular contexts. Recent data on the high rate of grants of summary judgment in employment and discrimination cases supports this view.[53] But the implications go beyond gender. The legal standards for summary judgment in Rule 56 are not sufficiently determinate, so judicial decision-making is bound to get out of control. In summary judgment, we are still playing out the classic tension between efficiency versus fairness. But efficiency goals are not necessarily met by the new summary judgment culture; more time may be spent on summary judgment motions than might be spent on trial.

Even if summary judgment is here to stay, the picture of gender and federal civil litigation presented in this chapter suggests the need to rethink summary judgment. At a minimum, this chapter suggests that district judges should pause and reconsider before granting summary judgment. Judges should exercise their discretion to deny summary judgment, even when it might be "technically appropriate"[54] or a "close case."[55] They should think carefully about the law and the evidence that is presented, look at the evidence holistically, resist the impulse to slice and dice the facts and the law, and consider the "public dimension" of federal civil litigation. Most significant, judges should try to get outside the limits of their own experiences in deciding whether no "reasonable juror" could support a determination in the plaintiff's favor. They should exercise all discretion in favor of trial. This historic presumption in summary judgment has been lost and must be vigorously reasserted in the federal courts. Gender cases provide disturbing examples of the dangers of the ways that summary judgment can reinforce implicit or explicit biases. These cases reveal the harm that abuse of this procedural device can wreak on individual litigants, as well as on our entire procedural system.

NOTES

Acknowledgment: This chapter is adapted from Elizabeth M. Schneider, *The Dangers of Summary Judgment: Gender and Civil Litigation*, 59 Rutgers L. Rev. 705 (2007).

1 For two representative reports, *see, e.g.*, *Final Report & Recommendations of the Eighth Circuit Gender Fairness Task Force*, 31 Creighton L. Rev. 9 (1997) [hereinafter *Eighth Circuit Report*]; *Introduction to the Ninth Circuit Gender Bias Task Force Report: The Effects of Gender*, 67 S. Cal. L. Rev. 739 (1994) [hereinafter *Ninth Circuit Report*].

2 *See* Symposium, *Feminist Jurisprudence and Procedure*, 61 U. Cin. L. Rev. 1139 (1993).

3 Barbara Allen Babcock, *A Place in the Palladium: Women's Rights and Jury Service*, 61 U. Cin. L. Rev. 1139 (1993).

4 Shirley S. Abrahamson, *Toward a Courtroom of One's Own: An Appellate Judge Looks at Gender Bias*, 61 U. Cin. L. Rev. 1209 (1993).

5 Harold Hongju Koh, *Two Cheers for Feminist Procedure*, 61 U. Cin. L. Rev. 1201 (1993).

6 *See generally* Patricia Wald, *Summary Judgment at Sixty*, 76 Tex. L. Rev. 1897 (1988); Brooke D. Coleman, *What We Think We Know Versus What We Ought to Know*, 43 Loy. U. Chi. L.J. (2012); Theresa M. Beiner, *The Misuse of Summary Judgment in Hostile Environment Cases*, 34 Wake Forest L. Rev. 71 (1999); Suja Thomas, *Why Summary Judgment Is Unconstitutional*, 93 Va. L. Rev. 139 (2007); Elizabeth M. Schneider & Hon. Nancy Gertner, *"Only Procedural": Thoughts on the Substantive Law Dimensions of Preliminary Procedural Decisions in Employment Discrimination Cases*, 57 N.Y. L. Sch. L. Rev. 767 (2012/2013).

7 *See generally* Brooke D. Coleman & Elizabeth G. Porter, *Reinvigorating Commonality: Gender and Class Actions*, 92 N.Y.U. L. Rev. 895 (2017); Schneider & Gertner, *"Only Procedural," supra* note 6.

8 *See generally* Schneider & Gertner, *"Only Procedural," supra* note 6.

9 *See generally* Judith Resnik, *On the Bias: Feminist Reconsideration of the Aspirations for Our Judges*, 61 S. Cal. L. Rev. 1877 (1988); Helen Hershkoff & Elizabeth M. Schneider, *Sex, Trump, and Constitutional Change*, 34 Const. Comment. 43, (2019).

10 *See generally* Abrahamson, *Toward a Courtroom of One's Own, supra* note 4; Martha Daughtrey, *Going Against the Grain: Personal Reflections on the Emergence of Women in the Legal Profession*, 76 Mont. L. Rev. 159 (2006); Hershkoff & Schneider, *Sex, Trump, and Constitutional Change, supra* note 9; Brooke D. Coleman, *A Legal Fempire? Women in Complex Civil Litigation*, 93 Ind. L.J. 1 (2018).

11 *See generally* Hon. Bernice B. Donald, *Judicial Independence, Collegiality, and the Problem of Dissent in Multi-Member Courts*, 94 N.Y.U. L. Rev. 317 (2019).
12 *See generally* Brooke D. Coleman, *#SoWhiteMale: Federal Civil Rulemaking*, 113 Nw. U. L. Rev 407 (2018); Hershkoff & Schneider, *Sex, Trump, and Constitutional Change*, *supra* note 9.
13 *See generally* sources cited *supra* note 12.
14 For a discussion of Judge Alex Kozinski's resignation and the appointment of the Working Group on Sexual Harassment in the Federal Courts, see Hershkoff & Schneider, *Sex, Trump, and Constitutional Change*, *supra* note 9, at 115. *See also* Helen Hershkoff, *Some Questions About #MeToo and Judicial Decision Making*, The Harbinger: N.Y.U. Rev. L. & Soc. Change (2019).
15 Kevin R. Johnson, *Integrating Racial Justice Into the Civil Procedure Survey Course*, 54 J. Legal Educ. 242 (2004).
16 Elizabeth M. Schneider, *The Dangers of Summary Judgment: Gender and Federal Civil Litigation*, 59 Rutgers L. Rev. 705, 707 (2007) (internal quotations omitted).
17 Matsushita Elec. Indus. Co. v. Zenith Radio Corp., 475 U.S. 574 (1986).
18 Anderson v. Liberty Lobby, Inc., 477 U.S. 242 (1986).
19 Celotex Corp. v. Catrett, 477 U.S. 317 (1986).
20 *See generally Eighth Circuit Report*, *supra* note 1; *Ninth Circuit Report*, *supra* note 1.
21 *See generally* Stephen B. Burbank, *Vanishing Trials and Summary Judgment in Federal Civil Cases: Drifting Toward Bethlehem or Gomorrah?*, 1 J. Empirical Legal Stud. 591 (2004).
22 365 F.3d. 107 (2d Cir. 2004). *See* Mark Hamblett, *Judging Motherhood: Beware*, Nat'l L.J., April 2004 at 4.
23 *Back*, 365 F.3d at 115.
24 *Id.* (alteration in original).
25 *Id.* at 117.
26 *Id.* at 119–20.
27 *Id.* at 120.
28 444 F.3d 255 (4th Cir. 2006).
29 *Id.* at 255.
30 *See* Jennings v. Univ. of N.C., 482 F.3d 686, 696 (4th Cir. 2007) ("Dorrance was not just any college coach. He was and still is the most successful women's soccer coach in U.S. college history, and he has coached the national team.").
31 *Jennings*, 444 F.3d at 263 (alteration in original).
32 *See id.* at 284, 290 (Michael, J., dissenting).
33 *See id.* at 289–90, 292, 294 (Michael, J., dissenting).
34 *Id.* at 282.
35 444 F.3d at 283 (Michael, J., dissenting).
36 482 F.3d 686, 702 (4th Cir. 2007).
37 *See Jennings* 444 F.3d at 274 (majority opinion).
38 The majority opinion references such remarks as "f*** of the week," "fat a**," and "Who are you f***king?" *Id.* at 260, 261, 263.

39 *Jennings*, 482 F.3d at 691–93.
40 *Id.* at 696.
41 187 F.3d. 553 (6th Cir. 1999).
42 *Id.* at 562–64.
43 *Id.* at 562–63.
44 444 F. 3d. 1104 (9th Cir 2006).
45 *Id.* at 1106.
46 *Id.* at 1105–06.
47 *See generally* Michael Selmi, *The Many Faces of Darlene Jeperson*, 14 Duke J. Gender L. & Pol'y 467 (2007).
48 422 F.3d 840 (9th Cir. 2005).
49 *Id.* at 842.
50 *Id.* at 845.
51 *Id.* at 846.
52 *Id.*
53 Memorandum from Joe Cecil & George Cort. Federal Judicial Center, to Hon. Michael Baylson, on Estimates of Summary Judgment Activity in Fiscal Year 2006 (Apr. 12, 2007; revised June 15, 2007).
54 Jack H. Friedenthal & Joshua E. Gardner, *Judicial Discretion to Deny Summary Judgment in the Era of Managerial Judging*, 31 Hofstra L. Rev. 91, 93 (2002).
55 Beiner, *The Misuse of Summary Judgment*, *supra* note 6, at 132.

32

Summary Judgment, Factfinding, and Juries

SUJA A. THOMAS

Summary judgment is one of the most important procedures in the court system.[1] Despite its acceptance, however, in most instances, its use is unconstitutional because the procedure usurps the role of the jury.[2]

Consider this case.[3] Among other alleged actions, the male supervisor of a female deputy in a sheriff's department "tried to kiss her . . . and called her a 'frigid bitch' when she refused," "lifted her over his head," "rubbed up against her and reached across her chest," "chased her around the . . . office," and "asked her over the Sheriff's Department telephones if she was dressed or naked."[4] A jury did not decide if the plaintiff experienced sexual harassment. Instead a judge dismissed the case on summary judgment. Affirming the trial court's decision, the appellate court held that the 16 actions of the supervisor over four years were not sufficiently severe or pervasive to constitute sexual harassment.[5]

Before a jury has the opportunity to hear a case and generally after discovery has occurred, a judge can order summary judgment on a claim such as the one brought by the deputy. Effectively, if granted, this procedure results in the litigant losing and being unable to recover for the alleged wrongdoing committed against her.

When parties move for summary judgment, they argue a reasonable jury could not find for the person who brought the claim. In federal courts, in about 17 percent of cases, the motion is made with respect to some or all claims, and judges grant summary judgment for some or all claims in about 65 percent of those cases.[6] In certain types of cases, summary judgment is granted even more often. For example, in employment discrimination cases, summary judgment is granted in full or in part about 77 percent of the time.[7]

Some judges have questioned the prevalent grant of the procedure in factually intensive cases and discussed the potential infringement on the right to a jury trial. For example, District Judge Jack Weinstein of the Eastern District of New York has stated "[t]he increasing use of . . . summary judgments . . . to limit jury fact finding . . . poses a threat to the continued viability of the Seventh Amendment jury trial."[8] District Judge William Young has further stated "[c]ourts ought be especially wary of granting summary judgment upon the rationale 'no jury could possibly find. . . .' In all too many cases, this is a thinly disguised form of judicial factfinding, forbidden by the Constitution in a jury case."[9] When he was a federal judge, Mark Bennett also described that "[t]he federal courts' daily ritual of trial court grants and appellate court affirmances of summary judgment in employment discrimination cases across the land is increasingly troubling to me. I worry that the expanding use of summary judgment, particularly in federal employment discrimination litigation, raises the ominous specter of serious erosion of the 'fundamental and sacred' right of trial by jury."[10]

Scholars have also questioned its use. For example, Arthur Miller warned that "a motion designed simply for identifying trial-worthy issues has become, on occasion, a vehicle for resolving trial-worthy issues. . . . The effect is to compromise the due process underpinnings of the day-in-court principle and the constitutional jury trial right without any empirical basis for believing that systemic benefits are realized that offset these consequences."[11] John Bronsteen has also teased that "[s]ummary judgment might be a wonderful procedure were it not inefficient, unfair, and unconstitutional."[12]

But some scholars disagree, arguing that the procedure is essential. For example, Randy Kozel and David Rosenberg have contended that summary judgment should be imposed to prevent bad cases from being settled.[13] Further, Bill Nelson has asserted that it is necessary to protect entrepreneurs and investors.[14]

In 2007, in an article published in the *Virginia Law Review*, I argued that summary judgment is unconstitutional. Since then, litigants have raised the issue in several courts. Two federal circuits have briefly addressed the argument. The Eleventh and Sixth Circuits have rejected it—relying on previous United States Supreme Court decisions.[15] Despite this justification, the Supreme Court has never actually addressed this issue.[16]

Following the publication of my article, several academics responded to the unconstitutionality argument. Importantly, the crux of my argument—that in substance there is no historical equivalent to summary judgment—remains unchallenged.[17]

The following argument that summary judgment is unconstitutional is adapted from the above-mentioned article.[18]

I. The Seventh Amendment and the Common Law

The constitutionality of summary judgment is governed by the Seventh Amendment, which provides that "[i]n Suits at common law . . . the right of trial by jury shall be preserved, and no fact tried by jury, shall be otherwise re-examined in any Court of the United States, than according to the rules of the common law."[19] In its decisions interpreting the Seventh Amendment, the Supreme Court has stated that "common law" in the Seventh Amendment refers to the English common law in 1791, the year when the Amendment was adopted.[20] According to the Court, the Amendment does not require that the common law is "fixed"[21] or that, in other words, the "form"[22] of the common law is preserved. Instead, the Amendment requires that the "substance"[23] of the English common law in 1791 must be satisfied. Thus, a new procedure is constitutional if it satisfies the substance of the English common law jury trial in 1791. The Court has not, however, defined what constitutes the substance of the English common law jury trial in 1791. Instead the Court has individually compared various common law procedures to modern procedures.[24] Under this approach, the Court has approved every procedure that it has considered that removes cases from juries, before, during, or after trials, even though such procedures did not exist under the English common law.[25]

While the Court has not endeavored to set forth the substance of the common law jury trial, an examination of the common law demonstrates that this substance, or the core principles, of the common law is quite clear. First, . . . under the common law, the jury or the parties determined the facts. One party could admit the allegations or the conclusions of the evidence of the other party, or the parties could leave the determination of the facts to the jury. A court itself never decided the case without a determination of the facts by the parties or the jury, however improbable the evidence might be. Second, only after the parties presented evidence at trial and only after a jury rendered a verdict, would a court ever determine whether the evidence was sufficient to support a jury verdict. Where the court decided that the evidence was insufficient to support the verdict, the court would order a new trial. Another jury would determine the facts and decide which party won. The court itself would never determine who should win if it believed the evidence was insufficient. Third, a jury would decide a case with any evidence, however improbable the evidence was, unless the moving party admitted the facts and conclusions of the nonmoving party, including the improbable facts and conclusions.

II. Summary Judgment Is Unconstitutional

The Supreme Court has stated that new procedures that affect the jury trial right, like summary judgment, must satisfy the substance of the jury trial under the English common law in 1791. In its jurisprudence, however, the Court has failed to articulate what constitutes the substance of the common law. Instead, the Court has individually compared the new procedures to common law procedures and, under this approach, has held constitutional every new procedure that it has considered that removes cases from juries before, during, and after trial.

. . . [T]he common law procedures that the Supreme Court has attempted to favorably compare to . . . summary judgment [are inapposite]. First, summary judgment, under which the court considers only reasonable inferences from the evidence, contrasts with the common law demurrer to the pleadings and the common law demurrer to the evidence, under which the court must consider as true the allegations or facts and conclusions of the opposing party, however improbable those facts or conclusions may be. Second, summary judgment, under which the court dismisses the case with prejudice after deciding that the evidence of the nonmoving party is insufficient, contrasts with the common law nonsuit, under which the plaintiff voluntarily withdraws from a case without prejudice when he believes his evidence may be insufficient. Third, summary judgment, under which the court dismisses a case upon a determination of the general insufficiency of the evidence, contrasts with the common law compulsory nonsuit and the common law special case, under which the court would never dismiss a case based on the general insufficiency of the evidence. Finally, summary judgment, under which the court dismisses a case based on the insufficiency of evidence, contrasts with the common law new trial, under which the court did not dismiss the case but rather ordered a new trial if the evidence was insufficient.

[In addition,] . . . summary judgment violates [the core] principles, or the substance, of the common law. Summary judgment violates the first core principle that the jury or the parties determined the facts. The court itself would never decide a case without such a determination of the facts by the jury or the parties. Under summary judgment, contrary to this principle, the court decides the case without a jury or the parties deciding the facts. The court assesses the evidence, decides what inferences from the evidence are reasonable, and decides whether a reasonable jury could find for the nonmoving party.

Summary judgment also breaches the second core principle of the common law that a court would determine whether the evidence was sufficient to support the jury verdict only after the parties presented evidence at trial, and only after a jury rendered a verdict. Even then, the court would order only a new trial, not judgment, if the evidence was insufficient. In contrast, under summary judgment, a court orders judgment for the moving party prior to trial if the court determines that the nonmoving party's evidence is insufficient.

Finally, summary judgment violates the third core principle of the common law that a jury, not a court, decided a case that had any evidence, however improbable, unless the moving party admitted all facts and conclusions of the nonmoving party, including the improbable facts and conclusions. In contrast, under summary judgment the moving party does not admit the truth of the non-moving party's evidence. Instead, the court determines the reasonableness of the evidence and removes cases from the jury based on this assessment.

Using the test for constitutionality that the Supreme Court has articulated since the adoption of the Seventh Amendment in 1791, I have described how summary judgment violates the core principles or the substance of the common law and is therefore unconstitutional.[26]

NOTES

Acknowledgment: This chapter is updated and adapted from the article Suja A. Thomas, *Why Summary Judgment Is Unconstitutional*, 93 Va. L. Rev. 139 (2007).

1 Summary judgment also may be used in arbitration. Charles F. Forer, *Does Summary Judgment in an Arbitration Proceeding Avoid Delays and Expenses—Or Add to Them?*, American Bar Association, www.americanbar.org.

2 Suja A. Thomas *Why Summary Judgment Is Unconstitutional*, 93 Va. L. Rev. 139 (2007). This chapter contains an excerpt of this article.

3 This case and other cases alleging employment discrimination are discussed in Sandra Sperino & Suja A. Thomas, Unequal: How America's Courts Undermine Discrimination Law (2017).

4 Mitchell v. Pope, 189 F. App'x 911, 913 & n.3 (11th Cir. 2006).

5 *Id.*

6 Memorandum on Report on Summary Judgment Practice Across Districts with Variations in Local Rule from Joe Cecil and George Cort to Judge Michael Baylson, The Federal Judicial Center 2, 9 (Aug. 13, 2008).

7 *Id.* at 9. Some statistics are even more stark. In 2011 and 2012, in the federal court in the Northern District of Georgia, in cases where there was a motion for summary judgment in an employment discrimination case, respectively 95 percent and 93 percent of those cases had claims dismissed in whole or in part. Barrett & Farahany, LLP, Analysis of Employment Discrimination Claims for Cases in Which an Order was Issued on Defendant's Motion for Summary Judgment in 2011 and 2012 in the U.S. District Court for the Northern District of Georgia 4 (2012).

8 In re Zyprexa Products Liability Litigation, 489 F. Supp.2d 230 (E.D.N.Y. 2007).

9 In re Nexium (Esomeprazole) Antitrust Litigation, 309 F.R.D. 107 (D. Mass. 2015); *see* S.E.C. v. EagleEye Asset Mgmt., 975 F. Supp. 2d 151, 155 (D. Mass. 2013) (summary judgment was inappropriate even though "overwhelming evidence [was] proffered at that stage by the SEC").

10 Mark W. Bennett, *Essay: From the "No Spittin, No Cussin and No Summary Judgment" Days of Employment Discrimination Litigation to the "Defendant's Summary Judgment Affirmed Without Comment" Days: One Judge's Four-Decade Perspective*, 57 N.Y.L. Sch. L. Rev. 685, 691 (2013). Former judge and Harvard professor Nancy Gertner stated "[j]udges recognize that divining a person's intent is messy and complex and that this issue usually involves a material dispute of fact for a jury to decide. Employment discrimination cases, in contrast, are typically resolved on summary judgment, although discriminatory intent may be more difficult to identify on a cold record than is the intent of a contract's drafters or a putative tortfeasor's state of mind." Nancy Gertner, *Opinions I Should Have Written*, 110 Nw. U. L. Rev. 423, 429–30 & n.12 (2016).

11 Arthur Miller, *Simplified Pleadings, Meaningful Days in Court, and Trials on the Merits: Reflections on the Deformation of Federal Procedure*, 88 N.Y.U. L. Rev. 286, 312 (2013).

12 John Bronsteen, *Against Summary Judgment*, 75 Geo. Wash. L. Rev. 522 (2007).

13 Randy J. Kozel & David Rosenberg, *Solving the Nuisance-Value Settlement Problem: Mandatory Summary Judgment*, 90 Va. L. Rev. 1849 (2004).

14 William E. Nelson, *Summary Judgment and the Progressive Constitution*, 93 Iowa L. Rev. 1653, 1660 (2008).

15 Jefferson v. Sewon America, Inc. 891 F.3d 911, 919–20 (11th Cir. 2018) ("an amicus curiae, Professor Suja Thomas, advances the radical argument that summary judgment is always unconstitutional. Nonsense. The Supreme Court made clear long ago that 'summary judgment does not violate the Seventh Amendment.' Parklane Hosiery Co. v. Shore, 439 U.S. 322, 336 (1979) (citing F*id.* & Deposit Co. v. United States, 187 U.S. 315, 319–21 (1902))"). McDaniel v. Kindred Healthcare, Inc., 311 Fed.Appx. 758 (6th 2009) ("[w]e reject McDaniel's argument, drawn from a law review article written by Professor Suja A. Thomas . . . that summary judgment violates the Seventh Amendment. This argument lacks merit. We agree with a prior panel of this court that recently examined the same law review article and rejected the same argument: Although the historical examination that Professor Thomas provides is interesting . . . [t]he Supreme Court has held that summary judgment is constitutional. . . . Thus, it would be inappropriate for us to hold that the summary judgment standard is unconstitutional." *Cook v. McPherson*, 273 Fed.Appx. 421, 425 (6th Cir.2008).) A state judge has been more sympathetic. Judge Colleen Mary O'Toole of the Ohio Court of Appeals dissented in a case ordering summary judgment in an employment discrimination case. Citing the article, she stated "[j]udges extensively utilize summary judgment to clear their dockets of cases they deem meritless. . . . This is a case of 'he said, she said' which should not be resolved through summary judgment." Weber v. Ferrellgas, Inc., 2016-Ohio-4738, ¶ 68, 68 N.E.3d 207, 218; see also Vidovic v. Hoynes, 2015-Ohio-712, ¶ 90, 29 N.E.3d 338, 354. A justice on the Wisconsin Supreme Court has recognized the importance of questioning summary judgment in other arenas including the termination of parental rights. He stated that "[s]cholarship on this subject is urgently needed." 749 N.W.2d 168, 180 (2008) (Prosser, J., concurring).

16 Thomas, *Why Summary Judgment Is Unconstitutional*, *supra* first unnumbered note, at 163–77.

17 Suja A. Thomas *Why Summary Judgment Is Still Unconstitutional: A Reply to Professors Brunet and Nelson*, 93 Iowa L. Rev. 1667 (2008) (discussing Nelson, *Summary Judgment and the Progressive Constitution*, *supra* note 13, where he acknowledges that my historical argument is correct and explaining Edward Brunet, *Summary Judgment Is Constitutional*, 93 Iowa L. Rev. 1625 ((2008)), where he incorrectly compares trial by inspection or trial by examination to summary judgment). Brian Fitzpatrick does not question my analysis under Supreme Court precedent but instead argues that an originalist analysis would include "a frame of reference that informs why the practice might or might not have been understood to be constitutionally required." He does not, however, provide the frame of refer-

ence or make a conclusion regarding the issue. Brian T. Fitzpatrick, *Originalism and the Constitution*, 71 Ohio St. L.J. 919, 920–21 (2010). Luke Meier attempts to distinguish probability and confidence analyses by judges on summary judgment but does not recognize that, historically, judges could not make such a sufficiency-of-the-evidence analysis prior to trial. Luke Meier, *Probability, Confidence, and the Constitutionality of Summary Judgment*, 42 Hastings Const. L.Q. 1 (2014); see also Edward Brunet, John Parry & Martin Redish, *Summary Judgment: Federal Law and Practice* § 2.1 (2018).

18 The rest of the article that is not included here describes arguments to justify summary judgment and then shows how those contentions are not correct. *See* Suja A. Thomas, *Why Summary Judgment Is Unconstitutional*, 93 Va. L. Rev. 139 (2007).

19 U.S. Const. amend. VII.

20 *See, e.g.*, Gasperini v. Ctr. for Humanities, Inc., 518 U.S. 415, 435–36 & n.20 (1996); Galloway v. United States, 319 U.S. 372, 388–92 (1943); Gasoline Prods. Co. v. Champlin Ref. Co., 283 U.S. 494, 497–98 (1931); Slocum v. N.Y. Life Ins. Co., 228 U.S. 364, 377 (1913).

21 *Gasperini*, 518 U.S. at 436 n.20.

22 *Gasoline Prods.*, 283 U.S. at 498.

23 *Id.*; *see also*, e.g., Colgrove v. Battin, 413 U.S. 149, 157–60 (1973); Galloway, 319 U.S. at 392.

24 *See* Thomas, *Why Summary Judgment Is Unconstitutional*, *supra* first unnumbered note, at 166–77.

25 Suja A. Thomas, *The Seventh Amendment, Modern Procedure, and the English Common Law*, 82 Wash. U. L.Q., 695–702 (2004).

26 To read the other parts of the article, please refer to Thomas, *Why Summary Judgment Is Unconstitutional*, *supra* first unnumbered note, at 160–80.

33

The Disparate Racial Impacts of Color-Blind Juror Eligibility Requirements

KEVIN R. JOHNSON

The right to trial by jury guaranteed by the Fifth and Sixth Amendments of the US Constitution stands as a proud testament to the nation's commitment to democracy. To that democratic end, juries are "drawn from *a fair cross section of the community*."[1] The United States Supreme Court has held that this requirement (i.e., to empanel juries drawn from a fair cross section of the community) prohibits the systematic exclusion of African American and Latinx persons from jury service.[2] The Court also has prohibited the use of peremptory challenges to remove prospective jurors on account of their race.[3]

Critical Race Theory posits that people of color have distinctive life experiences shaping a distinctive "voice."[4] Despite the express ban on the *systematic* exclusion of people of color from juries, restrictions on juror eligibility still disparately exclude voices of color from jury service. The uneven racial impacts of the color-blind US citizenship and English-language requirements for jury service, and the disqualification of felons and persons with disabilities from jury service, warrant reconsideration. Reform of the juror eligibility requirements could move juries toward more fully incorporating voices of color and better approximating the jury's democratic ideal.

The Exclusion of Immigrants from Jury Service

The US Constitution does not mandate US citizenship for jury service. Today, however, federal and state laws uniformly restrict jury service to US citizens. Little consideration has been given to the purposes served by the citizenship requirement. Speculation, not evidence, supports the notion that noncitizen residents, as a group, are any less committed than citizens to the proper application and enforcement of the laws, fidelity to the US justice system, and prevailing community values. Nonetheless, courts have consistently rejected challenges to the across-the-board exclusion of noncitizens from jury service.[5]

The citizenship requirement has the most striking effect on juries in major metropolitan areas with large immigrant populations. Moreover, the requirement has a racial impact. In Los Angeles County in 2010, for example, more than one-third of the residents were foreign-born, with the majority from Mexico; unless naturalized, these residents were barred from jury service.[6] Similarly, the state of Texas, straddling the United States–Mexico border and with one of the largest Mexican immigrant populations of all the states, not surprisingly prohibits those who are not US citizens from serving on juries.[7]

Federal law (28 U.S.C § 1865(b)(1)) requires a juror to be "a citizen of the United States." Every state in the union today requires jurors to be US citizens.[8] No legal challenges to the citizenship requirement have succeeded.

Federal and state laws deny immigrants the opportunity to participate in resolving legal disputes and even having their disputes decided by juries of their peers. Congress and state legislatures could change that by eliminating the US citizenship requirement for jury service. In 2013, the California legislature passed a bill that would have permitted lawful permanent residents to serve on juries.[9] However, the California governor refused to sign the bill on the ground that "'[j]ury service, like voting, is quintessentially a prerogative and responsibility of citizenship.'"[10]

Expanding juror eligibility to lawful permanent residents would allow juries to look more like our communities and add voices of color to juries. Moreover, immigrant communities likely would view jury verdicts as more legitimate than they currently are. And noncitizen jurors would be integrated into—rather than excluded from—a major social institution.

The Exclusion of Non-English Speakers from Jury Service

Federal and state laws generally require jurors to be able to read, write, understand, and speak the English language. Today, "8% of the United States population (25.1 million) is considered limited-English proficient (LEP)" and may not qualify for jury service.[11]

Because "the inability to speak English coincides neatly with race,"[12] the English-language requirement has a disparate racial impact on jury pools. "Although the widespread requirement that jurors speak English affects many different racial groups, the burden of language exclusion is borne predominantly by Spanish-speaking Latinos."[13]

Federal law (28 U.S.C. § 1865(b)(2), (3)) requires that, to be eligible for jury service, a person must be able "to read, write, and understand the English language" and "to speak the English language."

Although holding that the Constitution bans the exercise of peremptory challenges to strike potential jurors because of their race, the Supreme Court in *Hernandez v. New York*[14] rejected a challenge to a prosecutor's use of challenges to strike bilingual Spanish/English speakers, ostensibly on the ground that bilingual jurors might disregard the official translations of Spanish to English.[15]

Consistent with federal law, the states, with one exception, require English-language proficiency for jury service. For example, California excludes from jury service "[p]ersons who are not possessed of sufficient knowledge of the English language."[16]

With a large Spanish-speaking population, New Mexico is the only state that does not require English-language proficiency for jury service. To the contrary, the state constitution provides that "[t]he right of any citizen of the state to . . . sit upon juries, shall never be restricted, abridged or impaired on account of . . . inability to speak, read or write the English or Spanish languages."[17] The New Mexico courts provide interpretation services "to non-English-speaking jurors by certified court interpreters during all phases of trial."[18]

The English-language requirement for jury service denies representation of voices that are part of the community and has a racially disparate impact. To ensure that juries better reflect a fair cross section of the community, consideration should be given to expanding juror eligibility to non-English speakers.

Admittedly, translation of testimony and documents into languages other than English adds costs to the judicial system. Despite the costs, such services would allow non-English speaking citizens to serve on—and, as Critical Race Theory posits, add a distinctive voice to–juries. New Mexico has determined that the inclusion of non-English speakers on juries outweighs the costs of translation.

The Exclusion of Felons from Jury Service

Federal and state laws generally render convicted felons ineligible for jury service. Two principal rationales have been offered for the exclusion. First, as one federal court of appeals explained, the government has a "legitimate interest in protecting the probity [honesty and integrity] of juries" by excluding felons from jury service.[19] The second rationale is that felons are presumptively biased in favor of *criminal* defendants.[20] That rationale, however, cannot justify the exclusion of felons from *civil* juries.

Critical Race theorists roundly condemn the disparate impacts of the modern criminal justice system on African American and Latinx persons.[21] For example, as of 2010, nearly 20 million people, representing roughly 8.6 percent of the adult population and one-third of African American males, had been convicted of a felony and were presumptively barred from jury service.[22] By disparately excluding people—and voices—of color, the felon exclusion makes jury pools less representative than they otherwise would be.

Consistent with the claim that the felon exclusion does not constitute unlawful racial discrimination, one federal court of appeals held that the defendant failed to prove the intent to discriminate against African Americans through the felon exclusion,[23] as required by Supreme Court precedent.[24] Critical Race theorists have criticized the discriminatory intent requirement because it places an onerous evidentiary burden on persons seeking to prove discrimination.[25]

The US Constitution requires neither exclusion nor inclusion of felons on juries. However, under federal law (28 U.S.C. § 1865(b)(5)), a person cannot serve on a jury if he "has a charge pending against him for the commission of, or has been convicted in a State or Federal court of record of a crime, punishable by imprisonment for more than one year and his civil rights have not been restored."

A majority of states permanently bar felons from jury service. A number of states, including Colorado, Oregon, and Washington,[26] impose less strict restrictions on the exclusion of felons from jury service. In stark contrast to the general bar on felons from serving on juries, 45 states recognize that a convicted felon can be rehabilitated and is not permanently disqualified from practicing law.[27]

Maine is the only state that does not restrict a felon's eligibility for jury service.[28] One study found that jurors with a felony conviction in Maine strive to judge impartially.[29] Another study concluded that the service of felons on juries "may enhance [jury] deliberation quality."[30]

Because the criminal laws are unevenly enforced along racial lines, we should examine whether the exclusion of felons from juries undermines the goal of pulling jurors from a fair cross section of the community. The Maine experience suggests that the felon exclusion may not be necessary to protect jury integrity and that its elimination may add important voices to juries. Moreover, eliminating the felon exclusion "would . . . help integrate citizens who have completed their criminal sentences into democratic society."[31]

Exclusion of Persons with Disabilities from Juries

Federal and state laws restrict the service of persons with disabilities on juries. This is the case even though such persons regularly testify in trials.[32] As of 2017, more than 40 million people in the US, nearly 13 percent of the population, have some form of disability.[33] African Americans are overrepresented among them. "Blacks had a higher prevalence of disability (34.9 percent) than non-Hispanic Whites (31.5 percent) and Hispanics (24.6 percent)."[34]

Bars to jury service by persons with disabilities are in tension with modern antidiscrimination law. The Americans with Disabilities Act of 1990 (ADA) provides that "no qualified individual with a disability shall, by reason of such disability, be excluded from participation in or be denied the benefits of the services, programs, or activities of a public entity, or be subjected to discrimination by any such entity."[35] The Rehabilitation Act of 1973 similarly prohibits discrimination against persons with disabilities.[36]

Consistent with the antidiscrimination laws, courts today determine whether a person with a disability, with accommodations, can render satisfactory jury service. Expanding the ability of persons with disabilities to serve on juries would add a distinctive voice to the jury room.

Under federal law, a prospective juror is not eligible to serve if he or she "is incapable, by reason of mental or physical infirmity, to render satisfactory jury service."[37]

In the 1800s, many states automatically excluded blind or deaf persons from juries.[38] Courts today generally make case-by-case determinations about whether a disability might affect a person's ability to perform the duties of a juror. In many states, persons may not be automatically excluded from jury service solely because they are deaf, blind, have medical conditions, or because they suffer from a disability that impairs their mobility or ability to communicate.[39] Rather, a person with a disability may be excused only if the judge finds that the person is incapable of performing the duties of a juror.[40] To that end, Colorado requires a person seeking to be disqualified from jury service based on disability to submit a letter from a physician or nurse "stating the nature of the disability and an opinion that such disability prevents the person from rendering satisfactory jury service."[41]

Federal disability law applies to state courts and helps ensure that some persons with disabilities are not barred per se from jury service. In *DeLong v. Brumbaugh*,[42] for example, a deaf person who read, wrote, and understood—but could not speak—English successfully challenged her dismissal in a state court proceeding from jury service.[43] In *People v. Caldwell*,[44] a juror had a visual impairment that prevented her from seeing details in witnesses' faces and made it impossible for her to read standard print.[45] The court concluded that the juror's "vision limitation did not render her automatically unqualified for the jury and that the court had an obligation to 'reasonably accommodate' her pursuant to the" ADA.[46] The court further found that the juror could be reasonably accommodated by having witnesses describe evidence in detail and for the attorneys to provide large-print copies of exhibits.

To accommodate persons with disabilities, some states mandate sign-language interpreters, computer-aided transcription, or assistive listening devices for deaf or hearing-impaired jurors. A few states require that readers be available for jurors with visual impairments. Some states require communication services, such as spokespersons on communication boards, for jurors with speech impairments.[47]

Reasonable accommodations for persons with disabilities have improved their representation on juries. Several states have adopted the American Bar Association's recommendation[48] to make reasonable accommodations for persons with disabilities.[49] To ensure compliance with the growing federal law barring discrimination against persons with disabilities, states should reconsider their rules on jury service by such persons.

Conclusion

Current jury eligibility rules exclude large swaths of the US population from jury service. They make juries less, not more, representative of the general population and undermine the ability of the nation to fulfill its democratic commitment to pull jurors from a fair cross section of the community. Moreover, the juror eligibility requirements disparately exclude people of color, as well as other marginalized groups, from jury service.

Jury eligibility requirements should be reexamined with an eye toward the lessons of Critical Race Theory. Juries are designed to include different voices—including voices of color—representing a fair cross section of the community. Notions of democratic representation militate in favor of allowing immigrants, non-English speakers, felons, and persons with disabilities to serve on juries. Their exclusion has a disparate racial impact, excludes voices of color from the jury room, and undermines the legitimacy of the justice system.

NOTES

1 Taylor v. Louisiana, 419 U.S. 522, 527 (1975) (emphasis added).

2 Hernandez v. Texas, 347 U.S. 475, 480–82 (1954); Strauder v. West Virginia, 100 U.S. 303, 310 (1879).

3 Batson v. Kentucky, 476 U.S. 79, 89 (1986); Edmonson v. Leesville Concrete Co., 500 U.S. 614, 616 (1991).

4 Alex M. Johnson, Jr., *The New Voice of Color*, 100 Yale L.J. 2007, 2012–14 (1991).

5 Amy R. Motomura, Note, *The American Jury: Can Noncitizens Still Be Excluded?*, 64 Stan. L. Rev. 1503, 1516–19, 1545 (2012).

6 Quick Facts, Los Angeles County, California, U.S. Census Bureau, www.census.gov. Mexican persons, as well as Latinx persons generally, have been socially constructed as a race distinct from whites. *See generally* Laura E. Gómez, *Manifest Destinies: The Making of the Mexican American Race* (2d ed. 2018) (examining the social construction of persons of Mexican ancestry in the United States as a race separate from whites).

7 Tex. Gov't Code § 62.102 (2019).

8 *See* Motomura, *supra* note 5, at 1504 n.1 (citing authority).

9 Assemb. B. 1401, 2013 Leg., Reg. Sess. (Cal. (2013)). A lawful permanent resident generally is eligible to become a US citizen after five years of residence in the United States. 8 U.S.C. § 1427.

10 Jennifer Medina, *Veto Halts Bill for Jury Duty by Noncitizens in California*, N.Y. Times, Oct. 7, 2013, www.nytimes.com (quoting Governor Jerry Brown).

11 Kimberly Scamman, *Spanish Speakers in the United States (Infographic)*, Telelanguage (Sept. 4, 2018), www.telelanguage.com.

12 Bill Ong Hing, *Beyond the Rhetoric of Assimilation and Cultural Pluralism: Addressing the Tension of Separatism and Conflict in an Immigration-Driven Multiracial Society*, 81 Cal. L. Rev. 863, 874 (1993).

13 Jasmine B. Gonzales Rose, *Language Disenfranchisement in Juries: A Call for Constitutional Remediation*, 65 Hastings L.J. 811, 815 (2014).

14 500 U.S. 352 (1991).

15 *Id.* at 359–61.

16 Cal. Civ. Proc. Code § 203(a)(6).

17 N.M. Const. art. VII, § 3.

18 Jasmine B. Gonzales Rose, *The Exclusion of Non-English-Speaking Jurors: Remedying a Century of Denial of the Sixth Amendment in the Federal Courts of Puerto Rico*, 46 Harv. Civ. Rts.–Civ. Liberties L. Rev. 497, 548 (2011) (footnote omitted).

19 United States v. Arce, 997 F.2d 1123, 1127 (5th Cir. 1993).

20 Rubio v. Superior Court, 593 P.2d 595, 600 (1979).

21 *See, e.g.*, Michelle Alexander, The New Jim Crow: Mass Incarceration in the Age of Colorblindness 56–60 (2010).

22 Sarah Shannon, Christopher Uggen, Melissa Thompson, Jason Schnittker & Michael Massoglia, *Growth in the U.S. Ex-Felon and Ex-Prisoner Population, 1948 to 2010*, at 11–12 (2011).

23 United States v. Barry, 71 F.3d 1269, 1271–72 (7th Cir. 1995).

24 Washington v. Davis, 426 U.S. 229, 239 (1976).

25 *See, e.g.*, Charles R. Lawrence III, *The Id, the Ego, and Equal Protection: Reckoning with Unconscious Racism*, 39 Stan. L. Rev. 317, 360–62 (1987).

26 Co. Rev. Stat. § 13-71-105(3) (2019); Or. Rev. Stat. § 10.030(3)(E) (2019); Wash. Rev. Code Ann. § 2.36.070(5).

27 James M. Binnall, *Convicts in Court: Felonious Lawyers Make a Case for Including Convicted Felons in the Jury Pool*, 73 Alb. L. Rev. 1379, 1390 (2010).

28 Me. Rev. Stat. Ann. tit. 14, § 1211 (2019).

29 James M. Binnall, *Felon-Jurors in Vacationland: A Field Study of Transformative Civic Engagement in Maine*, 71 Me. L. Rev. 71, 89–96 (2018).

30 James M. Binnall, *Jury Diversity in the Age of Mass Incarceration: An Exploratory Mock Jury Experiment Examining Felon-Jurors' Potential Impacts on Deliberations*, 25 Psych., Crime & L. 345, 357 (2018).

31 Paula Z. Segal, *A More Inclusive Democracy: Challenging Felon Jury Exclusion in New York*, 13 N.Y.C. L. Rev. 313, 316 (2010).

32 Jasmine E. Harris, *Sexual Consent and Disability*, 93 N.Y.U. L. Rev. 480, 532–46 (2018) (presenting empirical data showing that persons with mental disabilities testified in the vast majority of cases involving the capacity to consent to sex).

33 U.S. Census Bureau, *What Can You Learn About Counties From the American Community Survey?*, www.census.gov.

34 Danielle M. Taylor, *Americans with Disabilities: 2014*, U.S. Census Bureau 5 (Nov. 2018), www.census.gov.

35 Americans with Disabilities Act of 1990, Pub. L. No. 101–336, § 202, 104 Stat. 327, 337 (1990).

36 Rehabilitation Act of 1973, Pub. L. No. 93–112, § 504, 87 Stat. 355, 394 (1973) (codified at 29 U.S.C. § 794(a)).

37 28 U.S.C. § 1865(b)(4).

38 *See, e.g.*, Rhodes v. State, 27 N.E. 866, 868–69 (1891).

39 *See, e.g.*, Cal. Civ. Proc. Code § 203(a)(6) (2020).

40 *See, e.g.*, Cal. Civ. Proc. Code § 228(b) (2003).

41 Colo. Rev. Stats. § 13-71-105(2)(c) (2019).

42 703 F. Supp. 399 (W.D. Pa. 1989).

43 *Id.* at 401–04.

44 603 N.Y.S.2d 713 (N.Y. Crim. Ct. 1993).

45 *Id.* at 713–14.

46 *Id.* at 714.

47 Kristi Bleyer, Kathryn Shane McCarty & Erica Wood, *Access to Jury Service for Persons With Disabilities*, 19 Mental & Physical Disability L. Rep. 249, 249–54 (1995).

48 American Bar Association, Standards Relating to Juror Use and Management 64–65 (1993).

49 Bleyer, McCarty & Wood, *supra* note 47, at 249.

PART V

Litigation and Arbitration

The joinder of claims and parties—whether through intervention, class actions, or other procedural mechanisms—can empower litigants to tell their stories, protect their interests, pool their resources, and bolster each other, among other benefits. The chapters in Part V shed light on the importance of joinder and aggregation to marginalized groups. Danielle Holley-Walker (chapter 34) describes how important intervention is for some students of color seeking to defend race-conscious affirmative action plans. Sergio Campos in chapter 35 challenges us to embrace class actions, despite their seeming contradiction with the "day in court" right we are often taught to idealize. Next, Brooke Coleman and Elizabeth Porter (chapter 36) highlight how the modern class action rule and its commonality requirement have affected the capacity of US feminists to advocate for working women over the course of half a century and through four waves of feminist movements. Together, these chapters demonstrate the power of collective action via procedural mechanisms.

Building on that theme, the remaining chapters explore alternative dispute resolution (ADR). ADR was initially thought to hold promise for underrepresented populations. Allowing claims to be resolved outside of a system fraught with structural inequality seemed like a viable alternative. Yet, as these chapters reveal, ADR, while bestowing some benefits, has also entrenched inequities. And while ADR may have begun as an "outsider" idea, it has become mainstream. Eric Yamamoto (chapter 37) reveals how arbitration—and the Supreme Court's pro-arbitration jurisprudence—has become part of a larger system of procedures that business interests use to effectively manufacture immunity from liability. Similarly, Stephanie Bornstein, in chapter 39, chronicles how the Supreme Court's arbitration jurisprudence has defeated statutory regimes that were intended to remedy structural discrimination. In chapter 38,

Michael Green departs from arbitration and instead illuminates how race and racial stereotypes can impact—both positively and negatively—negotiation tactics and results. Together, these chapters paint a complicated picture of how ADR, in its various forms, can both restrict and augment access to justice.

34

The Power of Narrative Through Intervention in Affirmative Action Cases

DANIELLE HOLLEY-WALKER

The narratives of the parties in higher education affirmative action litigation are so well known that the average layperson may be able to describe the plaintiff's claims. The story of the litigation typically begins when a Caucasian applicant seeks admission to a college or graduate school. The Caucasian applicant is denied admission but is aware that the college or graduate school has an affirmative action policy under which the school considers race or ethnicity in the admissions process. The Caucasian applicant then files suit against the university and its officers, claiming that the university's consideration of race in its admissions process is unconstitutional. It is this seemingly straightforward narrative that has come to define higher education affirmative action litigation.

The second narrative in higher education affirmative action cases is the narrative of the university defendant. This narrative is almost as well known as the plaintiff's. The university defendant's narrative centers around a defense of affirmative action on the basis that racial diversity is a compelling governmental interest, as required under Fourteenth Amendment Equal Protection Clause analysis, because racial diversity is integral to the university's educational mission. Its narrative attempts to demonstrate that racial diversity allows different perspectives in classroom discussions and that producing a racially diverse group of graduates provides state benefits, such as professionals who will work in underserved communities. The university defendant's story rarely includes a discussion of the university's or state's history of racial discrimination or any explanation of the connection between the university's current affirmative action program and the university's past racial discrimination.

The third narrative of the higher education affirmative action lawsuit is not as well known and has become marginalized in the public and academic debates surrounding these cases. The third narrative is the story of the minority students[1] who are the direct beneficiaries of these race-conscious admissions policies. The minority students' narrative is sometimes introduced into the litigation through intervention, which allows a person or group with an interest in the lawsuit to become a party even though the existing litigants have not named the person or group as a party.

Similar to the university defendant, the minority students' narrative focuses on defending the affirmative action policies. The minority student intervenors often tell a story about the value of racial diversity to a university community. However, the minority students' narrative diverges from the university defendant's in an important way. The former often attempts to connect current affirmative action policies with the state's and/or university's past and current racially discriminatory policies or practices.

The minority students' narrative also serves as an alternative viewpoint regarding the individualized effects of affirmative action admissions policies. While the Caucasian student plaintiff's narrative describes individualized harm as a result of the university's considering race in admissions, the minority student intervenors' narrative describes individualized harm as a result of the university's not considering race in admissions via an affirmative action program.

Intervention is a procedural device intended to enable a party or group with a substantial interest in the subject of litigation to become a party in the case to protect their rights. Intervention is often compared to other procedural devices that recognize that "a lawsuit is often not merely a private fight and will have implications on those not named as parties."[2] Although intervention does not create a cause of action, intervenors have rights similar to those of parties. Intervenors may file motions, participate in discovery, introduce direct testimony, conduct cross-examination, and appeal adverse rulings. An intervenor's ability to add witnesses and present separate and sometimes conflicting positions on existing issues often leads to the litigation becoming more complex. Due to the increased burden on the court and existing parties, the rule itself, and courts interpreting the rule, have standards to determine when a party should be allowed to intervene.

Federal Rule of Civil Procedure 24 provides for two types of intervention: intervention as a matter of right, and permissive intervention. Under FRCP 24(a), intervention as a matter of right is allowed when a federal statute confers a right of intervention to the applicant for intervention, or when the applicant is able to demonstrate that it has an interest in the subject matter of the transaction and that its ability to protect that interest may be substantially impaired by the court's disposition of the case.[3] The majority of circuits use a four-part standard to determine whether a party's motion to intervene as a matter of right under FRCP 24(a)(2) should be granted: (1) timeliness of the motion; (2) whether the proposed intervenor claims an interest relating to the property or transaction that is the subject of the litigation; (3) whether the disposition of the litigation may impair or impede the proposed intervenor's right to protect that interest; and (4) whether the proposed intervenor's interest is adequately represented by the existing parties.[4]

Minority students and public interest organizations have sought to intervene as a matter of right and permissively to defend affirmative action admissions policies in many higher education affirmative action cases. They argue they had a substantial interest in the university's being allowed to continue to consider race as a factor in admissions, as well as that their interest was not adequately represented by the university defendants.

However, minority students' narrative has been marginalized in higher education affirmative action cases. Courts at varying levels have either refused to hear the minority students' narrative via the denial of intervention or marginalized the narrative of minority students who have intervened.

Invisible Interests and the Denial of Intervention: *Hopwood v. Texas* and *Students for Fair Admissions v. Harvard*

In some cases, minority students' narrative has been invisible because intervention was denied. For example, in *Hopwood v. Texas*,[5] a Caucasian applicant to the University of Texas Law School filed suit against the state of Texas, the Board of Regents of the Texas State University System, and the University of Texas Law School, claiming that the law school's admissions procedures that considered race as an admissions factor were unconstitutional. Two groups representing minority students, the Thurgood Marshall Legal Society and the Black Pre-Law Association, sought to intervene in the lawsuit.

The district court denied the motion to intervene, and the Fifth Circuit affirmed the denial of the motion, finding that the intervenors failed to establish that the law school would not adequately represent the intervenors' interests. The Fifth Circuit concluded that the proposed intervenors failed to demonstrate that the law school would not strongly defend its affirmative action policy or that the intervenors had a separate defense for the program based on a past discrimination argument.

Despite the common goals of the University of Texas Law School and the minority applicants for intervention to maintain the race-conscious admissions policy, the minority students presented a narrative that was far from identical to that of the university. The proposed intervenors argued that they had an interest in both maintaining the law school's then-existing admissions policy, as well as in eliminating vestiges of past discrimination. The proposed intervenors also proffered that race-conscious remedies were necessary responses to the past discriminatory practices of the state and the university. The proposed intervenors further claimed that their unique narrative would provide better evidence of such past discrimination.

Even when minority students have been designated amici, this is not an adequate substitute for intervention. For example, in *Students for Fair Admissions v. Harvard*,[6] minority applicants and current students were denied intervenor status, but granted amicus curiae status. Although the minority students and applicants, as amici, were able to put on crucial evidence about the use of legacy admissions at Harvard, they were not able to fully explicate their narrative.

Students for Fair Admissions v. Harvard College was filed in 2014 by conservative activist Edward Blum, who formed Students for Fair Admissions to become plaintiffs in an affirmative action case against Harvard. They argued that Harvard's admissions policy discriminates against Asian American applicants in violation of Title VI of the Civil Rights Act of 1964.[7]

The Lawyers' Committee for Civil Rights moved on behalf of minority applicants and students to become intervenors in the litigation.[8] The students argued for intervention as a matter of right and in the alternative for permissive intervention. The minority students' position was that they needed to be parties to the case because, while they ultimately agreed with Harvard's goal to maintain a race-conscious admissions policy, they did not believe that Harvard would properly explain the role that legacy admissions plays in the overall Harvard admissions policy or that Harvard would strongly represent the views of minority students.

Ultimately, the district court denied the motion for intervention,[9] convinced that the minority students' interests would be fully represented by Harvard. The district court instead gave the minority students "amicus plus" status, which allowed them to present their own briefs related to summary judgment and to put on their own witnesses at trial. Organizations, such as the NAACP Legal Defense Fund and the Asian American Legal Defense and Education Fund were also granted amicus curiae status to represent the narrative of minority students.

While amici status provided Black and Latino students with some representation that was critical to the district court's ruling in favor of Harvard, amici status is not as favorable as intervenor status. For example, as intervenors, the Black and Latino students would have been able to craft their own theory of the primary case.

Marginalized Interests and Compromised Intervention: *Grutter* and *Gratz*

Even where minority students successfully moved to intervene, their narratives have been marginalized. In such cases, courts largely ignored the students' arguments, witnesses, and evidence. This includes the two University of Michigan affirmative action cases: *Grutter v. Bollinger*[10] and *Gratz v. Bollinger*.[11]

In 1997, Caucasian plaintiffs filed two separate lawsuits challenging admissions procedures at the University of Michigan Law School and the College of Literature, Arts, and Science.

In *Grutter*, plaintiff Barbara Grutter claimed that the law school's admissions process violated the Equal Protection Clause of the Fourteenth Amendment and Title VI of the Civil Rights Act of 1964 by considering an applicant's race or ethnicity in the admissions process. A group of 41 individual minority students, plus three pro–affirmative action coalitions, applied for intervention, contending that the law school could not adequately represent their interests. Specifically, the applicants argued that the law school would fail to raise several defenses—including its past discriminatory practices and the continuing use of racially discriminatory admissions criteria—and would not be able to produce sufficient evidence related to segregation and resegregation of educational institutions.[12]

The intervenors in *Grutter* and *Gratz* presented a unique narrative characterized by three aspects: the link between the race-conscious admissions programs and the university's history of overt racial discrimination unlikely to be raised by the university; the institutional racism undergirding the use of LSAT scores and GPA as admissions criteria; and the state's unitary education system of K–16.

The district court in *Grutter* initially denied the applicants' motion to intervene as a matter of right, finding—similar to the Fifth Circuit in *Hopwood*—that the applicants failed to establish that they had a different interest from the law school defendants or that the defendants would not adequately represent the applicants' interest. The court concluded that the applicants had the same "ultimate objective" as the defendants: to preserve the current admissions policy that takes race and ethnicity into consideration.[13]

Similarly, the district court in the related *Gratz* case also denied the intervenor applicants' motion to intervene. The applicants in *Gratz* included 17 African American and Latino/a high-school students, who intended to apply or had already applied to the College of Literature, Arts, and Science, plus one organization, the Citizens for Affirmative Action's Preservation. The court concluded that the applicants lacked a substantial interest in the outcome of the litigation and had failed to demonstrate that the university defendants inadequately represented their interests.[14]

Hearing a consolidated appeal on the intervenor applicants' motions to intervene in *Gratz* and *Grutter*, the Sixth Circuit reversed and held that the intervenor applicants in both cases met the requirements for intervention under FRCP 24(a). The Sixth Circuit used "a 'rather expansive notion of the interest sufficient to invoke intervention of right'" and found that the applicants' interest in maintaining race and ethnicity as a factor in the admissions process was sufficient to meet the intervention requirements.[15]

However, the right to intervene is not a panacea; courts do not treat all intervenors with the same respect with which they treat other parties. The *Grutter* district court is the only court during the course of the litigation that directly addressed the intervenors' narrative—both their presentation of facts and legal arguments. The court held that creating racial diversity was not a compelling interest that would allow the law school to constitutionally consider race as a factor in admissions. After a detailed treatment of the plaintiffs' and defendants' evidence and legal arguments, the court provided a separate analysis of the intervenors' witnesses, exhibits, and legal arguments.

The court acknowledged that, while the reasons for the GPA and LSAT gap between Caucasians and the minority groups were "complex," much of it is "due to the fact that disproportionate numbers of Native Americans, African Americans, and Hispanics live and go to school in impoverished areas of the country." The court reasoned that, even if one accepts the intervenors' factual assertions, their arguments failed as a basis for upending the law school's admissions policy because the United States Supreme Court has rejected general societal discrimination as a justification for "race conscious decision making."[16]

In contrast to the district court's detailed—although disparate—treatment of the intervenors' evidence and legal arguments, the Sixth Circuit largely ignored the intervenors. Although the Sixth Circuit found that diversity was a compelling interest in the creation of the law school's admissions policy, it never addressed the intervenors' contention that the policy was justified based on past discrimination.

The Supreme Court affirmed the Sixth Circuit's opinion that the law school's use of race and ethnicity in its admissions policy did not violate either the Equal Protection Clause or Title VI. The Supreme Court found that, while the use of race is subject to a strict scrutiny analysis to assure its compliance with the Fourteenth Amendment, creating diversity in the law school environment is a compelling government interest and the law school's 1992 policy was narrowly tailored to meet this goal. The majority opinion completely ignored the intervenors' past discrimination as an alternative justification for the law school's admission's policy. Moreover, in the factual and procedural history of the case, the majority failed to even acknowledge that the intervenors applied for intervention and that, after being included in the case, presented thirty hours of testimony at trial.

Conclusion

Since the inception of FRCP 24, the most prominent policy reason underlying intervention is the need to protect the interests of third parties that are not present in the lawsuit. In the realm of public law litigation, and specifically affirmative action litigation, intervention is necessary to allow minority students who would be affected by the outcome of the litigation an opportunity to be heard by the courts.

Despite this policy reason, intervenors remain outsiders in such litigation. Trial and appellate courts in higher education affirmative action cases, even after intervention, have treated the litigation as private (bipolar-type) litigation. In the *Grutter* and *Gratz* cases at the University of Michigan, the courts responded to the litigation framework established by the original parties to the lawsuit—the plaintiff and the university defendant. The original parties generally asked the courts to address a single question: Is the university entitled under the Fourteenth Amendment to use race as a factor in admissions to enhance the diversity of the student body? As a result, courts have made the diversity justification the central issue in all of these cases.

The intervenors attempted to broaden the framework of the litigation by including additional justifications for the race-conscious admissions program: namely, past discrimination and the discriminatory effects of current admissions criteria. The trial and appellate courts essentially rejected the intervenors' attempts to add information outside of the framework set up by the plaintiff and defendant. In this way, the court reacted to the intervenors' arguments in the mode of private rights litigation.

Courts' efforts to limit the framework or scope of litigation by ignoring intervenors' facts and legal arguments displaces the balance of interests that should be considered on a motion to intervene. The court should balance the interests of the original parties and the court in a streamlined, less complex case, on the one hand, against the interest of the intervenors in a more accurate and fuller determination of the legal and factual issues on the other. However, once the court has decided that the interests weigh in favor of allowing intervention, the court should fully consider the evidence and legal arguments presented by the intervenors as a guide and an aid to the court.

NOTES

Acknowledgment: This chapter is updated and adapted from a previously published article: Danielle R. Holley, *Narrative Highground: The Failure of Intervention as a Procedural Device in Affirmative Action Litigation*, 54 Case Western Res. L. Rev. 103 (2003).

1 This chapter uses the phrase "minority students." In all of the cases discussed in this chapter, the intervenors or putative intervenors are focused primarily on protecting the interests of Black and Latino/Latina students. This is an important distinction, because in *SSFA v. Harvard College* the plaintiffs claim to represent the interests of Asian applicants and students.

2 Michigan State AFL-CIO v. Miller, 103 F.3d 1240, 1245 (6th Cir. 1997).

3 F.R.C.P. 24(a).

4 Trbovich v. United Mine Workers, 404 U.S. 528, 538 (1972).

5 21 F.3d 603 (5th Cir. 1994).

6 308 F.R.D. 39 (D. Mass. 2015).

7 *Id.*

8 Brief in Support of Students' Motion to Intervene, SFFA v. Harvard College, 308 F.R.D. 39 (D. Mass. April 29, 2015) (No. 1:14-cv-14176-ADB).

9 Order granting "amicus plus" status, SFFA v. Harvard College, 308 F.R.D. 39 (D. Mass. June 15, 2015) (No. 1:14-cv-14176-ADB).

10 *Grutter V*, 123 S. Ct. 2325 (2003).

11 123 S. Ct. 2411 (2003).

12 *Grutter V*, 123 S. Ct. at 2332; Grutter v. Bollinger (Grutter IV), 288 F.3d 732, 735 (6th Cir. 2002).

13 Opinion and Order Denying Motion to Intervene, Grutter v. Bollinger (Grutter I), 16 F. Supp. 2d 797 (E.D. Mich. Aug. 17, 1998) (No. 97-CV-75923-DT).

14 *See* Gratz v. Bollinger, 122 F. Supp. 2d 811 (E.D. Mich. 2003).

15 Grutter II, 188 F.3d 394, 398 (6th Cir. 1999) (quoting Michigan State AFL-CIO v. Miller, 103 F.3d 1240, 1245 (6th Cir. 1997)).

16 Grutter v. Bollinger (Grutter III), 137 F. Supp. 2d 821, 865, 869 (E.D. Mich. 2001), *rev'd*, 288 F.3d 732 (6th Cir. 2002), *aff'd*, 123 S. Ct. 2325 (2003).

35

Class Actions and the "Day in Court" Ideal

Class Actions as Collective Power Against Subordination

SERGIO J. CAMPOS

The white firefighters watched the case from the sidelines. The case, *Ensley Branch of the NAACP v. Seibels,*[1] was a consolidation of two class actions filed on behalf of black firefighters in Birmingham, Alabama. Both alleged that the City of Birmingham administered a test to screen firefighter applicants that discriminated against African Americans[2] in violation of Title VII of the Civil Rights Act.[3] After a trial on some issues, the parties entered into a consent decree with the city, "provid[ing] for goals for promotion of blacks within the fire department."[4] The white firefighters challenged this decree as amicus curiae.[5] After the consent decree was entered as a judgment, the white firefighters filed two lawsuits alleging that the consent decree *itself* violated Title VII because its employment goals would result in "reverse discrimination" against them.[6]

The latter lawsuit, *In re Birmingham Reverse Discrimination Employment Litigation,*[7] was dismissed by the district court as an "impermissible collateral attack" of a consent decree.[8] However, the Eleventh Circuit reversed, relying on "the policy against requiring third parties to submit to bargains in which their interests were either ignored or sacrificed."[9] The United States Supreme Court, in *Martin v. Wilks,*[10] affirmed the Eleventh Circuit, citing "our 'deep-rooted historic tradition that everyone should have [their] own day in court.'"[11]

On the one hand, class actions such as *NAACP v. Seibels* allow the US civil litigation system to address structural harms like the subordination of African Americans in employment markets. On the other, to accomplish such systemic change, class actions may appear in tension with the "deep-rooted historic tradition" of the individual's right to their "day in court."[12]

Critical Race Theory's Interrogation of Class Actions

The initial lawsuits challenging the Birmingham Fire Department's employment practices were litigated concurrently with the emergence of Critical Race Theory,[13] a scholarly movement that seeks to bring to light how formally equal aspects of the law can have subordinating effects on racial groups.[14] One goal of Critical Race Theory is to challenge the "curiously constricted understanding of race and power" dominant in mainstream legal thinking by challenging the terms of the "traditional civil rights discourse."[15]

As recognized by other scholars,[16] a critical approach is particularly useful in analyzing class actions because these procedures self-consciously challenge any "deep-rooted historic tradition that everyone should have their day in court." As explained below, class actions challenge the day-in-court ideal because they are innovations that deal with situations where the right to one's day in court is itself problematic. This ideal can undermine the enforcement of substantive rights. One can say that class actions are examples of the critical approach in action, as they arose precisely from a critical examination of unchallenged mainstream legal thinking.

The "Day in Court" Ideal

In writing for the Supreme Court in *Martin v. Wilks*, Justice Rehnquist prefaced his invocation of the "day in court" tradition by noting that "[a]ll agree that '[i]t is a principle of general application in Anglo-American jurisprudence that one is not bound by a judgment in personam in litigation in which he is not designated as a party or to which he has not been made a party by service of process.'"[17] The quoted language is technical, but it clearly expresses the day-in-court ideal. In essence, the quote states that a judgment cannot apply to a person unless that person is formally made a *party* to the proceeding, either by consent or service of process. In other words, a court cannot enter a judgment affecting a person's rights unless that person has been afforded a day in court.

But despite its foundational place in our concept of procedural due process, the ideal is only one facet of access to justice. Indeed, an over-simplified vision of an individual standing before a judge and having their day in court can pose a barrier to justice. Put simply, we can't all go it alone. And—as seen in *Martin v. Wilks*—the concept of one's day in court may be used as a sword, not a shield, against civil rights judgments.

Martin v. Wilks highlighted how prior litigation could potentially compromise the interests of persons who were not parties to that litigation. One commonsense solution to this problem is to allow affected persons such as the white firefighters to *participate* in the prior action. A right to participate—to have one's day in court—would allow a party to defend their own interests[18] and not be at the mercy of existing parties who may have their own, conflicting agendas.

Although the day in court is a "principle of general application in Anglo-American jurisprudence," the Supreme Court has also stated that "there is a recognized exception that . . . the judgment in a 'class' or 'representative' suit, to which some members of the class are parties, may bind members of the class or those represented who were not made parties to it."[19] What makes the class action an "exception"? Under FRCP 23, the federal class action rule, "[o]ne or more members of a class may sue or be sued as representative parties on behalf of all members" if certain requirements are met[20] and the proposed class action fits within one of three categories.[21] In other words, a party can sue on behalf of a nonparty, and have a court adjudicate that nonparty's rights, without the participation of that nonparty. Accordingly, a class action by definition is a procedure that permits one party to take away another person's day in court, which is what has led the Supreme Court to view the class action as a "recognized exception."[22]

Class Actions as a "Day in Court" Problem

Arguably, one can view a class action as simply facilitating one's day in court, rather than taking it away.[23] For example, Rule 23(b)(3) defines a category of class actions that may be maintained if, among other things, common issues "predominate" and the class action is "superior" to other procedures.[24] If a Rule 23(b)(3) class action is certified, Rule 23 further provides that "the court must direct to class members the best notice practicable under the circumstances" and that the notice must inform the class members "that the court will exclude from the class any member who requests exclusion."[25] Thus, Rule 23(b)(3) can be read as preserving a party's day in court unless the party consents to the class action by not opting out.

But this facilitating view of the class action does not fully capture the class action in operation. First, Rule 23 does not require notice or an opportunity to opt out for the other categories of class actions, including the Rule 23(b)(2) class actions utilized in *Martin v. Wilks*.[26] Second, the consent provided by the Rule 23(b)(3) opt-out is weak at best. By its terms, Rule 23 requires only the "best notice that is practicable under the circumstances," and the reality is that the notice provided in actual class actions is often difficult to understand and ignored.[27]

But the most important reason why a class action, even a Rule 23(b)(3) class action, should not be viewed as facilitating a day in court surfaces when one examines the class certification process more closely. Consider, for example, the classic example of when a class action is justified—litigation in which "small recoveries do not provide the incentive for any individual to bring a solo action prosecuting his or her rights."[28] The Supreme Court has stated that facilitating small claims litigation is "[t]he policy at the very core of the class action mechanism."[29]

Small claims litigation involves situations where a day in court is valued the *least*, because by definition the litigation involves claims that are too small to motivate the filing of a lawsuit. As colloquially put by Judge Posner, "only a lunatic or a fanatic sues for $30."[30] If anything, the class action enables small claims litigation by effectively *denying* each plaintiff their right to a day in court or, more precisely, by assigning that right to someone else. Although each individual plaintiff has a right to opt out of a (b)(3) class, they have no incentive to bring an individual suit. By contrast, a class action attorney has such an incentive because they can obtain a fee award that is typically a percentage of the damages for the class as a whole.[31] Thus, as recognized by the Supreme Court, a class action enables small claims litigation "by aggregating relatively paltry potential recoveries into something worth someone's (*usually an attorney's*) labor."[32]

The class action does more than provide plaintiffs an incentive to finance the litigation. It also serves an important regulatory function.[33] In the absence of a procedure to force the parties to share the costs of common issues, the litigation never happens, thereby allowing, say, a manufacturer to escape liability for its wrongful conduct. Accordingly, in the absence of a class action, that manufacturer has no incentive to care about the safety of its potential customers when the harms are too small to provide an incentive to bring an individual lawsuit.[34]

Put another way, in the small claims context, preserving the abstract ideal of a day in court *causes* more injuries, not fewer, because it prevents the forced sharing of costs necessary to enable litigation. Under these circumstances, the day in court, ironically, is an obstacle to vindicating the rights of the class members rather than acting as the safeguard that our "deep-rooted tradition" presumes.

It is important to note that the same problem can arise in actions involving injunctive relief, as in *Martin v. Wilks*. Admittedly, one can sympathize with the white firefighters not wanting to be bound by consent decrees they had no voice in—decrees that would potentially diminish their employment prospects. But their interests in preserving the status quo was vigorously defended by the City of Birmingham itself.

Indeed, the Supreme Court's holding protecting the white firefighters' participation rights has the effect of delaying the implementation of consent decrees by "expos[ing] every decree to the risk of subsequent challenge, actually to an almost endless series of challenges."[35] The result might be not only to delay implementation of such decrees but also to discourage the filing of lawsuits in the first place. Here, protecting a day in court would have little effect on the city's employment practices.

The small claims and *Martin v. Wilks* examples above show how a day in court can make matters worse, not better. This is because, in both situations—each involving a single defendant harming numerous plaintiffs—the myth of the sanctity of one's day in court may prevent the plaintiffs from holding the defendant accountable. The class action solves these problems by in effect reducing the days in court of affected individuals so that they do not undermine the collective goal of determining the most just resolution.

When the "Day in Court" Is Itself the Problem

If the right to one's "day in court" can be problematic, then what process is due? One answer is suggested by *Hansberry v. Lee*.[36] This case, decided in 1940, concerned an African American family who moved to an area of Chicago that was subject to a racially restrictive covenant.[37] The covenant, however, was only enforceable if "'95 per cent of the frontage' within the described area" signed on to it.[38]

Residents filed suit to enjoin the Hansberrys from moving in to the area, contending that the requisite number of residents had signed the covenant.[39] To prove this, the residents contended that the 95-percent-of-the-frontage issue had already been decided in a prior class action, *Burke v. Kleiman*.[40] Accordingly, the Hansberrys, who were included as members of the class in *Burke v. Kleiman*, were *precluded* from relitigating the issue.

The Supreme Court concluded that precluding the Hansberrys violated due process. Specifically, the Court concluded that the Hansberrys' interests obviously were not adequately represented in *Burke v. Kleiman*.[41] Unlike the Hansberrys, the class representative in *Burke* sought to enforce the covenant, not challenge it.[42] Thus, to preclude the Hansberrys based on the prior class action—to pretend that the class in *Kleiman* represented their interests when in fact it fought directly against them—would offend due process.[43]

Hansberry defined "due process" in terms of whether "the procedure adopted . . . fairly insures the protection of the interests of absent parties who are to be bound by it."[44] Put another way, due process requires "not a day in court but the right to have one's interest adequately represented."[45]

Shifting the due process focus from the right to a day in court to the *function* of the day in court has a number of advantages. First, and most obviously, it provides courts flexibility when a procedural right such as a day in court is counterproductive. Second, such a shift provides for a more direct assessment of what is at stake. A blinkered focus on the day in court as the lodestar of due process can lead a court to lose sight of the reasons why a day in court is insisted upon in the first place.

This functional approach to due process is not only consistent with Critical Race Theory; arguably, it is the approach that animated the creation of the modern class action. The modern version of Rule 23, the federal class action rule, first promulgated in the 1966 amendments to the Federal Rules, was enacted precisely "to shake the law of class actions free of abstract categories . . . and to rebuild the law on functional lines responsive to those recurrent life patterns which call for mass litigation through representative parties."[46] Indeed, one goal of the amendments was to facilitate the civil rights litigation then working its way through the federal court system.[47] Such an approach is the very essence of Critical Race Theory and one worth continuing to take toward all procedures.

NOTES

1 Ensley Branch of the NAACP v. Seibels, No. S:74-CV-00212, 1977 WL 806, at *1 (N.D. Ala. Jan. 10, 1977), *aff'd in part, vacated in part, rev'd in part*, 31 F.3d 1548 (11th Cir. 1994).

2 *Ensley Branch*, 1977 WL 806 at *1.

3 *Id.* at *19–20.

4 Martin v. Wilks, 490 U.S. 755, 759 (1989).

5 *Id.*

6 *Id.* at 759–60.

7 No. S:84-CV-00903, 1985 WL 56690, at *1 (N.D. Ala. Dec. 20, 1985).

8 *Id.* at *24.

9 *Martin*, 490 U.S. at 761.

10 490 U.S. 755 (1989).

11 *Id.* at 762 (quoting 18 Charles Wright, Arthur Miller & Edward Cooper, Federal Practice and Procedure § 4449, at 417 (1981)).

12 *Id.*

13 *See Introduction* to Critical Race Theory: The Key Writings that Formed the Movement, at xxx (Kimberlé Crenshaw, Neil Gotanda, Gary Peller & Kendall Thomas eds., 1995).

14 *Id.* at xiii.

15 *Id.* at xiv–xv.

16 *See, e.g.*, Francisco Valdes, *Procedure, Policy and Power: Class Actions and Social Justice in Historical and Comparative Perspective*, 24 Ga. St. Univ. L. Rev. 627, 629 (2008) (focusing on the class action as an "antisubordination procedural device"); *see also* Roy L. Brooks, Critical Procedure 183–204 (1998) (applying a critical race theoretical examination of class actions).

17 Martin v. Wilks, 490 U.S. 755, 761 (1989) (second alteration in original) (emphasis omitted) (quoting Hansberry v. Lee, 311 U.S. 32, 40 (1940)).

18 Arguably the white firefighters in *Martin v. Wilks* did have a day in court but chose not to defend themselves by declining to intervene early in the litigation. *See* 490 U.S. 755, 772–73 (1989) (Stevens, J., dissenting).

19 *Hansberry*, 311 U.S. at 40–41 (citations omitted).

20 Fed. R. Civ. P. 23(a)(1)–(4) (requiring a showing of numerosity, commonality, typicality, and adequacy of representation).

21 Fed. R. Civ. P. 23(b) (defining three categories of permissible class actions).

22 *Hansberry*, 311 U.S. at 41.

23 Diane Wood Hutchinson, *Class Actions: Joinder or Representational Device?*, 1983 Sup. Ct. Rev. 459, 459 (1983).

24 Fed. R. Civ. P. 23(b)(3).

25 Fed. R. Civ. P. 23(c)(2)(B).

26 *See* Maureen Carroll, *Class Action Myopia*, 65 Duke L.J. 843, 847 (2016) (noting that current debates fail to distinguish among different categories of class actions).

27 Fed. R. Civ. P. 23(c)(2)(B); *see, e.g.*, Myriam Gilles, *Class Dismissed: Contemporary Judicial Hostility to Small-Claims Consumer Class Actions*, 59 DePaul L. Rev. 305, 316 (2010).

28 Amchem Prods., Inc. v. Windsor, 521 U.S. 591, 617 (1997).

29 *Id.* at 617; *see also* Amgen Inc. v. Conn. Ret. Plans & Trust Funds, 568 U.S. 455, 478 (2013).

30 Carnegie v. Household Int'l, Inc., 376 F.3d 656, 661 (7th Cir. 2004).

31 Principles of the Law of Aggregate Litig. § 3.13 cmt. b (Am. Law Inst. 2010).

32 *Amchem Prods., Inc.*, 521 U.S. at 617 (emphasis added).

33 *See* Harry Kalven, Jr. & Maurice Rosenfield, *The Contemporary Function of the Class Suit*, 8 U. Chi. L. Rev. 684, 720 (1941).

34 David Rosenberg, *Mass Tort Class Actions: What Defendants Have and Plaintiffs Don't*, 37 Harv. J. on Legis. 393, 404–08 (2000).

35 Owen Fiss, The Law as It Could Be 110 (2003).

36 Hansberry v. Lee, 311 U.S. 32 (1940).

37 *Id.* at 37–38.

38 *Id.* at 38.

39 *Id.* The fact was actually stipulated by the parties, and the facts showed that "only about 54 percent of the frontage had signed the agreement." *Id.* at 38.

40 *Id.*

41 *Id.* at 45.

42 *Id.* at 44.

43 *Id.* at 45.

44 *Id.* at 42.

45 Fiss, *supra* note 35, at 112.

46 Benjamin Kaplan, *A Prefatory Note*, 10 B.C. L. Rev. 497, 497 (1969). Kaplan was the reporter for the 1966 Amendments. *Id.*

47 David Marcus, *Flawed But Noble, Desegregation Litigation and Its Implications for the Modern Class Action*, 63 Fla. L. Rev. 657, 695–97 (2011).

36

Reinvigorating Commonality

Gender and Class Actions

BROOKE COLEMAN AND ELIZABETH PORTER

The modern class action, the modern feminist movement, and Title VII of the Civil Rights Act of 1964 were all products of the creativity and turmoil of the 1960s. As late as 1961—one year after Justice Felix Frankfurter rejected new law-school graduate Ruth Bader Ginsburg as a law clerk because she was a woman—the United States Supreme Court unanimously upheld the constitutionality of a Florida statute that required men, but not women, to serve on juries, on the ground that women's primary role was in the home.[1] As Betty Friedan put it in 1963's *The Feminine Mystique*, "In almost every professional field, in business and in the arts and sciences, women are still treated as second-class citizens."[2] But change was imminent. The Equal Pay Act of 1963, Title VII of the Civil Rights Act, the founding of the ACLU Women's Rights Project, and a rising social and intellectual feminist movement brought women's equality into the national conversation. Simultaneously—at least in part in response to the civil rights movement and the Civil Rights Act—an (all-male) Judicial Conference and Supreme Court in 1966 ushered in the modern era of collective litigation by promulgating Federal Rule of Civil Procedure 23, and more specifically, Rule 23(b)(2), which provided a formal structure for civil rights plaintiffs to seek aggregate relief for violations of federal and state antidiscrimination laws. Together, these phenomena gave impetus to communities of women to combat legal and cultural injustices through the courts. The result has been widespread improvement in the lives of working women—and men—across many industries.[3]

This chapter examines the interplay of Rule 23(b)(2) class actions, feminism, and Title VII sex discrimination doctrine since that period to show that the theoretical concept of commonality—cohesion, unity—in the women's movement has had a significant impact on the ability of women to seek collective redress for workplace discrimination. As Anita Hill has contended, "Class action lawsuits can force industry-wide change, even in the most entrenched, male-dominated industries."[4] Or at least they could at one point. The continuing trends toward tightening certification requirements, minimizing reliance on statistics, and shunting suits into individualized arbitration threaten to undermine the enforcement function that is central to Rule 23(b)(2).

The Waves of Feminism and Class Actions

Although it is difficult to confine diffuse social movements within narrow time periods, scholars and activists describe four periods, or waves, of US feminism—or perhaps three and a half. The first wave, which is often dated to the Seneca Falls Convention in 1848, sought fundamental legal rights for women: the right to vote, to own property, and to have custodial rights over children.[5] This groundbreaking phase of US feminism took place without the benefit of either the Civil Rights Act of 1964 or Rule 23. With the establishment of a birth control clinic in 1916 by Margaret Sanger, this wave of feminism also laid the foundation for reproductive rights. Notwithstanding these milestones, women were systematically excluded from power in the workforce during this time, an exclusion that was doubly harmful for working-class women and women of color.[6] Although interest in organized feminism waned after the passage of the Nineteenth Amendment extending the franchise to women, feminists continued to push for social change during the interwar period, proposing the Equal Rights Amendment (ERA) and joining labor movements. Even during this early period of US feminism, however, there was a cultural divide between (generally more privileged) "equality feminists," who prioritized seeking formal legal equality with men through developments like the ERA, and the so-called social justice feminists, who were more focused on the pragmatic needs of working-class women and women of color. These differences persisted throughout the 1940s and 1950s.

Feminism's second wave—the modern women's rights movement—gained momentum in the 1960s, resulting in the passage and enforcement by courts of Title VII, the formation of the National Organization for Women and other women's rights groups, and the 1968 bra-burning at the Miss America pageant.[7] It is during this second wave that the amended Rule 23 came into being and matured. Second-wave feminists radically altered the legal and cultural landscape for US women, successfully advocating for battered women's shelters, reproductive rights, equal access to jobs that explicitly or functionally excluded women, sexual harassment policies (indeed, coining the term "sexual harassment"[8]), women's studies departments in colleges and universities, and equal funding for education and extracurricular enrichment, among other things. Some—though by no means all—of these victories came in the form of Title VII class actions brought by the Equal Opportunity Employment Commission (EEOC), by labor unions, and by individuals. During this period, feminists also developed (or redeveloped) theories of gender as a social construct, of systemic gender discrimination, and—among the rising number of feminist lawyers—of feminist jurisprudence. The second-wave feminist movement was one of the nation's largest social movements. Despite, or perhaps because of, the movement's size, feminism lost its focus under the resurgence of conservative politics under President Ronald Reagan in the 1980s.

In this sense, feminism's third wave—which emerged in response to the outrage surrounding Justice Clarence Thomas's 1991 confirmation hearings—was in part a reaction to, and an oversimplification of, the second wave. "Younger feminists argued that the second wave was almost exclusively white (ignoring second-wave feminists of color), overly puritanical . . . (ignoring diverse second-wave perspectives on sexuality), and prescriptive . . . (ignoring the multiplicity of second-wave feminisms, plural)."[9] The third wave was defined by individualism and intersectionality, and its goals—perhaps because discrimination had become less explicit than it was during the age of single-sex job descriptions—were more difficult to tie to a unifying political theme or action. In fact, it is unclear whether this third wave can really be described as a feminist movement at all; many women of this generation refused to self-identify as feminists. The glass ceiling and the pay gap persisted for women, but the concept of feminism became tainted or, at a minimum, antiquated. The effects of this individualism permeated the legal academy, where feminist theory tapered off, although several influential scholars continued their work and new voices drew on social science literature to critique the systemic, implicit barriers to freedom from discrimination.

Activists have identified the current age of feminism—characterized as the fourth wave—with social media and podcasts, with intersectionality and internationalism, with fluidity of gender and sexual orientation, with marriage equality, and with ongoing battles against sexual assault, particularly—though not only—on college campuses.[10] In those areas, activists and scholars have accomplished sweeping change, often with vital assistance from courts.[11] Despite (or perhaps because of) this wide embrace, for a time it remained unclear whether these impulses would coalesce into a wide-ranging feminist movement with social and legal influence such as Black Lives Matter. The 2017 Women's March on Washington, which adopted a consciously intersectional and inclusive agenda and spurred similar marches across the country, may have signaled the onset of a newly invigorated, national movement; time will tell.

Parallels in Class Action Doctrine

Neither the amended Rule 23 nor Title VII existed during the first wave of feminism. Once Rule 23 was adopted, however, the second wave of feminism was marked by a significant number of Title VII class actions, as courts grew increasingly comfortable with the new procedural vehicle and were willing to confront the widespread, generally explicit, discrimination against working women that persisted into the 1980s. Indeed, there were more second-wave class action cases adjudicating women's rights under Title VII than in the third or fourth waves combined.[12]

The cases during this period are held together by some notable common themes. First—in line with the goals of second-wave feminism—"second-wave" Title VII class actions for gender discrimination tended to challenge explicit bias against women (or, on occasion, men) as embodied in facially discriminatory employment policies or practices. In other words, rarely was a case brought that challenged structural sexism or implicit bias. Instead, these early Title VII class actions challenged policies such as gender-based job classifications and requirements, gender-differentiated pension fund contributions, and sex-discriminatory promotion practices.

Second, notwithstanding the offensive jocularity that surrounded the inclusion of "sex" in Title VII,[13] and the initial reluctance by the EEOC to prioritize sex discrimination, courts during this period were by and large receptive to the efforts of women to obtain redress using Rule 23. This positive reception was due partly to the auspicious conflation of courts' acceptance of the class action device and a robust, activist feminist movement.

Reinforcing this procedural receptivity was a vigorous, nationwide feminist movement—described above—that provided political and theoretical support for women's workplace equality. Rule 23 may have been undertheorized at this time, but women's equality was not. The Department of Justice, the EEOC, Congress, and the courts were all responsive to an active, organized movement advocating for women's equality. As a result, many second-wave Title VII class action plaintiffs prevailed. District courts taking a narrow view of discrimination in these cases were reversed with surprising frequency. Perhaps the emblematic second-wave Title VII class action was *UAW v. Johnson Controls, Inc.*, in which the Supreme Court held that the defendant company's policy of excluding women, but not men, of childbearing age from jobs that might expose them to lead violated Title VII. The Court found the bias in the policy to be "obvious," and it rejected the company's defense that the policy was necessary for fetal protection.[14] Notably, in upholding the women's claims, the Court never even analyzed Rule 23's requirements. During the heyday of second-wave feminism, Title VII plaintiffs made substantial gains for women in the workplace, including through the use of the new Rule 23.

But just as the third wave of feminism—starting in the early 1990s—was less unified and weaker than its predecessor, Title VII class actions also entered a more complex phase during this period. Notably, one result of courts' lack of Rule 23 analysis in early cases was a smaller corpus of cases broadly supporting (and explaining) certification, including the requirement of "commonality" and the scope of Rule 23(b)(2)'s reach. Though it became a routine element of federal litigation, Rule 23 remained something of a cipher. Similarly, the blatant nature of the discriminatory policies in the 1970s and 1980s made the cases of that era only somewhat informative of the less obvious, more subjective forms of discrimination that permeated Title VII class actions starting in the 1990s for plaintiffs in race discrimination cases as well as sex discrimination cases. In addition, the political landscape shifted during the 1990s, as both feminism and class actions suffered backlashes.

Nevertheless, in practice, many courts in the 1990s adhered to their earlier, pragmatic approach to class certification. As a result of these contradictory trends, class actions during the third wave of feminism present a mixed picture. Courts in many third-wave Title VII sex discrimination cases certified classes where the alleged discrimination was based on discretionary promotional or other employment practices across a company, frequently finding expert statistical evidence sufficient to establish Rule 23(a)(2)'s commonality requirement.[15]

With the addition of potential compensatory and punitive damages to Title VII, some courts sought to balance classwide and individualized harms by certifying hybrid classes, with Rule 23(b)(2) governing the claims for declaratory and injunctive relief and Rule 23(b)(3) covering compensatory claims. Other courts—foreshadowing the Supreme Court's tone in *Wal-Mart v. Dukes*[16]—rejected commonality in situations where discretionary decisions were at play. These courts were skeptical of statistical experts, yet they also found anecdotal evidence insufficient. Often this hostility to commonality appeared when the class included women with significantly different job descriptions. On a deeper level, though, some of the cases rejecting commonality among classes of women evince disbelief that gender discrimination—rather than individual choices or a multitude of other factors—were causing the statistical differences.[17] At the same time, the divided, inwardly focused generation of third-wave feminists no longer presented a unified political or theoretical stance that could combat this skepticism.

The Supreme Court's decision in *Wal-Mart*—a case that sets the standard for Title VII class actions in feminism's fourth wave—combined and enshrined these various strains of skepticism. In one strike, the Court simultaneously contracted both its Rule 23 and Title VII jurisprudence. Indeed, as the third wave of feminism came to a close, the auspicious conflation of a flexible approach to Rule 23 and an active feminist movement had given way to class action skepticism and fractured feminism.

Entering the fourth wave, feminism and Title VII class actions continue to present a complicated story. On the bleak side, courts addressing Title VII class actions post–*Wal-Mart* have undoubtedly been affected by the *Wal-Mart* majority's cramped definition of commonality. Unsurprisingly, this is most apparent in cases, such as *Wal-Mart*, where there is no written or stated corporate policy of discrimination but instead an allegation that lower-level managers are exercising their discretion in variant discriminatory ways. As one court plainly explained: "[W]here persons who are afforded discretion exercise that discretion differently, commonality is not established."[18]

Yet, there is also hope: lawyers and courts are distinguishing *Wal-Mart* and finding ways to construct Title VII class actions that can withstand heightened scrutiny. *Ellis v. Costco Wholesale Corp.*,[19] for example, involved a nationwide class of women alleging discrimination in promotion and hiring. The *Ellis* class consisted of just two closely related management positions, and it alleged that Costco's decisions were guided by specific practices that came from top-level management. In this way, the case was different enough from *Wal-Mart* to survive certification; perhaps that is a sign that Title VII impact litigation can survive.

Much like the current wave of feminism—where the movement is at once atomizing and attempting to coalesce—the limitations placed on Title VII class actions threaten to reduce the effectiveness of this kind of litigation for all women. That *Ellis* helped only management-level women and relied on executive-level policies means that women in lower-paying jobs—those who are often discriminated against on the basis of inherent bias wielded through discretionary acts—may not be able to use Title VII class actions to remedy the discrimination they experience. In other words, current Title VII class actions and feminism suffer the same critique: they appear to help predominantly the haves rather than the have-nots.

Conclusion

Movements require new ideas and new people—new blood—to survive. Feminism and Title VII class action doctrine both need to harness the wisdom that middle age implies, as well as the ingenuity of a new generation of theorists and litigants. As history has demonstrated, when feminist scholars actively engage in the debate surrounding legal procedure and substance—as occurred in early Title VII litigation—courts will listen. Without scholarship that can theorize and translate feminist thought into the language of procedure, however, courts may fill that theoretical vacuum with holdings that indicate judicial doubts about the ongoing existence and severity of sex discrimination in the workplace. As in *Wal-Mart*, courts may presume that women "as women" lack commonality and that systemic bias is either overblown or a relic of the past—or both.

Despite a decade or more of backlash against feminism and against class actions, Title VII class actions under Rule 23(b)(2) remain a vital mechanism for eradicating sex discrimination in the workplace. It is possible to describe *Wal-Mart* as a bookend to an era of aggregate gender discrimination law—an era that made only partial progress and left many women behind. We hope that a new generation of lawyers, litigants, scholars, and activists will resist that narrative and will instead reinvigorate the concept of commonality among women.

NOTES

Acknowledgment: This chapter is updated and adapted from a previously published article: Brooke D. Coleman & Elizabeth G. Porter, *Reinvigorating Commonality: Gender and Class Actions*, 92 N.Y.U. L. Rev. 895 (2017).

1 Hoyt v. Florida, 368 U.S. 57, 58, 62 (1961) (upholding murder conviction by an all-male jury of woman who killed her husband).

2 Betty Friedan, *The Feminine Mystique* 374 (1963).

3 *See* Vicki Schultz, *Taking Sex Discrimination Seriously*, 91 Denv. U. L. Rev. 995, 1009 (2015).

4 Anita Hill, Opinion, *How to Disrupt Silicon Valley Sexism*, N.Y. Times, Aug. 9, 2017, at A19.

5 *See* Martha Minow, *Introduction: Finding Our Paradoxes, Affirming Our Beyond*, 24 Harv. C.R.-C.L. L. Rev. 1, 2–3 (1989).

6 *See* Angela Y. Davis, *Women, Race & Class* 159–60 (1983) (describing class and racial divides of first-wave feminist and suffrage movements); Penina Migda Glazer & Miriam Slater, *Unequal Colleagues: The Entrance of Women Into the Professions, 1890–1940* (1987).

7 In fact, the police barred the women from actually burning bras. *See* Nell Greenfieldboyce, *Pageant Protest Sparked Bra-Burning Myth*, Nat'l Pub. Radio (Sept. 5, 2008, 2:21 PM), www.npr.org.

8 *See* Gillian Thomas, *Because of Sex: One Law, Ten Cases, and Fifty Years that Changed American Women's Lives at Work*, 84–85 (2016) (describing how three

Cornell professors coined the term, which was picked up by a reporter and first appeared in the *New York Times* in August 1975).

9 Dorothy Sue Cobble, Linda Gordon & Astrid Henry, *Feminism Unfinished: A Short, Surprising History of American Women's Movements* 170 (2014).

10 *See, e.g.*, Roxane Gay, *Bad Feminist*, at xii–xiv (2014).

11 *See, e.g.*, Obergefell v. Hodges, 576 U.S. 644, 674–75 (2015) (holding that the Fourteenth Amendment mandates recognition of same-sex marriages).

12 The authors conducted a Westlaw search in the federal appellate court database for reported "class action!" decisions involving "women" or "gender" or "female." The results were then categorized by feminist-wave dates. The first wave of feminism included zero cases; the second wave included 126 cases; the third wave included nine cases; and the fourth wave included 22 cases. This research is on file with the authors and the *New York University Law Review*.

13 *See* Schultz, *supra* note 3, at 1014–21 (discussing and calling into question the story that some congressmen attempted to defeat the adoption of Title VII with the last-minute inclusion of sex discrimination).

14 499 U.S. 187, 197 (1991).

15 *See, e.g.*, Hnot v. Willis Grp. Holdings Ltd., 241 F.R.D. 204, 210 (S.D.N.Y. 2007) (relying on statistical evidence to find commonality in disparate impact case).

16 564 U.S. 338 (2011).

17 *See* Vicki Schultz & Stephen Petterson, *Race, Gender, Work, and Choice: An Empirical Study of the Lack of Interest Defense in Title VII Cases Challenging Job Segregation*, 59 U. Chi. L. Rev. 1073, 1124 (1992).

18 In re Wells Fargo Residential Mortg. Lending Discrimination Litig., No. 08-MD-01930, 2011 WL 3903117, at *4 (N.D. Cal. Sept. 6, 2011).

19 285 F.R.D. 492 (N.D. Cal. 2012).

37

Critical Procedure

Alternative Dispute Resolution and the Justices' "Second Wave" Constriction of Court Access and Claim Development

ERIC K. YAMAMOTO

In my 1996 article "ADR: Where Have the Critics Gone?,"[1] I described a hastening rush toward alternative dispute resolution (ADR) paired with a notable decline in mainstream scholarship critical of key aspects of ADR. I observed then that the ADR train had left the station and that critics of its impacts on societal "outsiders" were not welcome aboard.

Writing during a "First Wave" of efficiency procedural reforms in the 1980s through the mid-1990s, and drawing on the insights of pioneering scholars,[2] I asked whether this "ADR Express" undermined legal discourse and policy decisions critical of ADR's overall efficacy. ADR's overpowering salutary narrative, it appeared, tended especially to exclude, or at least overlook, those critical of ADR's harmful effects on marginalized social groups.

I cast these perceptions in preliminary fashion. Many have since materialized into procedural reality. This reality, as others and I now suggest, is integral to larger "Second Wave" procedural changes that commenced around the mid-2000s and continue today. A spate of restrictive United States Supreme Court rulings sharply constricts court access and claim development, so much so that some characterize it as a deformation of procedure[3] reflecting a sharply "restrictive ethos."[4]

During the ongoing Second Wave, a monumental ADR decision, *American Express Co. v. Italian Colors Restaurant*[5] (*AMEX*), dramatically, and perhaps traumatically for some, altered the justice landscape. *AMEX*, along with its predecessor *AT&T Mobility LLC v. Concepcion*[6] (*Concepcion*), through tight enforcement of small-print arbitration clauses in a wide array of contracts under the Federal Arbitration Act,[7] compels private arbitration of nearly all small claimant–versus–large business disputes and, moreover, compels those claimants' waiver of class adjudication.

These cases epitomize ADR's privatization (without judges, full discovery, or public scrutiny) and individuation (without broad joinder or cost-sharing) of claims by employees, consumers, tenants, small businesses, and discrimination claimants against more powerful businesses and institutions. The consequences are in-your-face startling. Backed by other cases, *AMEX* and *Concepcion* effectively block fair resolution of a wide range of potentially meritorious claims possessed by those of lesser societal stature or economic power. In doing so, they erect for many an insurmountable threshold barrier to justice. Moreover, the combined procedural rulings undercut major businesses' and institutions' substantive legal liability and diminish their public accountability—thereby undermining the rule of law.

These practical consequences do not result from fully vetted, formal procedural rulemaking. Rather, they emerge from the singular votes of a slim conservative majority of the Supreme Court—that is to say, significant procedural change by judicial fiat.

For this reason, and other reasons discussed below, alternative dispute resolution, through *AMEX* and *Concepcion*, now takes center stage in a conservative majority–generated deformation of procedure that, in Judge Weinstein's words, "under the guise of procedural efficiency . . . burden[s] the weak and the aggrieved unfairly, and . . . ultimately will undermine the legitimacy of the legal system."[8] In this Second Wave setting, the time is ripe through critical procedure inquiry to assess *AMEX* and *Concepcion* and the contemporary relevance of "ADR: Where Have the Critics Gone?".

Critical Procedure: An Analytical Framework

A developing critical procedure offers analytical tools for interrogating the often underexplored facets of present-day ADR—particularly how the Court's *AMEX* and *Concepcion* rulings are integral to the Second Wave's overall constriction of court access and claim development for those of comparatively lesser power. Critical procedure provides a contextual lens for this inquiry. As a complement to and departure from traditional legal analysis, it posits that "formalist notions of efficiency, neutrality and fairness have obscured the cumulative effects and attendant value judgments of procedural reforms."[9] From the vantage point of those lesser empowered, it interrogates:

> [W]hat is really at stake, who benefits and who is harmed (in the short and long term), who wields the behind-the-scenes power, which social values are supported and which are subverted, how political [or economic] concerns frame the legal questions, and how societal institutions and differing segments of the populace will be affected by the court's decision[s].[10]

Critical procedure emerges from critical legal studies and Critical Race Theory of the 1980s and 1990s[11] and new legal realism's continuing sociolegal study of the litigation process. Critical procedure advances a sharp "changing . . . narrative [in] civil procedure"[12]: "[A]ny attempt to understand procedural reform without attention to the legal and political philosophies [and interests] of its supporters and opponents, and without setting it in broader social [and political] context, is doomed."[13] Critical procedure thus explicitly and systematically integrates "changing social dynamics and consequences"[14] into its assessments.

Viewed in this light, critical procedure serves as a framework for realistically evaluating the impact of procedural changes. That framework is operationalized through insights into a given procedure's (or group of procedures') genesis, interpretation, application, alteration, and consequences.

Empowering/Disempowering

The first critical procedure insight highlights procedure as an "instrument of power." It stimulates inquiry into the impacts of litigation procedure on the empowerment or disempowerment of social groups. More specifically, it reveals ways that the litigation process enables people to coalesce because of group commonalities (including identity or similar harms) in joint pursuit of claims or forces them to disaggregate and pursue claims in isolation. It inquires into ways that procedure empowers communities to deploy litigation as a centerpiece for social justice organizing or compels them to individually litigate hypertechnical pieces of a controversy devoid of larger social content. And it assesses how procedure enables claimants to seek behavior-altering group remedies or impels them to craft narrow, individualized relief that, even when awarded, tends to preserve the institutional status quo.

Exposing the Myth of Inherent Neutrality

The second critical procedure insight dispels the myth of inherent procedural neutrality. Procedure's patina of neutrality (it is only process, not substance) at times disguises significant substantive consequences.

Critical procedure lifts the veil of inherent neutrality to reveal an often politicized process of rule formation and alteration. This veil-lifting exposes parries and thrusts over "neutral" efficiency procedural shift maneuvers that alter the impact of substantive law by affecting court access and claim development in ways that benefit some over others. It thus expands procedural inquiry beyond ordinary costs and burdens into the realm of social and economic consequences for individuals, organizations, governments, communities, businesses, and the judiciary itself.

Advantaging/Disadvantaging Some over Others

The third, and related, critical procedure insight reveals how procedure's differential effects, at times by design, substantively advantage those more economically powerful and disadvantage outsiders of lesser power, especially those challenging established political, social, or economic arrangements. I observed during the First Wave that efficiency reforms tended to discourage litigants on society's margins by compelling privatized dispute resolution, imposing punitive sanctions for cutting-edge filings, requiring greater factual support for some civil right filings, and shrinking the "information-gathering process and erect[ing] tougher obstacles to juries. They have pared down the system of public adjudication"[15] in ways that benefited some but not others.

Professor Brooke Coleman's recent study finds that the procedural limits on court access are in fact preventing plaintiffs from pursuing substantively meritorious claims.[16] This insight opens to scrutiny the political and economic underpinnings of the fights over procedural reform. It casts an eye on how procedural changes are affecting who wins and who loses in terms of legal outcomes as well as broad social and economic consequences.

Articulating Public Values/Shaping Public Consciousness

Building upon the others, the fourth critical procedure insight identifies the importance of the litigation of cutting-edge claims to public values articulation and to a reshaping of mainstream public consciousness about what is right and just. It underscores the dynamic interplay of pleadings, discovery, motions, and trial with parties, judges, community advocates, and media in imbuing social meaning to the "public" in public law litigation. For this reason, the fourth insight sees courts as more than forums for dispute resolution. They are also dynamic sites of "cultural performances."[17]

The litigation process, through subpoena power, enables participants to discover previously private information and develop claims and defenses. Through pleadings, discovery, motions, and the trial itself, parties are empowered to organize, assert, and publicize counternarratives that challenge dominant understandings, or master narratives, undergirding unfair political or social arrangements. In this way, public law litigation is not merely a process for resolving disputes; it is also a process that sometimes transforms narrow legal claims into larger public messages about social justice.

Highly public litigation becomes a vehicle for those without effective access to elective or bureaucratic power to participate actively in public debates about social controversies and to shape larger societal understandings and policy makers' actions over time.

Acknowledging Politics and Ideology Matters

The final critical procedure insight is that politics and ideology sometimes matter. This insight connects the others, and it reflects a twist on the familiar idea that "context matters." When procedural shifts generate markedly non-neutral impacts, substantially advantaging some over others, the idea that *ideology matters* explicitly directs inquiry toward the politics of procedure. That inquiry examines political and economic influences, with an emphasis on underlying value preferences that determine practical consequences.

This is because procedure is neither value-free nor a technical science. Both in formulation and operation, procedural systems embody often contested value choices about the importance of resources (or lack thereof) in resolving disputes; about whether similarly situated individuals should be allowed to band together to enter the courthouse and access the tools of factual discovery (particularly for discovery of private information located in defendants' files); about the significance of preliminary injunctive relief in forestalling damaging conduct at the risk of disrupting business or government operations; about the impact of the legal process in reshaping seemingly oppressive social relations and thus about the importance of boundary-shifting social justice claims; and about the storytelling, public-educating functions of the legal process.

These insights direct inquiry into the proclivities of those behind procedural decision-making. At its most basic, critical procedure undertakes a realist assessment of the extent to which procedural changes by legislators, rule makers, and judges are guided, at least partly, by ideological preferences for those of greater social and economic power over those of lesser stature and power, or vice versa. Politics—with a small *p*—sometimes matters.

Critical Consequences

Early ADR critics, myself included, worried about the unstated politics of ADR and its "hidden disadvantages for the already disadvantaged."[18] Amid the First Wave of efficiency procedural reforms, we worried about the "'quality' of justice" for outsiders over time and whether arbitration, in particular, might prove less the "salvation of federal . . . litigation" and more—at least in some situations—a case of the "emperor ha[ving] no clothes."[19]

The Supreme Court's Second Wave *AMEX/Concepcion* rulings significantly deepen those concerns. They extend ADR's deleterious impacts well beyond the cautionary scenarios imagined by the early outsider critiques. Critical procedure underscores the significance. Its attention to the power of procedure to generate differential impacts and reflect ideological preferences—all under the guise of ostensibly neutral efficiency reforms—reveals how and possibly why a conservative Court majority deployed compelled arbitration to privatize and individualize a wide swath of claims against major businesses and institutions. As Justice Kagan's *AMEX* dissent intimates, and as critical procedure inquiry illuminates, *AMEX* and *Concepcion* are key drivers of the Second Wave's constriction of court access and claim development—a designed narrowing of the legal process by judicial fiat.[20]

Assessed through a critical procedure lens, the consequences are profound. At bottom, the rulings force many small to moderate-size claimants—often those of limited social or economic power—to abandon meritorious claims. They abandon those claims because of the *AMEX/Concepcion* triple whammy: those claimants are compelled to waive public litigation in favor of private arbitration; are compelled to waive class treatment and litigate individually once in arbitration; and are no longer allowed to avail themselves of the "effective-vindication rule" even if individual arbitration costs far exceed potential recovery.[21] This claim suppression flows from Justice Scalia and the conservative majority's "jiggery-pokery" in favor of big business.

Critical Conclusions: The Ideological Deployment of Procedure—"Do Not Be Fooled"

In short, *AMEX/Concepcion*'s procedural rulings morphed mandatory arbitration into a do-it-yourself claim suppression guide for large companies. More so, the conservative majority's decisions substantially benefit large businesses by keeping out of the public eye dirty legal laundry sought to be aired by employees, consumers, tenants, small businesses, and discrimination claimants.

Justices Kagan, Ginsburg, and Breyer objected strenuously. American Express and other similar businesses, they observed, would be insulated from widespread liability, even when they clearly violated the law and harmed many in identical ways. For the dissenting justices, after *AMEX* and *Concepcion*, pursuit of small to modest-value claims against large businesses or institutions is "a fool's errand."[22] And without legal liability and public accountability, those businesses and institutions possess little incentive to stop profitably violating the law.

Critical procedure's rejection of the myth of the inherent neutrality of facially uniform procedures and its attention to context and consequences help unearth *AMEX/Concepcion*'s ideological underpinnings. Critical procedure sees the expanded arbitral regime as integral to the broad Second Wave's constriction of court access and claim development—significantly disadvantaging the claims of those less powerful under the guise of neutral efficiency reforms. Looking behind bland procedural language at differential group impacts shows, for some, what ostensibly efficiency-driven arbitrator rulings are actually designed to be: "[A]n alternate system of justice"[23] that strongly favors large companies and institutions while treating "the weak and the aggrieved unfairly."[24]

Critical procedure inquiries into empowerment/disempowerment, differential group impacts, the myth of inherent procedural neutrality, public values articulation, and consciousness-raising—all backstopped by contextual interrogation of ideology—disrobe *AMEX/Concepcion* and Justice Scalia's efficiency rhetoric. Those ADR cases are not isolated rulings about more efficient dispute resolution. Instead, the regime of mandatory privatized, individualized arbitration—dramatically expanded by five justices—lodges squarely amid, and markedly advances, the conservative majority's Second Wave of procedural constraints on courthouse entry and claim development. That regime is close kin to heightened fact-pleading, elevated barriers to class certification, diminished court personal jurisdictional reach over out-of-state manufacturers, narrowed preliminary injunctive relief, and expanded defendant summary judgments.

In sum, critical procedure reveals the impact of the *AMEX/Concepcion* rulings and the conservative majority justices' "Second Wave" constriction of court access and claim development. In the words of Judge Young, "[o]minously, business has a good chance of opting out of the legal system altogether and misbehaving without reproach."[25] And Judge Weinstein aptly highlights what is at stake: this "erection of barriers to court access under the guise of procedural efficiency . . . undermine[s] the legitimacy of the legal system."[26] In the end, it is not only about procedure; it is about power and substantive advantage for some over others. It is about injustice—or justice—for people and communities. "Do not be fooled."[27]

NOTES

Acknowledgment: This chapter is updated and adapted from a previously published article: Eric K. Yamamoto, *ADR and the Justices' "Second Wave" Constriction of Court Access and Claim Development*, 70 SMU L. Rev. 765 (2017).

1 Eric K. Yamamoto, *ADR: Where Have the Critics Gone?*, 36 Santa Clara L. Rev. 1055, 1056 (1996).

2 *Id.* at 1058–62 (outlining early critiques of ADR by Owen Fiss, Richard Delgado, Marjorie Silver, Trina Grillo, John Esser, Carrie Menkel-Meadow, and Kim Dayton).

3 Arthur R. Miller, *Simplified Pleading, Meaningful Days in Court, and Trials on the Merits: Reflections on the Deformation of Federal Procedure*, 88 N.Y.U. L. Rev. 286, 357–71 (2013).

4 A. Benjamin Spencer, *The Restrictive Ethos in Civil Procedure*, 78 Geo. Wash. L. Rev. 353, 358–59 (2010).

5 American Express Co. v. Italian Colors Restaurant, 570 U.S. 228 (2013).

6 AT&T Mobility LLC v. Concepcion, 563 U.S. 333 (2011).

7 Federal Arbitration Act, 9 U.S.C. §§ 1–16.

8 Jack B. Weinstein, *After Fifty Years of the Federal Rules of Civil Procedure: Are the Barriers to Justice Being Raised?*, 137 U. Pa. L. Rev. 1901, 1906 (1989).

9 Eric K. Yamamoto, *Efficiency's Threat to the Value of Accessible Courts for Minorities*, 25 Harv. C.R.-C.L. L. Rev. 341, 345 (1990).

10 Eric K. Yamamoto, *White (House) Lies: Why the Public Must Compel the Courts to Hold the President Accountable for National Security Abuses*, 68 Law & Contemp. Probs. 285, 291–92 (2005) (characterizing critical legal inquiry).

11 "Critical legal studies" and "critical race theory" have both played a significant role in advancing critical legal analyses. *See* Richard Delgado & Jean Stefancic, Critical Race Theory: An Introduction 3–5 (2d ed. 2012) (engaging critical theory analysis in race and law); Emma Coleman Jordan & Angela P. Harris, Beyond Rational Choice: Alternative Perspectives on Economics (2006) (employing critical legal theory to critique and remake standard economic analysis of justice issues); Eric K. Yamamoto, *Critical Race Praxis: Race Theory and Political Lawyering Practice in Post-Civil Rights America*, 95 Mich. L. Rev. 821, 827–28 (1997) (calling for pragmatic linkage of Critical Race Theory to frontline legal justice practice); Joseph William Singer, *Legal Realism Now*, 76 Calif. L. Rev. 465, 532–33 (1988) (review essay) (describing critical legal theory inquiry with roots in legal realism); Elizabeth M. Schneider, *The Dialectic of Rights and Politics: Perspectives from the Women's Movement*, 61 N.Y.U. L. Rev. 589, 597–98 (1986) (employing critical legal theory to assess and advance the feminist deployment of the litigation process).

12 Stephen B. Burbank & Sean Farhang, *Federal Court Rulemaking and Litigation Reform: An Institutional Approach*, 15 Nev. L.J. 1559, 1563 (2015).

13 *Id.*

14 *Id.*

15 Yamamoto, *supra* note 9, at 344.
16 Brooke D. Coleman, *The Vanishing Plaintiff*, 42 Seton Hall L. Rev. 501, 503 (2012).
17 Eric K. Yamamoto, Moses Haia & Donna Kalama, *Courts and the Cultural Performance: Native Hawaiians' Uncertain Federal and State Law Rights to Sue*, 16 Haw. L. Rev. 1, 6 (1994).
18 Yamamoto, *supra* note 1, at 1062.
19 *Id.* at 1061–62.
20 Am. Express Co. v. Italian Colors Rest., 570 U.S. 228, 247 (2013) (Kagan, J., dissenting).
21 *Id.* at 240.
22 *Id.*
23 Jessica Silver-Greenberg & Michael Corkery, *A "Privatization of the Justice System,"* N.Y. Times (Nov. 2, 2015).
24 Weinstein, *supra* note 8, at 1906.
25 Jessica Silver-Greenberg & Robert Gebeloff, *Arbitration Everywhere, Stacking the Deck of Justice*, N.Y. Times (Oct. 31, 2015).
26 Weinstein, *supra* note 8, at 1906.
27 *Am. Express*, 570 U.S. at 253 (Kagan, J., dissenting).

38

Reconsidering Prejudice in Alternative Dispute Resolution for Black Work Matters

MICHAEL Z. GREEN

Civil procedure contributes to employers defeating federal employment discrimination claims. The use of motions to dismiss, summary judgment, directed verdicts, and appeals of verdicts as procedural hurdles helps to prevent black workers' voices from being heard in the courts. But while the formal strictures of federal court may obscure or silence black workers' truths, other, less formal avenues for resolving workplace disputes—forms of alternative dispute resolution (ADR) including negotiation, mediation, and arbitration—carry their own risks. For example, critical race scholars have expressed concern that the lack of formality in ADR represents a major structural flaw for vulnerable participants.[1]

This chapter, an edited excerpt from a previously published article, identifies critical race concerns involving employment negotiation by black workers. Specifically, participants of color using ADR are more vulnerable because of stereotype threat, covering, unconscious bias, intersectionality, and a lack of diverse neutrals, among other challenges. These problems are not well understood by employers, courts, arbitrators, or others who adjudicate employment disputes. This excerpt also suggests ways to ameliorate these critical race concerns so that black workers can find racial justice in the workplace.

Negotiating While Black[2]

Many of the prominent studies that look at what it means to negotiate while being black have been conducted by Professor Ian Ayres. In a 1991 study, with a first report in 1991,[3] and then further analysis in a new and expanded audit of that study with resulting data and conclusions reported in 1995,[4] Ayres examined differences based on race by using pairs of testers—always including a white male versus someone of a different race—who were all trained to negotiate the same way and sent to purchase a new car at randomly selected Chicago auto dealerships.[5] Ayres found that black buyers were induced to pay much higher prices due to both the initial offer they received from the salesperson and also the final offer, which represented the lowest price offered by the salesperson after a number of rounds of bargaining.[6] Specific results demonstrated that "[b]lack female testers were asked to pay over three times the markup of white male testers, and black male testers were asked to pay over twice the white male markup."[7] Ayres also found that salespersons believed that white males had better search details and were more informed about the dealer's actual costs than black purchasers.[8]

Ayres has even more recently noted, in a 2011 unpublished paper with coauthors Mahzarin R. Banaji and Christine Jolls, that more nuanced and technical forms of negotiating, such as through electronic bartering and auction services like eBay, have also indicated biased results for black persons.[9] Ayres and his coauthors constructed a field experiment to test the effects of race on transactions involving baseball card auctions on eBay. The tester elements involved a display of photographs showing the same cards being "held by either a dark-skinned/African American or a light-skinned/Caucasian hand."[10] Their results indicated that the "[c]ards held by African-American sellers sold for approximately 20% ($0.90) less than cards held by Caucasian sellers."[11]

A similar study on the effects of race in negotiations was created by Jennifer Doleac and Luke Stein in the online sale of an Apple iPod.[12] These researchers "posted classified advertisements offering an iPod Nano portable digital music player for sale on several hundred locally focused websites throughout the US" and signaled race by the skin color of the hand holding a picture of the iPod being offered for sale in the advertisement.[13] This study differed somewhat from the Ayres eBay study because the eBay parties would never expect to meet and the purchases through eBay were insured by eBay. The participants in the iPod study would expect to meet in person to close the deal, and there was no insurance involved.[14]

The study undertaken by Doleac and Stein specifically used pictures of a man's black hand, or a man's white hand, or a man's white hand with a tattoo, each holding a new, unopened iPod Nano.[15] Potential buyers responded via anonymized email addresses. There was no formal bidding process, and "either party [could] cease communication at any time without facing any consequences."[16] About two hours after each advertisement was posted, the researchers sent an email message to each responder stating they received numerous responses and asked for their best offers.[17] From these results, Doleac and Stein concluded: "Black sellers receive 18% fewer offers than white sellers, whereas tattooed sellers receive 16% fewer."[18] Also, with respect to amounts, the mean offer received was $49.86 with a maximum offer of $54.05.[19] But, "[c]ompared with white sellers, black sellers receive average offers of $5.72 (11%) lower and tattooed sellers $5.53 (10%) lower."[20]

Further, Doleac and Stein concluded that the best offers that both "[b]lack and tattooed sellers" received were "also lower than whites', by $7.07 (12%) and $6.60 (11%), respectively."[21] Final conclusions from Doleac and Stein were that "black sellers suffer worse market outcomes than their white counterparts," including the receipt of "13% fewer responses and 18% fewer offers," and these negative results were "similar in magnitude to those associated with a seller's display of a wrist tattoo."[22] Also, this study found that "black sellers do better in markets with larger black populations, suggesting that the disparities may be driven, in part, by buyers' preference for their own-race sellers."[23]

A study in March 2000 by Marc-David Seidel, Jeffrey Polzer, and Katherine Stewart found that Black professionals negotiate less beneficial salary and benefit agreements than white persons.[24] They noted that "'[d]iscriminatory wage differences between White and minority employees have been documented in many organizations."[25] These authors recognized several potential causes for this wage discrimination, including overt organizational hostility based on race, manifested by efforts to cabin certain lower positions for minorities, as well as specifically choosing to give unequal pay for equal work.[26]

Seidel and his coauthors also decided to investigate whether salary negotiations may be infected by white assumptions that initial offers could be made lower to black applicants because they had less information about whether the employee's salary was negotiable and what the company's reservation price might be.[27] Also, this same study raised the question of whether direct racial bias by the company negotiator would make him less likely to give salary increases.[28] The authors also identified a concern about whether cultural differences in negotiating norms might explain the reason for lower salaries.[29]

Seidel and his coauthors tested their hypothesis that "[m]embers of racial minority groups will negotiate smaller increases to their initial salary offers than their White counterparts."[30] The authors also noted that "information about the employing organization may provide an advantage to a job candidate attempting to negotiate a higher starting salary."[31] More specifically, the authors described "[o]ne of the most useful sources of tailored, timely information may be a personal relationship with someone in the company, which can provide sensitive, detailed information that is not available through other sources."[32] Thus, social networks play a huge role in negotiations, and black persons with lesser social contacts than their white counterparts are disadvantaged by the impact of those social networks. A union, as a social or business network, or an identity caucus within a union might be able to help negotiate on behalf of black employees to help address the information imbalance.

However, black persons have unique issues that may arise in their workplace negotiations. There is an inherent concern or fear that one's actions in negotiations to obtain certain workplace benefits will reinforce negative stereotypes. This affects the negotiating posture of a black worker, and Professor Claude Steele has referred to this concern or fear that one's actions will reinforce negative stereotypes as "stereotype threat."[33] A black worker has an unusual worry about producing stereotype-confirming conversations if she pushes too hard in negotiating workplace benefits.[34] Specifically, "the existence of stereotypes diminishes an employee's workplace bargaining power, and thus, her ability to negotiate" her own work terms.[35]

And black persons, more likely than any other racial group, tend to find themselves pressured to "cover" or conform to norms that deny their racial identity at work.[36] This form of "covering" in workplace negotiations represents a tradeoff between the lesser of two evils related to racial stereotyping. She must act against her own financial interest to lose the battle for a higher negotiated salary in order to win the war of not losing out on overall professional opportunities for being viewed as incompetent or unqualified or lazy based on a racial stereotype.

Conclusions

Overall, one of the biggest concerns that should be addressed is the lack of information. One way for black persons to obtain additional information for fairer negotiations can be through receiving common information available to all parties, possibly through posting it on the internet and making sure that all parties have the same information. But as the study by Seidel and colleagues explained, companies may be unwilling to establish any policies aimed at correcting any information discrepancies related to salary negotiations because it "would result in higher payroll expenses."[37] Another way to improve the information disparity involves hiring more racially diverse employees as a whole so they can provide a social network for sharing information with same-race applicants. Unions also are able to balance the information-sharing process for racially diverse groups of employees.

With technological advances, the use of the internet may also help remove information disparities through developing social and electronic media networks that fairly disseminate information without consideration of race. Fiona Morton, Florian Zettelmeyer, and Jorge Silva-Risso studied an online referral service, Autobytel.com, to show that the use of that internet service helped to level the playing field in automobile pricing for minorities.[38] The authors noted that their findings, despite African American and Hispanic minorities probably being within the racial groups least likely to use the internet, suggest that those minorities who do use the internet to assist with auto purchases will benefit the most from doing so. While establishing that "disadvantaged minorities pay 2.0–2.3% more for their cars than do white consumers," the authors found that "this minority premium can be explained with differences in nonracial demographics and search costs between minority groups and white [people]."[39] Then, the authors asserted that when obtaining information through the internet via a referral service such as Autobytel.com, where party demographics are not known, this process eliminates most of the offline minority premium.[40]

As a result, unless the black person in the negotiation has as much information as a similar white counterpart, whether through social or internet networks or some other means, and the white person negotiating with her focuses on excising any conscious and subconscious race-based stereotypes from the process, negotiating while black—even in 2017 and even with relatively well-meaning counterparts—means that unproductive obstacles still exist. To the extent that companies do not find ways to address the "stereotype threat" that leads racial minorities to "cover" at work to protect themselves at their own expense in salary negotiations, those companies will lose out on finding and nurturing productive black talent in their workplaces.[41]

Kenji Yoshino and Dorie Clark suggest that organizations adopt a model that focuses on following four approaches to address covering in the workplace that could also help address racial consequences in negotiations: reflect, diagnose, analyze, and initiate.[42] While acknowledging that more study of stereotype threat involving racial minorities in the workplace must be done, since most studies have focused on stereotype threat for women, Elise Kalokerinos, Courtney von Hippel, and Hannes Zacher have found that identity-matching may help.[43] The authors also suggest a three-step approach in addressing stereotype threat in the workplace: (1) Focus on primary prevention; (2) diagnose and treat early stages of stereotype threat before it has long-term consequences; and (3) undo the consequences from those who have been subjected to stereotype threat.[44]

To capsulize these suggestions from Yoshino and Clark and Kalokerinos and colleagues, the best way to prevent covering and stereotype threat from infecting workplace negotiations over key concerns such as salary, a company should seek a very diverse leadership group, thereby providing many examples of people who look like and reflect the background of the black person negotiating with that company. Then, black persons can identify with people who are successful and look and sound like them to ease any apprehensions about performing in a way that feeds into negative stereotypes. Through mentoring networks, identity caucuses, and/or unions, black persons can meet similar role models who provide a positive reflection and offer social or business information to level the negotiating playing field. These groups help combat the application of negative stereotypes and also encourage self-affirming opportunities to show that negative stereotypes do not match the individual black person involved.

NOTES

Acknowledgment: This chapter is updated and adapted from the article Michael Z. Green, *Reconsidering Prejudice in Alternative Dispute Resolution for Black Work Matters*, 70 SMU L. Rev. 639 (2017).

1 *See, e.g.*, Richard Delgado, *The Unbearable Lightness of Alternative Dispute Resolution: Critical Thoughts on Fairness and Formality*, 70 SMU L. Rev. 611, 627–31 (2017).

2 The text of this section was, in substantial part, first published as Michael Z. Green, *Negotiating While Black*, *in* Negotiator's Desk Reference ch. 41 (Christopher Honeyman & Andrea Kupfer Schneider eds., 2017).

3 Ian Ayres, *Fair Driving: Gender and Race Discrimination in Retail Car Negotiations*, 104 Harv. L. Rev. 817, 856 (1991) (describing salespersons were more likely to negotiate price of a new car with white purchasers versus black persons, as 61 percent of black persons did not know that sticker prices were negotiable versus only 31 percent of white persons who did not know the prices were negotiable); *see also* Ian Ayres & Peter Siegelman, *Race and Gender Discrimination in Bargaining for a New Car*, 85 Am. Econ. Rev. 304, 312–13 (1995) (further confirming findings from the 1991 study and suggesting reasons why black persons were subjected to much higher prices than white persons during negotiations).

4 Ian Ayres, *Further Evidence of Discrimination in New Car Negotiations and Estimates of Its Cause*, 94 Mich. L. Rev. 109 (1995).

5 Ayres & Siegelman, *supra* note 3, at 305.

6 Ayres, *Fair Driving*, *supra* note 3, at 819, 830 ("The tests reveal that white males receive significantly better prices than blacks. . . ."); Ayres & Siegelman, *supra* note 3, at 319 ("In negotiations for more than 300 new cars, Chicago car dealers offered black and female testers significantly higher prices than white males with whom they were paired, even though all testers used identical bargaining strategies."); Ayres, *Further Evidence*, *supra* note 4, at 116 ("The current study confirms the original study's findings that offers to black males and black females are significantly higher than those made to white males.").

7 Ayres, *Fair Driving*, *supra* note 3, at 828.

8 Ayres & Siegelman, *supra* note 3, at 317 (describing how assumptions about lack of information among black persons and white persons having a lower reservation price (the maximum amount the buyer was willing to pay) could have led to disparity in offers for automobile purchases based on race); Ayers, *Fair Driving*, *supra* note 3, at 848–50 (referring to reasons why car dealerships would charge white males less based on assumed higher search costs for black persons and women).

9 *See* Ian Ayres, Mahzarin Banaji & Christine Jolls, *Race Effects on eBay*, 46 Rand J. Econ 891 (2015).

10 *Id.* at 896.

11 *Id.* at Abstract.

12 *See* Jennifer L. Doleac & Luke C. D. Stein, *The Visible Hand: Race and Online Market Outcomes*, 123 Econ. J. F469 (2013).
13 *Id.* at F470.
14 *Id.* at F472.
15 *Id.* at F476.
16 *Id.* at F474.
17 *Id.* at F477.
18 *Id.* at F482.
19 *Id.* at F484.
20 *Id.*
21 *Id.*
22 *Id.* at F490.
23 *Id.* at F491.
24 Marc-David L. Seidel, Jeffrey T. Polzer & Katherine J. Stewart, *Friends in High Places: The Effects of Social Networks on Discrimination in Salary Negotiations*, 45 Admin. Sci. Q. 1, 1–24 (2000).
25 *Id.* at 1.
26 *Id.*
27 *Id.* at 3.
28 *Id.*
29 *Id.*
30 *Id.* at 3, 10.
31 *Id.* at 4.
32 *Id.*
33 *See* Claude M. Steele, *A Threat in the Air: How Stereotypes Shape Intellectual Identity and Performance*, 52 Am. Psych. 613, 614 (1997); *see also* Elise K. Kalokerinos, Courtney von Hippel & Hannes Zacher, *Is Stereotype Threat a Useful Construct for Organizational Psychology Research and Practice?*, 7 Indus. & Org. Psych. 381, 391–92 (2014).
34 *See* Devon W. Carbado & Mitu Gulati, *Conversations at Work*, 79 Or. L. Rev. 103, 109 (2000).
35 *Id.* at 110.
36 *See* Christie Smith & Kenji Yoshino, *Uncovering Talent: A New Model of Inclusion*, 1, 4–6 (Dec. 6, 2013), www2.deloitte.com (referring to data collected regarding "covering at work" and noting that "Black respondents" constituted the "cohort that reported the highest degree of covering"); *see also* Dorie Clark, *Why So Few Women and Minorities at the Top? Here's the Real Reason*, Forbes (Sept. 3, 2013), www.forbes.com (describing Smith and Yoshino study).
37 Seidel et al., *supra* note 24, at 22.
38 *See* Fiona Scott Morton, Florian Zettelmeyer & Jorge Silva-Risso, *Consumer Information and Price Discrimination: Does the Internet Affect the Pricing of New Cars to Women and Minorities?* 1, 3 (Nat'l Bureau of Econ. Rsch., Working Paper No. 8668, 2001).

39 *See id.* at 2.

40 *Id.* at 3.

41 *See* Michelle Marks & Crystal Harold, *Who Asks and Who Receives in Salary Negotiation*, 32 J. Org. Behav. 371, 372 (2011) (perceptions of fairness in job salary negotiation affect "job satisfaction and commitment" and eventually affect "performance and turnover"); *see also* Smith & Yoshino, *supra* note 36, at 11 (loss of talent results because covering "negatively impacts individuals' sense of self" and "their commitment to their organizations"); Tristin K. Green, *Discomfort at Work: Workplace Assimilation Demands and the Contact Hypothesis*, 86 N.C. L. Rev. 379, 413–14 (2008) (describing how covering involves suppressing "signals of identification with socially salient groups").

42 Smith & Yoshino, *supra* note 36, at 13.

43 *See* Kalokerinos et al., *supra* note 33, at 381–82, 384, 387 (stereotype threat can result in "unfavorable job attitudes, disidentification at work, altered decision making, and lowered career aspirations").

44 *Id.* at 395; *see also* Andrea Kupfer Schneider, Catherine H. Tinsley, Sandra Cheldelin & Emily T. Amanatullah, *Likeability v. Competence: The Impossible Choice Faced by Female Politicians, Attenuated by Lawyers*, 17 Duke J. Gender L. & Pol'y 363, 382 (2010) (suggesting additional ways to "fight the stereotype").

39

When Forum Determines Rights

Forced Arbitration of Discrimination Claims

STEPHANIE BORNSTEIN

The resolution of a civil lawsuit often impacts more than just the individuals involved. A suit may define the law for future claims or enforce the law against large actors to protect the public. Yet the ability of lawsuits to provide systemic redress is now in peril. Beginning in the late 2000s, the United States Supreme Court has issued a series of decisions forcing plaintiffs out of the courthouse and into private arbitration.[1] These decisions rely on the Court's view that, so long as plaintiffs can bring their legal claims in *any* forum, whether judicial or arbitral, plaintiffs retain the ability to enforce their rights.

The Court's new arbitration jurisprudence poses a special threat to federal civil rights claims, for which there is often no neat distinction between forum and substance. The Civil Rights Act of 1964 was an ambitious effort by Congress to root out racial discrimination in all its forms. Title VII of the act—which prohibits discrimination in employment based on race, color, sex, national origin, or religion—specifically allows for group-based claims and injunctive relief to redress systemic and structural discrimination.[2] Modeled after Title VII, federal statutes prohibiting employment discrimination on the basis of age and disability—the Age Discrimination in Employment Act of 1967 (ADEA) and the Americans with Disabilities Act of 1991 (ADA)—provide the same protections.[3]

The Court's arbitration jurisprudence has thwarted these statutory imperatives, threatening essential legal tools designed to fight systemic inequality. Forced arbitration imposes two requirements that dramatically limit the reach of federal civil rights statutes: confidentiality and individuality. These defining characteristics of arbitration benefit well-resourced defendants at the expense of civil rights plaintiffs and civil rights laws. Contrary to the Court's rationale, forum often dictates which substantive rights can be enforced when plaintiffs who allege discrimination are forced to arbitrate.

Separating Forum from Substance: Mandating Arbitration of Statutory Claims

The Supreme Court's embrace of arbitration relies on rigid application of the Federal Arbitration Act of 1925 (FAA).[4] When enacted, the FAA's purpose was to correct judicial hostility to arbitration and ensure that arbitration agreements would be treated the same as all other contracts. The statute requires that commercial contracts with arbitration clauses be enforced unless there is a legal basis in contract law for invalidating them—for example, fraud, duress, or unconscionability. For much of the twentieth century, such agreements remained the province of private contract law.

Beginning in the 1980s, the Court expanded the reach of the FAA significantly. While acknowledging that arbitration may not be appropriate for every claim, the Court held that any party that entered a predispute agreement to arbitrate statutory claims was required to do so unless Congress precluded arbitration in the statute in question.[5] This meant that parties could be required to arbitrate claims arising under federal public statutes governing antitrust, securities, consumer safety, and more.

In 1991, in *Gilmer v. Interstate/Johnson Lane Corp.*,[6] the Court held that the FAA applied to federal antidiscrimination claims brought by employees. Plaintiff Robert Gilmer's employer required him to register as a securities representative with the New York Stock Exchange; the registration materials included an agreement to arbitrate any employment dispute. When, after Gilmer was fired, he sued for age discrimination under the federal ADEA, his employer moved to compel arbitration. The Court ruled for the employer, holding that "[s]o long as the prospective litigant effectively may vindicate [their] statutory cause of action in the arbitral forum, the statute . . . serve[s] both its remedial and deterrent function."[7]

While the *Gilmer* majority's rationale purported to remove stigma about arbitration to provide *more* choices of forum in which to enforce statutory rights, FAA jurisprudence has evolved quite differently. *Gilmer*'s holding that an arbitral forum could provide redress for an individual discrimination claim has been grossly distorted to mean that statutory civil rights claims *need never* be litigated. Relying on its distinction between the existence of a federal statutory right and the legal forum—federal court or private arbitration—in which that statutory right is enforced, the Court issued a series of decisions that effectively foreclose litigation regardless of plaintiffs' claims.

This arbitration jurisprudence stands to upend federal civil rights law. The Court has held that the FAA's "liberal federal policy favoring arbitration"[8] applies broadly to all federal statutory claims, including those that provide plaintiffs with a private right of action essential to enforcing public laws. A Court majority so held despite dissenting justices' view that a federal statute's private right of action is a substantive right, not a procedural right—a "vital element" necessary to "vindicate[e] the important congressional policy against discriminatory employment practices," as Justice Souter described it.[9] Plaintiffs may now be forced out of the courtroom and into confidential arbitration even if they were not aware that they had waived a right to their "day in court" in a judicial forum. Thus, a union's agreement with an employer to arbitrate employment disputes waived an individual employee's choice of judicial forum, even for a discrimination suit that the union declined to pursue on behalf of the employee.[10]

The Court has also upheld clauses that mandate arbitration *on an individual basis*, even if that means as a practical matter that many claims will not be pursued at all. Thus, customers whose adhesive cell-phone service contracts waived their rights to pursue any classwide relief were required to arbitrate their fee claims individually, each being worth less than $30.[11] While state law would have struck down the contract as unconscionable, intended to "cheat large numbers of consumers out of individually small sums of money," the Court held that the FAA preempted it.[12] Likewise, small businesses were required to arbitrate federal antitrust claims against credit-card companies individually, even though each plaintiff's damages were at most $39,000 while the cost of expert testimony to prove any single case exceeded $1 million.[13] Slicing the line between forum and rights ever thinner, and overruling its own prior precedent requiring "effective vindication" of rights in arbitration, the

Court held that, where the cost of proving a case outweighs any potential remedy, that "does not constitute the elimination of the *right to pursue* that remedy."[14]

Yet another federal statute designed to foster group-based action was, according to the Court, preempted by the FAA. In *Epic Systems v. Lewis*,[15] a group of employees brought a collective action against their employer for wage violations. When the employer moved to compel arbitration, the employees argued that their mandatory arbitration agreements waiving class-based remedies violated the National Labor Relations Act's protections for workers "to engage in . . . concerted activities for the purpose of . . . mutual aid or protection" for fair wages.[16] The Court disagreed and compelled individual arbitration of each wage claim, holding that the FAA preempted any defense to forced arbitration that "would render an agreement 'illegal' as a matter of federal statutory law" because it "impermissibly disfavored arbitration."[17]

Hiding and Dividing: The Impacts of Mandatory Arbitration of Discrimination Claims

Two limitations created by the Court's arbitration jurisprudence now threaten the ability of the civil rights statutes to redress systemic injustice: *confidentiality* and *individuality*.

In stark contrast to the public nature of judicial proceedings, arbitral forums are almost always private. Arbitration agreements routinely include a clause requiring both parties to keep the proceedings as well as any results confidential.[18] The veil of privacy surrounding arbitration poses significant challenges for employees asserting discrimination claims. To even bring a claim, an employee must recognize that what they have experienced amounts to discrimination, which an employee often cannot discover if similar complaints are kept quiet. Confidential or private arbitration may also hide a pattern of discrimination—for example, serial sexual harassment or widespread race or gender discrimination in pay. And the financial and negative publicity risks of a lawsuit also create incentives for organizations to self-correct or tackle systemic problems of bias—incentives that are lost when employers can channel discrimination claims into confidential arbitration.[19]

Unlike judicial decisions, which are public documents, arbitral decisions are not published in any uniform, searchable way, and they are rarely precedential. This leaves antidiscrimination law stagnant and hampers the ability of both employees and employers to understand the law and prevent its violation. In 1991, in *Gilmer*, the Court dismissed such concerns, noting that "judicial decisions addressing ADEA claims will continue to be issued because it is unlikely that all or even most ADEA claimants will be subject to arbitration agreements."[20] Yet today this is no longer true. As Justice Ginsburg noted in dissent in *Epic Systems*, arbitration agreements "[w]ith confidentiality and no-precedential-value provisions" create confusion about employer obligations, leaving "irreconcilable answers [that] remain unchecked."[21]

While arbitration's confidentiality makes recognizing potential discrimination claims difficult, arbitration clauses mandating individuality may in effect bar some claims entirely. Under Title VII, the ADEA, and the ADA, plaintiffs can allege that an employer has engaged in a pattern or practice of disparate treatment or that its neutral policy or practice has a disproportionately negative impact on members of one protected class. Both the "pattern or practice" and the "disparate impact" claims authorized by the statute are usually brought as class actions; to prove either type of claim requires statistical evidence based on comparing groups of employees. And both types of claims focus on redressing institution-wide problems of discrimination that require broad injunctive relief. By authorizing employers to adopt mandatory predispute arbitration agreements that include class action waivers, the Court has now effectively eliminated plaintiffs' ability to enforce key Title VII statutory provisions. This goes beyond just dividing and conquering the claims of individual employees for whom bringing an individual claim may no longer be worth the effort; it eviscerates two key enforcement mechanisms of substantive federal civil rights laws.

In *Gilmer*, the Court also considered and rejected this concern, responding to the plaintiff's argument that individual arbitration failed to serve the ADEA's goals by glibly noting that "arbitrators have the power to fashion equitable relief."[22] The majority disregarded Justice Stevens's concern, in dissent, that most arbitration is "limited to a specific dispute between the particular parties," making classwide relief rare.[23] Yet "authoriz[ing] courts to award broad, class-based injunctive relief" is both "the cornerstone to eliminating discrimination in society" and "an essential purpose" of federal antidiscrimination statutes, Stevens warned: compelling arbitration "frustrate[s] the purpose" of civil rights statutes.[24]

In the decades since *Gilmer*, in each case in which the Court compelled individual arbitration for a statutory right requiring collective redress, a steady drumbeat of dissenting justices has picked up the Stevens mantle. Justice Breyer explained that the Court, by requiring individual arbitration where, as in the cell-phone consumer case, each plaintiff's injury was about $30 in fees, was "[in] effect depriving claimants of their claims."[25] Ignoring the fact that, as in the credit-card consumer case, the cost of an expert witness needed to pursue individual arbitration of antitrust claims would far exceed any recovery, Justice Kagan decried the Court's "betrayal" that would allow "arbitration clauses [to] chok[e] off a plaintiff's ability to enforce congressionally created rights" and become "backdoor waivers of statutory rights."[26]

Indeed, the inability of individual arbitration to address systemic discrimination was so apparent to Justice Ginsburg that, in her *Epic Systems* dissent, she expressed her belief that the majority's decision compelling individual arbitration of wage claims simply could not apply to some civil rights claims:

> I do not read the Court's opinion to place in jeopardy discrimination complaints asserting disparate-impact and pattern-or-practice claims that call for proof on a groupwide basis . . . which some courts have concluded cannot be maintained by solo complainants. . . . It would be grossly exorbitant to read the FAA to devastate Title VII . . . , and other laws enacted to eliminate, root and branch, class-based employment discrimination. . . . With fidelity to the Legislature's will, the Court could hardly hold otherwise.[27]

Yet the majority agreed to no such limitation. And while this issue has yet to come squarely before the Court, recent arbitration jurisprudence leaves little room for optimism. At least one circuit court has compelled arbitration in a case alleging systemic sex discrimination because it viewed a pattern-or-practice claim as "simply refer[ing] to a method of proof,"[28] mistakenly equating the plaintiff's ability to introduce group-based evidence in her individual arbitration with the statute's substantive provisions for broad remedial action and injunctive relief.

Accessing Justice: Responses to Forced Arbitration of Discrimination Claims

The Supreme Court's unwavering support for mandatory predispute arbitration agreements has, unsurprisingly, impacted employer behavior. Between the 1991 *Gilmer* decision and the early 2000s, the portion of the workforce covered by mandatory arbitration agreements grew from a mere 2 percent to nearly 25 percent.[29] By 2018, more than 56 percent of the nonunionized, private sector workforce—more than 60 million workers—were required to arbitrate their statutory legal claims.[30] Nearly one-third of employers mandating arbitration barred class actions even *before* the Court's *Epic Systems* decision.[31] Because class action waivers are more common among large employers, this translates to nearly one-quarter of all private sector employees, or 24.7 million workers, for whom individual arbitration is the only option to enforce their statutory rights.[32] And this number is expected to rise: one study estimated that by 2023 the proportion of private employees subject to class action waivers would grow to exceed 80 percent.[33]

What is worse, mandatory arbitration requirements are more commonly applied to workers at the lower end of the pay scale (i.e., an hourly wage of $13 or less) and in "industries that are disproportionately composed of" of black and female workers (e.g., education and health)[34]—the very employees most likely to need the ability to bring class-based wage or discrimination claims. Forcing such employees to arbitrate claims individually is intended to deter all complaints by making the cost to pursue a claim not worth its potential remedy.

Interestingly, plaintiffs' attorneys have started to fight back, filing hundreds or thousands of individual arbitration claims for employees they would have otherwise represented as a class against companies with forced class waivers, including Uber, Lyft, Postmates, and Chipotle.[35] Repeating individual employee arbitration claims on a massive scale is time-consuming, yet it comes at a far greater cost to employers, who—to ensure that their mandatory arbitration agreements withstand court scrutiny—generally agree to pay the full cost of arbitration, to the tune of a few thousand dollars per case. In one such case, attorneys filed 6,000 arbitration claims against DoorDash on behalf of workers for unpaid wages, which would have cost the company $9 million in arbitration fees. In response, DoorDash sought to get out of the very arbitration agreement it had forced on its employees, but a federal district court upheld the agreement, compelling DoorDash to arbitrate.[36]

And some federal legislators have attempted to amend the FAA to abrogate the Court's arbitration jurisprudence, including by excluding certain types of claims (e.g., consumer, employment, civil rights), prohibiting compelled rather than voluntary arbitration, or barring confidentiality agreements for certain types of arbitrations (e.g., sexual harassment).[37] To date, however, no proposed legislation has made it out of both houses of Congress, leaving discrimination claimants who wish to pursue systemic claims on behalf of a group with little recourse.

As it stands today, then, Court jurisprudence on forced arbitration poses an existential challenge to federal antidiscrimination law. Congress intended federal civil rights laws to be enforced by a private right of action that allows for group-based claims with broad injunctive relief—essential enforcement tools to root out structural causes of discrimination. If a plaintiff needs complex discovery, public pressure, or—most important—the ability to bring a case collectively with others to right systemic wrongs, forcing her into individual arbitration means the case will likely go unpursued. In the context of civil rights claims, barring access to a federal court is often not just denying plaintiffs their preferred forum; it is denying them access to justice at all.

NOTES

1 *See* 14 Penn Plaza LLC v. Pyett, 556 U.S. 247 (2009); Rent-A-Center, West, Inc. v. Jackson, 561 U.S. 63 (2010); Stolt-Nielsen S.A. v. Animalfeeds Int'l Corp., 559 U.S. 662 (2010); AT&T Mobility LLC v. Concepcion, 563 U.S. 333 (2011); Am. Express v. Italian Colors Restaurants, 570 U.S. 228 (2013); Epic Sys. Corp. v. Lewis; 138 S. Ct. 1612 (2018).

2 42 U.S.C. § 2000e-6(a); *see* Int'l Brotherhood of Teamsters v. United States, 431 U.S. 324 (1977); Griggs v. Duke Power Co., 401 U.S. 424 (1971).

3 *See, e.g.*, Thompson v. Weyerhaeuser Co., 582 F.3d 1125, 1126 (10th Cir. 2009) (ADEA); Hohider v. United Parcel Serv., Inc., 574 F.3d 169, 182–83 (3d Cir. 2009) (ADA).

4 Pub. L. No. 68–401, 43 Stat. 883 (codified at 9 U.S.C. §§ 1–16).

5 *See* Gilmer v. Interstate/Johnson Lane Corp., 500 U.S. 20 (1991).

6 *Id.*

7 *Id.* (citing Mitsubishi Motor Corp. v. Soler Chrysler-Plymouth, Inc., 473 U.S. 614, 637 (1985)).

8 *Epic Sys.*, 138 S. Ct. at 1621.

9 *Pyett*, 556 U.S. at 278, 281 (Souter, J., dissenting) (citations omitted).

10 *Id.* at 260–68 (majority opinion).

11 *Concepcion*, 563 U.S. at 336–348.

12 *Id.* at 340, 343–348 (citing Discover Bank v. Superior Ct., 113 P.3d 1100 (Cal. 2005)).

13 *Am. Express*, 570 U.S. at 228.

14 *Id.* at 235–237.

15 Epic Systems v. Lewis, 138 S. Ct. at 1623–24.

16 Pub. L. No. 74–198, ch. 372, § 7, 49 Stat. 452 (1935) (codified at 29 U.S.C. § 157).

17 *Epic Sys.*, 138 S. Ct. at 1623.

18 *See* Christopher R. Drahozal, *Confidentiality in Consumer and Employment Arbitration*, 7 Y.B. Arb. & Mediation 28, 40–41 (2015).

19 *See, e.g.*, Stephanie Bornstein, *Disclosing Discrimination*, 101 B.U. L. Rev. 287, 306–308, 306 n.107 (2021).

20 *Gilmer*, 500 U.S. at 32.

21 *Epic Sys.*, 138 S. Ct. at 1648 (Ginsburg, J., dissenting).

22 *Gilmer*, 500 U.S. at 21.

23 *Id.* at 41–42 (Stevens, J., dissenting).

24 *Id.*

25 *Concepcion*, 563 U.S. at 365 (Breyer, J., dissenting).

26 *Am. Express*, 570 U.S. 228, 240, 244 (Kagan, J., dissenting).

27 *Epic Sys.*, 138 S. Ct. at 1648 (Ginsburg, J., dissenting).

28 Parisi v. Goldman, Sachs & Co., 710 F.3d 483, 487–88 (2d Cir. 2013).

29 Alexander J.S. Colvin, *The Growing Use of Mandatory Arbitration: Access to the Courts Is Now Barred for More Than 60 million American Workers*, Econ. Pol'y Inst. 1–2, 4 (Apr. 6, 2018), https://files.epi.org.

30 *Id.*

31 *Id.* at 2, 5.

32 *Id.* at 2, 6.

33 Rachel Deutsch, Kate Hamaji, Celine McNicholas, Elizabeth Nicolas, Margaret Poydock & Heidi Shierholz, *Unchecked Corporate Power: Forced Arbitration, the Enforcement Crisis, and How Workers Are Fighting Back*, Econ. Pol'y Inst. & Ctr. for Popular Democracy 4, 22 (May 2019), www.epi.org.

34 *Id.* at 2, 7–9.

35 Andrew Wallender, *Corporate Arbitration Tactics Backfires as Claims Flood In*, Bloomberg Law (Feb. 11, 2019, 6:06 AM), https://news.bloomberglaw.com; Michael Corkery & Jessica Silver-Greenberg, *"Scared to Death" by Arbitration: Companies Drowning in Their Own System*, N.Y. Times (Apr. 6, 2020).

36 Erin Mulvaney, *DoorDash Got Its Arbitration Wish, Costing Millions Up Front (2)*, Bloomberg Law (Feb. 12, 2020, 11:00 AM), https://news.bloomberglaw.com.

37 *See, e.g.*, Arbitration Fairness Act, S. 2591, 115th Cong. (2018); Forced Arbitration Injustice Repeal Act, S. 610, 116th Cong. (2019); Mandatory Arbitration Act, S.647, 115th Cong. (2017); Ending Forced Arbitration of Sexual Harassment Act, H.R.4734, 115th Cong. (2017).

ACKNOWLEDGMENTS

We would like to thank our contributors, without whom this compendium would not be possible. We appreciate their generosity and willingness to share their work with us and the world. We have enjoyed working with you and have learned so much from each and every one of you. Your work is making a difference!

We are also grateful to the many student research assistants who contributed to this project every step of the way. From the University of Colorado Law School, we thank Hillary Bernhardt, Amanda Blasingame, Angela Boettcher, Kyle Cotteleer, Lauren DiMartino, Shane Fitzgerald, Emely Garcia, Leanna Gavin, Mariel Rotbart, and Erin Vanek. From Seattle University School of Law, we thank Rafael Bultz, Denise Chen, Julia Doherty, Doreen Fadaeiforghan, Chandler Gordon, Ilana Korchia, Nicole Rash, Sarah Schweitzer, Cole Story, Emily Tatum, and Rayshaun Williams. From the University of Washington School of Law, we thank Jessica Lederman. And from Boston College School of Law, we thank Kyle Angelotti, Sabrina Arsalane, Jackson Barnett, Caitlin Calvo, Tyler Creighton, Lydia Cuddeback, Gillian Fisher, Christina H. Fuleihan, Katherine Grisham, Mia Harris, Alesha Ignatius Brereton, Doug Illsley, Megan E. Kira, Ellen Miller, Meghan McCarthy, Taylor Mckinnon, Monica Naranjo, Temi Omilabu, Helen Park, Katherine Pino, Raven Pitarra, Katherine Quezada, Troy D. Rayder, Ashley Riley, Mara Rosario-Salinas, Catherine Rutley, Peter Sheffer, Chase Shelton, Lisa Stern, Steven Crawford Young, and Emily Liu Zheng. Our respective administrative and library staff, Christina Baires, Kate Cochrane, Patricia Correia, Kelly Ilseng, Jyothi Nandakumar, Danyelle Stokes, Jane Thompson, Alena Wolotira, the staff of the Fineman and Pappas Law Libraries, and the Gallagher Law Library were also indispensable.

This project would also not have been possible with the generosity and an investment of significant resources into this project. Primary among these were Dean Angela Onwuachi-Willig (Boston College

School of Law), former Dean S. James Anaya (University of Colorado Law School), the Boston University Peter Paul Career Development Professorship, the Seattle University Summer Faculty Fellowship, and the University of Washington Charles I. Stone Professorship. We also thank the Annual Civil Procedure Workshop, and specifically the University of Arizona–sponsored workshop hosted by David Marcus. It was there that we discussed over a "feminist breakfast" the seeds of this project. And it was from there that the project grew into this anthology.

Finally, immense thanks to our family and friends who supported us throughout this wonderful, but long, process. We appreciate your patience as we took Zoom calls from vacation hikes, how you brought us coffee and homemade pumpkin chili as we edited deep into the night, and for your perpetual support of a project that you knew was so important to each of us.

ABOUT THE EDITORS

Brooke Coleman is an Associate Dean of Research & Faculty Development and a Professor at Seattle University School of Law. Her research and teaching interests focus on procedure and procedural justice. Coleman has received the university's 2021 Provost's Award for Excellence in Teaching and the law school's Outstanding Faculty Award in 2013, 2015, 2016, and 2020. Her work has been published in the *New York University Law Review*, *Northwestern University Law Review*, *Indiana Law Journal*, *Notre Dame Law Review*, and *Boston College Law Review*. She is the lead author of *Learning Civil Procedure*. She is the co-founder and co-organizer of the Civil Procedure Workshop, the former chair of the AALS Section on Civil Procedure, and coeditor of the Courts Law section for JOTWELL. Coleman was a Thomas C. Grey Fellow at Stanford Law School. She clerked for the Honorable David F. Levi, district judge in the Eastern District of California and then-chair of the Standing Committee on the Federal Rules of Practice and Procedure. Coleman practiced at Wilson Sonsini Goodrich & Rosati and at Gunderson Dettmer Stough Villeneuve Franklin & Hachigian in Palo Alto, California. She earned her JD from Harvard Law School.

Suzette Malveaux is Moses Lasky Professor of Law and Director of the Byron R. White Center for the Study of American Constitutional Law at the University of Colorado Law School. Malveaux previously taught at the University of Alabama School of Law, the Columbus School of Law at The Catholic University of America, and as a visiting professor at the University of Iowa College of Law and Washington and Lee University School of Law. She is a member of the American Law Institute (ALI). She teaches Civil Procedure, Complex Litigation, Civil Rights Law, and Fair Employment Law. She coauthored *Class Actions and Other Multi-Party Litigation: Cases and Materials* (2006, 2012) and has published numerous law review articles that explore the intersection of civil procedure and civil rights. Malveaux was a class action litigation specialist who has appeared before the United States Supreme Court and argued before the Eleventh Circuit Court of Appeals. She practiced at Cohen, Milstein, Hausfeld & Toll, PLLC and the Washington Lawyers' Committee for Civil Rights & Urban Affairs. Malveaux graduated magna cum laude from Harvard University. She earned her JD from New York University School of Law, where she was an Associate Editor of the New York University *Law Review*, a Root-Tilden Scholar, and a Center for International Law Fellow. She clerked for the Honorable Robert L. Carter of the United States District Court for the Southern District of New York.

PORTIA PEDRO is an Associate Professor of Law and a Peter Paul Career Development Professor at Boston University School of Law. Her research is in the areas of civil procedure, remedies, and federal courts. In 2019, she received the Dean's Service Award. She graduated from the University of California, Los Angeles. And she earned her JD from Harvard Law School, where she served as treasurer and vice president of the *Harvard Law Review* and as an editor of the *BlackLetter Law Journal* and the *Harvard Civil Rights–Civil Liberties Law Review*, and she is completing her PhD in law at Yale. Prior to her doctoral studies, she practiced law at Debevoise & Plimpton LLP, was a John J. Gibbons Fellow in Public Interest and Constitutional Law at Gibbons PC, and served as a clerk to the Honorable Joseph A. Greenaway Jr. of the United States Court of Appeals for the Third Circuit.

ELIZABETH PORTER is a Professor of Law, Interim Toni Rembe Dean and Co-Director, Appellate Advocacy Clinic, at the University of Washington School of Law. Her research focuses on civil procedure, as well as on the growing impact of visual media in briefs, judicial opinions, and other litigation documents. Her work has been published in journals including the *Columbia Law Review*, the *New York University Law Review*, and the *Cornell Law Review*. She graduated magna cum laude from Brown University with a concentration in East Asian Studies and received an EdM from the Harvard Graduate School of Education. She earned her JD from Columbia Law School, where she was an articles editor for the *Columbia Law Review* and received the

James Elkins Prize in Civil Procedure. She worked as a law clerk for Judge Sidney R. Thomas of the Court of Appeals for the Ninth Circuit and for Justice Ruth Bader Ginsburg of the United States Supreme Court. In 2014, she received a University of Washington Distinguished Teaching Award. She currently serves on the Rules Advisory Committee for the Ninth Circuit.

ABOUT THE CONTRIBUTORS

BARBARA ALLEN BABCOCK was the first woman appointed to the regular faculty, as well as the first to hold an endowed chair and the first emerita, at Stanford Law School. Babcock taught and wrote in the fields of civil and criminal procedure for many years. She also pioneered the study of women in the legal profession. Babcock was a distinguished teacher, being a four-time winner of the John Bingham Hurlbut Award for Excellence in Teaching at Stanford Law School. She was also a recipient of the Margaret Brent Women Lawyers of Achievement Award. Before joining the Stanford faculty, Babcock served as the first director of the Public Defender Service of the District of Columbia. She was assistant attorney general for the Civil Division in the United States Department of Justice during the Carter administration. She clerked for Judge Henry Edgerton of the United States Court of Appeals for the District of Columbia Circuit and worked for the noted criminal defense attorney Edward Bennett Williams. Babcock passed away in 2020.

RACHEL K. BEST is an Assistant Professor at the University of Michigan. She studies political responses to social problems, focusing on inequalities created by advocacy and culture. Her book *Common Enemies: Disease Campaigns in America* contends that Americans, when they come together to fight social problems, focus their largest efforts on diseases. Fighting one disease at a time has unintended consequences for health policy. Her current research uses computational methods to explore the relationship between disease stigma, advocacy, and policy outcomes. Another line of research investigates inequalities in employment litigation, with a current focus on disability law.

STEPHANIE BORNSTEIN is a Professor at the University of Florida. Her scholarship focuses on creative legal and administrative strategies to reduce structural gender and racial inequality in the workplace and to ensure access to justice in civil litigation. Bornstein's work has been cited in enforcement efforts by the United States Equal Employment Opportunity Commission, the United States Department of Labor's Office of Federal Contract Compliance Programs, and in amicus briefs filed in United States Supreme Court cases. Bornstein served as a Visiting Assistant Professor at the University of California, Hastings College of Law; as a Faculty Fellow and Deputy Director of the Center for WorkLife Law at UC Hastings; and as a staff attorney at the national public interest law center Equal Rights Advocates. Bornstein received her bachelor's degree magna cum laude from Harvard University and her law degree from the University of California, Berkeley, School of Law, where she served as a member of the *California Law Review* and Managing Editor of the *Berkeley Women's Law Journal*.

Roy L. Brooks is the Warren Distinguished Professor of Law and was twice selected as a University Professor. A graduate of Yale Law School Class of 1975, Professor Brooks teaches and writes in the areas of civil procedure, civil rights, jurisprudence, international human rights, and critical theory. He is the author of more than 110 articles and more than two dozen books, including *The Racial Glass Ceiling: Subordination in American Law and Culture*, published by Yale University Press; *Integration or Separation? A Strategy for Racial Equality*, published by Harvard University Press; *Racial Justice in the Age of Obama*, published by Princeton University Press; and *Atonement and Forgiveness: A New Model for Black Reparations*, published by University of California Press. His most recent book *Diversity Judgments* was published by Cambridge University Press.

Sergio J. Campos joined the University of Miami School of Law faculty in 2009. Prior to joining the faculty, he was a Charles Hamilton Houston Fellow at Harvard Law School and was in private practice. He also clerked for the Honorable Juan R. Torruella of the United States Court of Appeals for the First Circuit and the Honorable Patti B. Saris of the United States District Court for the District of Massachusetts. His research interests include civil procedure, federal courts, and remedies.

CHARLTON COPELAND is a Professor and M. Minnette Massey Chair in Law at the University of Miami School of Law. His scholarship has focused on the ways federalism as a constitutional and political structure is mediated in: the relationship between federal and state courts, the jurisprudence of remedies for state violations of federal law, and the relationship between state and federal implementation of federal policy. He has received the Dukeminier Award, the Michael Cunningham Prize from the Williams Institute at UCLA Law School, as well as the Richard Hausler Golden Apple Award. He was an associate at Hogan & Hartson in Washington, DC. He clerked for Justices Richard J. Goldstone and Catherine O'Regan of the Constitutional Court of South Africa and Judge R. Guy Cole Jr. of the United States Court of Appeals for the Sixth Circuit. Copeland graduated from Amherst College, Yale Divinity School, and Yale Law School. Copeland was a member and Chair of the Miami-Dade Commission on Ethics and Public Trust. He also served as Chair of the Law and Humanities Section of the American Association of Law Schools.

ANGELIQUE EAGLEWOMAN, (*Wambdi A. Was'teWinyan*) is a Professor at Mitchell Hamline School of Law, a legal scholar, and served as a pro tempore Tribal Judge in several Tribal Court systems. EagleWoman presents and publishes on topics involving tribal-based economics, Indigenous sovereignty, international Indigenous principles, and the quality of life for Indigenous peoples. As a professor at the University of Idaho College of Law, she established the Native American Law Emphasis program. She also formerly served as the dean of the Bora Laskin Faculty of Law at Lakehead University and was the first Indigenous law dean in Canada. As a practicing lawyer, one of the highlights of her career was to serve as General Counsel for her own Tribe. She graduated from Stanford University with a BA in Political Science, received her Juris Doctor degree from the University of North Dakota School of Law with distinction, and obtained her LLM in American Indian and Indigenous Law with honors from the University of Tulsa College of Law.

LAUREN EDELMAN is Agnes Roddy Robb Professor of Law and Sociology at the University of California, Berkley. At UC Berkeley, she served as Director of the Center for the Study of Law and Society from 2004–2009 and as Chair and Associate Dean for Jurisprudence and Social Policy from 2010–2013. Edelman is the winner of a Guggenheim Fellowship, has twice been a fellow at the Center for Advanced Studies in the Behavioral Sciences at Stanford University, and was a fellow at the Rockefeller Center in Bellagio, Italy. She has served as Secretary and President of the Law and Society Association, chaired the Sociology of Law section of the American Sociological Association, and was elected to the Sociological Research Association, an honorary society. Edelman's research addresses the interplay between organizations and their legal environments, focusing on employers' responses to and constructions of civil rights laws, workers' mobilization of legal rights, the impact of management practices on law and legal institutions, dispute resolution in organizations, school rights, empirical critical race studies, empirical sociolegal studies, and employer accommodations of disabilities in the workplace. Her publications appear in the *American Journal of Sociology*, *Law & Society Review*, *Law & Social Inquiry*, *Law & Policy*, *Annual Review of Sociology*, *Annual Review of Law and Social Science*, and numerous edited volumes. Her 2016 book *Working Law: Courts, Corporations and Symbolic Civil Rights* (University of Chicago Press) won the 2017 George R. Terry Book Award from the Academy of Management.

Robin Effron is a Professor at Brooklyn Law School and serves as Co-Director for the Dennis J. Block Center for the Study of International Business Law. Her articles have appeared in *Georgetown Law Journal*, *Alabama Law Review*, *William & Mary Law Review*, *Wake Forest Law Review*, and *Boston University Law Review*. Her work has been cited by several state and federal courts. She spent a year in Germany as a fellow in the DAAD Program for International Lawyers and worked with attorneys at a large investment bank to research questions of German and US law. Effron edits the *Civil Procedure and Federal Courts Blog* for the Law Professors Blog Network. Prior to joining the faculty at Brooklyn, Effron was a Bigelow Fellow and Lecturer in Law at the University of Chicago Law School. She served as a law clerk to Judge Alvin K. Hellerstein of the United States District Court for the Southern District of New York. In law school, she was an articles editor for the *New York University Law Review*.

SCOTT R. ELIASON was a Professor of Sociology at the University of Arizona. He received his PhD in sociology at Pennsylvania State University. He was known for his pathbreaking work in quantitative methodology and statistics, focusing in particular on models of discrete outcomes and causality. His work addressed social stratification, the sociology of work, economic sociology, the life course, the comparative welfare state, and the sociology of law. Eliason passed away in 2015.

SETH KATSUYA ENDO joined the University of Florida Levin College of Law in 2019 from New York University School of Law, where he was an Acting Assistant Professor of Lawyering and an Adjunct Professor of Clinical Law. Endo's primary scholarship and teaching interests include Civil Procedure, Election Law, Evidence, Federal Courts, and Professional Responsibility. Prior to his career in academia, Endo served as a Legal Fellow for Demos, a public policy organization, where he focused on campaign finance issues. He also was an Associate at Cleary, Gottlieb, Steen & Hamilton LLP in New York City.

MATTHEW L. M. FLETCHER is a Professor at Michigan State University College of Law and Director of its Indigenous Law and Policy Center. He sits as the Chief Justice of the Poarch Band of Creek Indians Supreme Court and also sits as an Appellate Judge for eight other tribes. He is a citizen of the Grand Traverse Band of Ottawa and Chippewa Indians. He is the Reporter for the American Law Institute's *Restatement of the Law of American Indians*. He is the author of the treatise *Federal Indian Law*, casebooks on tribal and federal Indian law, and volumes on the Indian Civil Rights Act and the Indian Child Welfare Act. Fletcher is the primary editor and author of *Turtle Talk*, the leading blog on American Indian law and policy. Fletcher received his JD and BA from the University of Michigan.

JUDGE NANCY GERTNER is a Senior Lecturer of Law at Harvard Law School and a former federal judge. She has published articles and chapters on sentencing, discrimination, forensic evidence, women's rights, and the jury system. Judge Gertner is a graduate of Barnard College and Yale Law School, where she was an editor for *Yale Law Journal*. She received her MA in Political Science at Yale University. She was appointed to the bench in 1994 by President Clinton. In 2008, she received the Thurgood Marshall Award from the American Bar Association, Section of Individual Rights and Responsibilities. She became a Leadership Council Member of the International Center for Research on Women the same year. In 2010, she received the Morton A. Brody Distinguished Judicial Service Award. In 2011, she received the Massachusetts Bar Association's Hennessey Award for judicial excellence. In 2014, she was a recipient of the Margaret Brent Women Lawyers of Achievement Award.

MYRIAM GILLES is a Professor and Paul R. Verkuil Chair in Public Law at Yeshiva University Benjamin N. Cardozo School of Law. Gilles specializes in class actions and aggregate litigation and has written extensively on class action waivers in arbitration clauses. She also writes on structural reform litigation and tort law. She is one of the most cited civil procedure professors in the country. Her articles have appeared in top law reviews, including at Chicago, Columbia, Michigan, and Penn. Gilles teaches Torts, Products Liability, and Class Actions & Aggregate Litigation. She has testified before Congress on consumer protections. Gilles served as Cardozo's vice dean from 2016–2018. She was a visiting professor at the University of Virginia Law School and in 2005–2006 was a fellow in the Program of Law and Public Affairs at Princeton University.

JASMINE GONZALES ROSE is a Professor of Law at Boston University School of Law and a Deputy Director of Research & Policy at the Center for Antiracist Research. She is a critical proceduralist whose research focuses on the intersection of race and language. She is the nation's leading expert on juror language disenfranchisement and juror language accommodation. She was twice selected as an inaugural Derrick A. Bell Fund for Excellence Scholar. She received the University of Pittsburgh School of Law's Distinguished Public Interest Professor Award twice and its Robert T. Harper Award for Excellence in Teaching. Gonzales Rose graduated from Harvard Law School, where she served as Editor in Chief of the *Harvard Latino Law Review* and as a member of the Harvard Legal Aid Bureau. She clerked for Judge Damon J. Keith of the United States Court of Appeals for the Sixth Circuit and Judge Héctor M. Laffitte of the United States District Court for the District of

Puerto Rico. She served on the Board of Directors of the American Civil Liberties Union of Greater Pittsburgh and the Abolitionist Law Center.

MICHAEL Z. GREEN is a member of the Texas A&M University School of Law faculty. His scholarship focuses on workplace disputes and the intersection of race and alternatives to the court resolution process. He previously served on the faculty of Texas Wesleyan University School of Law as its inaugural Associate Dean for Faculty Research & Development. Professor Green was a visiting professor at the University of Georgia School of Law and at Florida State University College of Law. His legal practice in Illinois and Kentucky focused on workplace disputes. Green was elected as a Fellow to the College of Labor and Employment Lawyers and as a member of the American Law Institute. He received the Paul Steven Miller Memorial Award for outstanding academic and public contributions in the field of labor and employment law. Green is a mediator and arbitrator who serves as a member of the American Arbitration Association's National Labor Arbitration Panel, the Federal Mediation and Conciliation Service Labor Panel, and as a hearing officer for the Dallas Area Rapid Transit Trial Board. He served as Secretary of the American Bar Association's Labor and Employment Section. Professor Green holds a LLM from the University of Wisconsin School of Law, a JD and a MS from Loyola Chicago, an MBA from California Lutheran, and a BS from the University of Southern California.

ANDREW HAMMOND is an Assistant Professor of Law at the University of Florida Levin College of Law. His research and teaching interests include civil procedure, legislation, administrative law, and poverty law. His articles have appeared or are forthcoming in *Lewis & Clark Law Review*, *Northwestern University Law Review*, and *Yale Law Journal*. Hammond holds degrees from the University of Chicago, Oxford University, where he was a Rhodes Scholar, and Yale Law School. In law school, Hammond served as Comments Editor of *Yale Law Journal* and a Coker Fellow for Civil Procedure. He clerked for Chief Judge Diane P. Wood of the United States Court of Appeals for the Seventh Circuit and Judge Robert M. Dow of the United States District Court for the Northern District of Illinois. Hammond has worked for the Sargent Shriver National Center on Poverty Law, where he practiced first as a Skadden Fellow and was later of Counsel. Hammond was a Senior Lecturer at the University of Chicago, where he helped direct the Law, Letters, and Society Program.

Jasmine E. Harris is a Professor of Law at Penn Law. Her research lies at the intersection of civil rights and social psychology, with a focus on disability antidiscrimination law. She is particularly concerned with the ways in which rules and procedures affect (and can shift) social norms. Harris sits on the Board of Directors of the Disability Rights Bar Association and advises the National Disability Rights Network and The ARC. She currently serves or has served in key elected leadership positions in the American Association of Law Schools' sections on Evidence and Law & Mental Disability. Harris graduated magna cum laude with a BA from Dartmouth College, where she was a recipient of the Andrew W. Mellon Foundation's Mellon Mays Fellowship. Harris earned a JD from Yale Law School, where she was a recipient of the Connecticut Hispanic Bar Association's Merit Scholarship, as well as the Lloyd N. Cutler Scholarship for Public Service. Harris clerked for the Honorable Harold Baer Jr. of the United States District Court for the Southern District of New York.

Danielle Holley-Walker is the Dean and Professor of Law at Howard University School of Law. She researches the governance of public schools and diversity in the legal profession. She was awarded the GWAC Trailblazer Award, the Lutie Lytle Conference Outstanding Scholar Award, and the University of South Carolina Educational Foundation's Service Award. She was twice awarded the Outstanding Faculty Member Award at the University of South Carolina. Dean Holley-Walker has served as Chair of the Board of Directors of the South Carolina HIV/AIDS Council. She is a Liberty Fellow through the Aspen Global Leadership network. She serves on the board of the Lawyers' Committee for Civil Rights. She earned a BA from Yale University and her JD from Harvard University. She clerked for Chief Judge Carl E. Stewart of the United States Court of Appeals for the Fifth Circuit. She practiced at Fulbright & Jaworski, LLP in Houston, Texas. She was the Associate Dean for Academic Affairs and Distinguished Professor of Law at the University of South Carolina.

Kevin R. Johnson is Dean and Mabie-Apallas Professor of Public Interest Law at University of California Davis School of Law, and Professor of Chicana/o Studies at UC Davis. Johnson has published extensively on immigration law and civil rights. He is the recipient of many awards and honors. At Harvard Law School, he was a magna cum laude graduate and editor of *Harvard Law Review*. Johnson earned an AB in economics from University of California, Berkeley, graduating Phi Beta Kappa. After law school, he clerked for the Honorable Stephen Reinhardt of the United States Court of Appeals for the Ninth Circuit and worked as an attorney at the international law firm Heller Ehrman White & McAuliffe. Since 1996, Johnson has served on the Board of Directors of Legal Services of Northern California and currently is President of the board. From 2006–2011, he served on the Board of Directors of the Mexican American Legal Defense and Education Fund. In 2003, Johnson was elected to the American Law Institute.

Deseriee Kennedy is the Associate Dean of Diversity & Inclusion and Professor of Law at the Touro College of the Jacob D. Fuchsberg Law Center. Prior to joining Touro, she was a member of the faculty for 12 years at the University of Tennessee College of Law, where she taught Civil Procedure, Family Law, Women and the Law, Domestic Violence, and Business Torts. Before starting her career in legal education, she was a commercial litigator and an Assistant City Solicitor in Philadelphia and with a private firm in Los Angeles. Her scholarship has been published in *Georgetown Journal of Legal Ethics*, *Arizona State Law Journal*, *Missouri Law Review*, *Southern California Review of Law and Women's Studies*, *Journal of Race*, and *Gender and Class*, among other journals. She received her BA from Lehigh University, her LLM from Temple University School of Law, and her JD from Harvard Law School.

Linda Hamilton Krieger is a Professor of Law at William S. Richardson School of Law. She served as Director of the Ulu Lehua Scholars Program from 2007–2017. Between graduating from law school in 1978 and entering law teaching full time in 1992, Krieger practiced as a civil rights lawyer in San Francisco, representing plaintiffs in race, sex, national origin, and disability discrimination class actions and individual cases at the trial and appellate levels. Many of her cases established important precedents in the areas of pregnancy discrimination, sexual harassment, the rights of workers subject to mass layoffs, and the health insurance–related rights of people with AIDS. Professor Krieger's legal scholarship explores how insights from the empirical social sciences can be used to inform civil rights law and policy, judicial decision-making, and the lawyer-client relationship. Krieger received an AB in psychology from Stanford, graduating Phi Beta Kappa. She earned her JD from New York University School of Law.

STEPHEN LEE is the Associate Dean for Faculty Research and Development and Professor of Law at the University of California, Irvine. Lee writes at the intersection of administrative law and immigration law. He is particularly interested in how enforcement realities constrain immigration law and policy across a variety of contexts and institutions, especially the workplace, the criminal justice system, and the food industry. Lee received his BA from Stanford University, his MA from UCLA, and his JD from the University of California, Berkeley, School of Law. A former Fulbright Fellow, Lee began his legal career at Skadden, Arps, in the Mass Torts and Insurance Litigation Group. After that, he clerked for Judge Mary Schroeder of the United States Court of Appeals for the Ninth Circuit, then completed a fellowship at Stanford Law School before joining the UCI Law faculty.

KATHERINE MACFARLANE teaches at the Southern University Law Center. Her scholarship focuses on how procedure creates inequality in civil rights actions, including those brought by prisoners. Macfarlane is a nationally recognized expert on patient rights and disability accommodations. She has testified in front of the Louisiana Legislature and participated in a Congressional Arthritis Caucus briefing. Her commentary has appeared in *Annals of Health Law*, *Ms.*, *Northwestern Magazine*, *Huffington Post*, the *Idaho Statesman*, *BUST*, and *The Mighty* and was anthologized in *Bodies of Truth: Personal Narratives on Illness, Disability, and Medicine*. Macfarlane received her BA, magna cum laude, from Northwestern University and her JD, cum laude, from Loyola Law School in Los Angeles. She was a Teaching Fellow at the Louisiana State University Paul M. Hebert Law Center. She is also an associate at Quinn Emanuel and an Assistant Corporation Counsel for the New York City

Law Department. Macfarlane clerked for the District of Arizona and the United States Court of Appeals for the Ninth Circuit. She is licensed to practice law in California and New York.

DAVID MARCUS is a Professor of Law at UCLA School of Law. His teaching and research interests include civil procedure, complex litigation, and administrative law. Prior to teaching at UCLA, Marcus taught at the University of Arizona James E. Rogers College of Law, where he was elected Professor of the Year by the student body in 2009, 2012, 2017, and 2018. Marcus received his BA from Harvard University and studied at the University of Cambridge before earning his JD from Yale Law School. After law school, he clerked for the Honorable Allyne R. Ross of the United States District Court for the Eastern District of New York in Brooklyn and the Honorable William Fletcher of the United States Court of Appeals for the Ninth Circuit in San Francisco. Marcus also represented plaintiffs in class actions at Lieff Cabraser Heimann and Bernstein. Marcus also participated in two large-scale studies of federal agencies handling mass adjudication and their relationships to the federal courts. His other scholarship focuses on class actions, especially those involving claims for injunctive relief brought in the public interest.

TONI M. MASSARO is the Milton O. Riepe Chair in Constitutional Law and Dean Emerita at the University of Arizona James E. Rogers College of Law and was named a Regent's Professor by the Arizona Board of Regents in 2006. Massaro served as Dean of the College of Law, the first woman to hold this post at Arizona. Her research focuses on constitutional law and procedure, with particular emphasis on freedom of expression, equality, and due process. Massaro also has written on law and emotion, with a focus on shaming as a means of criminal punishment. She is an eight-time recipient of the Teacher of the Year Award, a member of the American Law Institute, a former member of the Arizona State Bar Board of Governors, and the recipient of the Judge Learned Hand Public Service Award, as well as the inaugural 100 Women and Minorities Award, and was named by the State Bar of Arizona to honor pathbreakers in the Arizona legal profession. Massaro received her BS, magna cum laude, from Northwestern University, and her JD from the William & Mary Law School, where she served as Editor in Chief of *William & Mary Law Review*. She practiced at Vedder, Price, Kaufman and Kammholz in Chicago, Illinois.

ELIZABETH Y. MCCUSKEY joined the University of Massachusetts School of Law–Dartmouth faculty in 2019 as a nationally recognized expert in health law and civil procedure. Her research focuses on regulatory reforms for health equity and courts' roles in securing those reforms. McCuskey has published her scholarship in legal academic journals including *University of Pennsylvania Law Review*, *Ohio State Law Journal*, *Temple Law Review*, *Nevada Law Journal*, and *Nebraska Law Review*, in addition to the peer-reviewed interdisciplinary *Journal of Legal Medicine* and *New York University Review of Employee Benefits and Executive Compensation*. Her research merges procedure, federalism, and health policy. She was selected as a 2016 Health Law Scholar by the American Society for Law, Medicine & Ethics and received the University President's Award for Outstanding Contribution in Scholarship in 2018. McCuskey earned her BA and JD from the University of Pennsylvania. She managed a public benefits clinic for Philadelphia Legal Assistance and practiced law with Drinker Biddle & Reath LLP.

VICTOR QUINTANILLA is the Codirector of the Indiana University Maurer School of Law's Center for Law, Society & Culture, Professor of Law and Val Nolan Faculty Fellow, and an adjunct professor in the Department of Psychological and Brain Sciences. Quintanilla's research investigates access to justice, civil justice, and legal education by drawing on theory and methods within the field of psychological science. He served as a Fellow of the Center for Advanced Study in the Behavioral Sciences at Stanford University. He has presented his research at the Society for Personality and Social Psychology, the Society for the Psychological Study of Social Issues, the Conference for Empirical Legal Studies, the Association for Psychological Science, and the Law and Society Association. Quintanilla served as a trial attorney for the United States Department of Justice, Civil Rights Division; an associate of Sidley Austin LLP; a staff law clerk for the United States Court of Appeals for the Seventh Circuit; and a clerk for the Honorable Peter J. Messitte of the United States District Court for the District of Maryland. He received a

BBA and MPA from the University of Texas at Austin and a JD, magna cum laude, from Georgetown University Law Center.

DANYA SHOCAIR REDA is an Assistant Professor at the University of Law–Dartmouth. She is a scholar of procedural reform in the US civil system, alternative dispute resolution processes, and Islamic law. Before joining UMass Law, Reda was an associate professor at Peking University School of Transnational Law and an acting assistant professor in the Lawyering Program at New York University School of Law. She also worked as a civil litigator at Friedman, Kaplan, Seiler and Adelman LLP and Cleary, Gottlieb, Steen and Hamilton, LLP, and clerked for the Honorable Charles S. Haight Jr. at the United States District Court for the Southern District of New York. Her scholarship examining these questions has been published in *Fordham Law Review*, *Review of Litigation*, and *Oregon Law Review*, among other publications. Reda has served on the Federal Courts Committee of the Association of the Bar of the City of New York as the committee's liaison to the Task Force on National Security and the Rule of Law. After graduating Phi Beta Kappa and magna cum laude from Brown University, Reda was a Fulbright Scholar in Damascus, Syria. She holds a JD from Harvard Law School and a master's degree in Oriental Studies from the University of Oxford, where she studied Islamic law and philosophy.

ALEX REINERT is a Professor at the Benjamin N. Cardozo School of Law. Reinert has worked to advance the civil rights of people confined in prisons and jails throughout the United States since the early twenty-first century. In his work as both litigator and scholar, Reinert has developed a deep appreciation for the role that procedure can play in advancing justice. Reinert joined the faculty of the Benjamin N. Cardozo School of Law in 2007 after working as an Associate at Koob & Magoolaghan. Reinert argued before the Supreme Court in *Ashcroft v. Iqbal* and has appeared on behalf of parties and amicus curiae in many significant civil rights cases. In 2016, he became Director of the Center for Rights and Justice. His articles have appeared in *Indiana Law Journal*, *Northwestern University Law Review*, *Stanford Law Review*, *University of Pennsylvania Law Review*, *University of Virginia Law Review*, and *William & Mary*

Law Review, among other journals. Reinert graduated magna cum laude from New York University School of Law. After graduating from law school, he held two clerkships, first with the Honorable Harry T. Edwards of the United States Court of Appeals for the DC Circuit, and then at the United States Supreme Court for Associate Justice Stephen G. Breyer.

JUDITH RESNIK is the Arthur Liman Professor of Law at Yale Law School, where she teaches about federalism, procedure, courts, prisons, equality, and citizenship. Her scholarship focuses on the impact of democracy on government services, from courts and prisons to post offices, on the relationships of states to citizens and noncitizens, on the forms and norms of federalism, and on equality and gender. In 2018, Resnik received an Andrew Carnegie Fellowship, a two-year award to enable her to complete her research and write her new book, *Impermissible Punishment: Whipping, Isolating, and Debilitating*. She was also awarded an honorary doctorate from the University College London. Resnik chairs Yale Law School's Global Constitutional Law Seminar, a part of the Gruber Program on Global Justice and Women's Rights. She is also Chair of the Section on Law and the Humanities of the American Association of Law Schools, and she has chaired the American Association of Law Schools' Sections on Procedure, on Federal Courts, and on Women in Legal Education. She is a Managerial Trustee of the International Association of Women Judges. Resnik served as a founder and, for more than a decade, as a Cochair of Yale University's Women Faculty Forum, begun in 2001. She received her BA from Bryn Mawr College and her JD from New York University School of Law.

NEOSHIA R. ROEMER is an assistant Professor of Law at the University of Idaho College of Law, where she teaches Family Law and Native American Law. Prior to joining Idaho, she was Staff Attorney at the Indigenous Law & Policy Center at Michigan State University College of Law, where she supervises in the Indian Law Clinic and on the ICWA Appellate Project, mentored first-year students, developed and maintained effective pipelines to law, recruitment, and retention programs, and conducted scholarly research. She also serves as Adjunct Faculty at the Saginaw Chippewa Tribal College, where she teaches Violence Against Women in Native American Communities and Native American Children and Child Welfare, and serves as the Social Media Communications Coordinator for the Partnership for Native Children. Roemer is a 2013 graduate of Indiana University–Purdue University Indianapolis, and a 2017 graduate of the University of New Mexico School of Law, where she graduated cum laude, earned a Law & Indigenous Peoples Certificate, and served as a staff member on *Tribal Law Journal.* In 2017 she also received a Master of Arts in Latin American Studies from the University of New Mexico. Her scholarly interests include federal Indian Law policy, child welfare, children's rights, juvenile defense, and violence against women.

BRIANA ROSENBAUM is an Associate Professor at the University of Tennessee College of Law. Her research and writing interests include aggregate procedure, institutional design and reform, education justice, and transgender students and the law. She was a Thomas C. Grey Fellow at Stanford Law School. After graduating cum laude from Santa Clara University, Rosenbaum received her law degree magna cum laude from the University of California, Hastings College of the Law, where she served on the Hastings Law Journal, as a counselor for the Legal Aid Society, and as an intern for the California State Assembly. Rosenbaum clerked for two federal judges appointed to chair the Judicial Conference Standing Committee on the Rules of Practice and Procedure: Judge David F. Levi of the United States District Court for the Eastern District of California, and Judge Anthony J. Scirica of the United States Court of Appeals for the Third Circuit. Before moving into academia, Rosenbaum practiced in the San Francisco office of Bingham McCutchen. She primarily teaches courses in the advocacy concentration.

ELIZABETH M. SCHNEIDER is Rose L. Hoffer Professor of Law at Brooklyn Law School and has also been visiting professor of law at Harvard Law School and Columbia Law School. Much of her scholarship has focused on the impact of federal civil litigation on civil rights and employment discrimination cases. She is the coeditor of *Women and the Law Stories*, author of *Battered Women and Feminist Lawmaking*, which won the 2000 Association of American Publishers Professional-Scholarly Publishing Award in Law, and coauthor of the law school casebook *Domestic Violence and the Law: Theory and Practice.* Schneider was the founder and Director of the Edward V. Sparer Public Interest Law Fellowship Program. She graduated from Bryn Mawr College cum laude with honors in Political Science, was a Leverhulme Fellow at the London School of Economics, where she received an MSc in Political Sociology, and has a JD from New York University Law School, where she was an Arthur Garfield Hays Civil Liberties Fellow. She clerked for the late Judge Constance Baker Motley of the United States District Court for the Southern District of New York.

SHIRIN SINNAR is John A. Wilson Faculty Scholar and Professor of Law at Stanford Law. Her scholarship focuses on the role of institutions in protecting individual rights and democratic values in the national security context. She has written on the capacity of Inspectors General, civil rights offices, and other institutions within federal agencies to monitor and oversee national security conduct. She was corecipient of the inaugural Mike Lewis Prize for National Security Law Scholarship. Sinnar was also selected as the recipient of the John Bingham Hurlbut Award for Excellence in Teaching. She represented individuals facing discrimination based on government national security policies and unlawful employment practices as an Equal Justice Works Fellow at the Lawyers' Committee for Civil Rights of San Francisco and as a staff attorney with the Asian Law Caucus. She clerked for the Honorable Warren J. Ferguson of the United States Court of Appeals for the Ninth Circuit. She received her AB from Harvard and Radcliffe Colleges, summa cum laude, her MPhil from Cambridge University, and her JD from Stanford Law School.

BRIAN SOUCEK is a Professor of Law and Chancellor's Fellow at the University of California, Davis, School of Law. Soucek's published work spans from refugee/asylum law to constitutional and statutory antidiscrimination law to projects on law's aesthetic judgments. His articles have been cited by the United States Supreme Court and the Sixth and Seventh Circuit Courts of Appeals, referenced and excerpted in leading casebooks in Immigration Law and Sexual Orientation Law, discussed by the *Wall Street Journal*, and honored with the Dukeminier Award from UCLA's Williams Institute. He is a graduate of Boston College

(BA); Columbia University (PhD), where he was awarded the Core Preceptor Prize for his teaching; and Yale Law School (JD), where he was Comments Editor for *Yale Law Journal*, a Coker Fellow in Procedure, and won the Munson Prize for work in the school's immigration clinic. Prior to law school, Soucek taught at the University of Chicago. After law school, he clerked for the late Judge Mark R. Kravitz of the United States District Court for the District of Connecticut and the Honorable Guido Calabresi of the United States Court of Appeals for the Second Circuit.

Norman W. Spaulding is the Nelson Bowman Sweitzer & Marie B. Sweitzer Professor of Law at Stanford Law School. He is a nationally recognized scholar in the areas of professional responsibility, civil procedure, and federal courts. Spaulding's research concentrates on the history of the American legal profession and theories of adjudication. He received the John Bingham Hurlbut Award for Excellence in Teaching. He also served as the Covington & Burling Distinguished Visiting Professor of Law at Harvard Law School. In 2004, the Association of American Law Schools presented him with its Outstanding Scholarly Paper Prize. He is a member of the American Law Institute and the American Bar Association Standing Committee on Ethics and Professional Responsibility. Before joining the Stanford Law School faculty, he was a professor at the University of California, Berkeley, School of Law and an associate at Skadden, Arps, Slate, Meagher & Flom LLP. Spaulding served as a law clerk to Judge Betty B. Fletcher of the United States Court of Appeals for the Ninth Circuit and to Judge Thelton Henderson of the United States District Court for the Northern District of California.

A. Benjamin Spencer is Dean and Chancellor Professor at William & Mary Law School. Before becoming Dean at William & Mary Law School, he served on the faculty at the University of Virginia School of Law first as the Earle K. Shawe Professor of Law, as a Professor of Law, and as the Justice Thurgood Marshall Distinguished Professor of Law. His books on civil procedure are widely used by professors and students throughout the country. He formerly served on the Virginia State Bar Council and has served as Special Assistant United States Attorney for the Western District of Virginia, occasionally handling appellate cases in the Fourth Circuit on behalf of the government on a pro bono basis. In 2007, he was awarded the Virginia State Council of Higher Education Rising Star Award, given to the most promising junior faculty member among all academic fields at all colleges and universities in Virginia. He was the first law professor to receive this award. He received his BA from Morehouse College, his MS from London School of Economics, where he was a Marshall Scholar, and his JD from Harvard Law School. He also formerly worked as an associate in the law firm Shearman & Sterling and was a law clerk to Judge Judith W. Rogers of the United States Court of Appeals for the DC Circuit.

SUJA THOMAS is a Professor of Law at the University of Illinois College of Law. Her research interests include the Fifth, Sixth, and Seventh Amendment jury provisions, civil procedure, employment law, theories of constitutional interpretation, and consumer issues. Thomas earned her BA from Northwestern University and her JD from New York University School of Law, where she served as an articles editor on the *New York University Law Review* and received the Leonard M. Henkin Prize for her note on equal rights under the Fourteenth Amendment, the Mendes Hershman Prize for excellence in writing in the field of property law, and the William Miller Memorial Award for outstanding scholarship in the field of municipal law. Thomas practiced law in New York City with Cravath, Swaine & Moore, Vladeck, Waldman, Elias & Engelhard, P.C., and Weil, Gotshal & Manges, LLP. Thomas began her academic career as a professor at the University of Cincinnati College of Law and was a visiting professor at Vanderbilt University Law School.

ELIZABETH G. THORNBURG is the Altshuler Distinguished Teaching Professor and Richard R. Lee Endowed Professor of Law at SMU Dedman School of Law. Her scholarship focuses on the procedural fairness of the litigation process. She also writes and speaks in the areas of judicial ethics, comparative procedure, online dispute resolution, and the intersection of law and culture. Thornburg is coauthor of *Lawtalk: The Unknown Stories Behind Familiar Legal Expressions* (Yale University Press) in addition to a national study guide for civil procedure and two Texas procedure casebooks. She has also contributed chapters to books on civil procedure issues in consumer law, sports law, computer law, and classic civil procedure cases. She is a Civil Procedure Fellow for CALI (Computer-Assisted Legal Instruction). Thornburg also served Southern Methodist University as Director of the Center for Teaching Excellence, and in 2013 she received the University Scholar/Teacher of the Year Award. Thornburg is a member of the American Law Institute. She served as one of two US representatives to the international project "Teaching Civil Procedure in Common Law Countries." She has served as an officer of the Civil Procedure and Conflict of Laws sections of the Association of American Law Schools (AALS) and participated in the Global Class Action Exchange Research Group of the Law & Society Association. Thornburg has presented on procedure topics at the AALS and Law & Society conferences, has served as a commentator at the Civil Procedure Workshop, and contributes regularly to the Courts Law section for *JOTWELL*.

Eric K. Yamamoto is Fred T. Korematsu Professor of Law and Social Justice at the William S. Richardson School of Law, University of Hawai'i. He has published more than 100 articles and book chapters and has authored amicus briefs for the United States Supreme Court and Circuit Courts of Appeals. Yamamoto has received eight outstanding law teacher awards, as well as the Regents Medal for Teaching Excellence. He was also named the Haywood Burns Chair in Civil Rights for New York and was selected as a Rockefeller Foundation Resident Fellow in Bellagio, Italy. Yamamoto's other awards include the American Courage Award given by Asian American Justice organizations; the San Francisco Equal Justice Society's inaugural Scholar Advocacy Award; the Hawai'i Consumer Lawyers Patsy Mink Justice Award; the American Board of Trial Attorneys Ha`heo Community Justice Award; and the Japanese American Citizens League–Honolulu's Distinguished Community Service Award. He received his BA from the University of Hawai'i at Mānoa and his JD from the University of California, Berkeley, School of Law.

INDEX

Page numbers in *italics* indicate figures and tables

Printed in the USA
CPSIA information can be obtained
at www.ICGtesting.com
LVHW051228120823
755038LV00018B/262/J

9 781479 805938